Imitation: The Art of the Theatre

Imitation: The Art of the Theatre

Walter R. Stump and Loren K. Ruff

Hunter Publishing Company

Cover: *The Gamboling Jester,* Courtesty Stadt Museum, Munich, Germany.

Title Page: The Batemans, Kate (1843-1917) and Ellen (1844-1936). Under the management of their father, H.L. Bateman, both achieved prominence as child prodigies. Ellen retired at age 16 when she married; Kate became a successful adult actress. From *Dramatic Portrait Gallery,* 1885.

Printed in the U.S.A. by Hunter Publishing Company, Winston-Salem, North Carolina

Library of Congress Catalog Card Number 79-51023
ISBN 0-89459-050-2

Designed by Michael T. Slaughter

PREFACE

Shakespeare wrote that it is the attempt and not the deed that confounds us. So it is with this book. The authors are constantly reminded that many students who enroll in a theatre appreciation course do not have even a nodding acquaintance with theatre. For them theatre, its workings, and its people live in a world apart, and the closest reference is movies and television. As a result, these students tend to equate theatre with the movies or television, and fail to view Western theatre as an independent art form. This text is an attempt to clarify the image of the theatre and to bridge this gap.

This book is virtually the outcome of several years of teaching theatre appreciation at two universities. During that time, the students (roughly 1500) made input as to what they believed the course should or should not be. We have taken cues from the students and have incorporated their suggestions into the text. The chapters on theatre history are not intended to be inclusive but rather are designed to cover what the authors believe are the most important features of each period. Each chapter has a tear-out worksheet located at the back of the book. The worksheets are programmed and are intended to serve as a review of the chapter. The student should cover the answers at the right of the page and fill in the questions on the left. He can check his response by uncovering the answer. For items which are incorrect and for the key words listed at the top of the worksheet, we suggest that the students take a 3 x 5 card, create their own questions on one side and place the answers on the other. We have found the flashcard system very useful for students. In addition, each chapter has a pronunciation guide. Students, as well as professionals in the field, continually mispronounce names and terms, and this guide is an attempt to solve the problem. Ronald J. MacDougall, reference librarian at the University of Maine, has been an immeasurable source of help in determining the correct pronunciation.

On the surface, a book is the work of one or more authors. In reality, however, the manuscript is a contribution of many individuals. We would like especially to acknowledge Ernestine Godfrey and Donald Briggs for their efforts above and beyond the call of duty. With the deepest of gratitude we would like to thank Joseph "Mac" Dixon, Richard Weigel, William Walls, Minor Rootes, Carole Bohannon, Shirley Merritt, Nancy Davis, Anne Jordan and Judy Walls for their individual efforts. Randall Capps, Jim Brown, William Leonard, Whit Combs, Rebecca Ragland, Judith Siders, Gloria Duclos, Linda Betch, Stephanie Gould, Lynn Farrington, and Andria MacClean deserve special mention for their help. Others deserving mention are Victor Tagashov of the Soviet Embassy, Andrew Glaze and Mrs. Sally Viney of the British Embassy, and Robin Roseman of Sovofoto.

Last, but not least, we owe a special debt to our wives, Ann and Beverly, for their assistance, encouragement, and tolerance.

CONTENTS

CHAPTER ONE

The Nature of Theatre

This is a book about theatre. More precisely, it is about theatre and drama, which are two closely related but separate professions. Theatre signifies the physical building, the actor, the sets, the costumes, the lights, the properties, makeup, and music; drama denotes the script. Together, theatre and drama serve the same function — the representation of a play. Plays concern people and their lives. This is what theatre is all about: it is an art form which imitates the actions of life. That is why we call this book *Imitation: The Art of the Theatre*.

Theatre in its ritual form reflected, as well as imitated, primitive society: its hopes, its fears, its institutions, indeed, its very way of life. Today the theatre and its drama continue to sum up society's institutions, hopes, fears, and attitudes. Theatre is the pulse of human experience; it captures the growth of men and women — their goodness as well as their evilness. It allows us, the audience, to experience what past, present, and future civilizations have experienced and might experience. Theatre is thus much like a bridge, providing insight not only to other worlds and people, but to ourselves. It enables man, as does all art, to look into himself and say, "I Am."

But what is man? Blaise Pascal (1623-1662), French philosopher, mathematician, and physicist, says he is the weakest of reeds, but he is a thinking reed. And what is life? Shakespeare writes that life is but "a walking shadow," and thus has no real significance; therefore, we should not take life too seriously. Many dramatists express a similar viewpoint, while others feel life does have substance and meaning. Each generation seeks to answer the same haunting questions: Who are we? Why were we born? What is life? What is death? In exploring these questions, we are expressing our innermost thoughts — thoughts about who we are and what we are. And it is through art that we have learned to express ourselves best. These self-expressions, whether music, painting, dance, or theatre, are a record of man's search for his identity. Throughout the centuries man has posed many questions with few answers in an effort to find his identity. Yet the records remain for the next generations to read, examine, ponder, and ask. These records tell us that people are not very different. The questions asked by the Greeks are the same questions asked by modern Americans. Perhaps it is in the asking that humanity finds its greatest solace, for in raising these questions we have created a way of expressing our thoughts. And look what these thoughts have created: music, art, literature, theatre, medicine, and other devices for the benefit of mankind. But humanity's thoughts have not always been for the good. We have created war, bombs, guns, hatred, and similar tools of destruction which have hindered progress. Whether for good or evil, thoughts are the sum and substance of being. It is thoughts which give rise to actions. Theatre and drama concern actions, human actions. Of all the art forms, none express the actions of people better than theatre and drama. Only in the theatre can people watch their fellow beings enact life as though it were happening for the first time.

Opposite: Primitive mask used in the winter ceremonials by North American Indian tribes. From Ridgeway's *Dramas and Dramatic Dances of Non-European Races,* 1915.

Although we experience theatre as we do life, theatre is not life, but simply an imitation of life. Like life, theatre is absorbed through the senses. Thus, stage life has the capability of transcending into actual life, making the action on stage real and meaningful to the audience. Whereas a person's life consists of diverse action, drama structures action — that is, a dramatist condenses diversity into a few hours. Within those few hours, a play is presented which focuses on the significant events and ideas in the lives of certain people. These significant events and ideas do not merely entertain but also make a statement about the human condition. The statement may be in a tragedy or a comedy. It may be a profound comment about man and God, or it may be a simple observation about right and wrong. The point is that the events and ideas chosen by the dramatist combine to entertain and to make a statement about life.

The Aesthetics of Theatre and Drama

Inasmuch as theatre and drama imitate life, the question arises as to why we prefer imitation to the real thing. What fascination does art hold for us? To answer this question, we must first define art. A definition is better understood after an inquiry into how the term art has evolved.

Antiquity considered art to be a "useful skill which is systematically applied." This was a broad definition and included areas such as war, medicine, mining, and agriculture. Aristotle's treatise, *The Poetics* (c. 335-323 B.C.), was written to prove that art as a "species" was a useful skill which could be systematically applied. *The Poetics* proved to be the basis for determining the differences between theatre and drama as well as providing a method by which to formulate a drama.

In the eighteenth century, art was divided into two groupings. The first group was fine arts, also called polite or elegant arts. This group focused on the creation of art objects for beauty and pleasure. The second group was concerned with useful, practical, or industrial arts, and thus concentrated on creating useful art objects. Concomitant with this division of art was the notion that fine arts could not be taught and were products of genius. This placed the fine arts on a plane with the gods who communicated to a select group. Fine arts were thus thought to be products of inspiration (genius), whereas practical arts were considered the creation of perspiration.

The writing habits of two eighteenth century German writers exemplify the differences between the useful and polite arts. Johann Wolfgang von Goethe (1749-1832) relied greatly on perspiration in his creative efforts. He wrote, rewrote, and polished. Writing was a useful skill which he applied systematically. His contemporary, Johann Christoph Friedrich von Schiller (1759-1805), divined his writing; that is, he relied on inspiration from the gods. To acquire this inspiration, Schiller was said to have shut himself in an airtight room; whereupon, he would sniff a box of rotten apples until he reached what is popularly referred to as a "high." Then he would write.

Despite the separation and different approaches, art can and generally does serve two masters: it is both aesthetic and functional. Thus the chief function of fine arts is not only to "seek expression through beautiful or significant modes," but also to serve as a teaching tool. As fine arts, theatre and drama fulfill both functions.

Theatre's functions of teaching and pleasing (entertaining) have served society in many ways. Theatre is useful, for example, in rehabilitative therapy for the emotionally disturbed and physically handicapped. As a teaching tool, theatre serves to gain and sustain the interest of students. The business world has also utilized theatre. The theatre and its drama reflect the political, social, and economic attitudes of any society at any given time. Theatre audiences provide consumer information on standards and tastes, as well as political ideas and economic levels. Social sciences are also an outlet for theatre. Black and Chicano theatre, for example, dramatize problems, fears, and aspirations of minorities. When you dramatize minority problems, you must take into account social sciences such as sociology, economics, politics, history, and religion. No other form of communication affords us such an opportunity to interact visually, aurally, spiritually, and mentally with our fellow beings. Theatre and drama have universal appeal. They communicate to all people, regardless of the generation, language, or society, certain fundamental truths about life.

Hamlet (1601) and *A Death of a Salesman* (1949) are two tragedies which are hallmarks in theatre and drama and wherever they are produced, audiences, recognizing their merits, generally attend them in greater numbers than lesser-known works. The reasons underlying the strength of these dramas can be debated, but no doubt one of their strengths is that they communicate truths of life. These are fundamental truths to which audiences of any generation can relate; thus these plays have a universal appeal.

A factor which aids that appeal is a psychological state defined as aesthetic distance. This unique condition allows audience members to view events on stage with a semiobjective attitude (detachment). It is somewhat akin to tunnel vision in that audience members block out the world around them and immerse themselves into the world of the stage. Physically they are in the audience, but mentally they have entered into the world they are viewing. Samuel Taylor Coleridge termed this phenomenon "the willing suspension of disbelief." Audiences willingly give up their world (their reality) for that on stage, television, or the film screen. It is a curious psychological state which allows the audience to absorb the reality of one life while being temporarily suspended in their own world.

Theatre Origins

The origins of theatre are obscure. Inasmuch as drama was formally recognized and organized in Athens, Greece, the theories have centered on some aspect of Athenian society.

The fact that Greek theatre and drama were presented at a festival honoring the god Dionysus has influenced theorists to focus on that relationship in an effort to evolve a theory as to the origin of theatre and drama; namely, that Greek religion influenced the formation of theatre and drama.

Greek religion was not strong; it had no real authority, no sacred book or real dogma. It was a political religion and thus was controlled by the state. The leader of the state was also made guardian of the religious ceremonies. By the sixth century B.C., the state regulation of worship was organized to involve the entire population; for example, the festival honoring the god Dionysus. The coupling of dramatic performances with Greek religion has been the theoretical framework upon which the origins of theatre and drama have been formulated. Greek religion, however, was based largely on imagination and, hence, subject to interpretation. As a religion, its source was derived in part from primitive man's impersonation of those forces of nature which affect life. It also stems in part from the primitive idea of ritual as a means to communicate with those forces of nature. Also it seems that taboo was another factor affecting Greek religion — that is, certain things were to be considered sacred, clean, pure, and were not to be thought of otherwise. In addition to the above sources, the idea was added that the dead continued their lives in the grave and that these dead spirits continued to maintain the same power they held in life. Consequently, a hero cult arose which believed that the dead hero was the protector of all people. Therefore, the hero was to be honored with prayers, offerings and festivals in order that he would protect and avenge those whom he guarded.

By about the ninth century, Greek religion became anthropomorphic; that is, the powers of nature were conceived as gods and goddesses who had the same needs, desires, and faults of man. These deities lived on Olympus ruled by Zeus, and they controlled man's affairs according to their own personal inclination. This control, however, was subject to that quality in Greek religion termed fate — destiny, which was determined by Zeus, the will of the gods, or that person's birth-spirits *(parcae)*. Inasmuch as the gods were considered so influential, their worship became basic to Greek religion.

By the eighth century, the concepts of morality, mysticism, and justice became important, and hence, the notion of retribution, atonement, and guilt came into prominence. These latter ideas dominate Greek tragedy.

Although scholars have evolved different theories, they have agreed that theatre emerged from ritual. Reliable evidence is lacking, however, and thus the following theories must be accepted only in their theoretical framework.

The ritual theory has been the most widely discussed theory as to the origins of theatre. This concept was developed by the Cambridge School of Anthropologists and forwarded by Sir James Frazer (1854-1941) in his twelve-volume work, *The Golden Bough* (1890-1915).

Frazer's idea was to establish a relationship between the rituals and myths of primitive man and the theatre of the Greeks. Frazer suggests that all societies go through similar patterns of development and, consequently, one need only examine present-day primitive tribes to discover evidence about the rituals used in tribes a thousand years ago. It is in the development of ritual and myths that Frazer sees the origin of theatre. According to Frazer, primitive man, in dealing with his environment, was ignorant as to natural causes and their effects and, therefore, ascribed supernatural powers to those forces in nature which he did not understand. In seeking to gain the favor of these forces or gods, he developed systematic acts which were designed to curry favor. We term these systematic acts rituals. Some members of the tribes were more adept than others in dealing with rituals and they became known as the priests or chief actors. The stories that developed around the rituals were myths. The rituals disappeared, but the myths remain. They are the subject matter for drama.

These rituals were designed basically to insure fertility; that is, an abundance of children, crops, water, and animals to hunt. Underlying the concept of fertility was a recognition of death and man's desire to offset its powers. Death thus became evil and life (fertility), good. In many tribes, these two opposing forces became the subject of a mock battle called "The Year." One member of the tribe (the reigning king) would become an actor by representing the forces of winter (death, evil, etc.), and another member of the tribe (the king-to-be) would act the role of summer (fertility, good). This enactment or dramatic ritual was staged yearly, with good always winning. Although the winter king is slain, he is resurrected and spiritually lives on in his successor.

Dramatization of "The Year" ritual. From Ridgeway's *Dramas and Dramatic Dances of Non-European Races,* 1915.

The relationship between ritual and theatre is established through the worship of the god Dionysus, who was slain and resurrected. He was worshipped by the Greeks at festivals held throughout the year, as the god of wine, fertility, insanity, and catharsis. Inasmuch as drama originated in connection with one of these festivals (City Dionysia) held at Athens, Frazer sees the fertility rituals practiced by primitive man as having an influence on those rituals performed by the followers of Dionysus. These rituals, basically the dithyrambs, are said to have been the forerunners to tragedy and comedy.

A reaction to Frazer's ritual theory was that of archaeologist and writer, William Ridgeway (1853-1926). Ridgeway developed the tomb theory, which maintains that tragedy originated in performances at the tombs of deceased heroes. Based upon the hero-cult aspect of Greek religion, Ridgeway contends that dramatic dances and hero-cult lamentations were performed at these hero-tombs by a priest who became a medium for the hero's spirit. The priest was thus an actor playing a part. It is thought that rituals at the tombs were later absorbed by the worshippers of Dionysus who utilized similar ceremonies and concepts. Inasmuch as Aristotle contended that drama developed out of the worship of Dionysus, the rituals at the tombs, according to Ridgeway, were factors in shaping the form of drama. Aeschylus' *Persae* (472 B.C.) serves as a good example of a drama supporting Ridgeway's theory. Darius, the dead king, is to be summoned (second episode, lines 598-851) by a hymn of reverence sung by the chorus. When Darius' ghost appears, he addresses the chorus. Of importance to our discussion are his lines: "You are keening [lamenting] as you stand near my tomb and you are summoning me in piteous manner, singing the high-noted laments that raise the spirits of the dead." These lines indicate that a funeral ritual is being performed at the tomb of Darius, and hence involves the necessary dances, incense, incantations, and digging at the ground. The ritual seems to be much the same as that performed by the dithyrambic chorus in their worship of Dionysus.

Another theory which deserves mention is Gerald Else's (1908-) artistic theory. A classics professor and scholar, Else's new theory attributes the origin of theatre solely to the Athenians' artistic ability, which he contends was "rooted" in the wars in which Athens participated. Else sees no evidence to connect the worship of Dionysus with the origins of tragedy. The only relationship that exists, he contends, is that tragedy was presented at festivals honoring the god Dionysus. Furthermore, the fact that Aristotle contends that tragedy developed from the improvisation by the leaders of the dithyramb (a song or hymn in honor of the god

Dionysus) does not warrant consideration. In Aristotle's era, the dithyramb's connection to Dionysus was nil and it was simply a "narrative poem on heroic subjects." Historians have sought to transfer ritual performances from other countries to Greece in an effort to account for the influence on the Greek formation of tragedy. But as Else asserts: "Athens in the sixth century B.C. is the only place in the world that has ever given birth to tragedy. We must . . . take a closer look at Athens."

William Arrowsmith's (1924-) judicial metaphor theory is based upon the idea that the Greek tragic theatre's ritualistic origins warrant reexamination. Arrowsmith, an author and a scholar in the field of classics, argues that the origins are to be found in "a theatre shaped more by the law-court than by the altar." He points to the dominance of trial scenes in Greek tragedy and the plays of Euripides. In Euripides' plays, suggests Arrowsmith, the absence of a single hero can be observed. Instead, Euripides creates a formal clash between two central characters in the form of a debate *(agon)*. The theatre, then, is a metaphor for the Athenian courts, which may not have been the original creative force but certainly seem to have been a vital influence in the shaping of Greek tragedy.

There are other theories which concern the origins of theatre, but the focus of this book is simply to make the reader aware of the ambiguity surrounding the origins. Although the origins are obscure, the search for the theatre's roots has provided some insightful information concerning societal development. Contrary to Frazer's ritual theory, Claude Levi-Strauss (1908-), the noted French anthropologist, contends that not all societies developed similarly. His point is persuasive when one considers that not all societies developed theatre and drama past the ritual stage. While some societies remained static, others were dynamic in the use of theatre and drama. In these dynamic societies, the evolutionary stages of drama are unknown. A possible explanation as to the reason underlying the different stages of development in a society may be the particular methods used to transmit ideas from generation to generation. Historically, anthropologists recognize that rites which evolve in the course of human civilization are not hereditarily fixed, but rather are transmitted by tradition and must be learned anew by each succeeding generation. It seems, therefore, that societies generally have a fixed culture which is passed on from one generation to be learned by the next. A factor in maintaining that fixed culture is habit. When habit becomes ingrained in a society, it becomes a custom which traditionally creates fear when broken. Consequently, it appears that the static societies relied on ritual drama as part of the customs of their society, whereas the dynamic societies broke with old customs and developed newer forms of drama in keeping with their needs and purposes.

The Egyptians and the Greeks offer a comparison of static and dynamic societies. Although the Egyptians were an extremely sophisticated society, they never developed (formalized) theatre and drama past the ritualistic stage. The Greeks were the first to recognize theatre's potential as a specialized adjunct to their culture. The theatre provided the Greeks with a media whereby they could express their thoughts about life, death, and those forces which they believed shaped their destiny. A performance thus became more than just an art form; it became an expression of feelings, thoughts, and a way of life.

Javanese historical masks and puppet. From Ridgeway's *Dramas and Dramatic Dances of Non-European Races,* 1915.

Turkish karagoz shadow-play puppets. From Ridgeway's *Dramas and Dramatic Dances of Non-European Races,* 1915.

Theatre and Drama as Cultural Institutions

As cultural phenomena, theatre and drama form valuable assets to our society. Why should theatre and drama continue to be valued without any obvious practical purpose? A partial answer is offered by Aristotle who contended that imitation is natural and pleasurable and that man learns better from imitation. Another explanation is offered by the Swiss psychologist Carl Jung (1875-1961), who asserted that the value of theatre and drama is that they help us analyze our immediate environment. "A great work of art is like a dream," suggests Jung. That is, there is more to it than what is immediately seen. Moreover, the great work of art requires that you perceive it according to your own experiences and hence make your own value judgments (interpretations). Like Aristotle, Jung sees art as organic and related directly to man's nature.

It is not farfetched to suggest that we still retain a strong tie with primitive man and his use of ritual. A look at our religious services, political campaigns, parades, and sports events will testify to this. Our daily lives are ritualistic, as were those of primitive man. The relationship between ritual, symbol, and man is fundamental to theatre and drama. Although theatre and drama are not actual life, their ability to imitate life enables them to penetrate into the lives of the audience. On the one hand, audience members can respond emotionally to a situation. On the other hand, they can react intellectually to a particular social, political, or economic situation. In either case, the audience identifies and empathizes with the theatrical production through the characters, the settings, or the events. If characters in a drama are viewed as symbols of a society, then theatre and drama can be thought of as being expressions of a culture — that is, the meeting place where man's experiences are enjoined to symbolic representations. The characters, the settings, and the events are simply symbols; they represent life with all its problems and unanswered questions. The symbols of a theatre are developed according to the needs and purposes of a society. The complexity of modern society requires many more symbols than were required in a primitive society. This has led to newer forms of theatrical experimentation and a return to ritualistic drama in an effort to find some basic answers to some basic questions.

Selected Readings

Campbell, Joseph. *The Masks of Gods: Primitive Mythology.* New York, 1959.

Else, Gerald. *The Origin and Early Form of Greek Tragedy.* New York, 1965.

Hunningher, Benjamin. "The Primitive Phase," *Perspectives on Drama.* Eds. James L. Calderwood and Harold E. Toliver. New York, 1968. pp. 53-63.

Pickard-Cambridge, A.W. *Dithyramb, Tragedy, and Comedy,* 2nd ed., revised by T.B.L. Webster, Oxford, 1962.

Pronunciation Guide

The method used in this pronunciation guide is that of the *NBC Handbook of Pronunciation* which re-spells words according to their sound. This system is somewhat easier to deal with than the diacritical marks employed by dictionaries or the international phonetic alphabet familiar to students of linguistics. In our method the words, names or phrases are broken into their various syllables with the accented syllable appearing in capital letters. No attempt is made to reproduce such foreign sounds as the French *u*. Instead, a double *o* sound is given; thus the writer Camus becomes *kah MOO:,* a pronunciation not very French sounding, but one which has gained acceptance in English-speaking countries.

Here are the letters used for vowel sounds. In the right hand column is a familiar English word which will indicate the appropriate pronunciation.

a	cat	*igh*	fly
ah	father	*oh*	grow
ai	fair	*oy*	boy
aw	awful	*ow*	now
ay	hate	*oo:*	food
e	jet	*oo*	good
ee	feet	*uh*	away
i	it		

The last is the natural vowel sound that occurs in many unaccented syllables of English words. The letters used for consonant sounds should all be readily apparent with the possible exception of *zh* which is the French *j* (or sometimes g). This sound is heard at the end of a few English words such as garage and rouge.

Finally, we should point out that in many cases two or more pronunciations of a word may well be considered "correct." In such instances we have tried to select the one most commonly used throughout the United States. However, when it comes to dealing with foreign words we have tended to choose a version which retains some of the flavor of the original. For example, although the Greek word *himation* will be pronounced to rhyme with *my nation* when one anglicizes it to the extreme, the Merriam-Webster dictionaries give the pronunciation as *him-'at-e,an.* But we have chosen to use a broad *a* or *ah* in the second syllable, this being the standard sound denoted by the letter *a* in nearly all European languages.

Vocabulary

1. Dionysus	digh uh NIGH suhs
2. dithyramb	DI thuh ram
3. agon	AH gawn
4. Carl Jung	yoong
5. Levi-Strauss	LE vee strows

CHAPTER TWO

Dramatic Structure: Form and Style

Drama is a time art; that is, a composition requiring a lapse of time in order to comprehend it. However, drama is not life, but rather an imitation of life. Being concerned with life, it focuses primarily on people and their activities, whether the activities be past, present, future, or a combination of all three. All human activity involves either physical or mental change. When a person makes a change, action occurs; action is thus defined as change. Inasmuch as drama seeks to imitate life, it is concerned with action. Action in a drama has a dual nature: it includes acts and deeds done externally as well as the attitudes, thoughts, perceptions, and general awareness which take place within a character. The total action in a person's life, therefore, includes both external and internal activities.

Plot

Generally speaking, we are creatures of habit and thus try to impose order on our activities in an effort to control our lives. Life is so diverse, however, that the task seems a hopeless one. Drama simply imitates certain events in a character's life; in other words, drama focuses on selective actions. By limiting the action, drama can easily structure it. Whereas life consists of diverse action, drama is structured action — it is arranged and unified into a meaningful pattern. To unify in drama means to organize the parts of a play according to the dramatist's plan. That is how the dramatist sees life and how he or she plans to organize the characters to reflect that perception. One method for organizing drama is to use Aristotle's six basic elements: plot, character, thought, diction, sound, and spectacle. By unifying the characters — what they say, do, and think — according to a plan, the author is creating plot in drama. To put it another way, plot is concerned with structuring the thoughts, sayings, and doings of other people in accordance with the author's purpose for writing a play. The reader should think of plot as being a complete pie. It is the whole. The parts that make up the pie are like the six elements which make up plot. Plot organizes these six elements into a meaningful whole.

A dramatist may unify his plot in one, or a combination, of three ways: character, thought, and cause-effect. The use of the so-called classical unities (time, place, action), first insisted upon by Castelvetro (1501-1571), is often thought to be the most effective way to unify a play. The use of time and place to unify the characters, their thoughts, sayings, and doings is insufficient in creating an effective and understandable play. A more effective way is unity of character. This type of unity focuses on a character who is central to all the events and ideas in a play. Biography is a good example of this type of unity. Another method of unity is thought. The playwright focuses on a basic idea which becomes central to all the characters and their actions. The absurdist drama (so-called because life is considered absurd) by Eugene Ionesco, *The Bald Soprano,* serves as a good example. In this play the characters live in a seemingly illogical world where, for example, a clock strikes seventeen for nine o'clock; where doorbells ring when nobody is at the door, and yet when they don't ring, someone is at the door. Central to all this bizarreness are Ionesco's thoughts on the present state of humanity.

A third way, the most common way, is unity of action. Unity of action means that the actions within a play are organized according to a cause-effect relationship. A story, by definition, is a series of related incidents. It is an example of unity of action. A story is the traditional way of unifying a plot. Story and plot, however, are not the same. Plot is the overall organization, and story is one type of organization or plot. All stories have plots, but not all plots have stories. Plot depends upon three things: the author, the purpose, and the material. Unified action has a beginning, middle, and end. Aristotle's dictum that a play should have a beginning, middle, and end means that a play should be complete and self-contained; everything

Opposite: Iago as performed by famous American actor, Edwin Booth. From *Dramatic Portrait Gallery,* 1880.

you need to know about the characters, the events, and the actions should be included within the play's framework.

Beginning

The beginning of a play includes not only the beginning of the story but also the beginning of the main action. When a dramatist writes a play, he must choose which events of a story he will show the audience. He can show the entire story or he can show the middle or the end of the story. For example, in *The Three Bears,* the author could start the story as it is usually told, with Goldilocks entering the three bears' house, or he could start the story with the bears coming home. If he begins the play with the three bears coming home, then all the prior information must be told to the audience. Such information is exposition, which could be presented through a monologue by Goldilocks or perhaps in a dialogue between the bears and Goldilocks. Exposition is additional information which can be given throughout the play and is about events which have happened before the play started, about events which occur offstage during the production, or about events which happen between the acts. This information is needed if the audience is to understand the present situation. That place where the author chooses to start the story is known as the point of attack. Shakespeare uses an early point of attack; he tells the story from the beginning. In contrast, Greek tragedians use a late point of attack; they begin the play by dramatizing the final events in a story and use exposition to tell the audience what events have already transpired.

In addition to including the point of attack, the beginning of a play includes the start of the main action, the inciting incident. The inciting incident is an event which forces the central character (protagonist) from a static situation into an active one. In other words, everything is in balance or harmony until the inciting incident occurs and, like a seesaw, causes an imbalance. The inciting incident is that incident in a story that causes everything in the play to happen. Not all plays have an inciting incident; however, they do have some sort of focal point. Absurdist dramas are examples of plays which do not contain inciting incidents.

An example of traditional drama using a point of attack and an inciting incident is Euripides' *Hippolytus* (428 B.C.). The play opens with Aphrodite's prologue giving us exposition about her hatred of Hippolytus, who refuses to honor her and favors Artemis. She further describes how Phaedra, the wife of Theseus (Hippolytus' father), fell in love with Hippolytus. Angry over Hippolytus' refusal to honor her, Aphrodite plans to punish Hippolytus as well as kill Phaedra by revealing Phaedra's love for Hippolytus. The fact that Euripides begins the play after all the events described by Aphrodite have occurred indicates that this play has a late point of attack. Had he started with the first refusal of Hippolytus to honor Aphrodite or with Phaedra's marriage, then the play would have had an early point of attack. In Scene III the Nurse reveals Phaedra's love to an unsuspecting Hippolytus — this event is the inciting incident. It causes all the subsequent action.

Middle

The action created by the inciting incident constitutes the middle of the play. This action is made up of a series of complications. A complication is a factor which alters the course of action and occurs as a result of a discovery. Any change from ignorance to knowledge constitutes a discovery. A discovery may be related to an object, information, or to self (a realization). Discoveries are the basis for complications, and a play's progression hinges on complications. As the dramatist develops his script, he will create characters who will encounter complexities in their lives. The complexities themselves raise questions which eventually place the characters at a crossroad where they must make a decision. The decision made leads to solutions (answers) to the complication. This answer is a discovery; it answers a question. The answer to one question will serve to raise another question; this answer will in turn be the basis for yet another question, and so on throughout the play. Eventually these questions and answers will lead to the development of, and a solution to, the play's major question. Lesser questions and answers are thus directly related to the play's major question, which is answered at the play's end. Plays by writers such as Bertolt Brecht (1898-1956) are exceptions, since they are designed to end with a question which the audience is to resolve outside the theatre.

Let's examine how a discovery operates, again

using *Hippolytus* as our model. Phaedra has a tremendous problem. She loves her husband's son. A question is raised. What is she going to do? Phaedra's struggle to solve her problem has caused her unhappiness and she, therefore, decides to die. Maintaining silence about her love, she starves herself and becomes ill. Another question is raised — why is she sick? The Nurse discovers the answer, but the answer raises another question. What will the Nurse do? The Nurse reveals Phaedra's love to Hippolytus, thus answering one question but raising another. What will Hippolytus do? Raising questions and answering them constitute the basis for a complication. Discovery precipitates the beginning of a complication — Phaedra's self-discovery of her love for Hippolytus. In seeking to solve her question, a number of alternatives are considered — to die, reveal her love, or do nothing. The consideration of the alternatives, or the middle of the complication, creates tension and conflict (crisis) which lead to the climax (high point) of the complication — her enactment of one of the alternatives. When she decides to reveal her love, Phaedra answers the initial question but in so doing raises another. Answering one question marks the end of one complication and begins another. Complications, just as the whole of a play, are characterized by having a beginning, middle, end, a climax and resolution.

End

A dramatist develops action by weaving complications throughout the play. Questions are raised and may be answered quickly, or the dramatist may choose to leave them unanswered until later in the play. The time when a question will be answered depends upon whether all the possible answers have been considered for a particular complication. When only one remains, it will not only be the probable one, it will also be the necessary one. This answer or situation will thus be logical, believable, and consistent — that is, probable. This is what is meant by the term probability — the solution that must happen. If Hippolytus and Phaedra must die, if Phaedra's love is to be revealed, and if Theseus is to kill his son, then what must happen structurally is for the author to create situations where these events are logical, believable, and consistent. Eventually, the weaving of complications will lead to a major crisis — a turning point in the action. This turning point will lead to the end of the play.

The end of the play includes the resolution or denouement. It starts with the crisis which leads to a climax. A climax always follows a crisis, and is considered the high point of the play's action. This means that the central character (protagonist) is placed in a situation where the answer or solution to the play's major problem depends upon the protagonist's decision. That decision and the uncertainty as to the final outcome create the tension. This is the climax. The end of a play answers all questions and resolves all problems. Traditional dramas are structured to have all the unanswered questions, as well as the battle between the protagonist and antagonist, resolved in an obligatory scene. The obligatory scene follows the crisis and serves to restore the norm in the play. The climax is in this scene.

A scene from the Moscow Art Theatre's production of M. Gorky's *Lower Depths*. Pictured here are Konstantin Stanislavsky as Satin (hands up) and Vassili Kachalov as the Baron in a 1902 staging of the play. Courtesy Sovfoto.

Probability

Unity is a device used by the dramatist to make the play's action effective and understandable. Action in drama must not only employ unity, but that action must be probable as well. Probability means logical, believable, and consistent. But believability, logic, and consistency must be in terms of the play and not necessarily in terms of the audience. A dramatist may be inconsistent in his use of characters, ideas, and action, but as long as he is consistently inconsistent then his play is probable. Frequently the two logics will be in harmony; each play has its own probability, and it is the dramatist who determines the play's probability. For example, Superman, with his incredible feats of strength and his ability to fly, is believable to audiences only within a drama. Such a person does not exist nor do we as audience members believe he exists. Superman is not natural to us, but to the world created by the dramatist he is natural as well as real. Therefore, when an emergency arises and the only way it can be remedied is with Superman's help, his appearance becomes probable — that is, logical and believable. Superman serves as an example of how probability in our lives differs from that in a drama. Probability in drama should be thought of also in terms of the characters, the thoughts, the setting, the costumes and the lights.

In creating probability, a dramatist depicts a series of events which combine to make up one major event. If the writer has created his play correctly, each event raises a question which can be answered in a variety of ways — that is, a number of possibilities or solutions. Eventually all answers are ruled out but one. This is the necessary (logical) answer. It is the only one left.

Looking at probability another way, it is a way of creating or dispelling dramatic illusion; that is, the impression that actual life is occurring on stage. If the probability of the play is natural to our world, if the events and characters do and say things that are logical within the play's framework, then we tend to identify with the characters and events which occur. A bond is created by way of empathy — that is, we mentally enter into the feeling or spirit of a person or thing. This bond allows audiences to mentally escape into another world. Then too, the probability may be unnatural and deal with elements of fantasy. Although unnatural, the fantasy and make-believe world become probable if they are logical within the play's framework. Inasmuch as each play has its own probability, dramatic illusion may also be dispelled by this device. In a Brechtian drama, for example, dramatic illusion is broken by making the probability so unnatural as to alienate us. We are prevented from escaping into another world. Probability is concerned with the believability of the world which a dramatist creates within the framework of his drama.

If a play is to be effective as well as understandable, it should gain and sustain audience interest. Devices such as unity and probability do much in attaining that goal. But if the dramatist hopes to strike a responsive chord with the audience, he must create characters, ideas, events, and an environment which the audience will find meaningful.

Character

Since plot is concerned with structuring the play's action, the physical and mental human activity, it thus arranges characters. It arranges what they say, think, and do; that is, their actions. Characters are thus the material for creating plots. The way a dramatist chooses to differentiate his characters is known as characterization. Six levels of traits for characterization have been suggested by distinguished professor of theatre and drama, Hubert Heffner: (1) biological (male vs. female); (2) physical (age, height, weight, color, etc.); (3) environmental (social strata, religion, etc.); (4) emotional (feelings, desires); (5) psychological (attitude, disposition, habits, motives — a character's thoughts); and (6) moral (integrity, decision-making). Using Heffner's construct, the authors have expanded the moral level based upon psychologist Lawrence Kohlberg's theory of morality (1975). Accordingly, there are three levels of moral development.

The first level is preconventional: a person's moral behavior is based upon punishment. He obeys because of fear of being punished. For example, a person may drive at 55 mph because of fear of being arrested. The second is conventional: a person sees value in the rules and behaves out of loyalty to the system. This level enforces conformity and thus most people do not go beyond it. For example, a person may drive at 55 mph because he sees value in this speed limit — it saves lives and gas. The third level is postconventional: a person establishes his own rules which may or may not be the same as society's. At this level a person asserts his individuality rather than conforming for conformity's sake. Postconventional is thus the highest in terms of moral progression, in that it emphasizes the individual's own decision-making process. Morality is the highest level in affecting the decisions a character makes. Not only will the decisions that a character makes delineate his nature, but the type of decisions made will also aid in distinguishing the play's form (tragedy, comedy, melodrama). The characters in tragedies make moral (ethical) decisions, whereas the characters in melodramas and comedies make expedient decisions.

If a character is to serve adequately as an element of plot, the character must have not only varied traits but the traits must fit together. A character must first of all be good, not necessarily morally good but functionally good. Good, in this sense, means that decisions the characters make advance the action. In a tragedy, a character must make moral decisions if he is to be functionally good. The entire concept of good is directly related to a character's morality. He must make good decisions according to his ethical behavior depending upon whether he is a villain or a hero. The decisions a character makes must be congruent. That is, each new trait must fit with the other traits in terms of the kind of person he is — what he says or does, or what others say about him. When traits follow this pattern, they are termed appropriate. In addition, a dramatist strives to create characters who have likeness or unlikeness, and he tries to create characters who would likely appear in the situations he has devised. Lastly, the character's traits should be consistent. The character should exhibit a continuity throughout the play. Whatever happens to the character's situation, the character's traits should remain consistent to his nature. If the character is inconsistent by nature, then the dramatist should dramatize him as consistently inconsistent. For a character to be acceptable, he must be characterized in terms of being good, appropriate, like or unlike, and consistent.

Thought

Characters form thoughts. What a character thinks or feels is based upon his thoughts, which are expressed by his words and actions. Not only do characters form thoughts, but thoughts are the material for character. Thought appears in the play not only through the actions of the characters, but also as the overall meaning of the play. The character's reaction to his environment, his decisions, desires, emotions, attitudes, sayings, and doings, suggest relationships. These relationships help establish the play's meaning — the overall thought or theme. Thus thought is the play's significance, which in many plays is directly expressed through or by a character. If the play is organized totally upon a basic concept or thought, thought becomes the source of the play's unity. This is true of much modern drama, such as the plays of the absurdist writers or the works of Bertolt Brecht.

Diction

By shaping words into desired patterns, the dramatist creates a character's thoughts. Diction (dialogue) is how these thoughts are expressed. Diction can do much to affect a play's form. For example, Aeschylus' use of metaphor in *The Oresteia* serves to shape the play's action into a tragedy. Pace or speed help establish form as well as characters within that form. Pace in comedy is usually more rapid than it is in tragedy. In a Greek tragedy, for example, the actor must be aware of pace as he may be required to deliver a rapid-fire exchange known as *stychomythia*. Keep in mind that speed in language must never be such that the meaning is lost or misunderstood. Clarity is thus another important aspect of diction. Diction reveals the character's mood for the moment as well as his mood in terms of the entire play. For example, an actor saying, "Come in," may deliver the line fearfully, angrily, or whatever, and thus reveal the character's present state of mind. More in-depth dialogue or soliloquies would serve also to reveal the character's mental state or emotional stability. Another function or usage of diction is characterization. What sort of a person is the character? What motivates him? A dramatist assigns a particular pattern (rhythm) of speech to a character. The character may use his words in a clever way or in a boring manner. He may use slang or be extremely formal, or his actions may contradict everything that he says. A character's diction does much to provide clues to his environment, education, social position, and motives.

In drama a character's speech patterns (his choice of words, pace, and phrasing) underlie his lifestyle as well as the style of the play. A realistic play seeks to create characters whose speech is that of a contemporary society. The speech is conversational and is designed to relate to the speech patterns (rhythms) of everyday life. This means that if the characters are rendered by the dramatist as being realistic, the language should also be realistic. However, if the play's probability is such that a realistic character might speak in nonsense syllables, then the use of nonrealistic diction is acceptable and believable. Directors and actors should note a character's speech rhythms (recurring patterns), pace, and probability as the diction will provide clues not only to characterization but to the play's overall form and style.

Sound (Music)

As an element, sound can also mean music. Dialogue is rendered by the sound of an actor's voice. Within the sound, there is a tonal quality which is analogous to music. In response to a door knock (which is also a use for sound effects), a character may say "Come in" angrily or fearfully. The tonal quality (music) of the words does much to suggest a character's state of being at a particular moment. In *Cyrano de Bergerac,* Cyrano states that Roxane's name is like a bell. The actor can deliver these lines so that the musical quality of a bell is transmitted. The same concept is also true in poetry and verse dramas. Music can also be thought of as background music or music to forward the play's action, such as a tune to indicate a lapse of time. Sound as pure music, as tonal quality, as a dialogue, or as sound effects, is an integral part of the play's structure.

John Howard Payne (1791-1852), American dramatist whose work helped lay the foundation for native American drama. He wrote or adapted between fifty and sixty plays, was the author of the song "Home Sweet Home," and was the first American dramatist to achieve international success. From Coleman's *Players and Playwrights,* 1890.

Spectacle

Whereas plot, character, thought, and diction (when properly utilized) form structured action or drama, spectacle is the representation of that action.

In representing the dramatic action, all the aspects which help transfer the written word to the stage are brought into force. The actor uttering dialogue, the set designer, the lighting designer, the costumer, the propmistress, and the theatre itself are considered part of spectacle. Spectacle is theatre. It represents the structured human action of the drama. The object of the specialists in theatre (those in charge of lights, costumes, sets, etc.) and the specialist in drama (the playwright) is to complete a whole. For example, the set designer, the lighting designer, and the costumer will try to complement each other rather than seek to be individually outstanding. The functions of each part of spectacle will be discussed later at length, but it is important to note that each aspect seeks to enjoin itself as part of the whole and never seeks to be the completed whole. Only when the actor is present is that whole completed.

Form

To form means to arrange, to organize. When a dramatist forms, he is organizing human activity. He organizes the people in his play with the help of the six basic elements of dramatic structure: plot, character, thought, diction, sound (music), and spectacle. The parts are arranged according to the author's purpose; specific arrangement will give a specific form such as tragedy, comedy, or a third form, the most dominant of which is melodrama. Although specific arrangement of the basic elements of drama will create a tragedy, comedy, or melodrama, no two plays, whatever their form, are alike. Each play is unique and, although classified into a specific form, is nonetheless to be considered not in terms of the form but rather as an individual work. Many tragedies, for example, are inferior to many melodramas; conversely, a melodrama should not be judged superior to a comedy or a tragedy. Each play must be judged for its merits. Then too, some dramas defy labeling or do not fit into the traditional molds. Harold Pinter's early plays, for example, are labeled by him as comedies of menace; Ionesco's plays are called anti-plays and tragic-farces. The plays of Pinter and Ionesco do contain the six elements of drama; they have been arranged to create a seemingly different form. The difference lies in how the author perceives his world and how he chooses to dramatize that perception. Traditionally, authors have sought to place their plays in the molds of tragedy, comedy, or melodrama. Modern plays have sought to depart from that tradition as modern dramatists perceive life differently. Nevertheless, all plays display aspects of the three major forms — tragedies, comedies, or melodramas.

Charlotte (Lotte) Crabtree (1847-1924), American actress who began her career at age eight by performing in mining camps. In 1864 she became a major star in New York. She was a versatile performer who could sing, dance, play the banjo, and act. She is pictured here in one of her most memorable roles, Musette. From *Dramatic Portrait Gallery*, 1880.

Tragedy

Tragedy is concerned with a genuinely serious action, one of extreme importance in the lives of one or more characters. It is an action that is long-lasting and raises questions about man's existence, his moral nature, or his social and psychological relationships. The action in a tragedy is thus one that extends past the limits of the play; it is a universal action. For the action to be genuinely serious, it must involve a protagonist whom we can admire. He must possess admirable traits but must not be perfect. The protagonist is thus an above average person, although he is subject to error by not being perfect. The protagonist possesses traits which make him a believable character as well as one with whom the audience can identify. Aristotle termed it likeness; the character must be like us. This is important, for the audience's ability to identify with the protagonist will affect the arousal of the emotions pity and fear, which are characteristic of a tragedy. Pity is aroused when the protagonist encounters undeserved misfortune, struggles and is defeated. Fear is aroused when a threat occurs to the happiness or well-being of a leading character. The threat must be of such a nature as to jeopardize the existence of the protagonist. As a result of that threat, the protagonist begins his struggle to overcome the threat. In his struggle, the protagonist encounters a situation which forces him to make a moral decision. Moral decisions are fundamental to tragedies; they make the action genuinely serious. Thus the decision has lasting import, and its results will continue to affect the life of the protagonist long after the play has ended. A moral decision, then, is a decision of a universal nature (life, death, and man's relationship to a god are examples). It is made by the protagonist out of ignorance and thus contributes to the protagonist's undeserved misfortune. Before being made, a moral decision is usually preceded by the protagonist's deliberation about the decision's outcome. In spite of the deliberation, the decision will lead to the character's downfall because it is based on an error in judgment on the part of the central character. That error in judgment stems from a weakness in the character; that is, a flaw in his nature. This is known as the tragic flaw *(hamartia).* In Shakespeare's *Othello,* Iago is able to destroy Othello by arousing Othello's jealousy. Once his jealousy is aroused, Othello is convinced emotionally (not logically) that his wife is unfaithful. He therefore kills her. Another interpretation suggests the term fault rather than flaw. The argument is that the character is placed in these circumstances and is a victim of his environment rather than his mental processes. *Oedipus Rex* illustrates this concept. Oedipus unknowingly kills his father and marries his mother. The murder occurs when Oedipus and Laius (his father) arrive simultaneously at the three crossroads in Phocis. Each refuses to yield the right of way and Oedipus, in a fit of temper, kills Laius. If Oedipus had arrived at the crossroads five minutes sooner or later, he would not have encountered his father and subsequently killed him.

When the protagonist is threatened and is defeated in his struggle, the emotions of pity and fear are aroused. Aristotle used the term "such emotions," which indicates that pity and fear include a whole range of emotions — uncertainty, suspense, foreboding, apprehension, compassion, horror, and terror. For the action to be complete in tragedy, the emotions aroused must be reduced or removed. The concept of reducing or removing the emotions produced by a dramatic action is termed catharsis or purgation. To purge emotions produced by a play, however, does not mean that the audience's emotions must be purged. Purgation is an internal principle which must occur within the structure of the play if the play's action is to be complete and satisfying. Purgation occurs in the audience only after it has occurred within the play. To purge emotions, the initial cause for arousal must be determined. In the case of a tragedy, the threat to the central character creates fear. As audience members, we identify with the leading character and thus feel fear for that character's safety. When the character suffers undeserved misfortune, we feel pity for the character. To remove or end fear in a tragedy, the threat must be removed. In a tragedy this usually involves the defeat of the central character; this represents one way to remove the fear. With the defeat of the protagonist, the threat is removed. Pity, however, is not completely removed; it is changed. With the demise of the protagonist, we no longer pity but instead rationalize about the protagonist's defeat as well as his fate. Thus pity is usually changed to admiration. We admire the heroics of the chief character or are satisfied that his name and image will survive and give meaning to his death.

Comedy

Comedy requires a deviation or contradiction from what is normal. What is normal to you or your friends may be different, however. Norms also differ between countries, cultures, and generations. Normal is therefore relative. This is why a comedian from one country may not succeed in another. His comic references may be in terms of his own country and culture, his concept of what is normal. A joke about the president with allusions to peanuts may create laughs in present-day America, but such a joke may be ineffectual in another country or in another era.

As with all drama, comedy may be unified through character, thought, and action. A comedy of character may have normal characters in an eccentric world, use the converse, or even create characters who contradict expectations. The latter is a device of the Irish dramatist, George Bernard Shaw (1856-1950), and a good example is his *Arms and the Man.* The opening scene is devoted to establishing a stereotyped image of a soldier in war. The image is created through a description of the exploits of Major Sergius Saranoff, who is depicted as charging into battle, being patriotic, and cruel to his enemies. This image is satirized by Captain Bluntschli, who enters backwards through the window into the bedroom of the heroine, Raina. Contrary to Sergius' image, Bluntschli is running from battle, cringes when Raina scolds him, and carries chocolate candy instead of ammunition.

Another form of comedy is that of thought, better known as satire. The use of language to deride or ridicule some abuse in society by means of irony, sarcasm, puns, or double-entendre creates a deviation from the normal or literal meaning of words and their intended meaning. A third way of unifying comedy is deviating from accepted behavior — comedy of incident or farce. In such comedy the emphasis is on the character's actions and not the character or his thoughts. Although many plays emphasize one element, many comedies will use a combination of any two or all three.

In addition to deviations from the norm, the comic action produced must not render any harm to those involved. Any threat of a serious nature will preempt laughter.

Dramatists, as well as audiences, must be objective about writing and viewing comedy. Henri Bergson, in his essay "Laughter" (1900), suggests that we cannot have sympathy with the events on stage and must, therefore, have an "anesthesia of the heart." That is, we cannot be emotionally involved or identify with the characters or their situations as we do in tragedy. Dramatists must play down the empathetic aspect in a character in order to arouse laughter. A prime example of Bergson's concept is the comedian Vaughn Meader. During the early 1960's, Meader's imitations of President John F. Kennedy and jokes about the president and his family had earned him immense fame. With Kennedy's assassination, however, Vaughn Meader's career ended abruptly. The jokes were no longer funny; people were too emotionally involved. It has taken fifteen years for Vaughn Meader to resume his career.

Inasmuch as comedy is a deviation from the norm and reaction to the deviation is laughter, laughter then seems to serve as a corrective force, a type of catharsis. Laughter is aroused by emphasizing abnormal characters, situations, or creating characters whose behavior can be held up for ridicule. Ridicule is by definition designed to arouse laughter. Thus ridicule and laughter and their catharsis are the emotions aroused by comedy. If the abnormality aroused these emotions, then the catharsis of these emotions will restore the abnormal back to normal.

Unlike tragedy, the action in comedy is not of a highly serious nature. It is not usually concerned with man's relationship to his god, morality, or life and death. The issues involved in comedy seem to focus on what the dramatist considers the vices and follies of man — his mores, manners, and societal institutions. The action tends to be of a temporary nature, which means that it will be resolved before the play's end. Consequently, the action is only deemed serious, and not highly serious as it is in tragedy. Since the action is only serious, the characters make decisions which are expedient rather than moral. The decisions made will affect the characters only momentarily; they are decisions which affect the action throughout the play. At the play's end, however, the decisions will have little or no bearing upon the characters' lives. They are not catastrophic.

Melodrama

Much of what we see today whether in the theatre, movies, or television is melodrama. Because the name melodrama suggests the villain in a stovepipe hat who demands the young maiden if the mortgage is not paid, it has fallen into disrepute. The term given to melodrama today is drama, but structurally it is melodrama.

Unlike tragedy, melodrama focuses on a serious (not a genuinely serious) action. The action is not catastrophic and is only temporary. Its serious nature will no longer be serious at the end of the play, whereas in tragedy the serious nature will continue past the play's end. There are no moral decisions in melodrama, only expedient ones. The play's action is initiated by the villain who threatens or poses a threat to the hero. Throughout the play, the

Franz Molnar's *Liliom* as produced by the Straight Wharf Theatre, Nantucket. Directed by Joseph "Mac" Dixon. *Liliom* was adapted by Rogers and Hammerstein into the musical *Carousel* in 1945. Courtesy Joseph "Mac" Dixon.

Frank Chanfrau (1824-1884), American actor whose portrayal of Mose, the Bowery Boy, the New York fireman in Baker's *A Glance at New York* (1848), made Chanfrau's name synonymous with the Mose character. The play itself had numerous sequels because of its popularity. From *The Interviewer's Album,* 1881-1882.

hero and the villain do battle; the hero is placed in situations from which he seemingly cannot, yet does, escape. This is a characteristic of melodrama — good triumphs over evil. Good winning over evil not only characterizes melodrama but underlies its purpose of teaching a moral lesson.

The continual escape of the hero or heroine is termed chance probability, which is unlike the natural probability of tragedy. Inasmuch as the hero displays character traits with which we can identify (in other words, he is like us), we fear for the hero's safety and hate the villain for causing trouble. The emotions aroused by melodrama are thus fear, hate, and their catharsis. The catharsis, or the purging of fear and hate, is affected by what is termed the double-ending. The double-ending occurs at the conclusion when the villain is punished and the hero is rewarded. No other form of drama distinguishes more clearly between the concept of good and evil. In tragedy good and evil are probed, but in melodrama they are represented by the villain and the hero. This concept of good and evil extends to other aspects of melodrama. The use of signature music, for example, is a trademark of melodrama. It is background music which identifies whether characters are good or bad, and whether the situation a hero is about to enter will produce harm to him. We are all in tune to this use of music, and the moment we hear it during a production, we are able to determine if the ensuing events will be anxiety producing.

Style

Tragedy, comedy, and melodrama are all considered forms, whereas literary movements such as romanticism, realism, naturalism, and other "isms" are termed styles. (These movements will be discussed in later chapters.)

Style may be defined as a distinctive or characteristic mode of construction or execution in any art or work. Style in theatre and drama encompasses not only literary movements but anything which in execution displays unique definable properties. This would include the style of the individual dramatist, for each writer has a particular method of writing. In theatre and drama, style also affects the theatrical production — the director, actor, costumer, lighting designer, set designer, and others who make up a production. Not only is style far-ranging in theatre, it is also relative. It is relative to those involved in the theatre as well as to the era. What is romantic or realistic to one generation is not usually appropriate to other generations. Nineteenth century melodrama, with its stereotype villain who wore a black mustache, cloak and hat, aroused fear in the audiences of that time. Today such a figure is not real to us and we tend to be amused by his appearance. Similarly, what we consider romantic today may not be romantic in the next generation. Hence, realism and romanticism are relative.

Considering the variables in a theatrical production and the relativity of style, it is the task of the director to determine in what style he wishes to stage the production. Each specialist then contributes his portion according to the style the director has suggested in order that the overall production will consistently demonstrate the characteristics of that style. The director may suggest stylizing the production, which means deviating from what is considered realistic at the time. Stylizing (stylism) is often referred to as a style and is defined as a departure from realism. Realism, however, is a style and departures from realism can be conceived in a number of ways. To stylize a production thus does not define precisely in what manner the production's departure from realism will be shaped. Stylizing can mean any style and to refer to it as a style is paradoxical and somewhat confusing. Stylizing in terms of expressionism or naturalism can be thought of as being more precise. Although many plays will display more than one style, most plays lend themselves to one particular style, and that style has been determined by the dramatist. The style of any play is therefore affected by the dramatist and the director. Thus, a play may have a dramatic style as well as a theatrical style. A tragedy, for example, may be written in a realistic style but the director may choose to represent the dramatic action in an expressionistic style. Form and style are thus two separate entities affecting the staging of a play.

Inasmuch as dramatic form and style vary from generation to generation, and inasmuch as dramatic form and style reflect the social, political, and economic institutions of a society, beginning with the Greeks, we will consider various aspects of a particular society's social, political and economic institutions and how they shaped that society's theatre and drama.

Selected Readings

Heffner, Hubert C., Samuel Selden, and Hunton D. Sellman. *Modern Theatre Practice: A Handbook of Play Production.* 4th ed. New York, 1959.

Olson, Elder. *Tragedy and the Theory of Drama.* Detroit, 1961.

Smiley, Sam. *Playwriting: The Structure of Action.* Englewood Cliffs, New Jersey, 1971.

Teleford, Kenneth. *Aristotle's Poetics: Translation and Analysis.* Chicago, 1961.

Vocabulary

1. catharsis	kuh THAHR sus
2. Eugene Ionesco	ee uh NE skoh
3. Aphrodite	a fruh DIGH tee
4. Theseus	THEE see uhs
5. Bertolt Brecht	BAIR tawlt BREKT
6. *Oresteia*	aw RES tee uh
7. stichomythia	stik uh MITH ee uh
8. Cyrano de Bergerac	SEE ruh noh duh BAIR zher ak
9. Henri Bergson	AHN ree BAIRG suhn

CHAPTER THREE

The Greeks
From Ritual to Formalized Drama

It was the Greeks who first took theatre and drama from the ritual stage to its present form. One of the great mysteries is why the Greeks were the first to formalize theatre and drama. Many sophisticated civilizations existed prior to that of the Greeks, yet in these other societies the concept of theatre and drama did not develop past the ritual level. The answer as to why the Greeks, specifically the Athenians, were the first may lie in the concept of the *polis,* which made the Greeks uniquely different from other societies.

A geographical concept, the polis has been equated to a county. Thus every polis was different, just as every county is different. Within that area was located one major town, often walled, a fortified citadel, and a marketplace. For example, Attica was a polis whose major town was Athens. The citizens comprising the polis were the ruling class, whether a democracy, aristocracy or oligarchy. In addition to the citizens, there were other social classes such as slaves and foreigners. Since the Greeks believed the polis was descended from a common male, women were not considered real citizens. In fact they were not considered at all. As Thucydides indicates, it was a woman's duty "to be spoken of as little as possible among men, whether for good or ill." Each polis was comprised of the entire citizen body, and loyalty to the polis was first and foremost to the Greek citizen. This loyalty meant being involved in the daily operations of government. Inasmuch as the citizens made up the state, the name of the state came from the citizens and not the territory. Therefore, the Greek state of Athens is referred to as Athenians, which indicates the people of that state and, in this case, the geographical area also. As Thucydides states, "Men are the polis and not the walls or ships without men in them."

The polis affected every part of Greek society and hence directly affected Greek culture. Of importance to theatre and drama is the town of Athens. In the sixth century B.C., the tyrant Peisistratus (who ruled Athens continuously from c. 560 B.C. to 527 B.C.) reorganized the City Dionysia festival to include dramatic performances. These performances were coupled with a religious ceremony worshipping the god Dionysus, and were designed first of all to enhance Athens' growing power and reputation. They seem also to have been instrumental in neutralizing the power of the old ruling clans and their attempts to regain that power. Under Peisistratus, programs such as dramatic performances were instituted to encourage patriotic duty and loyalty to the polis among the people. The people of Attica thus attached their loyalties to the polis and its functions as a whole rather than to the narrow clans.

Opposite: Vase from fifth century, B.C., depicting satyrs dancing. Metropolitan Museum of Art, Fletcher Fund, 1924.

In 508 B.C. clan power was finally dissolved under Cleisthenes, who reorganized the four existing tribes into ten tribes, based upon residency rather than loyalty or kinship. The political basis of this reorganization was the *deme* — the smallest unit of the polis. These demes were much like our modern wards, and were scattered throughout Attica and were self-governing. The demes in turn were organized in *trittyes* (thirds), and though the number of demes in trittyes varied, three trittyes made up one of the new tribes; thirty trittyes made up the ten tribes. Inasmuch as the new tribes were composed of citizens from various parts of Attica, loyalty to the demes and tribes superseded that to the old tribes. Theatrical productions were organized at various demes and it seems likely that the motive in part was to encourage loyalty to the polis as a whole and the deme specifically.

As a dramatic form, a basic function of Greek tragedy was to provide an effective means by which the people could deliberate on life and death. Aeschylus, in his work, *The Oresteia,* concluded that though human suffering is inevitable, it must be viewed as part of some divine purpose. Right and wrong are also brought into question as is the status of women in society. Many of these same ideas are expressed in the works of Sophocles. *Antigone,* as well as *Ajax,* discusses the authority of the state in matters pertaining to religion. Oedipus, in *Oedipus Rex,* is a portrait of a man whose arrogance leads to his downfall. *Oedipus Rex* is also a drama that stresses man's resignation as the best approach to life and death — man's destiny is in the control of a higher force.

Whereas Aeschylus and Sophocles suggest adherence to formal religion and conventional ethical and social standards, Euripides is generally more skeptical. *Medea,* for example, dramatizes the plight of women as second class citizens in Greek society. His criticism of formal religion as well as war is taken up in *Iphigenia in Tauris* and *Helen.* Greek tragedy thus focused on such topics as suffering in life, the acceptance of death, religious matters, the question of right and wrong, the limits of human ability and potential, and values in society. It provided a way to question; it was a medium for the Greeks to illuminate life.

A second closely-related function of Greek tragedy was to mold man into a perfect being. Man was to be a balanced individual and not given to excesses. Above all, man must not possess arrogance *(hybris).* This is a constant theme throughout the works of Aeschylus and Sophocles. The characters of Creon in *Antigone,* Oedipus in *Oedipus Rex,* and Agamemnon in *The Oresteia* serve as good examples of characters possessing arrogance and who, as a result, encounter disaster. Being balanced extended to all areas of human activity. Further, each area was to contribute to the whole man but could not be greater or less than any other area. Since all areas were to be interrelated, art, athletics, religion, politics, ethics, and architecture were ways to create harmony (balance) and, hence, perfection and beauty in man. Greek tragedy reflects that desire of the Greeks to create the perfect and the beautiful, not only in terms of content but structurally as well. Aristotle's *The Poetics* focuses on the creation of an art object which, when correctly made, is beautiful. Like an art object, man is considered the ideal in Greek society. He is the embodiment of all things. He is, as Protagoras noted, "the measure of all things."

Origins of Tragedy and Comedy

The origins of tragedy are conjectural. The term itself means goat song, perhaps implying that either a goat was sacrificed or that a goat was given as a prize for the best chorus performers. Aristotle states that tragedy originated out of the mimic representations by the leaders of the dithyrambic chorus *(exarchon).* The *dithyramb* was a story about the suffering and death of Dionysus and was sung by the chorus leader backed up by the other chorus members who sang the refrain. The dithyramb is thought to have been developed in Phrygia and to have come to Greece with the cult of Dionysus. Arion (c. 625-585 B.C.) is credited with changing dithyrambs into literary compositions at Corinth. What he probably did was to create a stationary chorus and have the chorus sing a titled poem on a well-defined subject matter. As a form, the dithyramb developed fully in Athens at the festivals of Dionysus. The first dithyrambic contests were held at the City Dionysia about 509 B.C. Thespis is thought to have improved upon the dithyramb by adding a prologue and dialogue, thus developing the first role for an actor. This innovation was probably responsible for his winning in 534 B.C. the first contest for the best writer of tragedy.

Aristotle credits the origins of Greek comedy "out of those who led the phallic procession." Phallic refers to the penis, which was adopted by the Greeks as a symbol of fertility as part of their religious ceremony honoring the god Dionysus, god of fertility. Further, each Athenian house had a bust of the god Hermes mounted on a flat stone slab with a large erect penis projecting from its center. Also, the City Dionysia festival had a procession in which large erect penises made of terra-cotta were carried while songs were sung to phallus. How a sexual ritual was transformed into formal comedy is not known. Epicharmus, who lived in Sicily, is credited with making the transformation about 480 B.C. It is also asserted that another influence was the mime from which the Athenians borrowed certain elements which they combined with their phallic choruses to develop comedy. By 486 B.C. Greek comedy was given official recognition, when contests for writers of comedy were instituted at the City Dionysia festival. The first winner was Chionides.

Festivals

The Greeks were a religious society who believed in many gods. Atheism is said to have been practically unknown. One of the gods who had a great influence upon the Greeks was Dionysus (Baccus), the god of wine, vegetation, and fertility. Dionysus was a Mycenaean god and his worship was taken over by the Mycenaeans from the Minoans and then brought from Asia Minor to Crete, where it was probably transferred to Greece as early as the thirteenth century. As a god, Dionysus was the son of a god who died to save mankind and then was resurrected. His followers ate the flesh and drank the blood of a bull, "sometimes a man," in divine communion.

To honor Dionysus, the Greeks held four festivals yearly: The *Anthesteria* (February-March); the *Lenaia* (January-February); The *Rural Dionysia* (December); the City or Great Dionysia (March-April). All were held in Athens except the Rural Dionysia, which was held in the various demes outside of Athens. During these festivals the Greeks gave themselves to drinking, dancing, wild processions, listening to the story about the death and resurrection of Dionysus, and other ritualistic activities celebrating their god. In 534 B.C. Peisistratus (? - 527 B.C.) reorganized the City Dionysia. Part of the reorganization included the addition of dramatic contests for the best writer of tragedy as part of the festival's activities. These contests were held at the Theatre of Dionysus. Of the festivals honoring Dionysus, the City Dionysia was the last instituted, the most important, and the most representative of the Greek world. When the festival was held, it was open to the entire Greek world. A national holiday was declared, which meant prisoners were freed on bail and no business was transacted. Athens was engaging in good public relations.

As to the Lenaia, drama was not added until about 440 B.C. Comedy seems to have been the chief attraction at the Lenaia, due chiefly to the time of year when it was held. The seas were unnavigable during the last part of January and early February and thus the festival became a local celebration for Athenians. As a local festival, it had more freedom of expression and less censorship; hence, old comedy with its licentious as well as satiric format thrived here. Contests for tragedy and actors may have begun as early as 400 B.C.

The Rural Dionysia was held in villages outside of Athens. The introduction of dramatic contests to this festival is uncertain, and not all villages attached dramatic presentations to this festival. Those which used drama are noted after 460 B.C., and served to try out new plays, revive old plays, and present plays rejected for the City Dionysia. The plays were performed by actors' companies which toured the villages. The oldest extant remains of a theatre which held dramatic performances for the Rural Dionysia seems to be Thorikos. It well might be the oldest theatre in Attica.

The Anthesteria was the oldest festival and also was the only one thought to have little or no connection with the development of drama during the fifth century. Some evidence, however, indicates drama was a part of this festival in the fourth century.

Drama was begun formally, therefore, at a religious festival. The fact that drama was incorporated into the festival honoring Dionysus has led to the conclusion that drama originated out of the worship of Dionysus. This cannot be assumed. Prayers are said before Congress convenes or before sporting and other similar events, but these cannot be construed as religious ceremonies.

Audience

During the fifth century, the theatre audience at the Theatre of Dionysus numbered 15,000 and consisted of Athenian citizens as well as foreign visitors. Although Aristotle would not have allowed boys to witness comedy, boys were present in the audience; doubt exists about women, however. Women were second class citizens in the Greek world. In fact, the Greeks' concept of women generally was that they were "deformed creatures," weaker than men, morally depraved, and genetically they made no contribution to the offspring they produced. Killing a female baby was thus not considered a crime. An alternative to killing a female baby was to send the young female into a life of prostitution. This strong dichotomy between men and women is suggested in the theatre, where historians disagree as to whether women were allowed and, if so, whether they sat apart from men or were forced to sit in the rear of the theatre. Apart from boys and women, the audience was composed of slaves (about thirty-three percent of the population), if accompanied by their masters; Greeks from the states outside of Athens; and foreign visitors. The bulk of the audience consisted of Athenian citizens, who comprised about ten percent of the population.

The use of tickets is debatable. Cash seems to have been used. For those who were too poor to afford the price of a ticket, a *theorikon* (a welfare fund) was introduced during the time of Pericles

Statuettes of Greek actors. Metropolitan Museum of Art, Rogers Fund, 1913.

(fifth century). Some of the seats were reserved for dignitaries, but generally all the seats were the same price — two obols — with the underlying idea that possibly certain classes sat in certain sections of the theatre: women apart from men, and prostitutes apart from other women.

The seats at the theatres were hard and, as with our football games, cushions were used. Although refreshments were available, with the performances beginning at dawn and ending in the evening, some may have even gone home for food. The refreshments consisted of wines, dried fruits (to throw at the actors), and candies. Aristotle proposed measuring the amount of food eaten during a performance to determine the success or failure of a play. In some ways, Greek audiences resembled audiences of today. They slept during a performance, were rude, were drunk, applauded that which they liked and made a great commotion about that which they disliked, such as hissing while kicking their heels against the seats. Some audiences made enough noise to prevent a play from continuing. To control such crowds, comic actors are said to have bribed the audience by throwing nuts to the crowd.

Management

When drama was incorporated into the festivals in 534 B.C., a system of management by the state was also instituted. The management extended not only to the finances but also to the actor, the director, the dramatist, and the critic as well. Thus, when drama was inaugurated into the festival, to insure that it operated smoothly, the state appointed one person, the *archon,* to head it. A primary responsibility of the archon was selecting those dramatists who would compete at the festival. How he selected each dramatist is unknown. Maybe he heard passages from the dramatist's works intended for competition. The archon had to select three writers for the tragic contest, and in 486 B.C., five writers for comedy; during the Peloponnesian War (431-404 B.C.) the latter number was reduced to three. The writers selected for the tragedy contest were required to present three tragedies. In 501 B.C. a *satyr* play was added. The satyr drama is said to have been invented by Pratinas, whom ancient sources credit with having written fifty plays, thirty-two of which were satyr dramas.

Satyr drama took its name from the chorus, who were costumed as half-beast, half-human creatures. Mythologically, satyrs were responsible for attending to Dionysus and thus were his companions. Their leader was Silenus, the father of satyrs. Essentially, satyr plays afforded comic relief from the tragedies presented before them and, therefore, were filled with satire on the gods and heroes as well as dancing and sexual innuendoes. Sometimes the story was connected to that of a tragedy just presented, but usually it was different. In addition to writing three tragedies and one satyr drama, the dramatist was also responsible for composing the music and dance for the chorus.

On the other hand, the five comedy writers needed to present only one play each. When five comedies were presented, four days were required for the plays, possibly extending the festival an extra sixth day. When the number of comedy writers was reduced to three (c. 425 B.C.), the dramatic festival took three of the five days given to the City Dionysia. The dramatic festival began about dawn and ended in the early evening. Greek is spoken more rapidly than English, and generally, what took the Greeks an hour and a half to perform would take about two and a half hours in English. Thus, not counting intermissions between the play, the running time for the productions was roughly six to eight hours for the three tragedies, one satyr play, and one comedy.

Once a dramatist was selected, the next step was to get a *choregos* for each dramatist. This was also the job of the archon. The choregos was much like a modern day "angel," in that his function was to provide most of the financing for the production.

Once nominated by the archon for the position of choregos, a citizen was obligated by law to fulfill that position. Although the citizen chosen was wealthy, he could be released from this obligation by challenging another citizen with the claim that the challenged citizen was wealthier.

The choregos had to pay for the masks, costumes, the chorus salaries, later a chorus trainer, a flute player, and sometimes "extras." In addition, he was responsible for employing a chorus and an *aulos* player. The aulos was an instrument similar to an oboe and was not a flute. The rehearsal was left to the author, who also served as director, choreographer, composer, and, at times, actor. Rehearsal appears to have lasted for a year. A playwright's success depended, to a large extent, upon the willingness of the choregos to spend money.

Each tragic dramatist was allowed only three speaking actors. This is known as the three actor rule. Comedy had three to five actors. All actors were men. The great roles of Antigone, Electra, Medea, and Phaedra were done by men. Boys were not used either. The high esteem of actors precluded women being allowed as actors. This esteem can be noted particularly in the Hellenistic period, when actors were immune from military service and often served as ambassadors because they were allowed free access between countries. The actors were rated according to their ability: first actor *(protagonist),* second actor *(deuteragonist),* and third actor *(tritagonist).* It appears that the dramatist and the first actor chose the second and third actors. The choice of the protagonist was probably assigned by the archon. In 449 B.C. awards were given to the best protagonist (the first winner being Herakleides), awards which may represent the beginning of the "Oscars." These awards undoubtedly contributed to the fact that by the fourth century the actor received greater acclaim than the writer.

Major Greek Dramatists

The outstanding dramatists of Greek drama were Aeschylus, Sophocles, Euripides, Aristophanes, and Menander.

Aeschylus

Aeschylus's (c. 525-456 B.C.) addition of the second actor to drama marks him as the real founder of Greek tragedy. Minor characters such as soldiers, attendants, etc., were not considered actors. Thus, with Aeschylus there are two actors and a chorus creating the dramatic action. Altogether he wrote about ninety plays (satyr dramas included); only seven survive, and all focus on those unseen forces which shape and control man's destiny. The earliest play, which is also the oldest extant drama, is *The Persians* (472 B.C.). This play is also the only extant work of Aeschylus which does not form part of a trilogy (three complete and related plays based upon a single story or theme). *Prometheus Bound* (after 468 B.C.), *Agamemnon, Libation-Bearers, Eumenides, Suppliants* (after 468 B.C.), and *Seven Against Thebes* (467 B.C.) constitute parts of trilogies. *Agamemnon, Libation-Bearers,* and *Eumenides* are grouped together under the title *The Oresteia* (458 B.C.), which is the only complete extant trilogy in Greek drama. Some have contended that this trilogy represents the finest achievement in all of drama. Aeschylus' death is said to have occurred when an eagle dropped a tortoise on his bald head, mistaking it for a stone.

As a dramatist, Aeschylus seemingly considered his accomplishments secondary to his contributions to the state. His epitaph (supposedly composed by him) reads "Aeschylus, Euphorion's son, Athenian, lies in this tomb, perished in wheat-bearing Gela. Of his valour and fair-fame the sacred grove of Marathon can tell, and the long-haired Persian who learned it there." In other words, Aeschylus's pride in being a member of the polis and making a contribution to the same marked him as a loyal Athenian first, and a dramatist second.

Sophocles

Sophocles (c. 496 B.C.-406 B.C.) was a man of great charm, handsome, wealthy, and is considered by many historians the finest of the Greek tragic dramatists. Upon his death, he was worshipped as a hero. This esteem continued for generations. The poet Shelley (1792-1822), for example, had a volume of Sophocles in his pocket when he drowned.

His innovations to Greek tragedy include the addition of the third actor, the first use of scene painting, discontinuing the use of connected trilogies, and increasing the size of the chorus from twelve to fifteen.

Unlike the comic chorus which numbered twenty-four, the size of the tragic chorus is held in question. The tragic chorus was probably twelve. This number was raised to fifteen by Sophocles. He wrote 123 dramas of which seven are extant — *Oedipus Rex* (c. 430-425 B.C.), *Antigone* (c. 441 B.C.), *Ajax* (c. 450-440 B.C.), *Electra* (c. 418-410 B.C.), *Philoctetes* (409 B.C.), *Women of Trachis* (c. 413 B.C.) and *Oedipus at Colonus* (406 B.C.). In addition, a portion of a satyr play which he wrote, *The Trackers,* is extant. He won twenty-four contests and never finished lower than second. Whereas Aeschylus preferred the trilogy and focused on the concept of fate, Sophocles wrote individual works and concerned himself with the psychological nature of man. It is Sophocles' play, *Oedipus Rex,* which serves as the model for Aristotle's treatise, *The Poetics,* which focuses on what constitutes good dramatic structure.

Euripides

Unlike Sophocles, Euripides (c. 480-406 B.C.) was said to be a gloomy individual. Born on the day of the great naval battle at Salamis, Euripides died in Macedonia where he reportedly was accidentally torn to pieces by hunting dogs. He wrote ninety-two plays of which eighteen survive; he won first place five times. His satyr play, *The Cyclops* (date unknown), is the only complete extant satyr drama. Structurally, Euripides' plays are considered weaker than those of Aeschylus and Sophocles. The chorus serves no real function in Euripides' plays, even though the number of chorus members is raised to fifteen. His real concern is a strong psychological study of man, even more than that of Sophocles. It is an investigation into the motives of a character that dominates the plays of Euripides. In addition to psychological character studies, Euripides also favored realistic subjects and costumes. Consequently, Euripides is often considered the first of the realistic writers in drama. Euripides' later plays — for example, *Electra* (c. 417-408 B.C.) and *Hippolytus* (428 B.C.) — demonstrate a turn toward melodrama, which as a form has a contrived ending. In Euripides this contrived ending is noted in the use of the *deus ex machina* (god from the machine) at the end of the play. Deus ex machina refers to an actor who, in representing a god, was hoisted by a crane-like device atop the stage building at the end of the play. His function was to resolve the play in a manner suitable to all characters and the audience. This type of contrived ending represents an early stage of the contrived ending in melodrama, in which the rewarding of good and the punishing of evil became the standard. Euripides' plays served as a model for Greek New Comedy, and his *Andromeda* (c. 430-415 B.C.) is also the first play in which love interest motivates the action.

On the one hand, historians have indicated that Euripides' departure from traditional tragedy forced him into exile. On the other hand, his popularity in antiquity is attested to by Plutarch (c. 46-c. 120 A.D.), who contends that on three separate occasions Euripides' popularity saved the day. The first event noted concerns Athenian prisoners at Syracuse who were set free because they could recite passages from Euripides. On another occasion, a ship pursued by pirates was unable to enter a Sicilian harbor for safety until some member on board could recite from Euripides. In 404 B.C. when Athens had been conquered by Sparta and was to be destroyed, the Spartan generals were so moved, it is said, by a Phoenician singing the first chorus from Euripides' *Electra* that the city was saved.

Euripides, Sophocles, and Aeschylus were responsible for Greece's Golden Age of Drama. Together they wrote at least 278 plays of which only 32 survive. Thus our conclusions about Greek tragedy remain on somewhat tenuous grounds.

Aristophanes

The central dramatist for old and middle comedy was Aristophanes (c. 448-380 B.C.). Old comedy abounds with social satire (society, politics, literature, and war), and is organized around a concept known as "the happy idea." The happy idea is an absurd solution which never really succeeds; for example, a sex strike to end war. The idea is proposed in the first part of the play. Next comes the agon or debate as to the merits of the idea. The decision of the debate always favors putting the happy idea into practice. The action of the play now stops, and the chorus directly addresses the audience, in the name of the writer, about some particular problem. This is called the *parabasis,* which finds its modern sequel in the term *raisonneur* (a character speaking for the author). Structurally, the parabasis divides the play into two parts. The first part is the conception of the "happy idea," and the debate as to its merits. The second part of the play puts the "happy idea" into practice to demonstrate its ridiculous nature. It consists of roughly four episodes which are unified through thought — the "happy idea." A komos, or a final scene of reconciliation, ends the play and all characters gather together for a feast and dancing. This last feature has led some historians to see a direct relationship between the phallic processionals connected to the worship of Dionysus and Aristophanic comedy.

Middle comedy is transitional comedy. The structure is similar in many ways to old comedy except mythology replaces comments on society's social, political, or economic institutions as the main subject matter, personal satire disappears, and the function of the chorus as an integral part of the play is eliminated. Middle comedy continues until roughly 336 B.C., at which time new comedy begins.

Our complete knowledge of Greek old and middle comedy is based upon the plays of Aristophanes. Only eleven of these plays exist out of the forty he is thought to have written. Nine of these plays make up old comedy, whereas *Plutus* (388 B.C.) and *Ecclesiazusae* (392-391 B.C.) constitute middle comedy. With only nine plays it is difficult to determine if Aristophanes' plays are typical of Greek old and middle comedy. Thus, like Greek tragedy, the conclusions made about Gree' old comedy are far from absolute.

Vase, early fourth century B.C., depicting actors. Metropolitan Museum of Art, Fletcher Fund, 1924.

Menander

The most noted dramatist of Greek new comedy (330-150 B.C.) was Menander (c. 342-291 B.C.) Of the more than 100 plays which he wrote, we possess fragments of about 85 plays and portions of four: *The Girl from Samos, Arbitration, The Shorn Girl,* and *Heroes.* The only complete extant work of Menander is *The Grouch,* which was produced in 317 B.C. at the Lenaian festival where it was awarded first prize. The only known script of *The Grouch* is a third century A.D. papyrus, which was found in 1957 by a Swiss banker who discovered it in an antique shop in Cairo, Egypt. He kept the script in his private library until 1959, at which time the first translation was made. Based upon this scanty information plus commentaries, historians have evolved some characteristics of Menander, and hence, Greek new comedy:

1. The setting is usually a street in or near Athens.
2. Emphasis is upon domestic affairs of middle class Athenians.
3. A conventional recognition scene serves to solve the problems of the characters. (For example, a lost daughter is reunited with her family; there are mistaken identities; twins are used to create situations.)
4. Language is everyday speech.
5. The chorus serves the function of entertainment between the episodes. The use of commercials between episodes on television is, in a sense, a continuation of that function.

Menander proved to be an influence upon the Roman dramatists Plautus and Terence, and hence influenced our modern situation comedy in film, television, and theatre, which contains the devices popularized by Menander in Greek new comedy. Ancient commentary has it that Menander drowned while swimming in the harbor of Piraeus.

Costumes and Makeup

The Greek actors as well as the chorus of tragedy, comedy, and satyr drama used masks, although they might not have done so from the beginning. Thespis is said to have painted his face with white lead and then hung flowers over his head. In the fifth century, masks were very naturalistic, made of cork or linen, artificially stiffened, and some covered the entire head. Aeschylus is reported to have colored them and made them terrifying. Perhaps the use of masks was a continuation of drama's ritualistic origins.

It seems likely that the dress for actors of tragedies was a sleeved chiton (a basic dress-like garment) worn at ankle-length, and a himation (a rectangular cloth garment) usually draped over the left shoulder and continuing about the body. The footwear was a boot which came in two styles: a loose pull-on boot and a laced boot. Female characters often went barefooted in tragedy. In a satyr play, the chorus, unlike the actors, wore tights with a tail and a phallus attached, and wore no footwear.

The dress and footwear in comedy varied from that of tragedy but were similar to the satyr chorus. The costume for old and middle comedy featured a phallus attached to padded tights, a short chiton, and a soft-soled slipper called a buskin. The costume for new comedy was a plain white chiton, which was cut longer than that used in old and middle comedy. A phallus and padded tights seem to have been eliminated in new comedy.

Architecture

The Theatre of Dionysus, which was excavated in the nineteenth century, is one of the few remaining theatres left for modern study. Although the best preserved Greek theatre is at Epidaurus, the Theatre of Dionysus commands the most attention, for all the extant Greek tragedies and comedies were first presented here during the City Dionysia. Built at Athens at the beginning of the fifth century, the Theatre of Dionysus was probably a temporary wooden structure at first; however, by 330 B.C. it became a permanent stone theatre.

The Greeks, being outdoor people who were primarily involved in agriculture, built outdoor theatres. Inasmuch as the plays were presented at different times of the year, in order to aid the actors' projection, the theatres were constructed on a hillside in accordance with either the prevailing sea breeze or land breeze. The theatres were designed so the air currents would move toward the audience. The first theatre was nothing more than a raised circle called an *orchestra* (dancing place). In the orchestra a chorus danced while the audience watched from the hillside. Located within this area was an altar *(thymele)* large enough to accommodate the slaughtering of a bull. Between the orchestra and the first row of seats was a drainage ditch for the rain from the sloping hillside as well as the orchestra. The seats became stone seats in the fourth century, and there were at least fifty rows. The seats were spread in a fan-like arrangement and were sectioned off in wedge-shaped areas by flights of steps. Roughly thirty-five rows up, an aisle which extended horizontally across the theatre separated the two main seating areas. This was called the *diazoma* (girdle). Today we

Epidaurus festival. Courtesy Greek Embassy.

consider the seating area the auditorium, but to the Greeks it was the *theatron,* the watching place, whereas to the Romans, it was the auditorium which means listening place.

Behind the orchestra was a building called the skene, a hut or tent where the actors dressed. During the fifth century, it most likely was temporary and thus was erected and then taken down with the beginning and ending of each festival.In addition to being a dressing area, the skene also served as a permanent scenic device. It has been definitely established that painted panels *(pinakes)* were in use during the fifth century, but the practice of changing the pinakes for each play has not been proven. Supposedly the pinakes were fitted into the door openings *(thyromata)* in the second level of the skene — called episkenion. By inserting or removing the painted panels, a new set could be created. This is similar to a scenic device used in the twentieth century known as a plug. Pinakes are the only scenic device established for the fifth century. *Periaktoi* (triangular prisms which, when rotated, revealed a different scene painted on each side) were another scenic device used in the fourth century. By the end of the fifth century, it seems likely that the skene had three doors to enable the actors to make entrances and exits. The central doorway served also for use of a device called the *ekkyklema* (thing wheeled out). This was a platform on wheels, which was rolled out through the central doorway to reveal characters killed offstage or to present a tableau. Additionally, the skene had a stage on the second level called the *theologeion,* which was an area for the god characters — as for the deus ex machina *(mechane* in Greek and *machina* in Latin).

Access to the orchestra area was via passageways called the parados, located to the right and left of the orchestra. In Greek drama, chorus as well as actors used the parados for entrances and exits. It has also been stated that the horses and chariots indicated in the scripts also utilized the parados. Such statements, however, are not easily documented. The Greeks did not have stirrups, and the rocky terrain of Greece made chariot warfare useless. Further, the entrances to the parados seem too narrow for chariots, especially if a fast exit was required. In many cases a ninety degree turn would be required to prevent the exiting charioteer from going over the hillside.

The orchestra, skene, auditorium, episkenion, logeion, and parados represent the basic architectural elements of the fifth century Greek theatre. Beginning in the fourth century, Greek theatre and drama underwent changes in which consolidation and extension occurred. Briefly, the Hellenistic period (336-146 B.C.), sometimes called Alexandrian because it began with the reign of Alexander the Great, brought new innovations: an increase in the number of festivals; a more professional theatre; the Artists of Dionysus (possibly formed at this time), which was an actors' guild and the forerunner to Equity; a high raised stage; costume changes including soled boots *(cothurnus)* and a high headdress *(onkos)*; and a more elaborate skene. By the second century B.C., the Roman influence began to be asserted and by the first century A.D., Roman standards forced Greek theatres to be remodeled. The Greek theatre endured a thousand years of continuous use — a truly remarkable feat.

Selected Readings

Harsh, Phillip W. *A Handbook of Classical Drama*. Stanford, Calif., 1944.

Kitto, H.D.F. *Greek Tragedy*. Garden City, N.Y., 1954.

Pickard-Cambridge, A.W. *The Dramatic Festivals of Athens*. 2nd ed. revised by John Gould and D.M. Lewis. Oxford, 1968.

———. *The Theatre of Dionysus in Athens*. Oxford, 1946.

Vocabulary

1. Antigone	an TI guh nee
3. *Iphigenia in Tauris*	i fi ji NIGH uh in TAH ris
3. phallic	FA lik
4. Lenaia	luh NEE uh
5. Anthesteria	an thes TAIR ee uh
6. Peisistratus	pigh SIS truh tuhs
7. Thespis	THE spis
8. archon	AHR kawn
9. satyr	SA ter
10. choregos	kawr AY guhs
11. protagonist	proh TA guh nist
12. deuteragonist	doo: ter A guh nist
13. tritagonist	trigh TA guh nist
14. Silenus	sigh LEE nuhs
15. Pratinas	PRAH ti nuhs
16. Aeschylus	E skuh luhs
17. Sophocles	SAW fuh kleez
18. Euripides	yoo RI puh deez
19. Agamemnon	a guh MEM nuhn
20. Eumenides	yoo: ME nuh deez
21. Philoctetes	fil uhk TEE teez
22. Andromeda	an DRAW mi duh
23. Aristophanes	a ri STAW fuh neez
24. deus ex machina	DAY uhs eks MAH ki nah
25. parabasis	pa RAH buh sis
26. raisonneur	ray zaw NER
27. Plutus	PLOO: tuhs
28. Ecclesiazusae	ek KLAY zee ahd zoo sigh
29. chiton	KIGH tawn
30. himation	him AHT ee awn
31. diazoma	dee AHD zoh muh
32. thymele	thigh ME lay
33. thyromata	thigh ROH mah tuh
34. pinakes	pin AH kayz
35. periaktoi	pair ee AHK toy
36. theologeion	thee uh LOH gee on
37. ekkyklema	ek KIK lay muh
38. mechane	may kuh NAY
39. episkenion	e pi SKI nee awn
40. parados	PAHR uh daws
41. paradoi	PAHR uh doy
42. cothurnos	koh THER nuhs
43. onkos	AWN kuhs
44. polis	PAW luhs
45. Oedipus	E duh puhs
46. Aulos	AW luhs
47. theorikon	thee OHR ik awn
48. Chionides	kigh awn IGH deez
49. Epicharmus	e pi KAHR muhs

CHAPTER FOUR

The Romans
From Formalized Drama to the Dark Ages

Whereas the Greeks focused first and foremost upon man, the Romans focused on nature. The woods, the rivers, the mountains, and the home were thought to contain spirits who controlled their specific domain. This sense of awareness created in the Romans an awe or anxiety about the presence of spirits, and hence, the idea of maintaining the proper relations with the gods prevailed.

Roman religion was highly ritualistic and detail oriented. The ceremonies *(ludi)* were scrupulously followed and had to be repeated if, for example, a priest's hat fell off his head or a rat squeaked. The ritual was thus more important than the deity worshipped. An important aspect of the ritual was that of vows. The Romans maintained a business-like relation with their gods and did not consider morality. They simply made a vow to give the gods a temple, an offering, institute games in their honor, or some other pledge if that god would fulfill their request.

Like the Greeks, the Romans kept religion and politics together. Oftentimes, Roman leaders told the people or other politicians that they had consulted the gods in order to implement their own ideas. The fact that church and state were not separate greatly aided Roman society. The business-like attitude and the exact fulfillment of religion promoted discipline and obedience to the state. The government in turn held annual state festivals honoring the gods and thus strengthened patriotism to Rome through religious sanctification. It was in these state festivals that theatre and drama were first offered to the Romans. It was also through theatre and drama that in the third century B.C. religious beliefs were undermined.

The Roman theatre was developed as a result of Roman territorial expansion. About 272 B.C., Roman armies conquered the town of Tarentum in the province of Calabria. If you look at a map of Italy, Calabria made up the heel of the Italian boot.

Opposite: The Théâtre d'Orange. Courtesy French Cultural Services.

Tarentum was populated by many Greek citizens and, consequently, those not killed by the Romans were brought to Rome as slaves. Inasmuch as the teacher was usually a slave, some Greek captives became teachers for the children of their Roman masters. One such Greek was Livius Andronicus (c. 284-204 B.C.), who is considered the father of Latin literature. He taught Latin and Greek and also translated Greek literature into Latin. In 240 B.C. he was requested to produce a tragedy and a comedy for the Roman games (ludi). These ludi were equivalent to the Greek Dionysian festivals. Basing the plays on Greek models, Livius Andronicus produced a tragedy probably fashioned after Sophocles or Euripides and a comedy modeled on the work of Menander. These first works, translations, mark the beginning of regular tragedy and comedy in Roman theatre.

Festivals

Like the Greek Dionysian festivals, the ludi were official religious festivals. Rather than honor one god at the festivals, however, the Romans honored many gods. Some of these gods were Greek gods; Dionysus, for example. To be effective, the ceremony worshipping the gods had to be performed with exact precision. Any mistake meant that the ritual or the festival had to be repeated. Records indicate that some rituals at the festivals were repeated as many as thirty times; the entire festival of the ludi Romani was repeated eleven times between the years 214-200 B.C., and that of the ludi Plebeii seven times in one year. The concept of repetition carried over into the dramatic performances which were connected to the religious festivals and therefore required precision. This concept of repetition of the ludi, including dramatic performances, was termed *instauratio*.

Although there were a number of festivals, only certain festivals contained dramatic performances, like the Greek City Dionysia as opposed to the

Greek Anthesteria. The oldest festival which presented scenic plays *(ludi scaenici)*was the *ludi Romani* (4-18 September, given in honor of Jupiter), established in the sixth century B.C. Although it had pantomimic dances in 364 B.C., the ludi Romani did not have regular drama until 240 B.C., at which time the plays of Livius Andronicus were presented. Initially, one day of the festival was devoted to dramatic performances. By 27 B.C., fifty-five days were devoted to theatrical entertainments and by 250 A.D., the number increased to 100 days.

Like the ludi Romani, as other festivals developed, the concept of dramatic performances was gradually instituted. For example, the *ludi Florales* (28 April-3 May, given in honor of Flora) was instituted in 238 B.C., and added dramatic performances in 173, devoting five out of six festivals days to plays (basically mime). Other festivals included the *ludi Apollinares* (5-13 July) which was instituted in 212 B.C. and added dramatic performances in 179, devoting eight out of nine days to these performances. The *ludi Megalenses* (4-10 April, given in honor of the Great Mother) began in 204 B.C. and added regular performances in 194. Six out of seven days were devoted to drama. The *ludi Cereales* (12-19 April, given for Ceres) started in 202 B.C. and, of the eight festival days, seven were given to plays. Lastly, the *ludi Plebeii* (4-17 November given in honor of Jupiter) was instituted c. 220 B.C. and added plays c. 200 B.C.

Dramatic Forms and Entertainments

The Roman theatre is comparable to American television in that it included everything from tragedy and comedy to acrobatics, juggling, trained animal acts, athletic events, violence, and sex. The Roman public was fickle and, much like our television switchers, they left one event for another and demanded diversions. Consequently, the regular forms of tragedy and comedy flourished for a time and then declined. The best period in Roman drama was during the Republic (509-27 B.C.), specifically 240-86 B.C. By 100 B.C. comedy ceased to be a form which could attract or sustain the interest of the audience. Tragedy seems to have faded by 22 B.C. The last writer known to have his plays acted was the Consular, P. Pomponius Secundus. With the demise of tragedy and comedy, minor forms ascended in popularity.

Atellan farce *(fabula Atellanae)* was one minor form to replace comedy. Essentially a Punch and Judy show, it was a one-act form and was originally nonliterary. During the first century B.C., Pomponius and Novius are said to have turned it into a literary form. By the first century A.D., the Atellan farce reverted back to its nonliterary form. With its stock characters, rustic settings, its language, and references to sex and other bodily functions, a relationship is said to exist between the Atellan farce and the sixteenth century commedia dell'arte. Its similarity to mime leads some historians to conclude that the Atellan farce was nothing more than masked mime.

The Atellan farce was usurped in its popularity by mime (*fabula Riciniata)*. As a form, mime was elaborate, obscene, spectacular, and was particularly associated with the ludi Florales. Our first evidence of this mime is 211 B.C. as a nonliterary (impromptu) form. In the first century B.C., mime was temporarily transformed into a literary composition by Decimus Laberius (c. 106 B.C.-43) and Publius Syrus. However, under the Empire (27 B.C.-c. 476 A.D.) it reverted to its original concept.

Mime was unique; it was the only form in which women acted and stripped off their clothes at the audience's request. The low opinion held of the theatre, plus the stripping, led to labeling these actresses as prostitutes. The stock themes of adultery and love affairs were realistically enacted along with other sexual (such as sodomy) and violent acts. Domitian, the Emperor (51-96 A.D.), for example, commanded that a real crucifixion be inserted into a performance. Real executions and sundry sexual acts were performed in the name of entertainment. Because no masks were worn, the sexual emphasis of mime affected how actors were chosen. Those who were handsome would be most desired in a performance involving sexual activity, whereas those who were ugly were used for comedy or violence. In addition to looks, the mime actors had to have good voices and know how to dance. The mime actors went barefooted, which was quite different from actors in tragedy and comedy. Those in tragedy wore a high soled boot called a *cothurnus,* and those in comedy wore a low shoe or sock called a *soccus*. Additionally, actors of tragedy and comedy wore linen masks called *persona*, and the parts of the play were labeled according to the masks — *dramatis persona* (masks of the play). The term is still in use today.

In terms of content, the mimes in both the Eastern Roman Empire and Western Empire satirized the Christians, public events, and emperors. The emperors were not so forgiving, however; Caligula had one writer burned alive in the arena. Domitian had the actor Helvidius Priscus, the younger, executed for satirizing the emperor's divorce. Mime remained a dominant form until the sixth century A.D., at which time the theatres were closed.

Whereas farce replaced comedy, pantomime *(fabula saltica)* replaced tragedy. Phylades and Bathyllus are credited with introducing this form in 22 B.C. It was a distinctly Latin form as noted by the Greek term for it — "Italian dance." The central figure was a masked actor who danced alone without speaking. While the chorus sang the specially written dialogue accompanied by some sort of musical instrument, the dancer conveyed a mythological story to the audience. Roman pantomime can thus be considered a forerunner to our modern ballet.

Audience

Although these festivals were religious, they were a signal for the populace to enjoy themselves. The noted Roman dramatist, Plautus, phrased it best when he wrote: "You may eat what you like, go where you like . . . and love whom you like, provided you abstain from wives, widows, virgins, and free boys."

Admission to the theatre was free and all classes and ethnic groups attended. The populace was made up of Greeks (some slaves and some freedmen), Frenchmen (Gauls), Jews, Egyptians, Syrians, Spaniards, Ethiopians from Africa, "tattooed savages from Britain," "barbarians" from Germany, Persians, Scythians from Russia, and a host of other ethnic groups from Europe and Asia. This heterogeneous group composing the theatre audience included married women, nurses with children, gentlemen, slaves, and prostitutes who tended (if allowed) to sit on the stage. Women were more honored in Rome than in classical Greece and were allowed in the theatre. It appears that prior to 145 B.C., the audience stood, as sitting in the theatre was considered tantamount to corrupting one's morals. In one Roman play, a character referring to the standing audience asserts, "Cut it short: the stalls are thirsty." The audience was generally unruly and actors had a difficult time sustaining the audience's interest. At times actors were forced to extremes. At the ludi Florales, for example, the audience wanted and got the female actors to remove all their clothes. Eventually, audience demands caused the demise of tragedy and comedy and encouraged the rise of spectacle-oriented forms.

The Flavian Amphitheatre, commonly called the Colosseum. Animals are pictured coming from their dens into cages, which are then lifted to the floor of the Colosseum. This lifting system is an early example of what we know as the counterweight system. From *The Flavian Amphitheatre,* 1876.

Spectacles

Contemporary sources on Roman history indicate that the terms theatre and amphitheatre were used interchangeably. Parallels existed between the two types of structures. They both produced similar entertainments; raised stages existed in both structures for usage by actors who sang, danced, and recited odes. The area beneath the stages in the theatre and amphitheatre was used for housing stage machinery. Of particular interest is the machinery used for those entertainments known as spectacles and performed mainly at the amphitheatres — sea battles, gladiatorial contests, wild animal hunts, athletic contests, and other events which exploited sex and violence. Statilius Taurus in 29 B.C. built the first permanent amphitheatre, which housed a variety of machinery that could well have been an influence on the Italian Renaissance, which, in turn, influenced modern stagecraft.

Amphitheatre at Pozzuoli, near Naples. Note the traps — those at the edge are for animals, the others are for men and dogs. Also note that each trap has a groove for a cover. This was probably used to make the arena watertight for sea battles (naumachia). The limestone or tufa wall in the background indicates that there was an awning over the galleries. From *The Flavian Amphitheatre,* 1876.

The arena (which in Latin means sand with which the amphitheatre floor was covered) had a removable wooden floor with trap doors. These traps were equipped with counterweight elevators, which raised and lowered the wild beast cages to and from the stage area. The traps were operated from below and gave the effect of surprise when they were opened and the animals sprung from the seemingly solid floor. Wooden frames (much like modern-day flats) with scenes on them, as well as three-dimensional scenery, were located beneath the cavernous stage area and were also sent up through the traps. When the traps were not used, the arena could be flooded for a sea battle — ships and all — and then quickly drained so the arena could be used for the next event. Windlasses were attached to a cradle-type device which was used to drag the vessels. This device was similar to that utilized by Torelli to shift scenery in the Italian Renaissance. The use of a crane and ropes to raise and lower scenery and to fly actors, although used by the Romans, was probably a carry-over from the Greeks. A last type of machinery used by the Romans was for rotating the stage area (not the entire building). They could thus exhibit plays in the afternoon and, by rotating the structure, make an amphitheatre for spectacles in the evening.

Physical Theatre

The basic feature of the Roman theatre was its wooden stage *(pulpitum)*. Plautus termed it a *scaena* (stage, scene building) or *proscaenium.* It was about five feet high, twenty to forty feet deep, and between one to three hundred feet in length. In front of the stage was the orchestra area, which had varying uses. Movable seats could be placed here for special visitors, the area could be flooded for sea battles *(naumachia)* or water ballets, and sometimes it was used for gladiatorial contests. The orchestra area was a semicircle directly attached to the auditorium *(cavea),* and held anywhere from 8,000 to 14,000 people. Before 55 B.C., when the first permanent theatre was constructed by Pompey (Theatre of Pompey), the Roman theatres were temporary, and thus were constructed and dismantled for the different ludi (at least five) which were given each year. One source indicates that in 58 B.C. a temporary stage three stories high was constructed, with the first story made of marble, the second of glass, and the third of wood inlaid with gold. It had 360 columns, 3,000 bronze statues, and held 80,000 spectators.

Unlike the Greek theatre, the Roman theatre was one complete unit. Thus the auditorium was attached to the stage house *(scaena frons).* Like the skene of the Greek theatre, the front walls of the scaena frons were the basic scenic unit for the Roman theatre. The stage house thus served as a scenic unit, a dressing area for the actors and, with its multiple door openings, represented entrances and exits to designated areas. In comedy, for example, the doors represented houses on a city street; in tragedy the doors represented entrances to a palace or temple. The scene was changed primarily through dialogue. If the actors stated they were in the country, the Roman staging convention was such that the stage and stage house represented the country. This idea of the facade of the stage house representing the basic scenic background was carried on into the Medieval and Elizabethan periods.

In addition to this scenic convention, the Romans also developed a type of air conditioning (air blown over water); an awning which stretched over the audience to protect it from the sun; and types of curtains — the front curtain *(auleum)* and the back curtain *(siparium)*. The front curtain, which historians credit as a Roman invention, is said to have been introduced in 133 B.C. Cicero refers to it in 56 B.C. as being raised at the end of a mime. The curtain appears to have been a type of drop curtain which could be lowered into a slot located near the front of the stage. This slot was actually a recessed area under the stage where the curtain could be stored. Raising and lowering it was accomplished via telescopic poles. After the second century A.D., the curtain was operated by a series of overhead ropes.

The back curtain was probably introduced to the theatre through the mimes. It seems to have been a scenic drop as well as a front curtain behind which mime actors could hide until their entrance. The actors made their entrance through a part, which represented a door, in the curtain.

Dramatists

The Romans tended to categorize their drama according to whether the drama was based on Greek life or on Roman life. Roman comedy which focused on Greek life was termed *fabula palliata* and, traditionally, those Roman tragedies which were modeled after Greek life were called *fabula crepidata*, although there is some question about the latter term. These two forms were distinguished by what the Romans believed to be typical Greek dress. The crepida was an everyday shoe similar to a sandal and was worn in comedy. There is thus speculation that *crepidata* should not be thought of as tragedy but solely comedy, and that the term for derivative Greek tragedy is lost. The *pallium*, however, was considered the characteristic everyday Greek dress, and inasmuch as comedy dealt with everyday affairs, the pallium was appropriate for comedy. Traditionally, fabula palliata refers to comedy and crepidata to tragedy.

Roman comedy based upon Roman settings, dress, manners and characters, but structurally based upon Greek new comedy, is called *fabula togata*. The form flourished in the second century B.C. and the chief writer was Afranius (c. 150 B.C.-?). The name togata is derived from the toga, which is thought to be the everyday dress for Romans. This derivation has caused some concern among some historians, however, who believe that the ceremonial toga was not typical everyday dress of the peasants, who dominated this form of comedy. Inasmuch as tabernaria refers to the private houses of the poor, and Roman comedy deals with everyday humble life, *fabula tabernaria* is thought to be a more precise term. Fabula togata, however, is the traditional term. Both forms of comedy existed and were confined to Roman comedy based on Roman life. The only togata comedy recorded as being acted under the Empire was *Fire*, in which a real house was built on stage, equipped, and then burned.

As to Roman tragedies based on Roman material, historians generally used the term *fabula praetexta*, the dress of some priests, magistrates, and free boys until they attained manhood. Its subject matter focused on Roman history. Naevius is given credit for its invention. The only extant example of a fabula praetexta is the tragedy *Octavia*, by an unknown dramatist.

Seneca

Born at Cordoba, Spain, Lucius Annaeus Seneca (c. 4 B.C.-A.D. 65), the philosopher, was educated at Rome in rhetoric and philosophy. He became a senator, quaestor (in charge of the state treasury), and a rhetorician in the courts. Caligula's jealousy of Seneca almost cost Seneca his life. And in 41 A.D., he was accused of a romantic intrigue for which he was banished to Corsica. He remained in Corsica until 49 when he was recalled to serve as young Nero's tutor. As Emperor, Nero listened to Seneca's advice, which kept Nero's reign from becoming worse than it was. In 65 Seneca was accused of conspiracy and ordered to take his life. He did so calmly and with dignity.

Amphitheatre at Pompeii as depicted in a fresco painting. Note the awning, a wine shop in front of the amphitheatre, and another entertainment center next to the amphitheatre. From *The Flavian Amphitheatre*, 1876.

Only ten Roman tragedies are extant. Nine of those are the work of Seneca. He is mistakenly assigned the authorship of *Octavia*. The plays which survive are *The Trojan Women, Medea, Oedipus, Agamemnon, The Phoenician Women, The Mad Hercules, Hercules on Oeta, Phaedra,* and *Tyestes*. These nine tragedies, whose dates are uncertain, are based on Greek originals *(fabula crepidata),* and were probably not produced in the Roman public theatres. They seem to have been written for a single reciter with the idea of demonstrating certain elements of rhetoric. Plays such as those by Seneca, which were read but never produced, have become known as closet drama.

Seneca flourished during the Empire and, though his plays were apparently never produced, he was nonetheless a major influence on Shakespeare and his contemporaries. That Seneca's plays were read, imitated, and even acted at the English universities during the sixteenth century is a matter of record. His tragedies were translated into English in 1581, and some were acted at Cambridge before this date. The first English tragedy was *Gorboduc,* which was modeled after Seneca's work and presented in 1562 before Queen Elizabeth. Seneca's influence thus came through the Elizabethans' interpretation of his plays which led to his influencing the modern theatre. The following characteristics are attributed to Seneca's influence:

1. The structuring of plays into five acts.
2. The use of violence and horror.
3. The use of magic, death, and supernatural events, such as ghosts.
4. Characters obsessed by a single emotion (e.g., Hamlet's revenge or Macbeth's ambition).
5. Interest in morality as noted in characters whose unchecked emotions destroy them (e.g., *Othello),* and in *sententiae* (short, pithy statements about the human condition).
6. The use of soliloquies, asides, and confidants (a neoclassical device whereby, in a love affair, servants act as go-betweens for their masters who have confided in them).
7. The employment of rhetorical devices such as forensic speeches (e.g., *Julius Caesar).*

In addition to Seneca, two other writers of tragedy should be noted. The first is Lucius Varius Rufus, whose play *Thyestes* was produced most likely at the ludi Romani in 29 B.C. and represents the last record we possess of a new Latin play being produced. The other writer of tragedy worthy of mention was Gnaeus Naevius (c. 270 B.C.-199 B.C.). Born in Campania, Naevius was the first native-born Latin writer of both tragedy and comedy. He began writing about 235 B.C. and, for the next thirty years, produced about forty plays, seven of which were tragedies. In 206-205 B.C., Naevius wrote a comedy and, as a result, was brought to trial, imprisoned, and eventually banished. This case against Naevius is the only recorded conviction against a Roman citizen for political abuse on the stage. Its significance is that it stopped other writers from political satire and, as a consequence, seriously hampered the growth of Roman drama.

Plautus

The immediate successor to Naevius in comedy was Titus Maccius Plautus (c. 254 B.C.-184 B.C.), which translated means Titus, the flat-footed clown. Considered the playwright of the people, Plautus earned his living initially as a stage carpenter as well as working in a flour mill. When not working, he wrote his plays which, like those of many other writers of the era, were based on Greek new comedy, primarily the works of Menander, Diphilus, and Philemon. Naevius' case ruled out the use of old comedy which abounded in political satire. On the other hand, coarseness and obscenity were allowed and Plautus was a master at broad humor. Between 205-184 B.C. he wrote roughly 130 plays, of which twenty-one survive. His most important works were *The Menaechmi*, which influenced Shakespeare's *Comedy of Errors*; *The Pot of Gold*, which influenced Molière's *The Miser;* and *Amphitryon,* which served to influence Dryden's *Amphitryon* or *The Two Sosias*. All of Plautus' works cannot be definitely dated but probably all were written between 205-184 B.C.

Characteristic of Plautus was his emphasis upon farcical elements, eavesdropping scenes, improbable events, slaves with more brains than their masters, reversals of fortune, overheard conversations, mistaken identities, colloquial speech, elimination of the Greek chorus, a prologue to explain everything in the play, and his extensive use of music. One of the prominent characteristics of Plautine comedy is the extensive use of song. Plautus' plays were, in fact, musicals; one third was dialogue and two-thirds was sung. Whereas his successor, Terence, used a total of twenty-five lines of song, Plautus used over three thousand lines or over sixty songs. This averages to about three songs per play. However, *Miles Gloriosus* has no song; *Curculio* has one, as does the *Asinaria*. Plautus' heavy use of song and dance created a musical revue which, in essence, is a forerunner to our modern-day musicals.

Terence

Whereas Plautus wrote for his audience, Publius Terentius Afer (c. 195/85 B.C.-159 B.C.) wrote more for a literary coterie which supported him. Born in Carthage, Terence probably belonged to an African tribe. A slave of Terentius Lucanus in Rome, Terence took his former master's name when Lucanus freed him. The reception to Terence's first play, the *Andria* (166 B.C.) enabled Terence to pursue a career as a dramatist. He wrote only six plays, all of which survive. These six plays, plus the twenty-one of Plautus, constitute the complete extant works of Roman comedy. Horace and Cicero quoted him and Caesar considered him a *dimidiate Menander.* Terence placed his emphasis upon more thoughtful comedy rather than farce, an emphasis which did not endear him to the public audiences. But Terence seems to have been more concerned with a romantic treatment of his characters. Unlike Plautus, he characterized his females, for example, as being sentimental and tender; even prostitutes demonstrated a willingness toward virtue. Structurally, Terence dropped the expository prologue used by Plautus, did not deal with Roman life to the extent that Plautus did, used little obscenity, employed psychological changes in characters, shied away from farce, and wrote well-constructed plots which demonstrated surprise, irony, and a contrast in characters' behavior. Terence's influence can be seen in plays of the seventeenth and eighteenth centuries, such as Wycherley's *The Country Wife* (1675), and in modern plays such as Thornton Wilder's *The Woman of Andros* (1930).

Closing of Theatres

Biological factors seem to have been a fundamental reason for Rome's fall. Granted morals, failing trade, despotism by the rulers, taxes, church opposition, and wars were all strong factors. But a serious decline in the population, along with the importation of non-Roman citizens into Rome to serve in the army, as slaves, or in various other capacities, seem to have been fundamental. Although credit is given to the church, Christianity's growth was "more an effect than a cause of Rome's decay." The internal decay of Rome made it too weak to resist the invading barbarians who pillaged Rome in 410 A.D. and 455 A.D. The Roman Empire continued in the East until 1453, but its empire in the West ended in about 476 A.D. With the decline and fall of Rome in the West, Roman theatre came to an end. The last record of a performance in Rome is 533 A.D. Theatre continued in the East, but in the West it was relegated to nomadic actors until about 900 A.D. (or what is considered the first stage of the Middle Ages), at which time the church resurrected theatre and drama for its own use.

Selected Readings

Beare, William. *The Roman Stage.* 3rd ed. London, 1964.

Bieber, Margarete. *The History of Greek and Roman Theater.* 2nd ed. Princeton, N.J. 1961.

Duckworth, George E. *The Nature of Roman Comedy.* Princeton, N.J., 1952.

Friedlander, Ludwig. *Roman Life and Manners under the Early Empire.* 3 vols. New York, 1910.

Roman theatre at Leptis Magna, Libya, built about 1-2 A.D. by Annobal Rufus. This theatre is similar to other Roman theatres in its architectural layout. Courtesy Libyan Embassy.

Top: Theatre at Dionysus. All the surviving Greek plays were presented at this theatre.

Bottom: Theatre at Epidaurus. This is the best preserved of all the ancient Greek Theatres.

Top left: Shelves filled with masks. This tenth century painting of masks from Roman comedy is believed to have been copied from a second century A.D. original and may provide some evidence about Imperial Roman Theatre (second and third centuries A.D.). Courtesy Biblioteca Vaticana.

Top right: The lower frieze represents Satyrs dancing. Note the musician at center; he is playing the double aulos, a reed instrument which is one of three musical instruments commonly used in Greek tragedy. The upper frieze shows the gods bringing gifts to Pandora. Krater, London, British Museum.

Bottom left: An actor looking at his mask. Note the high boot (cothornus) and long sleeves of the costume. This fragment of a vase from Tarentum dates from the fourth century B.C. Courtesy Martin von Wagner Museum of the University of Wurzburg.

Bottom right: Chiron being pushed up the stairs. This scene from a Phlyakes vase of the fourth century B.C. shows a raised stage. London, British Museum.

Top: Roman Theatre at Sabratha (Libya). Note the three rows of columns on the scaenae frons. Roger Wood, London.

Bottom: Theatre at Orange, built in the first or second century A.D. in France. It is the best preserved Roman theatre in France and is now being used again for theatrical performances. Courtesy French Cultural Services.

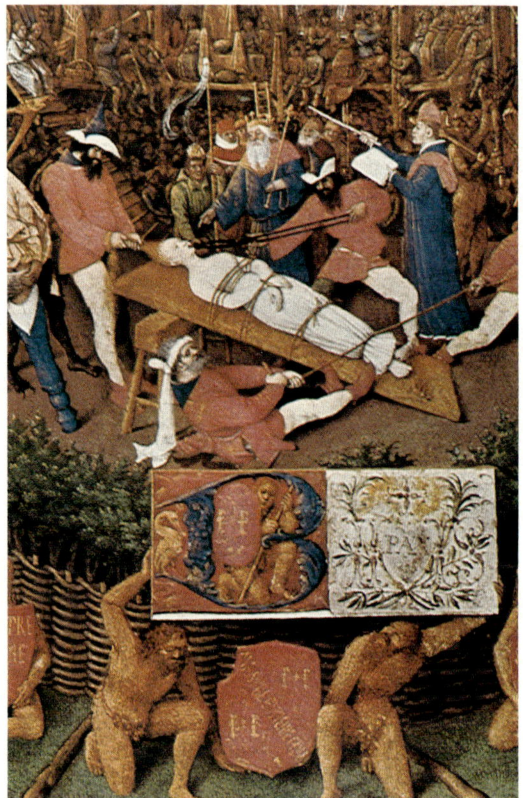

Top left: Martyrdom of Saint Apollonia, a miniature from the *Hours of Etienne Chevalier* by Jean Fouquet. Note the mansions illustrating the various stages of the saint's life. The actors and spectators seem to be intermingled. Musée Condé.

Hercules Furens. Classical works were rarely, if ever, produced during the Middle Ages. Hence the graphic artist attempted to portray various performances. Note the characters in the tragedy with Hercules in his lion skin in the upper portion of the miniature. The chorus is depicted at the bottom with the audience at upper and lower right. At center is the poet who, according to Middle Age thought, ostensibly read the dialogue as the actors mimed the action. Miniature from the codex Vaticanus Urbinas 355. Biblioteca Vaticana.

Bottom: General layout of the stage used for Valenciennes Passion Play; miniature from the *Mystere de la Passion.* Paris Bibliotheque Nationale.

Vocabulary

1. Tarentum	tah REN tuhm
2. Calabria	kah LAH bree uh
3. Livius Andronicus	LI vee uhs an DRAW ni kuhs
4. ludi Romani	LOO dee roh MAH nee
5. ludi Plebeii	LOO dee PLAY bee ee
6. ludi scaenici	SKIGH ni kee
7. ludi megalenses	me guh LEN sayz
8. ludi florales	floh RAY layz
9. ludi cereales	kayr ee AH layz
10. ludi Apollinares	uh paw luh NAY rayz
11. fabula riciniata	FAH boo luh ri kee nee AH tuh
12. Atellan	ah TEL uhn
13. soccus	SAW kuhs
14. dramatis personae	druh MAH tis per SOH nigh
15. Pylades	PIL ah deez
16. Bathyllus	bah THIL uhs
17. Statilius Taurus	stuh TIL lee uhs TAW ruhs
18. Titus Maccius Plautus	TIGH tus MAK ee uhs PLOW tuhs
19. Publius Terentius	POOB lee uhs ter EN tee uhs
20. Terence	TER uhnts
21. scaena frons	SKIGH nuh frawns
22. proscaenium	pruh SKIGH nee uhm
23. pulpitum	POOL pi tuhm
24. naumachia	naw MAY kee uh
25. cavea	KAH wee ah
26. Pompey	PAWM pee
27. auleum	OW lee uhm
28. siparium	si PAHR ee uhm
29. fabula palliata	FAH boo luh pah lee AY tuh
30. fabula togata	toh GAH tuh
31. fabula crepidata	cre pi DAH tuh
32. fabula praetexta	prigh TEX tuh
33. fabula tabernaria	ta ber NAIR ee uh
34. Seneca	SE ni kuh
35. Afranius	ah FRAY nee uhs
36. Hercules on Oeta	HER kyoo leez on OY tah
37. Gnaeus Naevius	GNIGH uhs NIGH wee uhs
38. fabula saltica	SAWL ti kuh
39. Diphilmus	digh FIL muhs
40. Philemon	FIL ay mawn

Carini.
Chreme.
Chrisidis
Do. symonis
Les.
Archi.
Liber.
Phoebus

Carini.
Chremetis
Chrisidis
Dom' symonis
Si.
Si.
So.
So.
Dro.
Da.
Phoebus
Liber.

CHAPTER FIVE

Middle Ages
The Rebirth of Theatre and Drama

Guided by the church, the Middle Ages held life to be a preparation for eternity; thus man was not to be concerned with worldly notions, but was to prepare himself spiritually. The idea that life was insignificant and that heaven was the goal pervaded the institutions of the Middle Ages. Thus, theological ideas dominated medieval life, and these ideas were reinforced by classical precepts. These precepts were imparted to medieval society through Latin manuscripts which were preserved throughout the Middle Ages. A prime characteristic of medieval society was its reliance on books, particularly those of earlier Latin writers which were used to bolster Christian learning.

That the medieval society was extremely organized, rigid, and orderly can be noted in its reliance on books for authority. The use of books was a way to provide a logical explanation about man and his universe. The logic that resulted was the notion of a fixed universe in which earth was the lowest point. From earth one advances upward through the finite universe. Because it is finite, it has shape — the perfect spherical shape — and everything within that shape is ordered. The universe is like a tall building and movement to the earth is down. You thus have absolute up and down, with earth being the very bottom. Man, because of original sin, has fallen from heaven to the earth where he remains imprisoned within his body atoning for his sin.

This notion also affected the medieval concept of history which viewed life as a continuum from Genesis to the present day. History was a story based upon the creation, fall, redemption and judgment. Medieval society thus lacked historical perspective. Hence, it wasn't important for costumes to be historically accurate in medieval drama. The past was Adam naked until he fell from grace; after that the past was in terms of their own age (classical influence was used only insofar as it reinforced Christian concepts; any other information which did not concur with this notion of history was rejected).

Opposite: Terence stages. It has been suggested that these stages were eventually enlarged to permit playing within the openings and that the openings gradually came together into one large opening or a single arch. From Cohen's *Le Théatre en France au Moyen Age*.

Spiritually then, the past was better than the present, for as the world continued, the sins of mankind became worse. Medieval man thus felt pleasure in the past, for it was a time when man's sins were not so grave, and he gloried in the future, for it brought him closer to judgment.

The Middle Ages went through three periods of development: (1) the rise of the Middle Ages — 300 A.D. to the eleventh century; (2) the High Middle Ages — about 1050 to 1350; (3) the Late Middle Ages — about 1350 to the fifteenth century. These changes correspond directly to Medieval theatre and drama. Under the church's guidance, theatre and drama were reborn, flowered, and then became secularized. A major contribution of this period was the rebirth of theatre and drama, which in turn influenced the Italian Renaissance and the Elizabethan period.

Reemergence of Drama

The collapse of the Roman empire is intertwined with the successful emergence of the Christian church. After 315 A.D. the Roman emperors Diocletian and Constantine lent the support of the Roman state to Christianity and thereby enabled Christianity to gain its needed foothold. With the rise of the Christian church and the collapse of the Roman Empire, theatre fell out of favor. From the sixth century to about the tenth century, Western theatrical activity went into a period akin to the Dark Ages. Although theatre continued to flourish in China, India, and Asia Minor, Western actors were relegated to wandering the countryside telling stories, juggling, rope dancing, and other such feats. By the tenth century, the church, which had tried so hard to suppress drama, was responsible for resurrecting it in church drama. This rebirth marks the beginning of medieval drama.

Medieval drama was didactic drama. Its main function was to teach man how to be saved. The logic behind the church's use of drama can probably be traced to the Fourth Lateran Council of 1215, which required all Christians to attend confession and communion once a year. To enforce this law and educate the priests, who were extremely ignorant of theology, and to educate the public in the doctrine of repentance, liturgical drama developed.

Liturgical Drama

In the first period of the Middle Ages, the religious ritual of the eighth, ninth, and tenth centuries made up the *liturgical* (church) drama. A ninth century bishop, Amalarius, used the mass theatrically by having the priests who participated in the mass enact the life, death, and resurrection of Christ. Mass was thus dramatic ritual. That the mass was used as drama seems to be indicated in a *trope* written in England for Easter mass. The trope, called the *Quem Quaeritis* (c. 925), which is the trope's opening words — "Whom Seek Ye" — has two meanings relating to liturgical drama. The first is its literary application. In this sense, it refers to the words and/or music added to the existing text of the church service. Trope can be defined as a choral addition to the music of the introit (musical composition at the beginning of the service). Translated from the Greek, trope means turn, and its second application relates to a memory device which helped choirs associate the words of the service with their turns or movements. Although the *Quem Quaeritis* exemplified mass as drama, evidence is missing to confirm that the clergy singing the trope were actors impersonating characters. Consequently, the *Quem Quaeritis* is considered by historians simply as the beginning of liturgical drama and not a play in and of itself.

The *Regularis Concordia* (965-975, harmony of the rule), compiled by St. Ethelwold, Bishop of Winchester, is considered the earliest extant medieval drama. The playlet is complete with directions which clearly indicate that the piece was to be acted. For example: "While the third lesson is being chanted, let four brothers dress themselves, of whom let one, clothed in an alb, enter as if to take part in the service." The *Regularis Concordia* appears to be designed to fortify the faith of the uneducated as well as to establish a uniform practice and purpose in the English churches and monasteries. This uniform practice led to Christianity being known initially as the Catholic (uniform) church.

In the first phase of the Middle Ages, not only were plays resurrected in the form of liturgical drama, but in the form of non-liturgical drama as well. In the tenth century, a Saxon nun, Hrosvitha of Gandersheim, wrote six plays modeled after Terence. Inasmuch as Hroswitha did not enter the convent until age twenty-five, these plays, in rhymed Latin prose, display a worldly view of human nature — for example, virginity is extolled. Although the plays do not seem to have been acted, they possibly could have been performed for and by the nuns of the convent as well as for the Saxon princesses who were in charge of the convent.

Analogous to the changes that characterize the three periods of the Middle Ages, medieval drama was resurrected in the first period. In the second period, it flourished as church drama, and in the third period it became secularized. Whereas the early Middle Ages, or first period, was marked by an agrarian society and political disintegration, the second period evidenced the beginnings of the modern bureaucratic state as well as rapid growth in all aspects of life. During this second period, liturgical drama flourished extensively within the church, and by the end of the tenth century, had spread throughout Europe and into Russia. For unknown reasons, liturgical drama moved outdoors by 1300. When the drama moved outside of the church proper, a new period of development gradually began to occur — the production of drama by non-church members.

Initially, the guilds produced liturgical drama in the vernacular under church supervision. However, as staging became more elaborate, the church relinquished its hold. Therefore the second phase of the Middle Ages is a transitional period for drama: liturgical drama flourished to its fullest potential and then gave way to the impending secular drama.

Mystery and Miracle Plays

When the church moved outdoors, dramatic production became a joint effort of the church and

Rustic stage comedy. Note the portable stage and the drawing on the curtain as well as the torches, which were used either for stage effects or possibly to ward off insects. From Cohen's *Le Théâtre en France au Moyen Age.*

state. Although the church and state were considered as one in the early Middle Ages, that concept was destroyed by the beginning of the twelfth century. With the separation of church and state came the growth of secular power bringing with it cultural change. Although the reason for moving drama outdoors is unclear, the attempts of the church to counteract secular power and reassert its control by going out to the people might be part of the answer. Two changes support this idea: first, the language of the drama was changed from the Latin to the vernacular (everyday language); second, in 1264, Pope Urban IV created the Feast of Corpus Christi to make the church more meaningful to the common man. Whatever the reason, moving the drama outdoors was in keeping with the period's extreme inventiveness. In fact, inventiveness was the chief characteristic of the second period of the Middle Ages.

With the move allowing drama to be presented outdoors came the emergence of the major forms of medieval drama — the mystery and miracle plays. Miracle plays were plays based upon the lives of saints and mystery plays were concerned more with Biblical subjects. Both are really Bible histories and were produced by the English trade guilds as part of the cycle dramas connected with the Feast of Corpus Christi.

The trade guilds responsible for producing these cycle dramas were trade or craft unions (consider the present-day union for motion picture actors, Screen Actors Guild), and in the thirteenth century nearly every major English town had one or more guilds. Being of a religious nature, the guilds had a patron saint, a chaplain, and a chapel. Thus they were likely choices for staging the mystery or miracle cycles. The larger guilds would each perform one play of the cycle, while the smaller ones (up to as many as six) would combine to do one play of the cycle. These cycle plays were performed on a wheeled wagon with scenery (called a pageant wagon). Either the wagons were fixed and the plays of the cycle were performed on or in front of them, or the wagons moved in a procession (much like our modern-day parades) with the actors on them, and stopped at a designated spot for the performance. The arrangement is unclear.

The only extant cycles are the mystery plays. In addition, the term mystery translated from the medieval French *mystère*, or from the Latin *ministerium*, means trade or craft. Inasmuch as the extant cycle plays were produced by the guilds and deal with Biblical subjects as opposed to the lives of saints, they are termed mystery plays. In Spain these plays were termed *auto sacramentale,* and in Italy, *sacre rapresentazione*. The reader should be alerted, however, to the use of the term miracle by many modern scholars to designate these same extant English cycle plays. For the reasons cited, the authors prefer the term mystery.

The four extant English cycle dramas are as follows:

1. The Chester plays established c. 1375, of which there were twenty-four.
2. The York plays, 1378, of which there were forty-eight. York had over fifty guilds.
3. The Wakefield cycle, 1403, of which there were thirty-two plays. A revision of the first York cycle is also called the Towneley cycle, after the name of the manuscript's owner who was a nineteenth century Lancashire squire.
4. The Ludus Coventriae, known as N-town or Hegge cycle. The *N* may stand for *nomen* (name) indicating that the blank is to be filled by the name of the town where the play was to be presented. For example:

   A Sunday next yf that we may
   At vi of the belle we gin oure play
   In N-towne.

   The town of Lincoln has also been suggested.

Of these four, the York cycle is the longest, most complete, and best known. Since 1951, a version lasting less than three hours has been regularly performed in York. The original version lasted all day.

Morality Plays

As a dramatic form, the morality play was popular in the fourteenth century, the third phase of the Middle Ages, and was concerned with improving human behavior through the teaching of moral lessons. The plays were like sermons in dramatic context, which led one individual to assert that "their very name is like a yawn." In keeping with the symbolism, the characters were dramatically represented in the form of an allegory (a story in a disguised form) in order to create greater interest and impact upon the audience. A good example of allegory is Bunyan's *Pilgrim's Progress.* Such allegorical characters include Sloth, Gluttony, Usury, Anger, Avarice, and a host of others which can be classified as either vice or virtue.

The basic differences between the morality and mystery plays are as follows:

1. The mystery plays generally did not tend toward allegory whereas morality plays did.
2. The mystery plays became meaningful only in terms of the complete cycle. The morality plays were unattached and individually could render a meaning.
3. Characters of the mystery plays were drawn from the Bible. Those of the morality plays were personifications (representing a thing or idea in form of a person) of virtue and vice and concerned the common man.
4. Conflict in mystery plays was in terms of the Biblical stories, whereas conflict in morality plays arose from the battle between vice and virtue over man's soul.
5. The emphasis in mystery plays was on the theological aspects of the Bible. In morality plays the emphasis was on molding human behavior through teaching about life via the example of the characters.
6. The mystery play tended toward the liturgical, and the morality play lent itself to the secular.

Massacre of the Innocents and the Flight into Egypt, taken from a frieze above the porch of the north transept to Notre-Dame Cathedral in Paris, c. 1250. Note the medieval costumes. Courtesy Martial Rose.

7. The mystery plays were performed by amateur actors, and the morality plays eventually became vehicles for professional actors.

Although a reference by Wycliffe to a dramatization (c. 1380) of the Lord's Prayer, and fragments of *The Pride of Life* (c. 1400), exist as examples of morality plays, the earliest complete extant morality play is *The Castle of Perseverance* (c. 1425). The best known morality play is *Everyman* (c. 1500), based on the Dutch play *Elkerliik*. Historically, the morality play marks a definite step towards completely secular drama in England, and its recognition and definition of good and bad within human nature (that is, externalizing these psychological forces) mark a major contribution to modern drama. This characteristic of the morality play can be noted today in melodrama, which makes up the majority of the television dramas. Like the morality play, the chief concern of melodrama is the struggle between good and evil with the eventual triumph of good. The intention of both melodrama and morality plays is to teach moral lessons by example.

Interludes

Although a variety of dramatic forms existed during the Middle Ages, the only other form (except possibly the disguising, which in the seventeenth century Ben Jonson turned into a court masque) to have impact upon succeeding generations was the interlude. The term itself appears to be derived from the Latin *ludus*, meaning play, and *inter* meaning between, among, or during. The definition suggests the interlude was a short play or plays placed between the intervals of a longer play, such

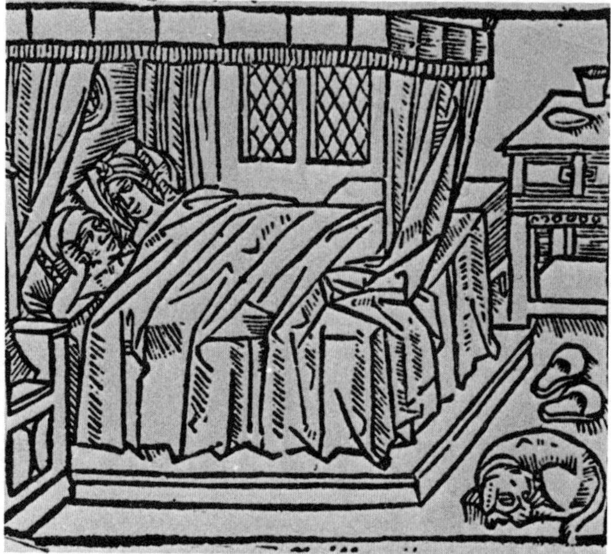

Scenes from *Pierre Patelin* (c. 1470), a French farce which was so popular it went through thirty editions. From the 1500 edition.

Top: The lawyer Patelin buying his cloth from Madame Guillaume.

Middle: Patelin, who pretends to be sick, and his wife Guillemette.

Bottom: Patelin pleading his case before the judge and his son, Greffier.

as a mystery play, or perhaps a short play between the courses of a banquet. In actuality, however, the interlude was any type of play presented during the Middle Ages, especially those plays first presented indoors in the "great hall" as after-dinner entertainment for the gentry.

Historically, the oldest extant English interlude is Henry Medwall's *Fulgens and Lucrece* (c. 1497). Like the morality play, the interlude was performed by professionals, and thus was associated with the rise of professional acting. By having a troupe of professional actors always available, the gentry could have an interlude performed at their discretion. For the professional actor being attached to a household as a servant meant a steady income. When not performing for their employer, acting troupes toured to make extra money. This attachment of actors to households proved to be of vital importance for the professional actor.

From approximately 1500 to 1572, the professional actor in Western Europe was denied official recognition by the church and state, and was therefore hard pressed to earn a livelihood. Consequently, the support rendered by individual noblemen or rich merchants enabled actors to survive. Also in this interim period religious drama became prohibited, which consequently led writers to choose other subjects. This choice of different subject matter for plays marks, on the one hand, the decline of medieval drama, and on the other, the rise of Renaissance drama.

Selected Readings

Chambers, E.K. *The Medieval Stage*. 2 vols. Oxford, 1903.

Lewis, C.S. *The Discarded Image*, Cambridge, 1964.

Wickham, Glynne. *Early English Stages,* 1300-1600. 2 vols. New York, 1959-1972.

Williams, Arnold. *The Drama of Medieval England.* East Lansing, Michigan, 1961.

Vocabulary

1. Amalarius	ah muh LAHR ee uhs
2. Quem Quaeritis	KWEM KWIGH ri tis
3. Regularis Concordia	re goo: LAH ruhs kuhn KAWR de uh
4. Hrosvitha of Gandersheim	rahs VI thuh of GAN der shighm
5. *Fulgens and Lucrece*	FOHL jens and loo: KREES
6. Ludus Coventriae	LOO duhs kuh VEN tree igh

CHAPTER SIX

Italian Renaissance
The Age of Scenes and Machines

In some ways the Italian Renaissance theatre was a continuation of the Middle Ages. First, plays in the vernacular were born in the Middle Ages and were carried over into the Renaissance where they were fully developed. Second, the use of stage machinery, called secrets in the medieval period, was also carried over and made more sophisticated by the Italians. Third, many of the Latin manuscripts preserved throughout the Middle Ages contributed significantly to the development of the theatre of the Italian Renaissance. Fourth, the major forms of Renaissance drama were derived in part from the Middle Ages. Fifth, the medieval novella was continued into the Renaissance.

In other ways, however, the Italian Renaissance represents a departure from the Middle Ages. Painting, sculpture, architecture, and the use of creative literature represent four areas in which the Renaissance departed. Underlying all shifts away from the Middle Ages was the fundamental thought of the Renaissance.

During the Renaissance, unlike the Middle Ages, life was viewed as something to be enjoyed. The Renaissance ideal, much like that of the Greeks, was the balanced life within one's self as well as society. The Renaissance desire to imitate antiquity altered the lifestyle and, consequently, affected theatrical development.

Two forces seem to have contributed to this change in world view: the revived interest in Roman life, and the use of ancient treatises for grammatical and rhetorical study. This renewed interest in antiquity was led by a group of scholars known as "humanists," whose overwhelming interest in Greek and Latin texts and the use of the Latin language constitutes the humanistic movement. The humanists' desire to "live again the ancient days" led them to shift away from the theological thought which dominated the Middle Ages to secular thinking. The fundamental tone of the Renaissance was secular — people were not as concerned with their souls as they were with their bodies. They wanted to enjoy life.

Opposite: Seventeenth or early eighteenth-century stage setting by Ferninando Galli-Bibiena (1657-1743), known as the "First architect and painter of Festivals and Theatres of Vienna."

With this new emphasis, theatrical productions moved away from the pure didactic of the Middle Ages to pure spectacle. As a result, the Italian Renaissance contributed significantly to many scenic innovations which influenced modern theatre. The most significant contributions of this period were scenic innovations, the formation of literary principles, and the commedia dell'arte.

Formation of Italian Renaissance Theatre

Two institutions contributed to the development of the Italian Renaissance theatre — the academies and the royal courts. The academies were half literary clubs and half academic societies and were composed of humanists who gathered together to hear speeches and work out common problems. Each of the academies was devoted to the study of a particular subject. Of importance to the Renaissance theatre was the Roman Academy, which was organized about 1460 under the leadership of Julio Pomponio Leto (1425-1498), who latinized his name to Pomponius Laetus. The academy focused upon Roman life and staged plays by Plautus. Members of the Academy also wrote plays modeled after the Roman dramatists Terence and Seneca. Under this academy's influence, *De Architectura* by Vitruvius (c. 50-26 B.C.) was published in 1486. Vitruvius was an architect who served in the army under Julius and Augustus Caesar. *De Architectura* was a treatise in ten books on Roman architecture. The manuscript was lost until 1414 when it was unearthed by Poggio Bracciolini (1380-1459) at a monastery in St. Gall. *De Architectura,* written about the first century, had twenty-three editions by 1600 and remained an unquestioned authority as a source for Roman architecture for many years. The importance of Vitruvius can be noted in the formation in 1526 of the Academy Della Virtu, which was devoted to the study of his works.

The second institution to have an influence on the Italian Renaissance theatre was the royal court. Italy was divided into independent city-states, each with its own capital city and court. These courts vied with each other in producing the most spectacular productions. These courts had, within the palaces, indoor theatres at which were developed many of the scenic innovations to emerge from this period. By 1500, every court had a temporary or a permanent stage. The characteristic form of entertainment to be presented at the court theatre was the *intermezzi*.

Intermezzi and Opera

The intermezzi were lavish entertainments similar to the English masques and were used to honor births, weddings, royalty, or other such engagements. They were inserted between the acts of the tragedy or comedy being presented, which meant that there would be as many intermezzi as acts in the play; thus, a five-act play would have five intermezzi. By the 1570's, when intermezzi became more popular than the plays being presented, the five intermezzi were combined together like a play. In terms of subject matter, the intermezzi emphasized spectacle and were not related to the tragedy or comedy being staged.

About 1580, intermezzi were absorbed by opera, which was developed by a group of musicians and literary individuals interested in music. This group included Vicenzo Galilei (the father of Galileo), Jacopo Peri, Guilio Caccini, and Ottavio Rinuccini (a poet). These individuals formed an organization known as the Florentine Camerata. (Camerata is a term used to designate a club of students.) Believing that Greek tragedies were sung in their entirety, the Camerata set about resurrecting the music of the ancient Greeks. Seeking to conform to what they believed was the Greek concept, they devised a style of music known as recitative, which emphasized solo voices intermittently singing and speaking. Vincenzo Galilei wrote the first compositions about 1590; unfortunately, they are now lost. The first short play was *Dafne* in 1594. Until 1637, operas were given only at court or under the auspices of the academies; in Venice the public was admitted to the performances. Due to the patronage of the Barberini family, opera gained in popularity. Through the intermezzi and the operas given at court theatres, perspective scenery, rapid changes of scenery, lighting devices, and stage machines were developed.

Sebastiano Serlio

Sebastiano Serlio (1475-1554) wrote *Architectura* between 1527 and 1547. Although there are five books, only a small section concerns the theatre. The second book, published in 1545, is considered the first Renaissance work to deal with the theatre. In this section on theatre, Serlio discusses perspective, how to construct scenery, a stage, and how to develop lights.

Perspective was the fundamental principle of the court theatre. The concept was rediscovered and developed by Filippo Brunelleschi (1377-1446), and seems to have been first used in 1486 in Ferrara for *The Menaechmi* by Plautus. The first treatise on perspective is *Della Pittura* by Leon Battista Alberti (1404-1472), who built one of the earliest, if not the earliest, court theatres, when he constructed a stage in the Vatican for Nicholas V. The best example of a Renaissance theatre utilizing perspective is the Teatro Olimpico at Vicenza, begun by Andrea Palladio (1518-1580) in 1580, and finished in 1584 by his student Vincenzo Scamozzi (1552-1616). It is the oldest surviving Renaissance theatre. Its characteristic feature is its five doorways with a perspective scene behind each door. The limitation, however, was the fact that the scenes could not be shifted.

The changing or shifting of scenery occurred first in 1637 at the public opera house, Teatro di San Cassiano, Venice. The major step toward the construction of a theatre suitable for changing scenery, however, was the Teatro Farnese, built at Parma by Giovan Battista Aleotti (1546-1636) in 1618-1619 at the request of Ranuccio I. Farnese. The significance of this theatre is that it is the first theatre known to have a permanent proscenium arch (a picture frame stage), which also served to hide a complex rigging system above the stage proper.

The basic unit of perspective was the house. Each house had to be equal distance from one another and wide enough to prevent the audience from seeing backstage. The first houses were to be

Serlio's tragic scene, from Serlio's *Architectura,* Book 2, 1569 edition. Courtesy Fine Arts Library, Indiana University.

opposite each other and parallel to the stage front; they were to be built against the stage left and stage right proscenium walls. At a predetermined ratio, a series of houses would be placed next to those of the first houses and would continue to progress on a raked (sloping) stage toward a vanishing point at the back wall.

Serlio recommended three types of houses, one per dramatic form. For tragedy, he stated that the houses must be of great persons because all the violence, death, and accidents which occurred in ancient and modern tragedies happened in the houses of kings and other royalty. For comedy, the houses should be of private citizens — middle and lower classes. In addition, three of the houses should be a tavern, a church, and a house of prostitution. For the satyric or pastoral play, Serlio recommended outdoor scenery, and huts in which rustics lived.

The use of houses and scenes painted on canvas-covered wooden frames (flats) marked the beginning of the "wing system." The problem of transferring a perspective picture to flat wings was solved in 1600 by Guido Ubaldus. The first application of Ubaldus' principles belongs to Giovan Battista Aleotti. He began using them as early as 1606

Serlio's comic scene. Courtesy Fine Arts Library, Indiana University.

in the Teatro dei Intrepidi in Ferrara, but they were not fully developed until 1619 when Aleotti used them in Parma at the Teatro Farnese. Today we use the term wings to refer to the offstage area, but wings were originally painted scenery.

In the Renaissance there were three types of wings:

1. The angle wing: a three-dimensional reproduction of a house which showed only two sides — a front and a side. Today the angle wing persists as a return and a tormentor.
2. The periaktoi or triangular wing: revolving triangular prism with a different scene on each side.
3. The flat wing: a series of flats placed at the back of the stage, parallel to the audience. Eventually, flat wings replaced angle wings as the scenery for the seventeenth century stage. The dominance of the flat wings marks the victory of the stage painter over the stage architecture.

Serlio's pastoral scene. Courtesy Fine Arts Library, Indiana University.

Nicola Sabbattini

The standard work on stage practices used at the Italian ducal courts in the late sixteenth and early seventeenth centuries was Nicola Sabbattini's (1574-1654) *Manual For Constructing Theatrical Scenes and Machines* (1638). In the second book of the *Manual,* Sabbattini turns his attention to the intermezzi, and a discussion of such devices as traps in the stage floor in which characters as well as scenery were raised and lowered, cylinders for dimming lights, ships moving on a rolling sea, a rainbow, clouds, lightning, wind, fire, flying actors, and the rapid shifting of scenery. Sabbattini recommends that when the scenery is to be shifted, someone be sent to the rear of the auditorium and, at the proper time, create a commotion or sound an instrument. In this way, the audience's attention will be drawn away from the stage, and they will not see the scenery changed.

As to the shifting of scenery, Sabbattini discusses four methods:

1. Dropping painted cloths over the scene.
2. Building grooves on the stage floor as well as

overhead, and then sliding the desired flat in front of the old one, or pulling the old flat offstage revealing the new flat behind it. The grooves and edges of the flats are soaped and two men per flat are needed for the shift.

3. Using periaktoi. The rotation of the periaktoi is accomplished by using two windlasses.
4. The fourth method relates to the flat wings and the shifting is similar to that in the second method. Flat wings eventually triumphed over the other scenic devices. For changing flat wings, Sabbattini suggested sliding a flat onstage or pulling one off by using a groove system. The back flat wings could be changed by opening and shutting the flats like a door, or they could be bolted together as one unit and raised and lowered like a curtain.

In addition to the flat wings, Sabbattini suggested the use of a painted drop and borders to help mask out the backstage area. Wings, borders, and drops continued into the twentieth century as the dominant means of scenic representation. They are the forerunner to the present day "box-set."

Giacomo Torelli

The complete shifting of the wings, drops, and borders required a coordination of movement which could not be achieved manually. Giacomo Torelli (1608-1678), a pupil of Aleotti, is given credit for perfecting the "chariot and pole system," which he perfected in 1641 at the Teatro Novissimo, and which is still in use at the Drottningholm and Gripsholm theatres in Sweden, and at Česky Krumlov, a court theatre in Czechoslovakia. The system involved cutting slots into the stage floor. Underneath these slots, which were placed parallel to the stage, were tracks for carriages (chariots). The carriages were frames, constructed out of poles, with wheels attached. Torelli conceived the idea of connecting all the wings, drops, and borders to a central winching system which one man could operate by cranking a handle. By 1650 this rapid change of scenery became the standard for public theatres throughout most of Europe except in England, the Netherlands, and some parts of Germany. These countries retained the "groove system," which Sabbattini discusses as his second suggestion for shifting scenery.

Torelli did most of his work between 1641-1645 in the public opera houses, which were the focal point of many of the new scenic ideas developed in the Italian Renaissance. Inasmuch as intermezzi were absorbed by opera, the intermezzi's emphasis on spectacle was also absorbed into opera.

One of the unique devices developed at opera houses was the cloud machine for creating various formations. Another device was the "glory," which was designed especially for lowering heavenly figures from the clouds. The figure could be suspended on a horse, sitting on a cloud, or riding in a chariot.

Joseph Furttenbach

Joseph Furttenbach (1591-1667) was a German who, like the English set designer Inigo Jones, studied in Italy and then took back to his native land the concept of Italianate scenery. Furttenbach's treatise, *The Noble Mirror of Art* (1663), is the only detailed account of stage lighting in the Renaissance. He discusses both the lighting equipment as well as where to place lamps on stage. For example, the discussion focuses on using individual candles with a reflector or grouping the candles in a chandelier. Although the melting wax doesn't smell and does give a better light, Furttenbach asserts there is the problem of wax falling on the audience members and ruining their clothes. He then suggests putting a plate or a bowl beneath each candle to catch the drippings. For aesthetic purposes, he recommends hanging the chandeliers at the sides of the stage so that they will not obstruct the audience's view of the stage machines and their effects.

In addition to candles, Furttenbach suggests using about one-fourth pound of olive oil with a wick. The latter will last twelve hours. One of the problems with this type of lighting is the bad smell given off by the burning oil. No matter what system is used, Furttenbach states that water in tubs and jars should be available beneath the stage, as well as above, for emergencies.

Literary Criticism

The literary principles formulated by Renaissance scholars formed the basis for French neoclassicism and English classicism. These principles were derived out of the Renaissance desires to justify creative literature, which the Middle Ages considered morally, aesthetically, and didactically unsound.

The medieval objections to creative literature were a reassertion of those stated by Plato in *The Republic*. Basically, Plato had three objections. Creative literature, he contended, arouses man's emotions, some of which are better not aroused. The ratings of movies today is a distant spin-off of this idea. Secondly, Plato objected to creative literature on the grounds of morality. This objection was based on Plato's assertion that Homer's work contained untruths, obscenity, and religious blasphemy. A third objection was the concept of reality. Literature is three times removed from reality (truth), contended Plato. The truth is in the mind of God, which is formed in life, and which in turn is imitated by the artist. In other words, the artist imitates life which imitates an idea in the mind of God. In addition to these ideas, the medievalists added a fourth — the value of creative literature in society. It was deemed to have no real function and, consequently, "the righteous man" was discouraged from engaging in such an occupation.
from engaging in such an occupation.

In an attempt to create a literature which could not be criticized on the basis of these objections, medievalists resorted to a fundamental concept of the age — symbolism. In interpreting literature, allegory was used. It was first popularized in the Middle Ages by Fulgentius in his *Mythologicon* during the first half of the sixth century. Liturgical and secular literature was thus interpreted and reinterpreted in terms of the allegorical method. Adam and Eve became symbols of virtue as well as of the moral struggle within man's soul. *The Aeneid* is treated like *Pilgrim's Progress* in that the travels of Aeneid symbolize the progress of the human soul from the beginning to final happiness. In the Middle Ages, therefore, literature was justified as an extension of theology. It was not an independent creative form and, therefore, there could be no literary criticism of it.

Aristotle's *The Poetics* (c. 335-323 B.C.) was responsible for instituting literary criticism. *The Poetics* appears to have been lost until about the thirteenth century, at which time an oriental version of *The Poetics* was translated into Latin. The next important translation was Alessandro de Pazzi's Latin

A Renaissance view of the Roman theatre. From Bapst, *Essai sur l'Histoire du Théâtre*, 1893.

version in 1536, which established Aristotle's influence. In 1549 Bernardo Segni translated *The Poetics* into the vernacular (Italian), paving the way for the innumerable versions which have transcended into the twentieth century. One of these versions was particularly influential, that of Castelvetro in 1570. His misinterpretation of Aristotle was responsible for many of the "rules" by which the French and English of sixteenth, seventeenth, and eighteenth centuries wrote drama.

In addition to *The Poetics,* Horace's *The Art of Poetry* (first century B.C.) played a part in the Renaissance justification of literature. The treatises of *Daniello* in 1536, *Minturno* in 1559, and Sidney's *The Defense of Poesie* (1595) display a justification of literature in terms of Horace. By combining Aristotle's *The Poetics* and Horace's *The Art of Poetry,* the Renaissance justified literature as a reputable, independent art form. Eventually, theories about what constitutes a good play, based on the concepts of imitation of Aristotle and Horace, resulted in firm rules which were the basis of French and English classicism. These rules established criteria for judging plays, and thus mark the beginning of literary criticism.

Commedia Dell'Arte

Commedia dell'arte means comedy of the profession, indicating that it was performed by professional actors. It was developed in opposition to the commedia erudita (learned comedy), which was performed by amateurs at the courts and academies.

Origins of the commedia dell'arte are unknown. Historians have variously linked it to the Atellan farce of the third century B.C., the wandering mime actors in the Middle Ages, and to the plays of Plautus and Terence. Complicating its history is the fact that it was known also as *commedia a soggetto* (comedy by subject), *commedia improvvisa* (improvised comedy), *commedia a braccio* (comedy "off the cuff"), comedy of masks, and Italian comedy. Although it was being performed as early as 1545, the earliest description of a commedia dell'arte performance is that written by Orlando di Lasso in 1568.

There were three standard groups of characters: lovers, servants, and old men. These groups were the mainstays and were supported by other individual types. Unlike the learned or scripted comedy, the commedia dell'arte used no finished script. The actors of the commedia had an outlined story (scenario) which was posted offstage and they simply improvised the action and dialogue around the scenario. The lovers (men and women) were cast according to their looks and youth. They wore no masks, and their costumes represented the latest upperclass fashion. Servants were divided not only by male and female, but also as first and second servants. The female servants were *zagne;* later they were called *fantesche* (maids) or *servette (soubrettes).* They wore no masks, and were noted for the variety of costumes they wore. Zagne were specialists in quick changes and disguises. Their male counterparts were the *zanni. Harlequin* (the second zanni) is perhaps the most noted of all the commedia characters. The earliest example of a Harlequin is dated about 1570 in a picture painted by Prolius the Elder. Brighella was the first zanni who functioned as the clever servant. The zanni wore masks and supplied much of the comedy through what was known as *lazzi* (stage business). For example, one actor would fill his mouth with water and another would slap the other's mouth.

The last group was the old men. *Pantalone* was the first old man, and the doctor was the second. Like the zanni, they wore masks, were generally in their sixties, fathers of families, and looking for a romantic escapade which led them to end up looking foolish.

Although commedia dell'arte continued into the eighteenth century, its peak of popularity was between 1570 and 1650. During that time there were numerous troupes, the most famous of which was the Gelosi company (1568-1604), which derived its name from *virtu fama ed honor ne fer gelosi* (zealous to please their audiences). Despite its decline, the influence of the commedia dell'arte on subsequent generations can be noted in the works of Molière and Shakespeare. In addition to the writers, modern comic actors owe much to the commedia dell'arte. The antics and slapstick comedy of Laurel and Hardy, Abbott and Costello, and the Marx Brothers echo the comedy of the commedia dell'arte.

Selected Readings

Artz, Frederick B. *Renaissance Humanism: 1300-1500.* Oberlin, Ohio, 1966.

Campbell, Lily Bess. *Scenes and Machines on the English Stage During the Renaissance.* Cambridge, 1923.

Hewitt, Barnard, ed. *The Renaissance Stage: Documents of Serlio, Sabbattini, and Furttenbach.* Coral Gables, Fla., 1958.

Weinberg, Bernard. *A History of Literary Criticism in the Italian Renaissance.* 2. vols. Chicago, 1961.

Vocabulary

Term	Pronunciation
1. commedia dell'arte	koh MAY dyuh del AHR tay
2. De Architectura	day ahr ki tek TOOR uh
3. Vitruvius	vi TROO vee uhs
4. intermezzi	in ter MET zee
5. Camerata	kah muh RAH tuh
6. *Dafne*	DAHF nee
7. recitative	re si tah TEEV
8. Sebastiano Serlio	se bah STYAH noh SAIR lee oh
9. Giovan Battista Aleotti	joh VAHN buh TEE stuh ah lay AW tee
10. Filippo Brunelleschi	fi LEE poh broo ne LES kee
11. Della Pittura	DEL lah pi TOOR uh
12. Leon Battista Alberti	lay AWN buh TEE stuh ahl BAIR tee
13. Teatro Olimpico	tay AHT roh oh LIM pee koh
14. Teatro Di San Cassiano	dee sahn kah SYAH noh
15. Vincenza	vin CHEN zah
16. Andrea Palladio	ahn DRAY uh pah LAH dyoh
17. Vincenzo Scamozzi	vin CHEN zoh skuh MAWT zee
18. Teatro Farnese	tay AH troh fahr NAY zay
19. Teatro dei Intrepidi	in TRE pee dee
20. Guido Ubaldus	GWEE doh oo BAHL duhs
21. Nicola Sabbattini	NEE koh luh sah buh TEE nee
22. Giacomo Torelli	JAH kuh moh tawr REL ee
23. Harlequin	HAHR luh kwin
24. Drottningholm	DRAWT ning hawlm
25. Gripsholm	GRIPS hawlm
26. Česky Krumlov	CHE skuh KROOM luf
27. Furttenbach	FOOR ten bahk
28. Mythologicon	mi thoh LAW gi kawn
29. Castelvetro	kah stel VE troh
30. Daniello	dah NYEL loh
31. Minturno	min TOOR noh
32. commedia erudita	koh MAY dyuh e roo DEE tuh
33. commedia a soggetto	ah saw JET toh
34. commedia all'improvvisa	ahl eem proh VEE zah
35. commedia a braccio	ah BRAH choh
36. zagne	ZAHN yee
37. fantesche	fahn TES kay
38. servette	ser VET
39. soubrettes	soo: BRETS
40. zanni	ZAHN nee
41. Prolius	proh LEE uhs
42. Grighella	gri GEL luh
43. lazzi	LAHT zee
44. Pantalone	pahn tah LOH nee
45. Gelosi	je LOH zee
46. Teatro Novissimo	noh VI see moh

CHAPTER SEVEN

English Theatre and Drama to 1642 The Golden Age

Historically, the Elizabethan period (1558-1603) represents a transition from medieval theatre and drama to modern theatre and drama. Its drama was a merging of two distinct forces, the classical drama as resurrected and developed by the Italian Renaissance, and the popular entertainments which were continued from the Middle Ages. At the beginning of the 1580's, these two forces came together to form what is now regarded as the Elizabethan drama represented by Shakespeare, Marlowe, and others. With regard to theatre and drama, the most outstanding contributions of the Elizabethan period were the development of significant dramatists and drama and the establishment or regularizing of the profession of acting.

The death of Elizabeth in 1603 technically ends the Elizabethan period. James I (who reigned from 1603-1625) ushered in the Jacobean period. This period is characterized by the works most notably of John Fletcher (1579-1625) and Francis Beaumont (c. 1584-1616). Also significant in this period is the Stuart masque, so named because James I was of the House of Stuart. These dramatic performances were popularized at his court and later at the court of his son, Charles I, who reigned from 1625-1649. Upon the death of James I, Charles I succeeded to the throne and the period became known historically as the Caroline period. During the reign of Charles I, the theatres were closed in 1642 and were not to reopen until 1660.

The Merging of Forces

Two forces contributed to the development of Elizabethan drama. The first was the native or popular drama performed by professional actors for the public theatre; it represented a continuation of the morality plays and interludes developed in the Middle Ages. In order to attract as many people as possible, the actors added to the popular drama diverse elements from romantic stories, classical myths, history, and the Bible, and also inserted comic scenes.

Opposite: The Globe Theatre about 1612. From *Londina Illustrata,* 1825.

On the other end of the spectrum was the second force which, unlike the public theatre, tended to be for a select audience. The actors were amateurs and the plays, written by teachers and students, were a result of the "new learning." Humanism, or "new learning," which began in Italy about the fourteenth century, was an important development in Europe; it established the educational system and the cultural tastes of the upperclasses during the sixteenth and seventeenth centuries. Thus education and refinement were the hallmarks of a person belonging to the elite class; money or inherited status were considered insufficient for a person to belong to this select group. Although the Italians borrowed this concept of what makes a superior person from the French aristocracy of the thirteenth century, they changed it enough so that in countries such as England, one wishing to become a truly Renaissance individual had to take lessons from the Italian humanists. Under Henry VII, a Tudor who reigned from 1485-1509, Italian humanists came to England to teach classical arts, literature, and philosophy. The effect was noted in the imitations and revivals of Roman drama at universities. The plays were written and performed in Latin as well as English, and their main subject matter focused on Roman life and literature. Two plays written at the universities are outstanding demonstrations of the influence of Roman comedy (Plautus and Terrence) — Nicholas Udall's *Ralph Roister Doister* (c. 1534-41) and a composition by "Mr. S" (perhaps William Stevenson) entitled *Gammer Gurton's Needle* (c. 1552-1563).

The universities were not the only institutions to be affected by humanism. Closely related to the universities were Inns of Court, which were schools to train upper-class gentlemen as lawyers as well as to instruct them in all the social graces, music, and dancing. The first English tragedy, *Gorboduc* or *Ferrex and Porrex* (1561), was written by

Howell's View of London, 1620. From Wilkinson's *Londina Illustrata,* 1825.

two students, Thomas Sackville and Thomas Norton, of Inner Temple, and displays an influence of the Roman dramatist Seneca. In addition to writing tragedy modeled after Seneca, the Inns presented contemporary Italian drama and staged court masques, which later flourished under James I.

About 1585, the native tradition (popular entertainment) and the classicai influence began to merge. This blending of the two dominant forces into Elizabethan drama was due to the efforts of a group of young playwrights known as the University Wits.

University Wits

Apparently the University Wits were so called because all were associated with the University and all possessed the faculty of wit, which in the Elizabethan period was defined as "smart knowing," repartee, joking, or invention. The outstanding members were Thomas Kyd (1558-1594), Christopher Marlowe (1564-1593), John Lyly (1554-1606), and Robert Greene (1558-1592). William Shakespeare was not a member of the University Wits.

Thomas Kyd is best remembered for his play *The Spanish Tragedy* (c. 1587), which popularized tragedy for the public theatre. Before Kyd, tragedy was confined to the upperclasses, but with *The Spanish Tragedy,* tragedy crossed the boundaries from the classical to popular entertainment. The play's success was due to the fact that it contained classical (Senecan) elements and was also popular entertainment. Kyd's use of a ghost demanding revenge and a play within a play indicates an influence on Shakespeare's *Hamlet.* Although Kyd was the only member of the University Wits not to graduate from a university, he was, nonetheless, extremely well educated.

The oldest member of the group was John Lyly. Lyly catered to the court, which favored love as a subject for dramatization. Consequently, the central theme of most of his plays is courtly love. His prose novel *Euphues* (1578) introduced the term *euphuism,* which is characterized by flowery prose based on mythology or nature, carefully balanced blending of elements, similes, alliterations, and antithesis. Antithesis is contrasting ideas; for example: "Extremism in pursuit of justice is no virtue, and moderation in pursuit of liberty is no vice." This use of flowery or euphuistic language is a chief characteristic of Lyly. His romantic comedies proved to be an influence on Shakespeare's *A Midsummer Night's Dream* and *As You Like It.*

Robert Greene disliked Shakespeare and indicated this in his pamphlet *A Groatsworth of Wit bought with a Million of Repentance* (1592), in which he called Shakespeare an "upstart crow." As a dramatist, Greene wrote primarily pastorals and romantic comedy, the best known romantic comedy being *Friar Bacon and Friar Bungay* (c. 1589). His masterpiece, *James IV* (c. 1591), is said to have been a forerunner to the development of English tragi-comedy.

Christopher Marlowe has been called by scholars the "most brilliant and interesting of the University Wits." His life and death are shrouded somewhat in mystery. His best known play is *The Tragicall History of Doctor Faustus* (c. 1588), and his *Edward II* (c. 1592) is considered the model for the chronicle play. Although other writers used blank verse, Marlowe perfected it as a medium for drama. Marlowe's work also emphasizes the construction of a play around a single character. The titles of some of his plays testify to this: *Doctor Faustus, Edward II, Tamburlaine,* Parts I and II, and *The Jew of Malta.* Christopher Marlowe's work represents, more than any of the University Wits, the culmination of classical and native traditions being blended. As a group the University Wits are to be credited for aiding the transitional period between medieval and Elizabethan drama as well as paving the way for the work of William Shakespeare.

William Shakespeare

William Shakespeare (1564-1616) is considered the best dramatist of all time. In addition to being a writer, he was an actor, owned shares in the Lord Chamberlain's Company, and owned part of several theatre buildings. He is one of the few figures of the Elizabethan stage not indebted to Phillip Henslowe, a pawnbroker, theatre owner, and general businessman.

Shakespeare's writing career spans the years 1591 to 1611, during which time he wrote thirty-eight plays. As a dramatist, he borrowed extensively, using titles, plots, and sometimes lines. His general education was not extensive and his plays indicate his lack of knowledge. He put a clock in *Julius Caesar,* gave Bohemia a seacoast, placed Aristotle in the third century B.C., and made numerous other errors. As a psychologist, he was first rate, however. His insights about life and human nature are as true today as they were then.

Shakespeare's masterful use of language is unsurpassed. His colleagues testified that Shakespeare never blotted a line, to which Ben Jonson quipped that he "wished to God [Shakespeare] blotted a thousand." His dialogue was not only poetic but particularly abounds with dramatic imagery. Perhaps his only match in the use of imagery was Aeschylus. Shakespeare's plays demonstrate wit, inventiveness, sensitivity, and thoughtfulness. He did not confine himself to one form, but wrote tragedies, comedies, chronicles, and melodramas. These dramas display characters from all walks of life; indeed, his plays imitate life. Perhaps one reason for Shakespeare's greatness is his range in stories, language, and characters, and his ability to relate them to his audience. For Shakespeare these audiences have been of every generation since he penned his work. His plays are timeless; they speak to everyone.

Shakespeare's plays were first published in 1623 by two of his fellow actors, John Heming and Henry Condell, whose intentions were "only to keep the memory of so worthy a friend." This first publication of thirty-six of Shakespeare's plays is known as the First Folio. The First Folio sold at the time for one pound; today there are 200 extant copies, each conservatively valued at more than 20,000 pounds. Only the Gutenberg Bible demands a higher price.

Despite the high regard we hold for Shakespeare, he was not always considered great. His reputation fluctuated throughout the ages. Milton, the poet, praised him in 1630, but when the theatres closed in 1642, his fame ceased. Later, seventeenth century English writers revived his work but were forced to revise it because society considered it too immoral for the age. Seventeenth

The Swan Theatre as it appeared in 1614. From *Londina Illustrata,* 1825.

century France cared little for Shakespeare, whereas eighteenth century German romantics praised him. In eighteenth century England, Shakespeare's reputation became established with a return to his original works. The first critical edition of his work and the first biography were published in 1709 by Nicholas Rowe. The nineteenth century romantics cemented Shakespeare's reputation in England and France. Although Shakespeare reigns supreme today, it was Ben Jonson who was considered the best dramatist while Shakespeare was alive.

Government Regulation

The political and religious struggle between the Church of Rome and England, and between the local and national governments which began in the reign of Henry VIII, continued during the reign of Elizabeth. How Elizabeth attempted to solve these struggles directly affected the rise of the professional actor.

One of the first edicts to affect actors was an order on May 16, 1559, banning all religious or political plays, presentation of unlicensed plays, and making all local officials responsible for performances in their areas. Two points should be noted here. First, the act was designed to curtail possible riot and rebellion against the government through the misuse of drama and to make sure that the heretofore uncertain enforcement of the Crown's policies by the local officials was corrected. Second, Elizabeth was constantly in need of money and loyal servants. The use of monopolies served to accomplish these aims best, since she could show favor and reward services at little cost by granting a license. The licensing of actors was such a favor.

Despite the 1559 act, London officials continued to suppress performances, citing reasons of health. The city was within its rights, since an act of Parliament had granted London officials the power to compel each house-owner to keep his premises clean. In actuality, the Lord Mayor of London believed himself to be the guardian of the city's morals. Moreover, city officials were concerned about the city's industry. The problem of plays drawing citizens from their jobs led officials to use the plague as an excuse to ban plays and actors.

The political-religious struggle was intensified in 1570 when the Pope excommunicated Queen Elizabeth. Concerned about the actor and his ability to spread sedition and heresy through drama, the government issued the 1572 Licensing Act. This act paved the way for the recognition of acting as a profession. The ordinance allowed actors a choice of two licenses: (1) they could belong to any Baron of the realm or "other honorable personage of greater degree"; (2) they could obtain a license from two justices of the peace in each town they played. As a result of the 1572 Licensing Act, religious plays were suppressed and the number of acting companies became limited; thus the keeping of actors became a status symbol. As for the justices of peace, it appeared that actors had to buy licenses from these local officials. The licensing system could therefore be used as a financial reward as well as a safeguard against the use of drama for antigovernment purposes. The licensing system was revised in 1574, 1584-1585, 1597-1598, and 1604. After 1604, only members of the royal family were allowed to keep acting companies.

Inasmuch as the 1572 act threatened the existence of those actors not attached to a household, a group of actors headed by James Burbage appealed to the Earl of Leicester to form a company. What resulted was the 1574 Licensing Act which granted to the Earl of Leicester the first royal patent. The act itself gave Leicester's company complete freedom to perform when and where they liked without interference except during time of "common prayer" or plague. The only stipulation was that the Master of Revels, an official of the Crown, approve the plays. This gave the Crown complete authority over plays and actors.

Public and Private Theatres

During the Elizabethan period, actors were guided by two traditions: the indoor and the outdoor. Since the late Middle Ages, these two traditions existed simultaneously, for while actors performed within halls, town houses, inns, and churches, they also presented plays in various outdoor areas — for example, innyards, streets, or village greens. To conclude that the actors adhered to playing solely indoors or outdoors is not warranted by the available evidence. Further, the assumption that innyards, baiting rings, or other theatre buildings were prototypes for the Elizabethan theatre is also untenable. The simultaneous tradition of outdoor and indoor performances led to the use of indoor and outdoor theatres, which is demonstrated in the public and private theatres.

The Old Tabard Inn, sketched shortly before its demolition. Actors possibly performed in innyards similar to this one. Thornbury, *Old and New London*.

Private theatres were indoor theatres. They were roofed, charged more than the public theatres, had an audience capacity which was roughly one-half of the public theatres, provided seats for all spectators, used candles, catered to an aristocratic audience, and were located within the city of London. Although the theatres were located within the city limits, they were not subject to the legal injunctions that the city officials imposed upon other playing areas. These theatres were situated within the "liberties," which means a self-governing community. The "liberties" belonged to monastic orders, but when Henry VIII broke with Rome he confiscated all church property and placed it under the control of the Crown. Thus these private theatres were protected by the royal government.

The private theatres were known by the monastic order which controlled the liberty wherein they performed. Thus, the first private theatre was known as the first Blackfriars, after the Dominican monks or Black Friars. The private theatre opened in 1606, called the Whitefriars, was named after the Carmelites or White Friars. The first Blackfriar's theatre opened in 1576 under the direction of William Farrant.

The next private theatre was the second Blackfriars which James Burbage built in 1596. This theatre is considered the most important private theatre because, up to that time, private theatres had been the domain of boys' companies, and Burbage intended his theatre as a winter home for his adult company — the Lord Chamberlain's men. Although local residents of the liberty prevented Burbage from opening by citing his use of adult actors rather than children, the concept of adult troupes performing at private theatres was eventually sanctioned by James I in 1608. At this time, the King's Men performed successfully at the Second Blackfriars. The success of an adult company (the King's Men) prompted others to build private or indoor theatres; eventually these theatres became the primary winter homes of the adult companies. While the adult companies used the private theatres from roughly mid-October to mid-May, they performed at public or outdoor theatres for the other five months.

The first public theatre was called The Theatre, and was built in 1576 by James Burbage and John Brayne. There were nine public theatres by 1615: The Curtain (1577), Newington Butts (before 1580), The Rose (1587), The Swan (1595-1596), The Globe (1599, rebuilt in 1614), The Fortune (1600-1621 rebuilt in 1623), The Red Bull (c. 1605), and The Hope (1613-1817). All of the public theatres had the following characteristics: (1) they were built outside of the city limits; (2) they catered to the general public; (3) they were open-air structures, (4) they were intended originally for adult troupes; and (5) they had various shapes — round, square, octagonal, or polygonal.

The dual tradition of acting had advantages and disadvantages. The advantages of indoor playing (private theatres) were, first, the actor and the audience were protected from the elements. Second, actors could perform with less fear of detection from city officials if they were performing at theatres within the city but outside of the liberties. Third, evidence indicates that the actors did not need a platform for a performance. Fourth, there were fewer inconveniences from crowds and vehicles. The chief disadvantages were the threat of plague and the possible loss of money due to the restricted size of the crowd.

The advantages of performing outdoors (public theatres) were: (1) the larger seating and staging area; (2) the reduction of the health menace which city fathers used in an effort to shut down the theatres; (3) open demonstration to the royal government that the plays did not contain sedition and heresy; (4) the use of daylight for performances; and (5) freedom from city officials. The chief disadvantages were possible interruption by bad weather and problems with large crowds.

Ben Jonson and the Court Masques

Ben Jonson (1572-1637) was England's first poet laureate in 1616. His first success was *Everyman in His Humour* (1598), a play in which Shakespeare acted. Humours referred to yellow bile, black bile, green phlegm, and red blood. These four fluids were thought to be within the body, and the predominance of one element over the others determined a person's behavior. By the end of the sixteenth century, the term came to mean whim or fancy. Jonson, however, used the term to denote an imbalance of the fluids; hence, his play *Everyman Out of His Humour* (1599). Should a person become ill, display emotional outbursts or any unusual behavior, the humours were considered out of balance and a purging or bloodletting was required to keep everyman in his humour.

Left: Frontispiece to Francis Kirkman's *The Wits; or Sport Upon Sport,* 1672. This drawing is believed to depict the inside of the Red Bull Playhouse and the characters probably represent the leading figures in a droll — a short, farcical work from a larger play. The droll was the primary form of entertainment from 1642 to 1660. Actor Robert Cox is thought to have played the role of Simpleton depicted in the drawing. From *Londina Illustrata,* 1825.

Below: A rare print of an entertainment at an Elizabethan inn yard. Cuthbert Burbage, who was responsible for the construction of the Globe Theatre in 1599, was the son of James Burbage, builder of the first public theatre, The Theatre, in England.

Fac-similes of the title page of Maroccus Extaticus, 1595, and of the rare engraving which represents Banks exhibiting the feats of his celebrated Dancing-horse in the yard of the Bel_Savage

Maroccus Extaticus.

Or,

BANKES

BAY HORSE IN

a Trance.

A Diſcourſe ſet downe in a merry Dialogue, between Bankes and his beaſt: Anatomizing ſome abuſes and bad trickes of this age.

Written and intituled to mine Hoſt of the Belſauage, and all his honeſt Gueſts.

By Iohn Dando the wierdrawer of Hadley, and Harrie Runt, head Oſtler of Boſomes Inne.

Printed for Cuthbert Burby.

1595.

Model of the original stage for Stratford, England. Courtesy British Tourist Authority.

Volpone, or The Fox (1606) rates as Jonson's best comedy and has been produced frequently. In 1977 it was on Broadway as *The Sly Fox.* His major efforts in writing, however, were the court masques.

The court masques were introduced into England by Henry VIII, but under Elizabeth they were relegated to occasional performances at the Inns of Court. During the reign of James I, however, one a year was produced, mostly at the Banqueting Hall at Whitehead Palace, and this was increased to two under Charles I, who built a special room for the masques. A favorite of James I, Jonson was responsible for writing the majority of scripts and Inigo Jones (1573-1652, England's first important set designer) undertook the design of the scenery.

The court masque placed its emphasis upon the courtier dancers. Because nobility did not wish to be labeled actors, they confined their theatrical activities to dancing and left the singing and dialogue to the court musicians, and the comic roles to the professional actors. As a form, the court masque consisted of lords and ladies who were masked and dressed as mythological characters, shepherds, or other figures. An entrance dance was performed by these nobles and then they went into the audience to dance many of the well-known dances of the day, called revels. There was also a "going out" dance. By wearing masks and costumes and dancing as the character they represented, the nobles were taking roles in a play. The masque consisted at first of disguised nobles acting out a role, not with dialogue but through the dances, which were symbolic of events or characters. As the masque developed and became more elaborate, dramatists developed allegorical stories into which were interwoven the dances as well as lines spoken by professional actors. In 1608 Jonson added another dimension to the masque when he introduced a comic dance with characters speaking satiric humor. This new form was known as the anti-masque. The anti-masque contrasted sharply with the formal masque and was probably performed by professional actors.

Scenery was considered a "special display" feature of the masque. For some plays, it was a special

Old inns of London. Plays were possibly staged in the yards of such inns during the Elizabethan period. Photograph by Walter Thornbury, *Old and New London.*

feature and, for others, an extra adornment. In the Caroline period, some masques did not use scenery. The scenic work of Inigo Jones, however, proved to be an influence on the development of scenery in the English public theatre. Jones went to Italy in 1600 and returned in 1604. When he came back, he brought with him the principles of Italianate scenery, which he used in his designs for court masques. His designs for the court masques included perspective scenery, a proscenium arch, rapid shifting of scenery, and machines. Despite their successes, Jonson and Jones quarreled, apparently over the importance of scenery with respect to the script. As a result, Jonson lost his patronage with the king and was forced to return to the public theatre. The last masque, *Salmacida Spolia,* was staged in 1640.

Not only did masques prove influential to the public theatre, they also exerted a part in the political fortunes of Charles I. Court masques were extravagantly produced by James I as well as Charles I. The money spent for these productions was a luxury Charles I could not afford. About 1640, when he was broke, he asked Parliament for additional funds which they refused. Civil war ensued. Inasmuch as the majority of the enemies of Charles I were Puritans who were also antitheatre, they used the civil war as an excuse for closing the theatres in 1642 for five years. In 1647 the Puritans gained control of the government and in 1649 Charles I was beheaded. With the Puritans in control, the public theatres remained closed until 1660 when Charles II was restored to the throne.

Selected Readings

Bergson, David M. *Shakespeare: A Study and Research Guide.* New York, 1975.

Chambers, E.K. *The Elizabethan Stage.* 4 vols., London, 1923.

Gurr, Andrew. *The Shakespearean Stage,* 1574-1642. Cambridge, Eng., 1970.

"Shakespeare: An Annotated Bibliography." *Shakespeare Quarterly* (1924-present).

Vocabulary

1. Jacobean	ja kuh BEE uhn
2. masque	mask
3. *Ralph Roister Doister*	ralf ROY ster DOY ster
4. *Gorboduc*	GAWR buh duhk
5. John Lyly	LIL ee
6. Thomas Kyd	kid
7. *Euphues*	YOO: fyoo eez
8. euphuism	YOO: fyoo iz uhm
9. *Doctor Faustus*	FOW stuhs
10. *Tamburlaine*	TAM buhr layn
11. Earl of Leicester	LE ster
12. James Burbage	BER bij
13. *Volpone*	vawl POH nee
14. phlegm	flem
15. Inigo Jones	IN i goh

CHAPTER EIGHT

The Birth of the Neoclassical Ideal

Many factors influenced the seventeenth century theatre and many developments occurring in the seventeenth century would influence the theatre to come. It was the Age of Reason with scientific breakthroughs of Kepler and Galileo. The visual arts were producing some of the great works of all time through the genius of Rubens, Vandyck, Rembrandt, El Greco and Vélazquez. But most of all the seventeenth century produced the birth of the neoclassical ideal which was to set the standard for drama during the entire period. It was a period of change, which saw the focus of power move from Spain to France, but not before the Spanish drama reached its apogee between the years 1580 and 1680, a period which has been designated the Golden Age of Spanish Literature.

Spain's Golden Age

The Golden Age produced two outstanding playwrights, Lope Félix de Vega Carpio, known as Lope de Vega (1562-1635), and Pedro Calderón de la Barca (1600-1681), called Calderón. Voltaire has placed Lope beside Shakespeare in the measure of his work. He does not deserve such an honor, qualitatively perhaps, but if quantity is any measure, Lope must rate high. He was one of the most prolific playwrights of all time, writing over 1800 plays of which more than 450 are extant.

Born in Madrid, Lope de Vega had an eventful, not always exemplary, life. His ability to turn out plays was phenomenal, to say the least. Cervantes is reported to have called him "monster of nature." Tradition has it that he composed ten plays in one week. Evidence does suggest that he wrote at least two a week during the latter part of his career. There is no question that Lope de Vega was the idol of Madrid. Crowds followed him and it is said that women and children asked for his blessing (he was an ordained priest). As with today's idols, his name was given to objects considered the best of their kind. There were Lope horses, Lope melons and Lope cigars.

Lope's plays are difficult to translate because they are written in rhymed poetry. For that reason, his fame is confined primarily to Spain. His most popular work for modern audiences is *The Sheep Well (Fuente Ovejuna,* c. 1614). *The Star of Seville (La Estrella de Sevilla)* remains his most famous play in Spain.

Lope's most challenging rival was Pedro Calderón de la Barca. Son of a finance minister under Phillip I and III, he was schooled at Salamanca by the Jesuits who, by the way, were the only religious order allowed to use drama in their teachings. While Lope was primarily associated with the public theatre, Calderón wrote for the court. His most famous secular play is *Life Is a Dream (La Vida es Sueno,* c. 1636), which is a philosophical allegory about the mystery of life.

Perhaps more than anything else, Calderón is noted for his religious plays called *autos sacramentales*. These plays were similar to morality plays in which human and supernatural characters met allegorical figures such as Sin, Grace, Pleasure, etc. The plays always demonstrated the validity of church dogma.

The theatres of seventeenth century Spain were called *corrales*. The corrales were not uniform in design, but there were many common features. Most were constructed around rectangular courtyards. The balconies of surrounding buildings were used to seat spectators, while standing room was provided in the courtyard or *patio* for men only; the women were forced to sit in a gallery called the *cazuela*. The stage was at the end of the yard.

Opposite: Francois Joseph Talma (1763-1826) as Manlius in a revival of *Manlius Capitolinus* (1806). Talma, a favorite of Napoleon and considered by many to rival Molière as the greatest French actor, was the first French actor to play Roman parts in historically accurate costume.

Right: The Actor by Vélazquez depicts Phillip II's court jester. Courtesy Museo del Prado.

Below: A representation of the Italian farce comedians at the Hôtel de Bourgogne around 1630. The male figures are the Frenchmen (extreme left) looking at the Spaniard (extreme right), who has fled from fear of the Frenchman. Turpulin (second from left), whose name means "unlucky," steals from Gaultier-Garguille, whose name means "great greedy mouth." Gros-Guillaume (second from right), whose name means "big Bill," is dressed as a tennis player and is acting the lover. Courtesy French Cultural Services.

Que ce Theatre est magnifique !
Que ces Acteurs sont inuentifs !
Et qu'ils ont de preseruatifs
Contre l'humeur melancolique !

Icy d'vne posture drolle
Ils nazardent le mauuais temps;
Et charment tous les Escoutans,
Auec vne seule parolle.

Icy l'ingenieux Gullaume
Contrefaisant l'homme de Cour,
Se plaist à gourmander l'Amour,
Troussé comme vn joueur de paume

Icy d'vne façon hagarde
Turlupin veut faire l'Escroq,
Et l'Espagnol de peur du choq,
Fuit le François qui le regarde.

Mais le vray Gautier les surpasse,
Et malgré la rigueur du sort,
Il nous fait rire après sa mort,
Au souuenir de sa grimasse.

The Birth of New France

By 1600 the Spanish Empire was in decline. Virtually every country in Europe began to look to France. After 1643, France offered an almost paranormal dominance over western Europe. Writers, painters, sculptors and architects made Paris their home away from home. Trends in fashion, manners and politics were set by the French government more so than at any other time in history. Much of what had occurred had been incubated by Richelieu, nurtured by Mazarin, and glorified by Louis XIV. After 1659 France became the most powerful nation in Christendom. The nation was confident in the skills of its people, the strategy of its soldiers, and the destiny of the king. It was the beginning of a period of almost unprecedented glory and an era that produced some of the greatest theatre of all time.

The French theatre, which had barely become an entity prior to the Religious War (1540-1598), was now to begin anew. Indeed, France's contribution to theatre during the seventeenth century was the most significant during the period. The Hôtel de Bourgogne, which had been built in 1548 by the Confrérie de la Passion, an amateur theatrical group that had acquired a monopoly on theatrical production in Paris, was the birthplace of the new theatre.

The first professional playwright of the new era was Alexandre Hardy (c. 1572-1632). In 1608 Hardy wrote for a troupe headed by Valleran LeComte; the troupe was called the King's Players *(Les Comédiens du Roi).* The troupe produced Hardy's plays at the Hôtel de Bourgogne. In many ways Hardy's plays were a transition from the medieval to the new classical style which was soon to dominate the stage. Hardy's plays were written for a popular audience and he adapted his plays for the common taste. He never really achieved greatness but he was certainly influential on those to follow.

In staging Hardy's plays there is some indication that individual scenic devices resembling mansions were probably used. This type of setting was called *décor simultane,* or simultaneous setting. A number of designs for this setting are extant. Most are by Mahelot, who worked for Valleran LeComte's troupe. Basically the stage had several scenic backgrounds, in front of which an actor might stand. Since the acting area was common to all scenic elements, the dialogue was the chief determinant in identifying a specific location. This type of staging is called platea, which lasted at the Hôtel de Bourgogne until around 1650.

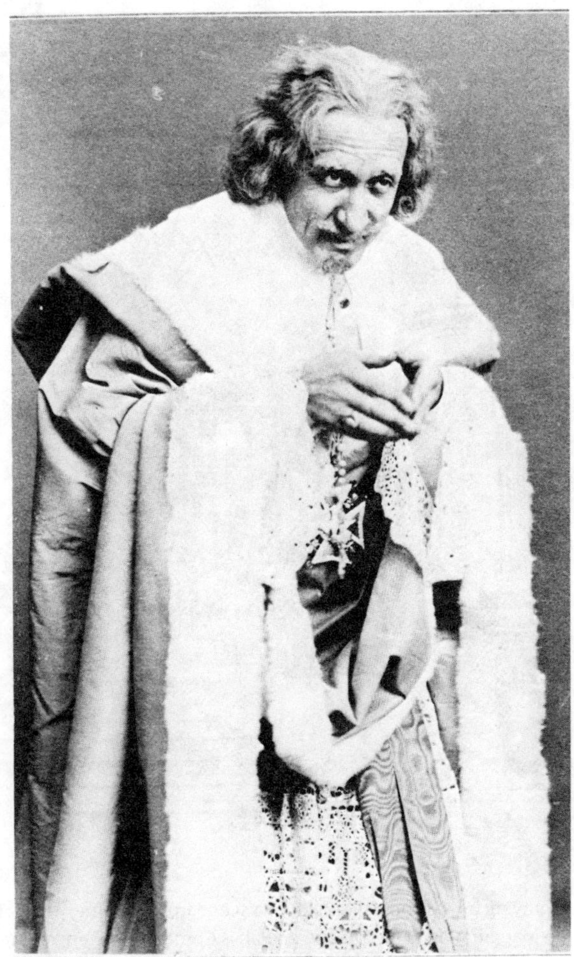

Cardinal Richelieu as portrayed by Edwin Booth. From *Dramatic Portrait Gallery,* 1880.

With the assassination of Henry IV in 1610, Louis XIII came to the throne at the age of nine. In 1620, the unquestioned power behind the throne, Cardinal Richelieu, began his reign. Richelieu quickly was able to concentrate almost unlimited power in the crown by taking power away from the aristocracy and the Protestants. Richelieu gathered his power over virtually all phases of French life. The arts were no exception.

Dealing with cultural affairs, Richelieu looked

Engraving by Stefano della Bella of a scene from Mirame, 1641. This tragi-comedy, by Desmaret de Saint-Sorlin, was performed for the inauguration of the Théâtre du Palais Cardinal. The engraving stresses the ceremonious and static quality of the performance and the elegant symmetry of the groups which harmonizes with the setting. Courtesy French Cultural Services.

toward Italy to guide the new programs. The new Italian scenic conventions were brought to France with the importation of designers such as Tomaso Francini. In 1641 Richelieu built in his palace a theatre of the Italian type containing the first proscenium arch in France. He called it the Palais-Royal and it was destined to become the home of Molière. Mazarin, who succeeded Richelieu in 1642, continued the importation of Italian designers with the arrival of Torelli to stage operas. In 1644 the second permanent theatre in Paris, the Théâtre du Marais, was rebuilt in the Italian style.

The French Academy

Several scholars and authors began to meet in 1627 at the home of Valentin Conrart, a secretary to the king. Richelieu openly encouraged the meetings and even offered to constitute the group as a public body recognized by the state. The group was eventually incorporated in 1635 as the Academie Française and is still in existence today. The group was charged with maintaining the purity of the language and being the final arbiter in things literary. It is the French Academy which determines the gender of new words added to the vocabulary. To become one of the "immortal forty," as members are called, is one of the truly great honors of all time. It was from the French Academy that the standards of drama, which were primarily of Italian origin, were postulated. These standards have come to be called neoclassicism.

Neoclassicism

In a sense, the standards of authority championed by Richelieu found the rigidity of neoclassi-

Engraving by Giovanni Burnacini depicting an allegorical scene at the theatre in Regensburg, Bavaria (Germany), about 1653.

cism made to order. Fundamentally, the neoclassical doctrine demanded that the playwright follow certain rules so that reality might be shown. The neoclassical doctrine had at its core the concept of verisimilitude. If you were a playwright in seventeenth century France, strict adherence to the concept of verisimilitude would certainly be desirable. Verisimilitude can be reduced to three basic ideas, reality, morality and abstraction.

First, your play would have to be concerned with life as the seventeenth century person saw it. You would be discouraged from writing about supernatural or mythical characters. In short, the material you chose for your play would have to be from real life. Consequently, it was essential that characters be portrayed realistically, but the kinds of characters that one might portray were restricted. Your portrayal must be consistent with the moral standards of the time. This forced the dramatists to create certain types of characters; ones who would display the moral precepts of the day. The underlying tone of seventeenth century French neoclassicism suggested a just God who rewarded good and punished evil. This concept implied that right would always be triumphant. On those occasions when justice did not emerge triumphant, seventeenth century rationalizing sought to explain them by asserting that these were accidents — designs by God for his special purpose and beyond the understanding of humans. Write about reality, then, but only those aspects of reality that demonstrate acceptable moral principles.

In addition, all dramaturgic development must be further modified by the concept of abstraction. The neoclassicist believed that no two things were exactly alike. On the other hand, all classes of things may be identified by certain characteristics which all members of a class share. For example, there are many different kinds of chairs — metal chairs, wooden chairs, plain chairs and highly ornate chairs. While each chair may vary a great deal from the other, all have certain characteristics in common which permit them to be classified as chairs. Those common elements are called essences. The neoclassicist believed it possible to find the essence of all things, including dramatic literature. For that reason, purity of dramatic types was essential. Tragedy must not contain comic elements nor should comedy be serious. All essences could be determined through analysis and study. It was believed that all societies had permanent aspects which were essences of human society in general. Therefore, the study of any of the trappings of historical accuracy was, in effect, irrelevant. What was relevant was isolating those aspects of society common to all. Neoclassicism, then, was concerned with those universal aspects of character and situation. Each character portrayed must be appropriate in terms of the universal standard of the norm that was being depicted. This rule was called decorum.

Along with decorum was a misinterpretation of Aristotle's *The Poetics,* in which the Academy decreed that a play should be unified in terms of time, place and action. Most good drama is unified by action, but to impose a limit as to time and place was not what Aristotle had intended. The neoclassical ideal called for an action which could take place within twenty-four hours and in one place, or two if the other could be reached in twenty-four hours. Most writers, if they were to maintain any kind of relationship with the Academy or their peers, wrote in accordance with the rules of neoclassicism.

The neoclassical ideal, then, was the purity of tragedy and comedy; strict adherence to verisimilitude and decorum; the observance of the unities of time, place and action; and the idea that each drama should teach with pleasure. The influence of these principles was to be felt in western theatre for quite some time. The influence in France was immediate and significant. The theatre under Richelieu's control attempted to follow the tenents of neoclassicism as rigidly as possible. Playwrights were loath to bring down the wrath of the Cardinal or the displeasure of the Academy.

Pierre Corneille

Pierre Corneille (1606-1684), a Jesuit trained lawyer, was one who dared defy the Cardinal. Richelieu had engaged Corneille and four other young writers in 1629 to write plays along the lines he suggested. Corneille frequently showed a great deal of independence in working from the sketches submitted to him. In 1636 Corneille wrote and performed a play which had not been suggested or encouraged by the Cardinal. The play, *El Cid*, was to become one of the most famous works in French literature. Based on Guillen de Castro's *Youthful Adventures of the Cid (Las Mocedades del Cid)*, Corneille's play became at the time a popular hit and a highly controversial *cause célèbre*.

The play is based on the life of Rodrigo Diaz, the half legendary hero called El Cid by the Moors. Chimene and Rodrigo (or Roderigue as he is called in the play) are desperately in love. Act I reveals Chimene's love for Roderigue through the technique of a confidant. Chimene confides her love to Elvise. Before the love can be revealed, Chimene's father, Don Gomes, quarrels with and insults Roderigue's elderly father, Don Diegue. Corneille's dramatic theme is primarily based on the ancient Spanish code of honor which demanded a death for every insult or seduction. Therefore, Roderigue was bound by his code of honor to avenge his father. He then challenges, fights and kills Gomes. Chimene, who is still deeply in love with Roderigue, feels that she must avenge her father and asks King Fernand to behead or banish Roderigue. Roderigue, upon hearing of Chimene's request, goes to her and in a stirring scene gives her his sword and invites her to slay him. Chimene cannot bring herself to run him through. Don Diegue persuades Roderigue to fight the Moors, who were converging by sea to capture Seville. Roderigue battles the Moors, defeats them, and returns to Seville in glory. All of Seville praises the hero Roderigue, save Chimene, who still demands his death. King Fernand refuses to order the execution of the man who defeated the Moors, so Chimene offers her hand in marriage to anyone who will challenge and kill the man with whom she is deeply in love. Sancho accepts and immediately challenges Roderigue. Roderigue decides to allow Chimene her revenge by letting Sancho kill

Scene from the first edition of Pierre Corneille's *Polyeucte* (1643), considered by many critics to be his masterpiece. Courtesy Lilly Library, Indiana University.

him. When Chimene learns of the plan, she repents of her revenge and begs Roderigue to defend himself. In the ensuing battle Roderigue overcomes Sancho but refuses to kill him. According to the code of honor, Roderigue's decision to spare Sancho satisfies Chimene's honor. Chimene, seeing Sancho come to her, believes Roderigue is dead. But King Fernand tells her the truth and Chimene is overjoyed. Roderigue and Chimene meet and agree to marry after a year's mourning period has passed.

Le Cid provoked an interesting controversy. Given classical standards, many critics felt that the play had a number of faults. Richelieu joined in the battle although his interests were probably more political than literary. After an exchange of pamphlets between Corneille and his enemies, the French Academy was asked to render an opinion on how well the play followed the neoclassical ideal. In December of 1637, the Academy published the "sentiments" called *The Views of the Academy on the Tragedy-Comedy of The Cid (Les Sentiments de L'Academie sur la Tragi-Comédie du Cid)*. The pamphlet was written by the acknowledged leader of the Academy, Jean Chapelain, and edited, according to some scholars, by Richelieu. The Academy admitted that there was beauty in the play and praised certain qualities. However, Chapelain felt that the play was weak because it contained neither ordinary nor extraordinary verisimilitude. The characters did not behave satisfactorily in terms of norms. In addition, he felt that there were perhaps too many events crowded into twenty-four hours, an observation with which many would heartily agree. The primary disagreement was an ethical one. There was objection to the apparent exaltation of romantic love, and Chimene's words to Roderique as he went to fight Sancho were thought to be indecent. They were, "Come victor from a combat of which Chimene is the prize."

While the controversy may seem silly from a modern vantage, it was of some significance: it encouraged Corneille to write critical observations on his art; it also furnishes the historian with invaluable information about Corneille and other playwrights of the period. Certainly the controversy established classicism as the standard of the period. Corneille never again challenged the concept of the Cardinal's Academy in his later works and was voted acceptance as a member in 1647.

Jean Racine

The second of the great seventeenth century dramatists was Jean Racine (1639-1699). Racine was the son of the controller of the state's salt monopoly at La Ferte-Milon. His mother was the daughter of an attorney at Villers-Cotterets. Both of Racine's parents died when he was young and Jean was raised by paternal grandparents. Because of the family's Jansenist bent (a religious order believing in predestination), Racine studied at the *petite ecole* in Port-Royal run by the Solitaries, to prepare for a religious life. He received intensive religious training and learned Greek, both of which were to influence him for the rest of his life. At the College d'Harcourt in Paris, Jean became fascinated with the plays of Euripides and Sophocles, philosophy, and young women, in that order. During this period Racine wrote his first play, which was presented to Molière. The play was never produced, but Molière gave the young poet a small stipend and encouraged him to try again. Racine's inclination to the theatre and young women prompted his grandparents to remove him from Paris. Racine traveled to Uzes in southern France, ostensibly to study for the priesthood. It was there that Racine commented in a letter to Jean de la Fontaine that the women of Uzes were "corpsus solidum et succi plenum" (flesh firm and succulent). By 1663 Racine had determined that his future did not lie with the priesthood, and returned to Paris, where much to the horror of his pious relatives, he turned back to theatre. An aunt who was a member of the sisterhood at Port-Royal-des-Champs admonished the young man, stating: "I have learned with sorrow that you frequent, more than ever, people whose name is an abomination to all who have any measure of piety, and with reason, since they are forbidden entry to the church, or access to the sacrament." All entreaties were to little avail, however, as Racine wrote his second play *The Thebans* (La Thébaide), which was produced in 1664 by Molière. From that moment on, Racine entered a period of great accomplishment. *La Thébaide* was followed by *Andromaque* (1667), which was recognized immediately as a masterpiece. *The Litigants (Les Plaideurs),* a comedy, followed in 1668 and one year later, *Britanicus,* which Racine always considered his most careful work. Among Racine's most famous works are *Berenice* (1670), *Bajazet* (1762) and *Iphigénie* (1674).

Jean Racine, as sketched by his eldest son. Courtesy French Cultural Services.

The play that is most performed of all Racine's work is, perhaps, the crowning achievement of the classical style, *Phèdre* (1677). In the long history of dramatic literature there has been a handful of roles that seem to attract actors. Referring to this phenomenon in English and American actors, Carl Sandburg once observed: "They all want to play Hamlet." But if you are female and you are French, the role that is most coveted of them all is Phèdre. Based on *Hippolytus* by Euripides, the Racine play made many significant changes to adhere to the neoclassical rules.

Racine attempted to show only those occurrences which could happen in real life, thereby complying with rules of verisimilitude. Only the sea monster, a part of the original myth, deviated from reality. Hippolytus of Racine is not the chaste woman-hating, shining paragon of virtue as was the Euripidean original, but a normal seventeenth century Frenchman with a girlfriend. Phèdre, while falling victim to almost uncontrollable love, still has a great capacity for moral feeling. She suffers her fate with great remorse which, for the most part, redeems her in the minds of the audience. Racine is primarily concerned with the universal in character, and therefore bothers little with delving into the idiosyncrasies of character. Racine was interested in the essence, only those things which focus on the emotions of a woman caught between desire and her own morality. There is no question that in *Phèdre,* Racine turned the prescribed restrictions of form to eloquent advantage by the manner in which he focused his drama through careful structure with a singular action and clarity of tone. Racine brought neoclassical tragedy to perfection and must rank among the great writers of all time.

French Manners

It was not only the contribution of neoclassical tragedy that gives seventeenth century France a

Marie Francoise Dumesnil (Mlle. Dumesnil), photographed between 1737-1770 as Agrippine in Racine's *Britanicus.* Courtesy French Cultural Services.

special place in history. Her manners, her morals and her fashion were duplicated by smart society throughout the western world. Indeed, France's contribution to theatre during the seventeenth century was the most significant during the period. Seventeenth century France was in many ways as puzzling as it was productive. It was an age of paradox and enigma, of strict manners and loose morals. Middle-class clothing consisted of a simple black coat covering most of the body, but in the elite, clothing was the signpost of status and was superb. Perhaps no other period in history produced a more effeminate costume for men. Large brimmed hats covering wigs of long curls down to the shoulders, silk cravats loosely tied about the neck and a long, highly ornamented vest down to the knees were the style. Trousers, ending at the knees where they were ribboned, were covered by a large coat with huge cuffs trimmed in lace. Silk stockings were worn along with boots on all occasions. Lace handkerchiefs were sometimes pulled from the sleeve and used to gesture with during conversation. Yet, for all their lace, most of the elite men were skilled swordsmen and quick to uphold their honor if challenged.

The dress of the women at court was, as one historian put it, "free and flowing to accord with their morals." Their dresses were richly embroidered and gaily colored with laced bodices designed to show more than ample amounts of womanly charms. Their hair was beautifully ribboned, jeweled, perfumed and curled. Since most marriages among the aristocracy were preplanned and arranged by parents on the basis of property, affairs of passion usually took place outside the marital bed. Almost every man who could afford it had a mistress, and the number of affairs managed over a given period was almost as important an indicator of masculinity as the number of battles fought. Women, too, found the number of admirers in pursuit of their charms a measure of their femininity and openly encouraged liaisons. And yet no other period refined the art of conversation to the degree that it was perfected under Louis XIV. At no other time had women been more encouraged to develop their intelligence as well as their beauty, and the ideal woman became one of educated wit. It was these idiosyncrasies of French society that fell under the satirical eye of one of the greatest playwrights of all time, Jean-Baptiste Poquelin, better known as Molière.

Molière

Molière was born in Paris on January 15, 1622, to Jean-Baptiste Poquelin III and his wife Marie Cresse. The elder Poquelin was superintendent of the royal upholstery and was charged with, among other things, the making of the royal bed. Jean IV was schooled at the Collège de Clermont under the Jesuits who, as mentioned earlier, were the only religious group permitted to use drama as a teaching device. Poquelin studied law for a time before turning his attention to the theatre. At this time Jean was living with Madeleine Béjart, who had a passion for the theatre. Her two brothers and Jean-Baptiste Poquelin signed a formal contract on June 30, 1643, establishing the Théâtre Illustrè. The Comédie Française regards this date as the beginning of what is now the longest continuing theatre company in the world. Because of the stigma attached to acting by the church, most actors took a stage name. Thus Molière was born.

The Théâtre Illustrè was hardly illustrious and Molière was arrested at least three times for debt before departing with his company for the provinces. For twelve years Molière learned the art of the theatre both in acting and in writing before returning to Paris in 1658. On October 24, 1658, Molière's troupe presented before Louis XIV Corneille's tragedy *Nicomede*. Voltaire maintains that Molière suffered from chronic hiccoughs, which often enhanced a comic character but spelled doom to the performance of tragedy. Whatever the cause, the tragedy was a disaster and the company would have been sent back to the provinces but for the performance of an afterpiece by Molière, which so delighted the king that he allowed the company to share a theatre with an Italian group. The fashions and morals of Paris caught the eye of Molière, particularly men and women making so much over delicate manners and perfumed speech. He began to chronicle the foibles of an age and on November 18, 1659, *Les Précieuses Ridicules* was produced at the Salle du Petit Bourbon. The play was an instant hit, but more than that, it marked the real beginning of one of the most beloved playwrights the world has ever known. Louis commanded three performances the first year and the play was performed forty-four times. When the Petit Bourbon was torn down, the King came to the rescue by assigning to Molière the Palais-Royal, which Richelieu had built and

Torelli had remodeled. Molière and the Troup de Monsieur remained at the Palasi-Royal from 1660 to 1673, where they produced some of the greatest comedies ever written. Although Molière wrote different types of comedy, his most admired works were his comedies of character and manners. His work in this area includes *The School for Husbands* (1661), *The School for Wives* (1662), *Tartuffe* (1664), *The Misanthrope* (1666), *The Miser* (1668), *The Learned Ladies* (1672), and *The Imaginary Invalid* (1673).

When one ridicules the foppery of an age, one is bound to accumulate ememies. *School for Wives* was attacked by the more conservative members of court. The King himself was young enough to enjoy its levity but others were shocked. Prince de Conti denounced the play as the most scandalous thing ever staged. Some magistrates advocated that the play be banned as an affront to morality and religion. Molière turned his satirical pen on his critics presenting on June 1, 1663, *The School for Wives Criticized (La Critique de l'Ecole des Femmes).* The play allows the critics to voice their criticisms but ridicules them through the exaggeration of their own arguments. The rival troupe at the Hôtel de Bourgogne continued the attack with the *Counter Critic*, to which Molière replied with *Versailles Impromptu (L'Impromtu de Versailles)* on October 18, 1663. Throughout all the point-counterpoint, Louis stood loyally by Molière, giving him an annual pension of a thousand livres.

The most heated criticism of Molière surfaced after the first performance of perhaps his greatest play, *Tartuffe*. Père Roullé, vicar of St. Barthelemy, suggested that for writing *Tartuffe* Molière "should be burned at the stake as a foretaste of the fires of hell." Louis did withhold permission for the play to be presented to the public of Paris, but soothed his friend's hurt pride by increasing his annual pension to six thousand livres and taking the troupe under his protection, calling it Troupe du Roi.

Tartuffe is a study in religious hypocrisy but was interpreted by many to be a condemnation of all religion. Molière himself added lines to the script pointing out that the satire was not of the faithful. He rewrote the play twice, once in 1667 and once in 1669, before Louis would allow it to be produced. On February 5, 1669, *Tartuffe* began a run of twenty-eight consecutive performances. Of all French classic plays, it is perhaps the most frequently produced.

Molière, the greatest actor and dramatist of France. Courtesy French Cultural Services.

There is a curious paradox in Molière's plays. While they satirize human foibles, there is always a touch of bitterness in the plays. Likewise there always seemed to be a touch of sadness in the man. By the age of fifty, Molière had lost two of his three children, had contracted tuberculosis, and was involved in a hectic marriage. He became sharp-tempered, melancholy and deeply tired. Despite his increasing cough, Molière decided to play the leading role of Argan in his final play, *The Imaginary Invalid.* On February 17, 1673, Molière's company saw that he was dangerously tired and pleaded with him to close his theatre and rest. Molière refused to close down and proceeded with the play. During the performance, he was taken with a fit of coughing and was barely able to finish. A young actor, Michel Baron, and Molière's wife rushed him home. Sensing death approaching Molière asked for a priest, but none came. The coughing continued until he broke a blood vessel and died. The failure of a priest to arrive caused a rather distasteful event in history to take place. In 398 A.D. the Council of Carthage decreed that ac-

Armade Bejart (1642-1700), wife of Molière, as the heroine in *The Princess of Elide* (1664). Courtesy French Cultural Services.

tors be forbidden the sacraments unless they foreswore their profession. After Molière's death Harlay de Champvallon, Archbishop of Paris, ruled that since Molière had not repented his profession, he could not be buried in consecrated ground. Armande, his wife, pleaded with the King at Versaille to intercede. Harlay received a message from the King and decreed that the body not be taken into a church for rites but be quietly buried in a remote corner of the cemetery of St. Joseph in the Rue Montmartre. In spite of an attempt to find and move Molière's remains to the present marker, no one knows the exact whereabouts of the body of one of the truly great dramatists of all time.

After Molière's death, Louis ordered the acting troupe at the Marais and the Molière troupes to combine at a new theatre in the Rue Guénégaud. This now meant that there were companies in Rue Guénégaud and at the Hôtel de Bourgogne. In 1679 Mlle. Champmeslé, the Bourgogne's principal tragic actress, bolted her company to join the troupe at the Guénégaud. Angry words were spoken between the two companies and a crisis was born. At that point Louis issued an order joining the two companies into the world's first national theatre. On August 25, 1680, at the theatre in the Rue Guénégaud, the Comédie Française gave its first performance. This troupe performs today and is the oldest continuing theatrical group in the world.

When first formed, the Comédie Française was given a monopoly on the performance of all spoken drama in French. This monopoly was to produce a bizarre chain reaction in the eighteenth century which would have a lasting effect on western theatre.

The English

While France rested in the glory of Louis XIV, England was undergoing considerable change. The beginning of the Civil War between the Royalists and the Puritans and the subsequent closing of the theatres by Parliament brought to a halt the glorious English theatre. The original proclamation halting theatrical activity was issued for a period of five years, during which time only a few performances were recorded. In 1647 performances resumed, only to be prohibited once more in 1649 when Parliament decreed that all actors be classified as rogues.

The next sign of theatrical activity of any consequence occurred in May 1656. William Davenant, who was one of the principal writers of court masques, staged what were probably the first operatic productions in England. *The Siege of Rhodes*, one of his offerings, marks the first use of the Italian style scenery for a public performance in England. When these operas, which had been presented at Rutland House (Davenant's Home), moved to the Cockpit, a proscenium arch was constructed and the production was staged in the Italian style. No action was taken against Davenant as there had never been a ban on musical entertainments, an oversight which was to plague the English government for a number of years.

The plight of Charles I was becoming more and more desperate. Cromwell's forces had captured a Royalist stronghold in Wales and defeated the

Scots at Preston in Lancashire. Charles was captured and offered freedom if he would consent to the sale of the Bishop's lands and resign his power to veto the ordinances of Parliament. He refused the offer and on January 19, 1649, he was tried and found guilty. Fifty-nine judges, including Cromwell, signed the death sentence and on January 30, 1649, King Charles I was beheaded.

While the middle class prospered under Cromwell's reign, he never was able to capture the love of his subjects. As British dominance on the sea extended her banner over the world, Cromwell and his government became hated as no other government had been hated. With Cromwell's death in 1658, Richard, his eldest son, was promoted to power but the people of England began to look, once again, for their King.

The Restoration

Charles II had escaped England in 1650 and had become a veritable vagabond. His mother, Henrietta Maria, and his sister, Henrietta Ann, received him in Paris where Louis XIV gave him a pension of six thousand francs. Charles loved the ways of Paris, frequenting the theatre and living life to the hilt. When Mazarin began to negotiate an alliance with Cromwell, Charles left Paris for Cologne, then Brussels. The elections in England had returned a royalist majority and on May 8, 1660, the Stuart line was returned to the throne. Bells rang throughout the land and the people of England rejoiced. The Fleet decked with pennants emblazoned *C.R., Carolus Rex,* took him on board from Holland and brought him to Dover into the arms of thousands upon thousands of Englishmen.

As soon as it became evident that Charles was to be returned, activity began in theatrical circles. Sir Henry Herbert resumed his position as Master of Revels, a member of the Lord Chamberlain's staff, and licensed three companies without the knowledge of the King. Charles, on the other hand, was in the process of committing one of the gross follies of all times. William Davenant, after leasing Lisle's tennis court, asked and received special privileges from the King. Both Davenant and Thomas Killigrew, who had been with the royal family for most of the exile, were granted a monopoly over theatrical productions in London. It was evident from his irresponsible action that Charles intended to make

Dorset Garden Theatre (earlier known as the Duke's Theatre and Lisle's Tennis Court, and as Lincoln Inn Fields Theatre). Depicted is a scene from Settle's *The Empress of Morocco,* (1673). From *Londina Illustrata,* 1825.

the theatre his royal property. Parliament let the edict go unchallenged as they debated for weeks on whom to hang for the death of Charles I. They finally arrived at twenty-three men including Cromwell, whose body was exhumed from Westminister Abbey, hanged, and decapitated. Charles' theatrical monopoly was granted to Davenant and Killigrew by virtue of Letters Patent. Charles' Letters Patent followed the precedent established by Elizabeth and James I by neglecting to obtain confirmation from Parliament. In addition, Charles made no provisions for the expiration of the monopoly at the death of the two recipients.

George Jolly, who had received a commitment from Charles during the Commonwealth years for a theatrical license, challenged the new monopoly. As a result, Jolly was granted a license to perform in London. By 1664, however, Davenant and Killigrew claimed they had purchased Jolly's license and Charles issued new patents in their names. The two theatres licensed by Letters Patent remained in operation until 1682 when Charles, in an attempt to save the theatres from ruin because of competition, united them by indenture. The ramifications of these monopolies were to influence the theatre of London, and all of England for that matter, for almost three hundred years.

There were a great many similarities between France and England under Charles II, and with reason. Charles' own character contributed a great deal to the manners and morals of English society. He was essentially French in both parentage and education. His mother was French and his father was the great-great-grandson of Mary of Lorraine. He lived in France or on the continent for fourteen years and was thoroughly indoctrinated with French manners and morals. With Charles setting the pace, it is no wonder that the Restoration Period in England became similar, in terms of manners and morals, to the France of Louis XIV. Like France, England produced some of the finest, if not the bawdiest, comedy of manners ever produced. Plays such as Sir George Etherege's (c. 1634-1691) *Love in a Tub* (1664), *The Man of Mode* (1676), and *She Would if She Could* (1668), are still banned on some stages. No other period prior to the twentieth century seems to have outraged critics, especially Victorian critics, more than Restoration Comedy. No other writer epitomized the style more than William Wycherley (1640-1715).

Wycherley was born to a royalist family of some wealth. When Cromwell came to power, young Wycherley was sent to France for his education. When he returned to England he was sent to Oxford; however, he left without a degree to become a playwright. His first success was *Love in a Wood* (1671), which he dedicated to Lady Castlemaine, a mistress of Charles II. After going to war in 1672, he returned to write the *Country Wife* (1675), usually considered the classic example of Restoration comedy. While Molière's *School for Wives* probably influenced the play, there is something decidedly original about *Country Wife*. The hero of the play, Horner, arrives at a happy idea. He plots to spread the rumor that he has lost his sexual potency in France and has become a eunuch. Husbands who are normally jealous of handsome young men allow him access to their wives. The results are both hilarious and scandalous and provided a delightful evening in the theatre for the Restoration Court. Another important Restoration Comedy, *The Way of the World* by William Congreve (1670-1729), is still frequently produced and is considered by most critics to be a bona fide masterpiece.

French influence was also felt on English tragedy. The heroic tragedy popular at the beginning of the Restoration, exemplified by Roger Boyle's *The Tragedy of Mustapha* (1665) and Nathaniel Lee's *The Rival Queen* (1677), gradually was replaced by neoclassical tragedy. English neoclassicism, never as rigid as its French counterpart, produced *All For Love* by John Dryden (1631-1700), a play considered to be the finest tragedy of the period.

Charles' reign ended on February 4, 1685. He renounced the Anglican Church, called for a priest, professed his Catholicism, and died. The manners and morals of England began a slow change through the rule of James II, who reigned from 1685-1688, and William and Mary who co-ruled from 1689 to 1702. As the lifestyle changes, so does the theatre. By the end of the seventeenth century a new drama and a different theatre were evolving.

The dominance and influence of France during the seventeenth century were manifold: first, Italian theatre architecture and scenic convention were adopted by the French and copied by the English; second, French neoclassicism became the dominant philosophy of the English theatre; third, the comedies of Molière set a standard for Restoration comedy; and fourth, Louis XIV, granting a monopoly to Comédie Française, may have influenced Charles to grant his monopoly. Certainly granting of monopolies in both countries was destined to create havoc in the eighteenth century.

Selected Readings

Lancaster, H.C. *A History of French Dramatic Literature in the Seventeenth Century*, 5 vols. in 9. Baltimore, 1929-1942.

Palmer, John. *Molière*. Cambridge, 1936.

Shergold, N.D. *A History of the Spanish Stage from Medieval Times Until the End of the 17th Century*. Oxford, 1967.

Summers, Montague. *The Restoration Stage*. London, 1934.

Vocabulary

1. Lope de Vega	LOH puh de VAY gah
2. Calderón	kahl de ROHN
3. auto sacramentales	AW toh sah crah men TAH lis
4. corrales	kaw RAH lis
5. cazuela	kah ZWAY luh
6. Richelieu	ree shuh LOO:
7. Mazarin	MA zah rin
8. Palais Royale	PA lay roy YAHL
9. verisimilitude	vai ruh si MI luh tood
10. Pierre Corneille	pyair kawr NAY
11. *Le Cid*	luh SID
12. Jean Racine	zhaw rah SEEN
13. La Thébaide	luh tay bah EED
14. Les Plaideurs	lay play DER
15. *Phèdra*	FAY druh
16. Hippolytus	hi PAW li tuhs
17. Jean-Baptiste Poquelin	zhaw bah TIST poh kuh LIN
18. Madeleine Béjart	mahd LAYN bay JAHR
19. *Les Précieuses Ridicules*	lay pray SYUZ ree dee KOOL
20. Molière	MAWL yair
21. Marais	ma RAY
22. Rue Guénégaud	roo gay nay GOH
23. Mlle. Champmeslé	shaw may LAY
24. Hôtel de Bourgogne	oh TEL de boor GOH nyuh

CHAPTER NINE

Government Interference Shapes the Eighteenth Century

Selecting the major contributions of eighteenth century theatre is difficult, as there were many rather influential minor developments. The first of these, the development of sentimental drama, was, in a sense, a reaction against the neoclassical standards. It reflected the philosophical revolution of David Hume and others who believed that man is by nature good, and that one must follow the dictates of the heart, of the instincts, to remain good. Plays were written to arouse a sympathetic response from the audience. Noble characters were placed in oppressing situations which they bore with admirable valor until they were eventually rescued. Sentimental drama reached its full formulation in *The Conscious Lovers* by Richard Steele (1672-1729). Steele's play deals with a penniless heroine, Indiana, who bravely undergoes suffering and humiliation, only to discover that she is the daughter of a rich merchant.

The second important development during the eighteenth century was the use of a middle-class protagonist in tragedy. While this phenomenon had occurred in isolated dramas as early as the sixteenth century, it was not widespread. George Lillo's (1693-1739) *The London Merchant,* Denis Diderot's (1713-1784) *The Illegitimate Son,* and Gotthold Ephraim Lessing's (1729-1781) *Miss Sara Sampson,* are all classic examples of the innovation.

The third development was the phenomenal growth of the German theatre. Johann Gottsched (1700-1766) and Caroline Neuber (1697-1760) combined to reform what had been a theatre of no consequence specializing in farce into one of the finest theatres in Europe.

Fourth, Italy's scenic technique continued its evolution from developments of the Renaissance. In addition, Italian commedia dell'arte became a literary form under the pen of Carlo Goldoni (1707-1793).

Opposite: Charles Macklin as Shylock in *Merchant of Venice,* Act IV, Scene 1. From *Dramatic Portrait Gallery,* 1880.

Fifth, the acting profession not only welcomed women for the first time, but produced many of the world's most famous actors. In Germany, F.L. Schröder (1774-1816) began his acting career with the Ackerman Troupe, one of the most popular acting companies in Germany. He is generally considered to have been the greatest German actor of the eighteenth century and, according to some, perhaps of all time. England produced David Garrick (1717-1779), James Quin (1692-1766), and Charles Macklin (1699-1777). Garrick, the foremost actor in England between 1741 and 1776, is credited with elevating the English theatre to a position of international esteem. Garrick made reforms in acting techniques, management, and scenic design and was an innovative forerunner to the modern director. He is considered by the British theatrical community to be one of the greatest English actors of all times. Quin was famous for his declamatory style and was one of the ranking tragic actors of the time. Macklin, who acted for seventy years, is most famous for his innovative interpretation of Shylock. This character from Shakespeare's *Merchant of Venice* had been played as a clown complete with red wig until Macklin played him sympathetically.

Finally, the eighteenth century saw the beginnings of American professional theatre, with the arrival in America of Lewis Hallam (1714-1756) from England. In September of 1752, Hallam's company fitted a theatre at Williamsburg and began a long professional career. It is interesting to note that the reason for Hallam's departure from England was governmental restrictions induced by the Licensing Act of 1737. As a matter of fact, eighteenth century governmental interference in France and England led not only to the arrival of professional theatre in America but to the development of operetta and melodrama, two new dramatic genre, which were to have a lasting effect on the theatre as we know it. Governmental interference in the theatre, and its ramifications, is the focus of this chapter.

Gotthold Ephraim Lessing, considered Germany's first significant dramatist, is best remembered for breaking the neoclassical tradition with his plays and criticism, particularly the *Hamburg Dramaturgy* (1767-1769). His most important works are *Miss Sara Sampson* (1775), *Minna von Barnhelm* (1767), and *Nathan the Wise,* which many regard as the finest philosophical drama of the eighteenth century. Courtesy German Information Center.

Scene from Lessing's *Minna von Barnhelm,* considered Germany's first comedy. Courtesy German Information Center.

Top: *Les Delices du Genre Humain,* oil on canvas, French school, 1670, Paris. The painting shows leading French actors, including Jodelet and Molière (extreme left), and several commedia dell'arte characters including Harlequin at left center. Comédie Française.

A student production of Shakespeare's *Romeo and Juliet* at Western Kentucky University, directed by Patrick Tucker of the Royal Shakespeare Company, London. Set by James Brown.

Top left: Mlle. Dumesnil (Marie-Françoise Marchand, 1713-1803) as *Phèdre.* She was probably the most famous French actress of the eighteenth century. Note the costume; French actresses wore the latest fashions regardless of the role. Comédie Française.

Top right: Mlle. Champmesle (1642-1698), considered to be the finest tragic actress of her time. She was very close to Racine and created the role of Phèdre. When she left the Bourgogne company, the motivation for the formation of the Comédie Française was created.

Bottom right: Henri-Lekain (1729-1778) in Voltaire's *L'orphelin de la Chine.* Lekain overcame vocal and physical shortcomings to be admitted to the Comédie Française in 1750. A friend of Voltaire, he became one of the finest tragic actors of the eighteenth century. Courtesy Comédie Française.

Some scholars date the beginning of French romanticism to the production of *Hernani* by Victor Hugo (1802-1885) in 1830. This sketch for the set is by J.B. Lavestre from the *Livre de régie*. Comédie Française.

The Good Woman of Setzuan by Bertolt Brecht. Gorham State College; masks by Alan Bray, direction by Walter R. Stump, scene design by Minor Rootes.

David Garrick, depicted as between tragedy and comedy *(left)* and portraying Richard III *(right)*. Garrick was not only a great actor, but inaugurated such innovations as concealing stage lighting from the audience and abolishing the audience from the stage. The Hogarth rendering *(right)* courtesy Fine Arts Library, Indiana University.

Below: Staging of athletic games at Naples, 1746, to honor Pope Clement XIII. This early theatre designed by Paoli Posi, is a prototype of the modern proscenium stage. Note that by extending the elliptical shape of the stage house (with its boxes for the audience) straight back from the stage proper, the theatre would approximate auditoriums from the nineteenth century onward.

The Government and the French Theatre

The monopoly in England by virtue of Charles' Letters Patent and Louis XIV's gift of legitimate drama to the Comédie Française and opera to the Royal Academy of Music had virtually stultified the development of the theatre. The rigidity of neoclassicism had not only manifested itself in the kind of drama being written, but, by virtue of the official edicts of the period, in the way in which a drama could be produced. The vitality of the neoclassical ideal quickly declined after 1700 largely because of its intractability. The excesses of Louis XIV's government in foreign affairs and the King's own iron rule created pockets of hostility. Furthermore, a new philosophical liberalism, which by its very nature was moving in the direction of new discoveries, began to take shape.

Theatre is a public institution. The theatre demands an audience that must react to it emotionally and intellectually. Since it is an imitative art, those actions imitated may well reflect all too well the foibles and errors of an age. For that reason, critics have tried to chastise theatre, politicians have tried to control it, clergymen have tried to close it, and fanatics have tried to gag it. Fortunately, like the mythical phoenix, the theatre always seems to grow out of its own ashes stronger, better, and slightly wiser. The restrictions of the eighteenth century did indeed kill one form of the drama, only to see two new forms rise up. The theatre profession has never been an easy life. Even the most successful of its people have probably experienced at some time the feeling of being on the brink of disaster. Consider this case in point.

The royal edicts had virtually banished the so-called legitimate drama from the many small theatres in France. At the Foire Saint-Germain and the Foire Saint-Laurent, the two great fairs in Paris, the managers of the theatres purposefully produced plays which violated all of the neoclassical rules in an attempt to circumvent Louis' proclamation. By 1705 the Comédie Française was feeling the competition of the fair theatres at the box office. They requested and obtained a new proclamation from the King extending the restriction to any dramatic entertainment with spoken dialogue. With their license to perform the spoken drama voided, the fair managers turned toward the productions of pantomime *(pièces a la muette)*. The success of the pantomime was immediate as was the backlash from the Comédie Française. Pressured once again by the national theatre, Louis banned pantomimes in 1709, an action which put the fair theatres out of business. The fair managers, faced with idle companies and dark theatres, reasoned that if they could not do pantomime or the *spoken* drama perhaps they could do the unspoken drama. The managers thus devised a method whereby the audience could understand and actually participate in the play. Two young boys dressed as cupids *(putti)* were dangled above the stage with placards in their hands. Couplets representing the actors' speeches were written on these placards, each set to a tune popular with everyone in the audience. Actors were planted throughout the audience and instructed to sing the tunes as soon as the orchestra began to play. The audience, delighted with the ruse, soon began to join the singers, performing, in effect, the dialogue which the actors had been forbidden to speak. This ingenious device was called *pièce à écriteaux* (play with placards or writing). It was later to be called *comédies-en-vaudeville*.

In 1714 the opera, in financial difficulty, received permission to sell the privilege of using dance, music, and spectacle to one of the fair companies. As a result, the placards could be removed and actors were allowed to sing the couplets. Beginning in 1715, the new form was called *opéra comique*. Alain-Rèné Le Sage (1668-1747) perfected *opéra comique* and it became both immensely popular and financially rewarding.

The arrival in Paris during 1716 of a group of Italian players introduced another new musical form called *opéra buffa*. Opéra buffa, originally an operatic satire, was now composed entirely by one composer and librettist, included recitative and airs, and was somewhat bawdy in character. The opéra comique, on the other hand, had no single composer and was made up of *vaudevilles*, or rewritten popular tunes. There was no recitative and the libretto was probably less bawdy than the Italian pieces. Both of these musical forms were to have an important effect on the English theatre.

By the turn of the century the English theatrical monopoly was in trouble. Legitimate drama had been deemphasized by the public's demand for novelty and imported dancers and singers. By 1708 some of the harlequins of the French fairs had arrived in London, where their performances were billed as "Italian Night Scenes." These pieces were later to form the basis for English pantomimes which, under the direction of John Rich (1692-1761), were destined to become one of the most popular theatrical entertainments of eighteenth century London. The importation of Italian *opéra serio* (serious operas) gradually changed the nature of native English opera. This influence reached a peak in the late 1720's with the works of George Frederick Handel (1685-1759). The reaction against Handel's adaption of the Italian form culminated in 1728 with the production of John Gay's ballad opera *The Beggar's Opera*.

The Beggar's Opera

John Gay (1685-1732) rose quickly from a merchant's apprentice to secretary to the Earl of Clarendon. A friend of the literary figures of the period, Gay was a recognized poet. His *Trivia, or The Art of Walking the Streets,* is still a delightful picture of early eighteenth century London. His *Poems,* published in 1720, was financially successful but he lost most of his money in the crash of the South Sea Company. In 1728, however, Gay was to make himself financially solvent for the rest of his life. His ballad opera, *The Beggar's Opera,* not only was the most popular piece of its day, but indirectly influenced the theatre for the next hundred years. As he did in *Trivia,* Gay made quiet fun of the London that he knew. The people of the eighteenth century England were a tough breed. Great fortunes were derived from smuggling, piracy, and even from capturing and selling slaves. English, French, Dutch, and Portuguese ships competed for the privilege of selling Africans to Americans. Gin drinking became a passion to the English, with some retailers promising to make their customers drunk for a penny, and even offering free beds of straw in the cellar. Robbery was rampant. Many eighteenth century playbills included reassurances the "there will be an armed guard on horseback to patrol the roads." If caught, thieves were punished with brutality seldom equalled since. Gallows were raised in virtually every district of London, and on many of them corpses were left to decompose or furnish a macabre morsel for the birds. Hangings frequently had the character of a festival and crowds would line the road to watch the condemmed ride the cart to Tyburn.

John Gay, poet, playwright and author of *The Beggar's Opera,* the most successful eighteenth century musical. Courtesy Harvard Theatre Collection.

Peddlers sold gin, nuts, and apples to the crowd as a kind of bizzare last tribute. Thieves who became successful were frequently made heroes by the public. Jack Sheppard, "Rob Roy" (Robert Macgregor), Dick Turpin, Jonathan Wild, all became legends in their own time. Many writers, including Henry Fielding, were to capitalize on the highwayman craze, but none so well as Gay.

The Beggar's Opera reads and plays like a Hogarth sketch, with vivid images of a London of the time. It begins with an introduction by a beggar who presents his own opera taking a slight poke at the Italian form. He states: "I hope I may be forgiven, that I have not made my opera throughout unnatural, like those in vogue; for I have no recitative . . . ."

Musically, the opera begins with a ballad by Peachum, a dealer in stolen goods, who many identified with Robert Walpole. Peachum's life is complicated by the fact that his daughter Polly has

Hogarth's *Gin Lane,* picturing the shop of pawnbroker S. Gripe, which is flourishing as is the gin cellar below and the distillery to the right. Above the entrance to the gin cellar is written: "Drunk for a penny, Dead drunk for twopence, clean straw for nothing." A barber has hanged himself (upper right) because the people can no longer afford his services. The working class is beset by murder, suicide, starvation, disease, and poverty, and Hogarth indicates that children are the worst victims. Note the mother feeding her child gin (extreme right center). Courtesy Fine Arts Library, Indiana University.

fallen in love with, and may have married, the handsome highwayman Captain Macheath. A marriage would interfere with the use of Polly in managing buyers and sellers. When it is found that she has indeed married Macheath, Peachum says, "Polly, do you think your mother and I should have lived comfortably for so long together, if ever we had been married? Baggage!" The rest of the play evolves around the attempt of Peachum to betray Macheath to the law. It is filled with humor and infectious tunes selected by Johan Pepsch and is a landmark on the English stage.

The ballad opera, in general, and *The Beggar's Opera,* in particular, are not, strictly speaking, either opéra buffa or opéra comique and yet the influence of both forms is clearly visible. From the opéra buffa came the bawdy nature of the piece itself with the humorous satire on Italian operatic devices such as recitative. The songs, with the exception of a march from Handel's *Rivaldo,* were set to traditional English and Scottish tunes, thus duplicating the method of the opéra comique. But the English added a twist of their own in the form of political satire. According to many contemporary sources, the first audiences who viewed *The Beggar's Opera* had little difficulty in recognizing Peachum, the gang's organizer, as Robert Walpole. *The Beggar's Opera* ran for sixty-three consecutive nights, a record for that period. The popularity of the piece was not limited to London alone, as it played in most of the major cities of England and played on Broadway as late as 1972. The success of the new form not only spawned Gay's own sequel *Polly,* but also the *Cobbler's Opera* by Thomas Walker, *Mormus Turn'd Fabulist* or *Vulcan's Wedding* by Ebeneezer Forest, and *The Highland Fair* or *Union of the Clans* by Joseph Mitchell. The political satire of *The Beggar's Opera* in some ways set the pattern for minor theatre for some time to come. Although it was indeed amusing to the masses, Robert Walpole found it less than amusing.

Walpole and Fielding

With the death of William in 1702, Queen Anne became the unwilling sovereign. Anne's own moral fibre helped produce a change in the character of the English court. Her avoidance of the theatre had some influence in improving the very nature of the legitimate drama. But perhaps the most far-reaching consequences of Anne's reign was the power she allowed her ministers to appropriate. From this time on, political battles were fought between Parliament and the ministers rather than Parliament and the sovereign. In order to prevent the restoration of the Stuarts at Anne's death, Parliament crowned George I of Germany as King of England. Robert Walpole initially assumed power under George I. When the King died in 1727, George II eventually rehired the minister. Walpole was the first to use the 10 Downing Street address. Walpole used whatever means necessary to buy members of Parliament, thus becoming one of the most corrupt ministers England has ever had. Still, there was a curious paradox about the man. While forbidding the publication of Parliamentary debates, he was tolerant, for the most part, of the many attacks on him in print. Such historic magazines as *The Craftsman* (1726), *The Grub Street Journal* (1730-37), and *The Gentleman's Magazine* (1731) all waged a journalistic war against his policies. To all this he remained relatively calm. But when the ridicule of the Prime Minister moved from the bookstore to the stage, the end of Walpole's patience was nearing. *The Beggar's Opera* did much to infuriate the Prime Minister, but it took the pen of the great satirist Henry Fielding to provide the proverbial straw.

Henry Fielding, born in 1707, arrived in London in 1727. Fielding was a handsome, personable man who enjoyed his life and his friends. He had everything it seems, but money, and in the pursuit of that necessity, he began to write. History remembers Henry Fielding primarily for his delightful novels. Few are aware that Fielding's first love was the theatre. Between 1729 and 1736 he wrote sixteen satirical plays and ballad operas. By 1736 Fielding established a landmark in the English theatre by taking over the little theatre at the Haymarket. When Fielding became manager, Drury Lane was under the management of Charles Fleetwood. Rich's company at Covent Garden was playing dramatic entertainments varied by light

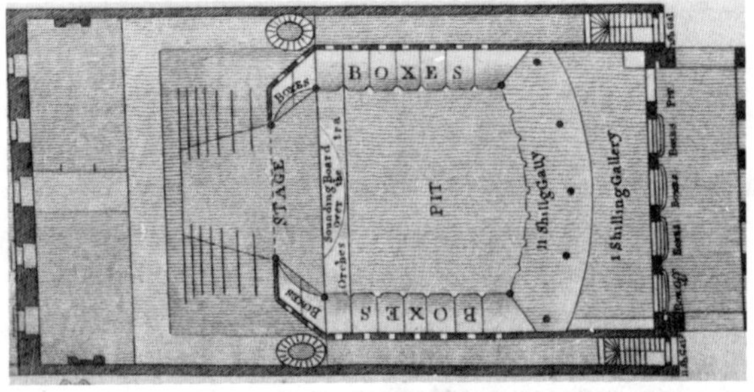

The Haymarket Theatre, originally built in 1720 by John Potter. Henry Fielding took over this theatre, called "The Little Theatre in the Hay," in 1730, but gave it up because of licensing problems. Pictured here is the interior of the Haymarket (rebuilt by John Nash), as it appeared on opening night July 4, 1821, for Sheridan's *The Rivals*. From *Londina Illustrata*, 1825.

comedy, opera, and occasionally tragedy. Another company at Lincoln's Inn Fields produced a rather close rivalry. In addition, there was a war between Farinelli's opera group in the Haymarket and Handel's company performing at Rich's theatre in Covent Garden. The Haymarket was not unknown to Fielding, as his ballad opera *Don Quixote in England* had been produced there in 1734. Fielding's management began on March 5, 1736, with the performance of his satirical farce *Pasquin*. *Pasquin* satirized, among other things, comedy and neoclassical tragedy as forms.

It is only natural to assume that Fielding, as a satirist, would use theatre as a sounding board for his talent, but it was also good business to do so. *The Grub Street Journal* and similar publications had popularized satire on many levels and had attracted an immense public following. Satire was in vogue, so to speak, and from past use of the form in the theatre, Fielding was well aware of its potential at the box office. Few aspects of English life were safe from Fielding's pen. Rich's pantomimes, for example, were satirized, as was the Poet Laureate, Colly Cibber. One of Fielding's favorite targets was Robert Walpole. Whenever possible, Fielding lampooned either Walpole or the Walpole administration. Some say that the whole object of the Haymarket management was the embarrassment of the Walpole regime. To deny that Fielding was a political animal and that the Walpole government was the object of much of his attention, would be to reject the facts. But it must also be conceded that Fielding's satire was not limited to politics nor was his season limited to political plays. Nevertheless, Walpole was getting the message and was waiting for the appropriate excuse to end the harassment.

Colley Cibber (1671-1757), Poet Laureate, actor, and one of the managers of Drury Lane Theatre. Cibber was famous for his plays, *Love's Last Shift* (1796) and *The Careless Husband* (1704). Courtesy Harvard Theatre Collection.

Fielding's company was an odd assortment of Grub Street eccentrics. The company included such personalities as Eliza Haywood, author of such enticing pieces as *Love in Excess* and *A Wife to be Let,* and Charlotte Charke, who had an affinity for male roles. So expert at playing male roles was she, that when her acting days were over, she spent two years as a gentleman's gentleman to a lord before being detected. Fielding also had an American in the company by the name of James Ralph. Ralph had gone to England with Benjamin Franklin and had joined the Fielding company after a breach had occurred between the two men over the attempted seduction of Ralph's mistress by Franklin. Franklin returned to America to help found the Republic and Ralph remained in England to become a mildly successful writer.

Along with Fielding, the combined talents of this unique group eventually provided Walpole with his excuse. Fielding's final hours in the theatre may have been his finest. In 1737 he wrote and produced a new satire which he called *The Historical Register for 1737*. Embodied in the play were attacks on both the political and social conditions of England. Among other things, Fielding ridiculed the office of the Poet Laureate by a parody on Colly Cibber's poetry *en vaudeville*.

The uproar resulting from *The Historical Register for 1737* united Rich, Cibber, and Walpole against

Fielding. In the meantime, Walpole had acquired a playlet entitled *The Golden Rump,* which ostensibly satirized the king. The satire, said to have been written by Fielding (it probably was not), was purportedly scandalous. Walpole read portions to Parliament as a prelude to the introduction of a new law called 10 George II, cap. 28, better known as the Licensing Act of 1737.

The Licensing Act of 1737

The Licensing Act of 1737 contained some very important provisions. First, it declared that no persons should perform or cause to be performed any

> tragedy, comedy, opera, play, farce or other entertainment of the stage, for gain, hire, or reward, other than, and except such person or persons in whom the right of property in and to the said Thomas Killigrew, Robert Wilks, Colly Cibber, and Barton Booth . . . is vested, and their respected deputies or servants, during the continance of the process and priviledges of them by their several Letters Patent respectively granted.

Players, then, could not perform unless their managers had been licensed by the Lord Chamberlain or Letters Patent. The most important feature of this statute, however, is the authorization by Parliament for the first time that plays be censored by the Lord Chamberlain. It provided that every stage play to be produced must first be sent to the Lord Chamberlain for his inspection and approval, and it gave him the power to prohibit the performance of plays of which he did not approve. In reality, the law did not give him a legal right to censor but the right of approval was taken to mean censorship by the office. Many members of Parliament, including Lord Chesterfield, objected to the bill. In one of the more eloquent speeches of the decade, Chesterfield declared:

> If poets and players are to be restrained, let them be restrained as other subjects are, by the known laws of their country; if they offend, let them be tried as every Englishman ought to be, by God and their country. Do not let us subject them to the arbitrary will and pleasure of any one single man, to judge and determine, without any limitation, without any control or appeal, is sort of power unknown to our laws, inconsistent with our constitution. It is higher, a more absolute power than we even trust to the King himself; and therefore I must think, we ought not to vest any such power in his majesty's Lord Chamberlain.

So it came to be that the Lord Chamberlain, an unelected servant of the King, was given the power of life or death over playwrighting on the English stage. Furthermore, the Chamberlain usually appointed an examiner with little or no experience in dramatic literature to read the plays. At one point in history, a former bank teller had control of the drama in the English speaking world, since banned plays were rarely, if ever, produced elsewhere in the eighteenth century.

The English stage, then, was entering into a period of governmental restriction which was to govern the nature of drama for years to come. But in France developments were taking a new twist.

Development of the Melodrama

The popularity of the new opéra comique had forced the Comédie Française to give short plays in imitation of the genre which the fair theatres had perfected. The Italians in the meantime had been given official status by the French government. Both official theatres, then, were imitating the minor genre thereby provoking a competition, and in 1745 the fair theatres were again closed.

With the closing of the opéra comique in 1745, the fair theatres returned to pantomime. In 1751, Louis XV authorized a return to opéra comique. Pergolesi's *La Serva Padrona* was produced in Paris by the bouffons Italian. It initiated such a craze for Italian music and opera that the fair theatres set out deliberately to supply the new demand. The controversy that followed was the famous "Querelle des Bouffons." The argument was between the supporters of the Queen who favored the Italian style opera and the supporters of the King who favored opéra comique. The peak of disagreement was reached in 1753 when an ingenious fraud was perpetrated by Jean Monet (1713-1785), director of the opéra comique, in which he had an opera written which was praised by the antinational (Bouffonist, Queen's corner) party; then Monet made it known that it was by the Paris poet Jean Vade (1719-1754) and the Paris composer Antoine Auvergne (1713-1797). This work, *Les Troquers,* is

Examples of dress for the opera in 1784.

considered the beginning of an era. It was one of the first French works to have recitative throughout, instead of spoken dialogue, and it has been called the first French comic opera with the libretto written by a poet and the score by a composer. Thus the opéra comique had become what was, and is, comic opera.

Again the success of the comic opera quickly led to its suppression at the fairs. In 1762 the Comédie Italienne was awarded the exclusive rights to the new genre. Some of the managers of the fair troupes began to open new theatres on the Boulevard du Temple and once again they turned to pantomime. The most important of the new theatres were those of Nicolas Medard Audinot (c. 1740-1801) and of Jean Baptist Nicolet (c. 1728-1796), the Théâtre des Associés, and the Variétés Amusantes. The new pantomime gradually assumed all of the characteristic traits of melodrama. The plots showed persecuted innocence, a villain, and the eventual triumph of good over evil. Music underscored the emotional qualities of scenes and accompanied the dances. By 1780, dialogue was reintroduced. The restrictions on the theatres were lifted shortly after the French Revolution and in 1800 René Charles Guilbert de Pixérécourt's plays fixed the form of melodrama.

The Contribution of the Fair Theatres

There can be little doubt as to the significance of the fair theatres as a catalyst in the development of dramatic forms. Furthermore, although there were other forces involved, they must be assigned an important role in the break from the neoclassical traditions. More than this, however, the fair theatres represented a reemergence of the popular theatre. The lower class was always to be found at the fair theatres. At the Comédie Française, on the other hand, the lower class was never welcome. It is a credit to the French people that the theatre was not permitted to remain in the hands of the few appointed ones and that the freshness and ingenuity of the fair managers were rewarded with admiration and loyalty. Thus, under the restraint of the French government and under the protective malleability of the Opéra Comique, the seeds of melodrama and romantic drama were planted. It is not surprising, therefore, that the English Licensing Act of 1737 produced its own fascinating mutate.

Fielding's Law

The situation in England was, of course, somewhat different from that of France. While the French government restricted the *form* of the drama, the English government set out to restrict the *place*. Basically, the law gave a monopoly for theatrical performances to the two patent theatres, Drury Lane and Covent Garden. Garrick's engagement at Goodman's Field and other performances by theatres outside Westminster created a menace to the patent houses. In addition to theatres, other popular amusements were cropping up throughout the suburbs. The nature of these entertainments was, in some instances, grotesque. In 1748, for example, two women fought for a new dress near Islington. The battle was won by a woman called "bruising Peg," who all but killed her opponent. In the summer of the same year, an extraordinary battle was fought in Spawfields by two women against two tailors for a guinea. The two women, who beat the tailors severely, won. A gown, a dress, and a pair of shoes were donated to the winner of a foot race between four elderly women, with at least one of the losers suffering a cardiac arrest. In addition to the above horrors,

Hogarth's *Strolling Actresses Dressing in a Barn* (1738) demonstrates how the 1737 Licensing Act was evaded. The Act (on the crown, left foreground) specified actors; the country company depicted thus used a cast of women and children. The playbill on the bed reveals that the company intended to present *The Devil to Pay in Heaven.* Courtesy Fine Arts Library, Indiana University.

fireworks were lashed to a bull with a cat tied to his tail.

In 1751 Henry Fielding, who had turned from the theatre to a judgeship, wrote *An Enquiry into the Causes of the Late Increase of Robbers,and c.* The pamphlet blames part of the lawlessness on the increase of luxury, which it considers to be a "moral rather than political evil" among the upper classes, and to require legislative interference only when it descends downward to the tradesmen, the mechanic, and the laborer. To protect the lower classes, Fielding issued a temporary law called *An Act for the Better Preventing Thefts and Robberies, and for Regulating Places of Public Entertainment, and Punish Persons Keeping Disorderly Houses.*

Several points about this act are worthy of notice. First, Fielding wrote it hastily to deal with an immediate situation and did not intend it to be permanent. Second, it allowed justices to license public entertainments. Third, the act failed to define precisely what was included in "Public Entertainment and the like."

It was just this kind of loophole contained in the phrase "the like" that permitted the spirit of the fair theatres to cross the channel in the form of the short *opéra buffa* or, as it was now called, the burletta.

The Burletta

The first burletta was produced in the late 1740's at one of the legitimate houses. After the passing of the Licensing Act there were only two legitimate theatres in London — Drury Lane and Covent Garden. The Haymarket was licensed in 1766 for summer performances only. At first, the unlicensed theatres attempted to get around the law by various liberal interpretations. Henry Gifford charged admission at his Goodman's Fields Theatre only for the concert; the play was free. Some of these ruses were tolerated for a while, but eventually performances were forbidden. It was the ability to license public entertainments under the Fielding law and the arrival of the burletta that eventually broke the back of the law.

In the beginning, it was difficult to determine what a burletta was. Opéra buffa was called burletta and in 1758, *La Serva Padrona,* a comic opera, was performed as a burletta. In 1761 the Irish writer, Kane O'Hara, produced what may be the first English burletta, *Midas. Midas* is written in recitative with airs in the opéra comique fashion. Its similarity to the nineteenth century operetta of W.S. Gilbert is unmistakable. By the 1770's, burlettas were becoming vogue, and with them many small theatres licensed by magistrates were performing "entertainments and the like" under Fielding's Law. The problem of circumventing the law presented an interesting challenge to the proprietors of the minor theatres just as it had the fair managers. In 1787 Phillip Astley, proprietor of Astley's Circus, where horse shows and musical entertainments were performed, asked for and received permission to add the term burletta to his amphitheatre license. By adding the title burletta to his equestrian dramas, Astley was able to add plot and music to his shows. Since pantomime was considered a legal form for the minors, the equestrian plays made use of the French melodramatic pantomime, although they were essentially comic. By 1802, the pieces were no longer restricted to comedy although they were still completely musical.

The proprietor of the Sans Pareil Theatre in Bullen Court applied to the Lord Chamberlain's office, asking and receiving permission to add to his license the word burletta "which have hitherto been performed under his present license for music, dancing, song recitative and pantomine with optical and mechanical exhibition." This request was brought up before the privy council and lawyers were called in to decide the meaning of the term and state the law regulating it. The results were indecisive and provided no real legal definition of burletta. The indecision of the privy council lawyers in defining the term created a new opening for the proprietors of the minor theatres. Soon a plethora of burlettas appeared all over London. Robert Elliston opened at the Royal Circus as Captain Macheath in a burletta melodrama in three parts, founded on *The Beggar's Opera.* He followed this with "A Grand Ballet of Action" with music founded on the *Macbeth* of Shakespeare. Soon a multitude of famous English tragedies, comedies, and melodramas were performed under the general description of burletta with a piano providing the background music. The inability of the patent theatres to combat the minor theatres eventually led to the defeat of the monopoly. In 1843, the Theatre Regulations Act restored the spoken dialogue to the minor theatres and their victory was complete. Macbeth need no longer have a tinkling piano supplementing the verse, but background music in the melodrama was continued forever.

Influences of Governmental Restrictions

The influences on the theatre by governmental restrictions, then, created some rather important results. First, the fact that both the minor theatres in England and the fair theatre in France were forced to experiment with new genres in effect released them from the rigidity of neoclassicism. In France these experiments led directly to the emergence of melodrama which, in turn, was the greatest single influence on the romantic technique of Dumas père and Hugo. In England the growth of the ballad opera and political satire were seriously restricted by the Licensing Act of 1737. The importation of burletta, however, as well as the antisuppression techniques of the fair theatres, enabled the English minor theatres to continue to search for new means of expression.

Second, both the fair theatres and the English minor theatres catered more to the common man

Astley's Amphitheatre about 1815. Dramatic presentations were staged both in the ring and on the stage. The theatre was especially noted for its equestrian melodramas. The entrance to the theatre is shown below. From *Londina Illustrata,* 1825.

who could not always attend the legitimate theatre.

Third, besides the development and popularization of melodrama and romantic drama, new genres in the form of comic opera in France and operetta in England evolved.

Fourth, in France and England the minor theatres played a major role in the development of social drama both in form and sympathy to the common man.

Thus a change from the structure of neoclassicism was rapidly developing. It was to reach its apex with the rise of the romantic ideal and the American and French revolutionary cries of equality, fraternity and brotherhood.

Selected Readings

Bernbaum, Ernest. *The Drama of Sensibility*. Cambridge, Mass., 1915.

Jourdain, Eleanor F. *Dramatic Theory and Practice in France, 1690-1808*. New York, 1921.

The London Stage, 1660-1800. 11 vols. Carbondale, Ill., 1960-1968.

Melcher, Edith. *Stage Realism in France Between Diderot and Antoine*. Bryn Mawr, Pa., 1928.

Vocabulary

1. Denis Diderot	duh NEE DEE duh roh
2. pièce à écriteaux	pyes ah ay kree TOH
3. opéra comique	OH pay ruh caw MEEK
4. foire Saint-Germain	fwawr san zhair MEN
5. foire Saint-Laurent	fwawr san loh RAHN
6. Charlotte Charke	shahrk
7. William Davenant	DA vuh nuhnt
8. querelle des bouffons	ke REL day boo FAWN
9. Jean Vade	zhaw VAHD
10. Antoine Auvergne	ahn TWUHN oh VAIRN
11. Les Troquers	lay troh KER
12. Théâtre des Associés	tay AHT ruh dayz ah soh SYAY
13. variétiés amusantes	vah ree ay TAYZ ah moo ZAHNT
14. Pixérécourt	peez ay ray KOOR
15. sans pareil	saw pah RAY

CHAPTER TEN

Romanticism
The Age of Revolt

When the words of America's Decalaration of Independence exhorting the equality of man are carefully analyzed, a philosophic influence can be seen. In a sense, much of the document is romantic in outlook. It is imbued with a combination of ideas which developed as early as 1689 when John Locke (1632-1704) wrote in *Second Treatise of Civil Government:*

> To understand political power aright, and derive it from its original, we must consider what state all men are naturally in, and that is a state of perfect freedom to order their actions and dispose of their possessions and persons as they think fit.

Burke, Rousseau and others, while not necessarily endorsing the concept of democracy, certainly contributed to the growing principles of equality and liberty from aristocratic governments. Burke defined natural society as "society founded in natural appetites and instincts, and not in any positive institution." The idea of natural instincts and the better society was, in many ways, a revolt against the neoclassical ideal and its concept of cold hard reasoning. Reasoning, at least neoclassical reasoning, had tended to uphold the status quo. Doubt was growing as to the morality of the existing political hierarchy. In England, for example, the census of 1801 estimated a population of some nine million people, divided into roughly seven different classes. First, there were some 287 persons who headed families totaling about 7,000 persons. This rank included princes, dukes, marquises, earls, viscounts and barons. Second, there were the spiritual lords, numbering about twenty-six bishops. The bishops along with the peers were entitled to sit in the House of Lords. Third were some 540 baronets and their wives who were entitled to add "Sir" and "Lady" to their names and to transmit their titles. The fourth group included knights and their wives, who were allowed the same prefix as baronets but were unable to transmit the title. Fifth were the approximately 6,000 squires or the gentry, as they were sometimes called. This group included the most numerous class of landowners and, along with the baronets, knights, squires and their wives, were considered the lesser nobility. These groups as a whole were considered to be the "aristocracy."

In addition to the aristocracy, there were some 20,000 "gentlemen" or "ladies" living on income without manual work, having a coat of arms, and assumed to be of gentle birth (born into old and accepted families).

Below these groups came the other eight and a half million members of the English population. When you consider that the 287 peers received twenty-nine percent of the national income in 1801, it is easy to understand that there was a great deal of skepticism about the fairness of the existing social order. The justice of aristocratic birthright was called to question by a rising middle class. They began to trace the development of these unfair political and social structures and, in doing so, tended to idealize primitive society. Primitive man, who was equal to his peers and free to follow the dictates of his own conscience, seemed the ideal.

Back to nature, then, became almost a rallying cry. Since according to the romanticist, nature and man are all part of a singular creation by God out of Himself, everything in existence has a common origin. To know truth one may study any individual aspect of creation and by doing so gain knowledge of the whole, so that it is possible to study a skylark, a cloud, daffodils, or even the west wind, and discover new truth about man. The more unspoiled the thing, the better the study. Nature's objects were popular subjects among writers, as was primitive, unspoiled man. Because a highly structured and bureaucratic society tended

Opposite: James Henry Hackett (1800-1871), American actor noted for his Yankee characters and the first American to appear in London as a star. In this photo he is playing Falstaff in Henry IV in London, 1833. Hackett was also manager of the Astor Place Opera House at the time of the Astor Place Riot. From *Dramatic Portrait Gallery,* 1880.

to foster unnatural restraints on the natural man, writers frequently concerned themselves with man in rebellion against despotic rulers.

Rise of Romanticism

As a literary movement, Romanticism began in Germany. The term was first used by a group of Berlin authors writing in the literary journal, *Das Athenaeum* (1798-1800). August Wilhelm Schlegel (1767-1845) is generally credited with formulating and disseminating romantic theory through a series of lectures and essays. It was Schlegel's ideas that were adapted by Samuel Taylor Coleridge in England and Mme. de Staël. It was Schlegel who considered Shakespeare the greatest of all dramatists and translated seventeen of his plays.

Perhaps the greatest of the German playwrights, Johann Wolfgang von Goethe (1749-1832) and Friedrich von Schiller (1759-1805), wrote in the romantic vein, although both denied being romanticists. Goethe is sometimes called the German Shakespeare and is generally considered to be the greatest of the German writers. He was a universal

Top: Johann Wolfgang von Goethe, Germany's greatest literary figure. A dramatist, novelist, and director, Goethe did most of his work at the Court Theatre, Weimar (1796-1817). He and Schiller were initially members of a romantic movement known as the Sturm and Drang (Storm and Stress). Courtesy German Information Center.

Bottom: Friedrich von Schiller, another of Germany's great dramatists. Schiller and Goethe formed artistic views which came to be labeled "Weimar Classicism." Courtesy Germany Information Center.

genius equally proficient in the arts, philosophy, and science. His work in botany is still considered valid. *Faust (Part I,* 1808; *Part II,* 1831), Goethe's most important play, stands as a classic. *Faust* deals with man's search for his own salvation. Written throughout Goethe's life, it records his own growth and change. It is a magnificent work that is probably the finest of the romantic plays.

Schiller wrote more plays in the romantic style, starting with *The Robbers* (1782). His drama *Don Carlos* (1787) attempted to encourage the development of freedom throughout the world. He also used historical topics in *Maria Stuart, The Maid of Orleans, William Tell,* and German history in the *Wallenstein Trilogy.*

Perhaps the most popular playwright of the early nineteenth century German romantics was Heinrich von Kleist (1777-1811). Among his best known works are *The Broken Jug* (1806), *Penthesilea* (1808), and *The Prince of Homburg* (1810).

The French Theatre

The French theatre was tainted by the excesses of revolution. Napoleon, who had a preference for neoclassical drama, attempted to stultify the minor theatres. But true to form, it was the minor theatres that were the most popular. René Charles Guilbert de Pixérécourt (1773-1844) established the form of melodrama which was to become the dominant dramatic type of the nineteenth century. It is important to note Pixérécourt's works were still considered a minor form and were not played by the Comédie Française. It was not until Romanticism arrived in France that melodrama became a legitimate form.

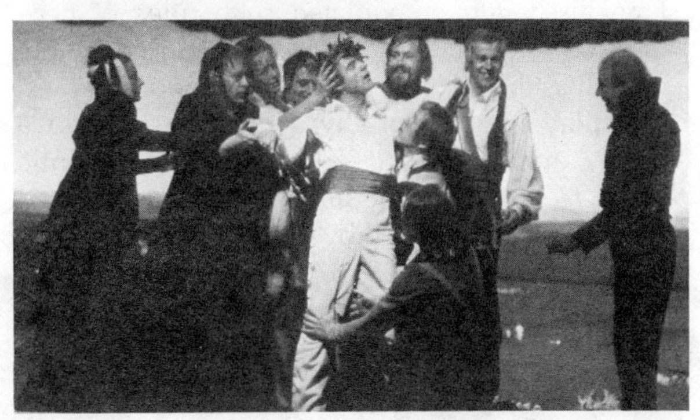

Top right: Johann Gottfried Herder (1744-1783), a leading dramatist of the Sturm and Drang romantic movement (1767-1787). Courtesy German Information Center.

Middle right: Heinrich von Kleist, a leading figure in the German romantic movement. Courtesy German Information Center.

Bottom right: A scene from Kleist's *The Prince of Homburg,* as produced by the Berlin Schaubühne. Courtesy German Information Center.

Georg Büchner (1813-1873), a major nineteenth century dramatist, was a forerunner of expressionism and naturalism. He wrote three plays: *Danton's Death* (1835), *Leonce and Lena* (1836), and *Woyzech* (1836: pronounced Voycheck). Courtesy German Information Service.

Germaine Necker or Mme. de Staël (1766-1817) is generally credited with introducing Romanticism to France when she published *Of Germany (1810)*.The book was suppressed by Napoleon but was republished after his downfall in 1814.

French Romanticism is considered to have begun in 1830. In that year Victor Hugo's (1802-1885) *Hernani* was produced by the Comédie Française. *Hernani* violated such rules of neoclassicism as the unity of time, place, and action, as well as the mixing of comic and serious moods. The play was essentially a melodrama with a happy ending, characteristic of most romantic plays. *Hernani* became an overnight success and set the pattern followed by such writers as Alexander Dumas père (1802-1870) and Alfred de Vigny (1797-1863). Dumas père is famous for such plays as *The Three Musketeers* and *Henri III and His Court.* Vigny is known for *Chatterton* and *The Marshal of Ancre.* Alfred de Musset (1810-1857) and his plays, particularly *No Trifling With Love,* have withstood the test of time.

Romanticism and the Theatre

While the political ramifications of Romanticism were manifest, its influence on the theatre was more subtle. There was first a gradual change in the depiction of women, and for that matter, morals in general. Reactions against the aggressiveness of women during the period of Louis XIV and the Restoration in England were epitomized in the writings of Rousseau.

Rousseau said, in effect, that the woman's place is in the home. She should accept her husband as a master, but in the home she should be supreme. In that way the health of the race would be preserved. Rousseau believed that the education of girls should aim to produce such women. Girls should be educated at home by their mothers; they should learn all the arts of the home, from cooking to embroidery. They should get much religion and as early as possible, for this would help them to achieve modesty, virtue and obedience. In any case, a girl should avoid philosophy and scorn to be salonnière. However, a girl should not be suppressed into dull timidity; she should be lively, merry, and eager; she should sing and dance to her heart's content. Let her go to balls, even to theatres — under proper supervision and in good company. Her mind should be kept active and alert if she would ever be a fit wife for a thinking man. And she should be allowed a certain amount of coquetry as a part of a complex game by which she might test her suitors and choose her mate. The proper study of womankind should be man.

Whatever the present-day reaction to these general thoughts from Rousseau's book *Emile,* several points can be made. First, the cry of equality did not necessarily include women, although many free-thinking women did evolve from the movement. Second, the literary concept of women became idealized or romanticized and that ideal was to set an artificial standard of morality for some time to come. Third, the artificial standard of morality was to affect the content of the English drama throughout the nineteenth century.

Ada Isaacs Menken (1835-1868), pictured here in *The French Spy,* 1866. She gained fame for her role in *Mazeppa* (1859), in which she appeared virtually nude, strapped to a horse. From *Dramatic Portrait Gallery,* 1880.

The romantic movement, with its concern for the ancient, stimulated a new interest in antiquarianism. The discovery of the long-buried cities of Herculaneum and Pompeii in 1706 gave birth to modern archaeology. In the theatre, historical accuracy, which because of neoclassicism had never been of concern, suddenly gained importance. James Robinson Planché (1796-1880) persuaded Charles Kemble (1775-1854) to use historically accurate costumes in his production of *King John*. Later, both historically accurate costumes and scenery were used in Kemble's *Henry IV, Part I*. Planché continued his work in costuming by completing research for the standard *History of British Costume* (1834).

A third important romantic influence was in playwriting itself. The Romanticist believed that art had enormous significance because it enabled man to glimpse an ideal existence or society even though the ideal might be well beyond his practical grasp. Because of man's human limitation, the ideal may only exist in art. Therefore, the artist-genius was a superior being capable of providing guidance for those willing to be guided. The romantic playwright looked to the past for inspiration. Just as the neoclassicist discovered the Greek and Roman writers, the romanticist looked for champions. It is not surprising that Shakespeare's plays became the needed model. Shakespeare had always been considered an inferior playwright by the neoclassicists. During the eighteenth century, his plays had been expunged of what was considered to be excessive verbage. In many instances, Shakespeare's plays were actually altered to make them conform more readily to neoclassical tenets. The classical example is Nahum Tate's version of

King Lear, in which Cordelia and Edgar are lovers from the beginning of the play and are united in marriage at the end and Lear is restored to the throne. This device, of course, fulfills the neoclassical demand for poetic justice.

The romantics, on the other hand, used Shakespeare as a model upon which to build. Not only were Shakespeare's plays revived, but the scripts were returned almost to their original state.

The Romantic Poets

Most of the romantic poets of England followed the Shakespeare model and attempted verse plays. Wordsworth (1770-1850) wrote *The Borderers* in 1795. John Keats (1795-1821) wrote *Otho the Great* in 1819. Samuel Taylor Coleridge wrote *Remorse* in 1813. Robert Browning (1812-1889) wrote *Strafford* (1837), *A Blot on the Scutcheon* (1843), and *Colombe's Birthday* (1853). Percy Bysshe Shelley (1792-1822) wrote *Prometheus Unbound* and *The Cenci* in 1819. All of these plays, with the possible exception of *The Cenci,* are singularly unexciting and uninspiring. The most popular of the romantic poets as a playwright was George Gordon, Lord Byron (1788-1824), who wrote *Marino Faliero* (1821), *Sardanapalus* (1821), and his most popular play, *Werner,* in 1830. *Werner* became one of William Charles Macready's prime theatrical vehicles.

Right: J.R. Planché's costume design for Charles Kemble's *King Henry IV,* 1824. This production marked the first use of *both* historically accurate costumes and sets. The first use of historically accurate costumes appears to have been in Kemble's 1823 production of King John, with Planché again the costume designer. Courtesy Lilly Library, Indiana University.

Opposite: Giovanni Battista Piranesi (1720-1778), who through his stage settings and engravings of Roman ruins stirred a new interest in the use of light and shadow, which contributed to the eerie mood effects of romantic dramas. These engravings (1765) depict the Forum of Nerva. Courtesy Lilly Library, Indiana University.

C

B
B
A

John Fawcett as Captain Copp and Charles Kemble as Charles II in John Howard Payne's *Charles II*, May 27, 1824, at Covent Garden.

Oddly enough, none of the great romantic poets achieved anything close to lasting fame for their efforts in the theatre. One of the most popular, if not *the* most popular English playwright of this period, was Edward George Bulwer-Lytton (1803-1873). Bulwer-Lytton combined melodrama with romanticism to form what was called "gentlemanly" melodrama. Lord Lytton is probably best known for his novels, particularly *The Last Days of Pompeii*. His influence on the English theatre, both as a reform member of Parliament and as an author, are exceptional.

Bulwer-Lytton and Macready

When George Edward Bulwer-Lytton invited Macready to call on him at Albany in February, 1836, to announce, as it were, the beginning of his try at playwrighting, he could expect to deliver himself as king to the king, for Lytton had one of the greatest literary reputations of the day. At the age of thirty-three, he was not only the most widely read and most admired novelist in England, but was also famous in Germany, Italy, France, and America as well. He had published ten novels in at least four distinct manners: witty novels of fashionable life like *Pelham;* Newgate melodramas such as *Paul Clifford* and *Eugene Aram;* the baroque philosophical romance of *Goldolphin;* and historical novels such as *Rienzi* and, perhaps the most popular of them all, *The Last Days of Pompeii.* His reputation was further enhanced by several volumes of verse, and by his two-year editorship of the *New Monthly,* a nineteenth century literary magazine.

Macready was also well known among literary circles of his time. He created, and scrupulously maintained, for himself the position of a gentleman. According to English statutes unrepealed from the reign of Elizabeth, an actor was little more than a "rogue and vagabond." Consequently, Macready was constantly bitter with the members of his profession who created public scandal and reaffirmed the old appellation. Macready was always considered to be prudent, frugal, sober, reliable, dignified, and self-respecting. Romantic drama featured the virtuous gentleman, the hero embued with English respectability. Macready became the epitomy of the romantic ideal both on and off stage; he became a sign of the times. It was to this man that the dramatic elite brought their plays not only to be acted, but also to be counseled in the planning and writing. He was proud, sensitive, intelligent, and ambitious. Though born into a theatrical family, he aspired from early boyhood to the gentlemanly profession of the church or the bar. Forced to leave Rugby school at the age of fifteen because of his father's financial collapse, and forced into the disagreeable labors of managing and performing in the provincial theatres of his father's circuits, he at first hated the theatre. He vehemently disliked the kinds of people he was forced to work with and tried to escape the theatre. Finding that impossible, he worked with fanatic devotion to improve his place within it. By 1820,

Edward George Bulwer-Lytton. From *Dramatic Portrait Gallery,* 1880.

William Charles Macready. Courtesy Harvard Theatre Collection.

he had become a leading actor in the country and distinguished himself at Covent Garden, and was ready to embark upon a more or less conscious and consistent program of transforming the theatre into an institution worthy of himself and his friends. Macready became one of the most successful theatre managers of his time. He managed Covent Garden from 1837 to 1839 and moved to Drury Lane from 1841 to 1843. Some of Macready's techniques will be discussed later, but it is important to remember that he was one of the first to impose stage movement on his actors. He was one of the first to collaborate with playwrights in the writing of plays. Macready's work with Lord Lytton produced the most popular plays in England during the first half of the nineteenth century.

The Macready-Lytton partnership produced six plays. The correspondence between the two men reveals not only the process of playwriting, but two essentially romantic minds at work. Macready concerned himself with helping Lytton with characterizations, especially characterizations of the hero. In each case it was Macready who created these roles. The plays were *The Duchess de la Valliere and Cromwell, The Lady of Lyons, Richelieu, The Sea Captain,* and *Money*. Because romantic plays illustrate a philosophical perspective which no longer exists, they appear to be contrived and overly sentimental. *The Lady of Lyons* was perhaps Macready's greatest vehicle. He played Claude Melnotte, a gardener's son who rose from poverty to win honor and the love of Pauline. It has, as one reviewer put it, "the one indispensible merit of the romantic play. It has in it the free plunge of life."

Macready was constantly trying to improve the repertory. He is credited with restoring many of Shakespeare's altered texts, although propriety seems to have governed what speeches were restored and what were not. For his efforts he became a national idol.

Macready gave up management in 1843 partly because he felt that he was not maintaining the quality of theatre that he desired. He began touring and eventually landed in America, where misfortune awaited him.

Royall Tyler and the American Theatre

The American theatre was primarily manned by the English actors who had fled the restrictions of the Licensing Act of 1737. But by the turn of the century, America began to develop a theatre of its own. The first American comedy to be professionally produced was Royall Tyler's (1757-1826) *The Contrast.*

Royall Tyler was born in the vicinity of Faneuil Hall, Boston, in 1757. His father, Royall Tyler the elder, was a graduate of Harvard and a prosperous Boston merchant. The elder Tyler was active in business and politics and served on the King's Council during the troubled days of the notorious Stamp Act, which was passed March 22, 1765. The elder Tyler died in 1770 and was buried in the churchyard of Kings Chapel, Boston, in a tomb sculptured with the family arms (Tyler was a Boston Brahmin).

At fifteen, young Tyler followed his father's footsteps to Harvard. He was handsome, had a beautiful voice, a volatile wit, great friendliness, and a gift of laughter. His wit was fully exercised at the expense of the Harvard faculty. On one occasion Tyler and his roommate, Christopher Gore, who later became a Massachusetts governor and senator, were perched in their rooms looking with fascination at a litter of pigs. It was decided that one of the pigs might be hooked with a piece of bent wire and a long string. The device was made and lowered to the ground. Unfortunately, before it reached the pig it reached a wig, the biggest wig of Cambridge — that of the Reverend President Langdon, who was just entering the building. The result of this act is not fully known. Tyler managed to graduate in 1776 with an A.B. degree from Harvard and he received simultaneously an A.B. degree from Yale. This fact has puzzled biographers and scholars for some time; the general agreement is that his outstanding scholarship had already extended itself throughout the area. One scholar has suggested, however, that the scalping of the Harvard president merited the recognition from New Haven.

Lithograph made in the 1850's of the stage Yankee, G.E. Locke.

George Handel Hill (1809-1849), considered the best of those portraying the Yankee character.

In 1779 Tyler was admitted to the bar and began his practice in Maine and Boston. He courted Abigail Adams, who was the daughter of John Adams, only to lose her to Colonel Smith of the American Legation in London. During Shay's Rebellion of 1787, Tyler was called up with the rank of major to pursue the rebels into Vermont. He continued to negotiate with the rebels both in Vermont and New York. While in New York City, Tyler saw a production of Sheridan's *School for Scandal* at the little red wooden playhouse on John Street. The performance made a great impression on the young lawyer and, in less than a month, Tyler wrote *The Contrast*. The John Street Theatre was occupied at that time by the American company under the tutelage of Lewis Hallam (c. 1740-1808) and John Henry (1738-1794). Apparently Tyler gave the play to Thomas Wignell (1753-1803), the principal low comedian of the company. The play was first performed on April 16, 1787, with Wignell playing the part of Jonathan.

The character of Jonathan became an immediate hit. In a sense, the play is a contrast between decadent England with its aristocracy and the romantic America represented by Jonathan. The first stage Yankee, Jonathan, represents the noble savage, the common man, the primitive. His unspoiled nature, in contrast to the polished decadence of Dimple, allows him to speak from the heart in romantic truths. Every American viewer could see in Jonathan a raison d'être for the revolution.

Napoleon's need for money greatly extended America's territorial limits when he sold France's lands west of the Mississippi. The Louisiana Purchase, the acquisition of Florida, Texas, Arizona, New Mexico, and California, extended the nation from the Mississippi River to the Pacific Ocean. The demand for theatrical activity increased proportionately. American playwrights were on the increase and along with them, the actors.

Charlotte Cushman

The first native-born actress to be internationally acclaimed was Charlotte Cushman (1816-1876). Originally an opera singer, she was to be considered the finest tragic actress of the English-speaking world during the nineteenth century. Cushman made her debut as an actress at the Bowery Theatre in New York in 1836. Between 1842 and 1843, she was the leading lady at the Walnut Theatre in Philadelphia. She was also its

Wood engraving of the John Street Theatre, which opened December 7, 1767, and remained the leading theatre in New York until the turn of the century. Courtesy Museum of the City of New York.

Charlotte Cushman, first American actress to be internationally acclaimed. Like Edwin Forrest, she relied heavily on her energy and her physical appearance to give her a commanding stage presence. From *Dramatic Portrait Gallery,* 1880.

manager, which made her one of the first female theatre managers in America.

William Charles Macready was so impressed with her acting that he urged her to go to London. She made her debut at the Princess in 1844 and became an overnight star. When she returned to the United States her reputation was established. Some critics called her a female counterpart of Edwin Forrest because of the physical and emotional power of her characterization, and others called her the "female Macready" because of the similarity in style.

Edwin Forrest

The first true star of the American stage among the native-born actors was Edwin Forrest (1806-1872). He was a man of imposing physical strength and he disliked what he called the "repressed" acting of Macready. Forrest's rivalry of Macready led to one of the most bizarre incidents ever to occur in the theatre. Forrest had gone to London with the idea of booking into Paris. After encountering abnormal difficulties in meeting with the Paris booking agent, Forrest immediately suspected that Macready had caused the problem. Later as Forrest performed *Macbeth* in London, with Charlotte Cushman as his leading lady, he detected noises in the audience. Enraged at what he thought to have been prearranged by Macready, he vowed to revenge himself. While Macready performed *Hamlet* at Edinburgh, Forrest, who had taken the week off, purchased a box seat in order to watch his rival perform. During a quiet scene Macready was unnerved by a rather loud hiss from Forrest's box. Forrest never attempted to hide his identity, thus infuriating his English rival.

The next collision occurred as Macready made a series of farewell performances in America. Macready was booked into the Astor Place Opera House and was set to open with *Macbeth.* The story of the feud between the two national idols was well publicized. The situation was further

Edwin Forrest as Spartacus in Robert Montgomery Bird's *The Gladiator,* 1831. From *Dramatic Portrait Gallery,* 1880.

complicated by the engagement of Forrest to open a simultaneous *Macbeth*. Newspapers added fuel to the fire by making the two performances a fight to the finish for theatrical supremacy. Most papers sided with Forrest, certain that the "unsophisticated energy of the daring child of nature" would win out over the "glossy polish" of the Britisher. Any good American preferred "the tomahawk to the toga."

The Astor Place Riot

Macready's opening night audience was literally infiltrated by Forrest's supporters, particularly in the gallery. The first two scenes were enthusiastically applauded as the American actor C.W. Clarke, who played Macduff, dominated the stage. At Macready's entrance, however, the Bowery B'hoys in the gallery went wild with hisses and catcalls. Macready was pelted with rotten eggs, potatoes, and copper coins; when these were exhausted, the Gallery began throwing chairs. The curtain was brought down and Macready was allowed to return to his hotel, resolving to leave for England on the next boat. A steady stream of visitors, including such literary figures as Washington Irving and Herman Melville, apologized for their fellow citizens and urged Macready to continue his run. Macready, the gentleman, was flattered by the response and agreed to continue, a decision he would live to regret.

The Forrest contingents were outraged and began to flood the city with handbills reading:

Workingmen
shall
Americans or English Rule
in this city.
Workingmen! Freemen!
stand by your
lawful rights.

The city was up in arms. The affair was taking on the dimensions of a revolt, pitting the true-hearted American primitive against an English blue blood which, of course, Macready was not. The police chief G.W. Matsell informed Mayor Caleb S. Woodhull that a riot might occur and the mayor urged the managers to cancel the performance. William Niblo (1789-1878) and James Henry Hackett (1800-1871), the managers, refused, citing the public's right to see and hear Macready. The mayor ordered Matsell to position a full police detail at the theatre, and a military force under General Sandford was to be held in readiness.

At curtain there were 1,800 spectators in the building, about 200 policemen inside the theatre, 50 police on the Eighth Street side of the building, and 75 at the main entrance. In addition there were 200 members of the Seventh Infantry Regiment, two troops of horses, plus a standby unit of hussars.

The first scenes went as before with the American actor being cheered, but when Macready entered, the galleries went wild. The police, in an attempt to restore order, arrested three of the most flagrant rowdies. Word of the arrests was passed to the angry crowd outside, and they began throwing sticks and bottles. The army was called and the cavalry unit attempted to clear the area. When they were forced to retreat by a hail of bricks, the infantry moved in with fixed bayonets but were driven back. The order was then given to fire over the heads of the rioters. The crowd moved back temporarily, but thinking that the troops were using blanks, soon returned with renewed hostility. The field commander, General Hall, ordered his troops to fire a second round at the legs of the rioters. Half of the troops balked at shooting Americans and the other half fired, dropping about a dozen people. The crowd charged again with the General ordering his men to fire at will. The cries of the wounded finally broke the spirit of the rioters.

Macready escaped the theatre, spent the night with a friend, took the train to Boston, and on Tuesday, May 22, 1849, sailed for home. never to return.

As for the rioters, thirty-one lay dead in the streets and forty-eight were injured badly enough to be hospitalized. Forrest had won, protesting that he was not responsible for the riot. He was flooded with congratulatory letters, for the most part, saying that the time was at hand when American actors would do American acting.

William C. Macready

Edwin Forrest

The Astor Place Riot, May 10, 1849.

Top left: Interior of Laura Keene's Theatre, New York, as pictured in *Leslie's Magazine,* 1856. The theatre opened November 18, 1856, and held 1800 people.

Top right: Engraving of the first Bowery Theatre, New York, which opened October 23, 1826, but was destroyed by fire May 26, 1828.

Middle left: The Arch Street Theatre, Philadelphia, which opened October 1, 1828, under the management of William B. Wood (1779-1861).

Bottom: McVicker's Theatre, which opened November 5, 1857, in Chicago. This photograph appeared in the *Chicago Illustrated,* October 1866.

Right: Playbill for Ford's Theatre the night President Abraham Lincoln was assassinated. This playbill was printed before it was known Lincoln would attend; after his plans were known, the playbill was reprinted to include a patriotic song and chorus to the soldiers.

Below: Edward Askew Sothern (1826-81), English actor pictured here as Lord Dundreary (*Our American Cousin*), a role with which he is always associated. From *Dramatic Portrait Gallery,* 1880.

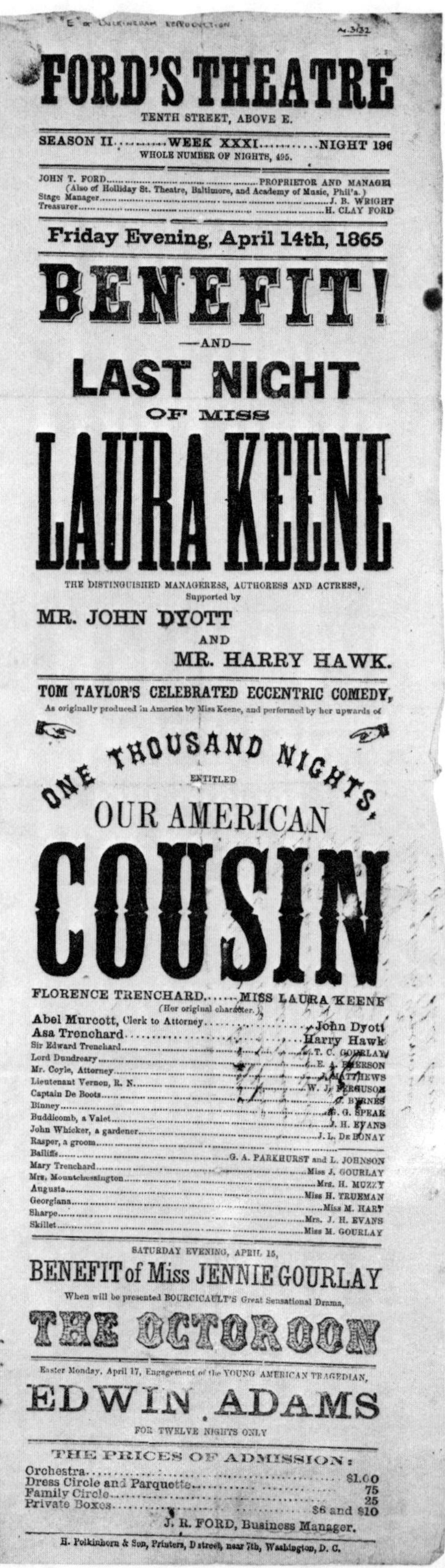

FORD'S THEATRE

TENTH STREET, ABOVE E.

SEASON II..........WEEK XXXI..........NIGHT 196

WHOLE NUMBER OF NIGHTS, 495.

JOHN T. FORD..........PROPRIETOR AND MANAGER
(Also of Holliday St. Theatre, Baltimore, and Academy of Music, Phil'a.)
Stage Manager..........J. B. WRIGHT
Treasurer..........H. CLAY FORD

Friday Evening, April 14th, 1865

BENEFIT!

—AND—

LAST NIGHT

OF MISS

LAURA KEENE

THE DISTINGUISHED MANAGERESS, AUTHORESS AND ACTRESS,
Supported by

MR. JOHN DYOTT

AND

MR. HARRY HAWK.

TOM TAYLOR'S CELEBRATED ECCENTRIC COMEDY,

As originally produced in America by Miss Keene, and performed by her upwards of

ONE THOUSAND NIGHTS,

ENTITLED

OUR AMERICAN

COUSIN

FLORENCE TRENCHARD..........MISS LAURA KEENE
(Her original character.)
Abel Murcott, Clerk to Attorney..........John Dyott
Asa Trenchard..........Harry Hawk
Sir Edward Trenchard..........T. C. GOURLAY
Lord Dundreary..........E. A. EMERSON
Mr. Coyle, Attorney..........J. MATTHEWS
Lieutenant Vernon, R. N...........W. J. FERGUSON
Captain De Boots..........C. BYRNES
Binney..........G. G. SPEAR
Buddicomb, a Valet..........J. H. EVANS
John Whicker, a gardener..........J. L. DE BONAY
Rasper, a groom..........
Bailiffs..........G. A. PARKHURST and L. JOHNSON
Mary Trenchard..........Miss J. GOURLAY
Mrs. Mountchessington..........Mrs. H. MUZZY
Augusta..........Miss H. TRUEMAN
Georgiana..........Miss M. HART
Sharpe..........Mrs. J. H. EVANS
Skillet..........Miss M. GOURLAY

SATURDAY EVENING, APRIL 15,

BENEFIT of Miss JENNIE GOURLAY

When will be presented BOURCICAULT'S Great Sensational Drama,

THE OCTOROON

Easter Monday, April 17, Engagement of the YOUNG AMERICAN TRAGEDIAN,

EDWIN ADAMS

FOR TWELVE NIGHTS ONLY

THE PRICES OF ADMISSION:

Orchestra..........$1.00
Dress Circle and Parquette..........75
Family Circle..........25
Private Boxes..........$6 and $10

J. R. FORD, Business Manager.

H. Polkinhorn & Son, Printers, D street, near 7th, Washington, D. C.

Top left: The Booth brothers at Winter Garden, New York, for *Julius Caesar,* five months before Lincoln's assassination. From left to right: John Wilkes (1839-1865), Edwin (1833-1893), and Junius Brutus, Jr. (1821-1883).

Top right: Frank Mayo (1839-1896), American actor who achieved his greatest success in Frank Murdoch's *Davy Crockett.* Mayo played the role from 1872 until his death; after 2000 performances, he stopped counting. From *Dramatic Portrait Gallery,* 1880.

Bottom left: Laura Keene (c. 1820-1873), born Mary Moss in England. Miss Keene, one of the first female theatrical managers in America, was playing Florence Trenchard in *Our American Cousin* at Ford's Theatre the night of Lincoln's assassination.

Victorian Morality and English Drama

The marriage of melodrama and romanticism continued to dominate the stage until the latter part of the nineteenth century. But in England another influence was to combine with this hybrid and affect the quality of the English drama well into the twentieth century.

George III, who had been politically discredited by the loss of the American colonies, was, from 1788 onwards, reduced to periodic bouts of insanity. After the death of his favorite daughter in 1811, he lived in pathetic seclusion, blind as well as mad, until his death in 1820 at the age of eighty-two.

Twelve of his fifteen children survived infancy. The oldest succeeded the King as George IV, and reigned from 1820-1830. George III's third son, Edward, Duke of Kent, who had reluctantly married Princess Victoria of Saxe-Coburg in 1818, was the only member of the Hanoverian family to produce an offspring. On May 24, 1819, shortly before his death, Edward became the father of a daughter, Victoria. Since there were no children to survive either the Prince Regent, George IV, or William IV who succeeded him in 1830, Victoria became Queen Regent in 1837.

The Victorian age set up ground rules for the theatre which puzzle the modern mind. Perhaps in no age have people been so concerned about the appearance of respectability as were the Victorians, and perhaps in no other age have people been so hypocritical. At the center of this hypocrisy was the middle class, who modeled their behavior and thought after the upper classes, or what they thought to be upper-class behavior and thought. Politically, the Victorians were chauvinistic and easily swayed by imperialistic designs. They professed manliness to a fault, yet their standards were based on a romantic conception of ideal femininity. In some ways, the Victorians emancipated women; in other ways, they took from women a vital place in society. Sexually, they were inhibited to the point of almost denying the existence of physical love, yet the average Victorian family was large.

These apparent contradictions in Victorian society manifested themselves in many other ways. Sexual intercourse and matters related to physical desires were treated as deeds of darkness, as matters which well-bred men and women never discussed. Gentility was thought antipathetic to the physical relationships between the sexes, a view which the medical profession and the clergy constantly reinforced. Doctors proclaimed the inevitability of cancer for those who overindulged in sex. Leading medical authorities cautioned women, in particular, never to indulge in sexual enjoyment. "The ideal English Mother," according to Dr. William Acton (1818-1875), one of the most famous doctors in nineteenth century England, "knows little or nothing of sexual indulgences. Love of home, children, and domestic duties, are the only passions she feels." Forbidden by these unwritten laws of the middle class to indulge in sex or to enjoy it when available, many women found themselves in the unenviable position of becoming child-rearing vehicles, while their husbands shelved their guilt and made use of the vast array of prostitutes, reputed to number 120,000 in London alone. It is small wonder that the middle class found the whole subject of sex taboo. Because of the repressive restraint on the subject, it became confused, even diffused, into other manifestations. The shape of a grand piano, for example, became indecent, and piano legs were frequently draped to avoid the possibility of offending young ladies.

The protection of young ladies, of course, was the prime justification for having a censor of English drama. With the romantic idealization of the virtuous woman and honorable man, the English language was subjected to an expurgation of words with even the slightest hint of sexuality. Hence, *breast* became *bosom* and even *naked necks. Legs* became *limbs* and the word *thigh* was removed from polite conversation altogether. Any article of underwear was referred to as an *unmentionable.* A whole new etiquette was brought into play in what had once been a simple boy meets girl situation. When sex ceased to be talked about openly, it went underground. Probably no society, with the possible exception of our own, has been as eager to welcome pornography and indecent engravings as were the Victorians. Since pornography was available through underground book sales, and since literature was free from any kind of pre-censorship, the burden of dramatizing middle class standards fell on the theatre. For that reason, the censorship of drama reached its apogee during the Victorian period.

English Censorship

De facto censorship of the English stage had been present since the advent of the Master of Revels office under Elizabeth. The Theatre Regulations Act of 1843 legitimized censorship while freeing the minor theatres from the domination of the patent houses. Since this act literally governed the English stage for well over a hundred years, its ramifications are important to the theatre student.

The second section of the act gives the Lord Chamberlain a power which he never had. For the first time in English theatrical history, he was legally able to license theatres; that is, to license theatre buildings rather than producers, players, or plays. This factor alone increased his power to an unprecedented degree. Further, while the justices of the peace had the right to license theatres outside London, the Lord Chamberlain could close them anywhere the sovereign happened to be in residence. The Lord Chamberlain was also given the power to close, without trial, any theatre in England for misbehavior if an unlicensed play were produced. He was also empowered to fine any manager in London for any breach of the Lord Chamberlain's rules. Allowing the Lord Chamberlain to set his own rules gave him legislative and judicial authority, as well as the right to define what constituted a theatre. In addition, the fact that actors could now be penalized for performing anywhere except a licensed theatre virtually returned them to the old rogue and vagabond status. But the most important of all sections was section fourteen which read:

> And it be enacted, that it shall be lawfull for the Lord Chamberlain for the time being, whenever he shall be of opinion that it is fitting for Preservation of good manners, Decorum, or of the public Peace so to do, to forbid the acting or presenting any Stage Play, or any Act, Scene, or Part thereof . . . anywhere in Great Britain, or in such Theatres as he shall specify, and either absolutely or for such time as he shall think fit.

This, in effect, gave the Lord Chamberlain control over the content of English drama. Being a man responsible for maintaining the royal household, the Lord Chamberlain was, and is, a busy man. Since he rarely had time to read even a small portion of the material submitted, the Chamberlain would appoint a play examiner to read the manuscripts. If the examiner wished a word or a paragraph changed, even a major alteration, the playwright would be obligated to follow instructions or have his license refused. Once refused, the playwright had virtually no right to appeal. The examiner's word was law. Playwrights either took it — or left it.

The Play Examiner

The Victorian gentlemen who became play examiners were particularly alert to the sensibilities of young ladies. William Bodham Donne, one of the nineteenth century examiners, always changed the word *God* to *heaven*. The word *Lord* was also changed to *heaven* on occasion. The phrase *fit for a Lord* in W.S. Gilbert's version of *Great Expectations* was changed to *chambers fit for heaven*.

Donne's replacement, Edward F. Smyth Pigott, banned, among other things, the *Oberammergau Passion Play* and Shelley's *The Cenci*. Pigott was particularly watchful of French pieces, and he censored far more French adaptions than English plays. In one instance related by George Bernard Shaw, Piggott refused to license a translation of a French play on the ground that the heroine, a married woman, had been guilty of an indiscretion in early life. The actress cast for the part visited Piggott and naturally used all her powers of persuasion to induce him to revoke his decision. Finally he consented on condition that the words, "I sinned but in intention" were introduced into her part. According to Shaw, "every night, during the burst of welcome which hailed her first entrance in the piece, the actress remarked confidentially to the conductor of the band, 'I sinned but in intention,' and thereby rescued her country from demoralization by French levity."

George Alexander Redford

Perhaps the most famous or infamous of the play examiners was George Alexander Redford, who had the dubious distinction of refusing a license to Sophocles' *Oedipus Rex,* Maeterlinck's *Monna Vanna,* Ibsen's *Ghosts,* Shaw's *Mrs. Warren's Profession,* and Gilbert & Sullivan's *The Mikado,* to name but a few.

Oedipus Rex was banned outright because Oedipus had married his mother, and it was several years before the ban was removed. The banning prompted the playwright Henry Arthur Jones to comment in *The Foundations of a National Drama:*

> If after the production of Oedipus, it is found that Englishmen are developing the habit of marrying their mothers, even if there is any noticeable tendency that way, then the Censorship must be held to have justified itself, and in this instance to have shown a sagacity and foresight which none of its other actions would lead us to imagine it possessed.

Monna Vanna was refused because of a scene in which Monna gives herself to the tyrant in order to save the city. Ostensibly she goes to the tyrant's tent wearing only a cloak. According to Redford, the fact that she was naked under her cloak made the play improper for the stage. The playwright Hall Caine commented: "On stage she comes in a cloak, and the evil is supposed to lie in the fact that the audience knows that under her cloak she is nude. Well, aren't we all nude under our clothes?"

The prohibition of *Mrs. Warren's Profession* because of the subject matter provoked an interesting story by George Bernard Shaw. According to Shaw, after he had been refused a license to perform the play in London, he attempted to have the play performed in New York. The word was printed in the papers that a banned play was to be performed. As a consequence, the worst elements of American society turned out to see the show. There were near-riot conditions and scalpers were demanding and receiving enormous prices for the tickets. As the curtain rose, the police arrived and arrested the entire company. The magistrate announced that he would adjourn the case until he had read the play, and publicly expressed his loathing of the task before him. At the next hearing he arrived and announced that he had read the play and had not found in it what he had expected. The final results were the following, as quoted by Shaw: "The defendants stand acquitted by the decision of the court, in which it is stated that there is nothing in the words themselves or in any particular phrase or expression which can be said to be indecent."

Perhaps the most damning incident involved the ban on Gilbert and Sullivan's *The Mikado.* Following the tradition of banning politically sensitive plays, Redford had disallowed *The Mikado* because of the Anglo-Japanese Alliance then being negotiated. Shortly after the ban, the Japanese warship *Tsukuba* anchored in the harbor at Chattham. Admiral Sir Gerald Noel, along with the chief military and naval officers of the station, was entertained aboard the Japanese man-of-war. Although these officers had issued imperative orders that their bands should not play any of *The Mikado* music, it was with selections from this very opera that the band of the Japanese regaled them.

Complaints by playwrights and critics against Redford's practice were bitter and in many cases irate. William Archer, playwright and critic, stated to a committee of Parliament in 1909 that, in his opinion, "the censor keeps serious drama down to the level of his own intelligence." Referring to his many roles as a playwright, journalist, author, and public speaker, Shaw perhaps said it best when he commented: "In all those capacities I may offend against the law, and I am responsible for what I do; but I am responsible to the law and not to Mr. Redford or the Lord Chamberlain."

There is no doubt that by the end of the century the world was already in the throes of a new revolution. The romantic era as a literary movement had long expired. But the romantic concepts of morality became somehow ingrained in the English theatre and, to some extent, France as well. In many ways, Victoria was the last vestige of a dying era. The Victorians really did not practice equality, fraternity, or brotherhood nor did they really believe in the essential goodness of man; yet, they always claimed to believe. They talked a great deal about virtue, so much so that for a while the middle class almost believed. But the realities of the world have a sobering effect and the dichotomy between what was being said and what was happening became too evident to be ignored. Sadly, the romantic ideal was seen for what it was — an ideal. When the truth was recognized, a new and exciting theatre began to take shape.

Selected Readings

Lacey, Alexander. *Pixérécourt and the French Romantic Drama.* Toronto, 1928.

Moody, Richard. *America Takes the Stage,* 1750-1900. Bloomington, Ind., 1955.

Odell, George C.D. *Shakespeare from Betterton to Irving.* 2 vols. New York, 1920.

Planché, J.R. *The Recollections and Reflections of James Robinson Planché.* 2 vols. London, 1872.

Vocabulary

1. Das Athenaeum	dahs ah tuh NAY uhm
2. August Wilhelm Schlegel	ow goost VIL helm SHLAY guhl
3. Johann Wolfgang von Goethe	YOH hahn VAWLF gahng fawn GER tuh
4. Heinrich von Kleist	HIGHN rik fawn KLIGHST
5. Germaine Necker	zher MAYN ne KAIR
6. Mme. de Staël	duh STAHL
7. Alexander Dumas père	ah leg ZAHND ruh doo: MAH pair
8. Alfred de Vigny	duh vee NYEE
9. Alfred de Musset	duh moo SAY
10. James Robinson Planché	plahn SHAY
11. William Charles Macready	muh KREED ee
12. *A Blot on the Scutcheon*	SKUH chuhn
13. *The Cenci*	CHEN chee
14. Edward George Bulwer-Lytton	BOOL wer LI tuhn
15. Covent Garden	KUH vent
16. Edward F. Smyth Pigott	SMIGHTH PIG uht

CHAPTER ELEVEN

Chaos and Poverty
The Rise of Realism

The chief contribution of the latter half of the nineteenth century is difficult to pinpoint because so many innovations in the theatre occurred. It can be safely concluded, however, that the rise of realism in the theatre served as the chief catalyst, if not the innovative force itself, behind these changes.

The seeds of the realistic movement in England were ingrained in the industrial revolution, which began the latter half of the eighteenth century. The Seven Years War insured Britain's supremacy of the sea and with it lucrative trade markets throughout the world. New and bigger merchant ships were constructed for the long voyages to China and India. To deal with increases in trade, industry moved out of homes and into larger factories, creating a private enterprise system spurred by the profit motive. The factory system began to dominate not only the economy of the country but the landscape as well. Hundreds of smokestacks rose over the new industrial centers of Manchester, Birmingham, Sheffield, Leeds, Glasgow and Edinburgh.

Poor Working Conditions

As increasing numbers of farmers poured into the city, the areas surrounding the factories became more and more depressed. For the worker, conditions were as poor as salaries. The work force during the first part of the century consisted primarily of women and children because they could be paid substantially less. Children, hired as chimney sweeps (among other things), rarely reached puberty before succumbing to lung disease. Cholera, contracted from the grossly-polluted drinking water, took a horrifying toll among the women and children. The disease raged in London until John Snow (1813-1858), a modest medical practitioner, published in 1849 the opinion that cholera was spread by the pollution of water by sewage. Only then were steps initiated to relieve this condition.

The agony of the industrial revolution was not confined to England. France and the newly unified German states were also affected. In Germany the factories multiplied, particularly in the Rhineland, and the fate of the worker equaled his English counterpart. The worker was championed by a young writer who also found time to castigate the Prussian royal house. For his trouble Karl Marx was expelled from the Rhineland to France, where he was ordered to leave in 1844. After being arrested in Brussels, he finally settled in London where he wrote *Das Kapital* at the British Museum. His attack on the capitalistic system found ample negative documentation in the industrial quagmire of London.

Marx was not the only one to realize that the workers' lot needed improvement. Reformers like Robert Owen warned Parliament that violence would be on the increase if factory conditions were not improved. Intolerable social conditions eventually led to revolt. Following the Silesian weavers, there were several uprisings in 1830 and still larger ones between 1845 and 1850. It became more and more evident that the workers would play a part in their own government.

Through the ages the theatre has always been a reflection of its society and the latter part of the nineteenth century was no different. Dramatists began to look to the problems of the working class with a seriousness that had formerly been reserved for the middle and upper classes. This change in approach from the idealistic man in a corrupt society to a realistic view of human problems and needs required not the dreamer but the scientist.

Positivism

The scientific method by its very nature was a reaction against the nebulosity of Romanticism. One of the first philosophers to take a stand against the past was Auguste Comte (1798-1857), who argued that the scientific method must be applied to

Opposite: Sarah Bernhardt (Bernard) (1844-1923), the most famous French actress of the nineteenth century. Her best-known role was Camille; she also achieved success as Tosca, Phèdra (1879), and Adrienne Lecouvreur (1880). From *The Theatre*, 1879.

social problems. He wrote: "Positive sociology is to concern itself with the investigation of the facts instead of leisured contemplation, certainty instead of doubt and indecision, organization instead of negation and destruction."

Comte's theories were called Positivism. Positive philosophy tended to equate the study of society with the study of nature, so that natural science, particularly biology, became the archetype of social theory. Social study was to be a science seeking social laws. Inherent in these ideas is the concept of natural cause and effect. Emphasis must be put on what can be experienced in terms of the five senses or objective reality. Comte believed in the concept of progress, but he felt that the laws of progress were part of the machinery of a given order, a natural order emanating from physical laws. He viewed the different stages of historical development as stages of a philosophical movement rather than of a social process. Comte's law of three stages illustrates this theory. History, he says, takes the inevitable path of first, theological rule (classical, medieval, Elizabethan); then metaphysical rule (Romantic); and, finally, positivist rule (realistic).

Darwin

The theories of Positivism were reinforced by Charles Robert Darwin's (1809-1882) controversial manuscript, *The Origin of the Species* (1859). Fundamentally the Darwinian theory operates on two basic premises. First, all forms of life have evolved from a common ancestry. Second, there is a process of natural selection which is moving toward perfection. Darwin states:

> As all the living forms of life are the lineal descendants of those which lived long before the Cambrian epoch, we may feel certain that the ordinary succession by generation has never once been broken, and that no cataclysm has desolated the whole world. Hence we may look with some confidence to a secure future of great length. And as natural selection works solely by and for the good of each being, all corporeal and mental endowments will tend to progress towards perfection.

While Darwin never intended his theory to be equated with social progress, the concept of progress had enormous influence on the thinking of the nineteenth century. England had already expanded her empire to a great degree. The concept of progress gave colonization a new raison d'être. The idea that western society was at a higher stage of evolution than other cultures seemed to give British imperialism an almost messianic fervor. If we accept the premise that one society is in a higher state of evolution than another, then the higher society may attempt to "civilize" the other. The idea of progress, then, was one of the most important ramifications of the Darwinian theory.

The concept that all forms of life evolved from a common origin cast considerable doubt about the existence of God, or at least God as conceived by the major religions of the world. This factor seriously questioned the concept of immortality and, therefore, underlined the importance of fulfillment in one's lifetime. It thus became important to improve the conditions of the present life, and science seemed to offer the best means of doing so.

Darwin's strong emphasis on heredity and environment as the most important factors in natural selection strongly influenced later thinkers. First, while little could be done to alter it, heredity was recognized as being responsible for certain character traits and actions. Second, the importance of environment as a controlling force in the development of the individual was postulated. The theory suggested a need for society to recognize the influence of an inadequate environment and work to improve it.

Perhaps the most far-reaching ramification of the Darwinian Theory was the reevaluation of man himself. For the first time in the history of western civilization, man was viewed as an animal. His status as a god-like creature was lost. The impact of this concept caused the western world to begin to rethink its whole moral structure. Prior to this time, man enjoyed a status superior to all other creatures. All things on this earth were thought to have been created by God for the exclusive use of man. Darwin's theory first suggested that incredible idea that other life forms might have a right to exist. In some ways the modern environmentalist was born with the publication of the *Origin of the Species*.

The Scribe Technique

The effect of these developments on art, in general, and the theatre, in particular, was gradual at first. The emphasis on observation of life in terms of the five senses demanded a dramatic form that would develop logically in a cause-effect manner. While not a realist himself, the French playwright Eugene Scribe (1791-1861) formed the ideal dramatic structure. Sometimes called the "well made play formula," Scribe's playwriting technique influenced realistic drama well into the twentieth century. The Scribean techniques employed cause-effect development geared to carefully prepared climax. Suspense and unexpected twists and endings were carefully woven into the script. Fortunate arrivals of persons or letters and foreshadowings were other devices. These techniques, along with expository preparation for developments to come, were included in virtually every respectable textbook on drama. Scribe's plays were extremely popular in France between 1811 and 1861 but have not survived the test of time. However, his influence is clearly shown in a number of realistic playwrights.

Alexander Dumas fils (1824-1895), who first became popular with his *The Lady of the Camellias,* better known as *Camille,* is a case in point. *Camille* is written in prose and sympathetically treats the central character who happens to be a prostitute. After *Camille,* Dumas fils wrote a series of "thesis" plays each studying current social problems and each using the cause-effect Scribean techniques. Emile Augier (1820-1889) and Victorien Sardou (1831-1908) both were to follow the Scribean formula and were quite popular during their lifetimes. But the writer who was to become the father of dramatic realism was a blustery Scandinavian by the name of Ibsen.

Henrik Ibsen, the father of modern drama. Courtesy Norwegian Information Service.

Ibsen — The Father of Modern Drama

Henrik Johann Ibsen (1828-1906) was born on March 20, 1828, in Skien, Norway. Ibsen lived in luxury until 1836 when his father fell into bankruptcy. The disgrace of his father's failure turned the sensitive boy into a near recluse. In 1844 Ibsen left home to become an apothecary's apprentice in the town of Grimstadt. While there the young apprentice read every book available to him and quickly acquired a good education. Ibsen remained at Grimstadt until 1850. Deeply influenced by the romanticists, Ibsen wrote his first finished play, *Cataline,* which was transported to Christiana by a close friend Ole Schulerud in the hope of publication. When all hopes failed, Schulerud had the scripts printed at his own expense and sent for Ibsen, who spent the next two years in the capital city. Despite the failure of *Cataline* in Christiania, Ole Bull, a national hero and world famous violinist, became interested in the young poet, and employed him to assist in creating a national theatre in Bergen. This position eventually led to Ibsen's first grant for study outside Norway. The playwright received 140 pounds for studying the theatre in Denmark and Germany, with the prospect of later becoming stage manager or director of the Bergen Theatre.

Upon his return to Norway, Ibsen continued to experiment with Romanticism. In 1857 he became artistic manager of the National Norwegian Theatre in Christiania and wrote the epic *The Vikings at Helgeland*. Another romantic play, *Love's Comedy*, was written in 1862. In 1863, he was granted his second travel stipend by the government. This grant was later augmented by private contributions collected by Björnstjerne Björnson, Bunker, and Johan Sverdaup, three literary friends of Ibsen. *The Pretenders* was completed before Ibsen left Christiania for Copenhagen. He then departed for Rome, where he wrote his great poetic masterpiece *Brand* (1866). This romantic drama eliminated the financial problems that had plagued Ibsen. Shortly after the success of *Brand*, he was granted a stipend by the Trondheim Scientific Association and a new travel grant by the Norwegian government. Beginning in 1866, Ibsen received an annual stipend from the government that made him financially solvent for the rest of his life. Between the years 1867 and 1874, Ibsen completed three plays, including his romantic masterpiece *Peer Gynt* (1867). *Peer Gynt* was later immortalized by Grieg's famous *Peer Gynt Suite*. Ibsen continued to travel, and was one of the first to pass through the newly constructed Suez Canal in 1869. After the publication of *Emperor and Gallilean* in 1873, Ibsen was made a knight of St. Olaf by King Oscar II.

Despite the honors showered on him, Ibsen was unhappy. His peers had attacked his poetry and had been highly critical of his last few poetic plays, including *Peer Gynt*. When the most famous poet of Norway, Björnstjerne Björnson, downgraded the quality of his poetry, Ibsen remarked: "If I am not a poet, then I have nothing to lose. I will try my hand as a photographer." Four years later in 1877 Ibsen published *Pillars of Society*, the first of his realistic plays. This play shows the influence of Scribe in terms of dramatic structure and established a structural technique that Ibsen generally followed throughout the rest of his career. It was not until the publication of *A Doll's House* (1879), *Ghosts* (1881), and *An Enemy of the People* (1882) that Ibsen established the reputation of social dramatist, which was to earn him the label "father of modern drama."

Ibsen and Realism

During this period in Ibsen's life, a significant book was being read throughout the world. This book, *The Subjection of Women* by John Stuart Mill, translated by Georg Brandes, was read by Ibsen and his Scandinavian contemporaries and it set off the same flare-up of controversy in Norway as it did all over the world. The nonsuffragist believed that if women were allowed more freedom, it would destroy their idealized status (romantic concept). The suffragists, on the other hand, objected to what they termed the "white slavery of women." In 1874, Aasta Hansteen, a pioneer suffragist in Norway, lashed out against the existing inequality of women. At first Ibsen was irritated at this outbreak, but basically he believed in individual as well as national freedom. Eventually he extended his demand of individual freedom to include women, whom he considered to be oppressed in their efforts at self-realization. In *A Doll's House* just such a woman, Nora, makes a decision to leave her husband because he will not allow her to exist as a person. When Ibsen published *A Doll's House*, he was branded a leader in the suffragist movement. He objected throughout his life to being categorized. He felt that he was a spokesman for all of humanity and not an evangelist for the few.

Later in life Ibsen replied to the label of suffragist while lecturing to the Women's Rights League in 1898.

> I am not a member of the Women's Rights League. Whatever I have written, has been without any conscious thought of making propaganda. I have been more poet and less social philosopher than people generally seem inclined to believe. I thank you for the toast, but must disdain the honor of having consciously worked for the Women's Rights Movement. I am not quite clear as to just what the Women's Rights Movement really is. And if you read my books carefully, you will understand this. True enough, it is desirable to solve the problem of Women's Rights along with the others; but that is not been the whole purpose. My task has been the description of humanity.

Ibsen was disturbed by the criticism that *A Doll's House* had received because of what he called "ecclesiastical narrow-mindedness" in Norway. Partly as an answer to his critics, Ibsen penned his third social play, in which the central character, Mrs. Alving, does not leave her husband but stays and is brought to tragedy because of that decision. Her son Oswald goes mad from syphilis ostensibly inherited from his father.

The world-wide reaction to *Ghosts* was tumultuous, to say the least. Some hailed the play and Ibsen with almost messianic fervor, while others called him a lunatic and pervert. Edward F. Smyth Pigott, the British play examiner between 1874 and 1895, was quoted as saying:

> I have studied Ibsen's plays pretty carefully, and all the characters in Ibsen's plays appear to me morally deranged. All the heroines are dissatisfied married women in a chronic state of rebellion against not only the conditions which nature has imposed on their sex, but against all duties and obligations of mothers and wives; and as for the men they are all rascals or imbeciles.

Janet Achurch (1864-1916), English actress who in 1889 presented the first unadapted version of Ibsen's *A Doll's House*. A champion of Ibsen's work, she was called by George Bernard Shaw "the only tragic actress of genius we now possess." From Dirck's *Players of Today*, 1892.

Needless to say, *Ghosts* was banned from the legitimate stage in England; however, it was given a performance at the Independent Theatre in London founded for the productions of new plays by J.T. Grein. The reaction to *Ghosts* in London was varied depending upon the reviewer. George Bernard Shaw and William Archer, among others, hailed it as a masterpiece. Some of the more Victorian critics were outraged. Clement Scott, a popular critic of the day, was particularly bitter. After viewing *Ghosts* he called it "a play that if presented to the general public would, if not hissed off the stage the first night, close the doors of any London theatre in a fortnight." He went on to say: "If it is desirable to drive decent minded women from the playhouse, and to use the auditorium as a hospital ward or dissecting-room, let it be so . . . But in our hurry to dramatize the Contagious Diseases Act let us first set about writing a good play." But the reaction of the play did not deter Ibsen from attacking social idols. In his next play he questioned the notion that the majority are right.

An Enemy of the People presents a town doctor who discovers that the baths, which are the economic heart of a resort community, are polluted. Not unlike John Snow who fought to convince the public that cholera came from polluted wells, Dr. Stockman attempts to convince the town to close the baths to prevent typhoid. When the town refuses, Stockman becomes the individual against society, much like Nora and Mrs. Alving.

Naturalism

Along with Ibsen and the development of realism, a parallel movement called Naturalism was taking place. The naturalists believed that all behavior is directly related to heredity and environment. Therefore the more scientific the approach in determining human nature, the better.

Émile Zola (1840-1902) became the chief spokesman for the new school. Zola was convinced that the dramatist scientist was the only hope in the search for the truth. He maintained that "we must look to the future, and the future will have to do with the human problems studied in the framework of reality. We must cast aside fables of every sort, and delve into the living drama of the twofold life of the character and its environment, bereft of every nursery tale, historical trapping, and the usual conventional stupidities."

There is, of course, much more to Zola's theories than can be explained here, but his principal points are: (1) in all things, the conditions of existence are determined in an absolute fashion; (2) an author must be a scientific observer and experimenter, taking all the facts, studying the data, and reproducing environmental circumstances without ever departing from the laws of nature; (3) the naturalistic author examines man's behavior, discovers the causes of the behavior, and ultimately learns to control the conditions of man's existence for the betterment of society.

As a playwright, Zola was not well received. His most famous play, *Thérèse Raquin* (1873), was an adaptation from a novel and marks the first attempt at a naturalistic drama. Other writers were to refine the style and bring it to its peak. Henri Becque (1837-1899) is probably the most famous of the French naturalistic writers. His *Vultures,* produced by the Comédie Francaise in 1882, has become a naturalistic masterpiece. Another important naturalistic writer was Gerhart Hauptmann, whose play *The Weavers* is based on the revolt of linen weavers in Silesia. Instead of emphasizing the individual, Hauptmann emphasizes the masses and creates a collective hero, making the play a drama of the group. The weavers as a group, stultified horribly by their environment, rise up against forces which they cannot control. The play reaches a startling climax as the weavers seek to destroy the machines which have become a symbol of the fate that has oppressed them.

With plays from both the realistic and naturalistic schools of thought being written, it became necessary to alter the techniques of the theatre itself in order to produce them. The new styles demanded several drastic changes. First, new scenic approaches utilizing more photographic reproduction to deal with the slice-of-life techniques were needed. Second, if the plays attempted to reproduce life as it is, new acting styles were needed. Third, to make all elements unified, an overseer, in the form of the Regisseur or director, was needed. Fourth, new theatres were needed because, as we have seen in England, the old theatres would not always produce the new plays and, in many instances, were too large for plays demanding intimacy.

The Scenic Arts

Realistic scenery had begun to evolve as early as the last of the eighteenth century with Phillippe Jacques DeLouthebourg's experiments in local color. Madame Vestris continued the evolution with the first use of the box set in England around 1832. Charles Kean (1811-1868), more than any other English producer, developed historical research in designing scenery. Beginning with *Macbeth* in 1853, Kean provided his audiences with a printed list of authorities he had consulted in striving for historical accuracy. His productions at the Princess Theatre did much to bring fashionable audiences back to the theatre as well as to refine the gentlemanly melodrama originally begun by Macready and Lytton.

Scenic development continued with the Bancrofts at the Prince of Wales. Mrs. Bancroft, born Marie Wilton (1839-1921), and her actor-husband, Squire Bancroft (1841-1926), were famous for refining the use of the box set and utilizing many small realistic properties.

Henry Irving (1838-1905), the first actor in English history to be knighted, is famous for his development of three-dimensional stage pieces and what has been called pictorial realism.

On the continent, Andre Antoine (1858-1943) concentrated his efforts toward achieving absolute fidelity to real life. A strong believer in the influence of environment on the individual, he designed his interior sets with the idea of absolute realism. He frequently used real properties — wind, running water, etc. — and attempted to unify the entire production to make it seem lifelike.

Antoine's ideas were given expression in America by David Belasco, who created sets with absolute fidelity to the original. In *The Governor's Lady* (1912) Belasco re-created New York's Child's Restaurant on stage, complete with restaurant apparatus and with food stocked daily by Child's for consumption during the performance. For his production of *The Easiest Way* (1909), an entire room from a boardinghouse (wallpaper and all) was transferred to the stage.

Early scenic projection as depicted in *Harper's Weekly,* 1864.

Sarah Siddons (1755-1831), who with her brother, John Philip Kemble, established the "classical" style of acting, so named because it emphasized dignity, grace, and nobleness. From *The Kembles and Their Contemporaries,* 1892.

1815 stage setting at the Royalty Theatre (built in 1787 by John Palmer). Note the proscenium doors at each side of the stage *(below).* Attempts to replace wooden machinery with metal date from 1840 at this theatre. From *Londina Illustrata,* 1825.

Ellen Terry (1847-1928), the first actress to be knighted (1925), gained fame as Henry Irving's leading lady at the Lyceum from 1878-1902. She is shown here as Portia in the *Merchant of Venice*. Miss Terry is the mother of Gordon Craig and grandmother of John Gielgud. From *The Theatre,* 1886.

Naturalism in scenic design, while still used in contemporary theatre, is more frequently utilized in cinema. As a matter of fact, naturalistic design has been the prevalent style until the more recent cinamatographic experimentation. Selective realism, in which enough realistic effects are seen to give the impression of realism, is more prevalent on the stage.

When a stage or theatrical environment is real to life, then the environment requires actors to function realistically within that environment. The illusion of reality in acting is not exclusively a nineteenth century phenomenon. Greek actors were frequently judged and compared as to their realistic styles. In many ways, the conception of realism through the ages is directly related to the kind of scenic environment within which, or in front of which, the actor moved. Hence, idealized scenic background, along with other factors such as theatre size and shape, produced a particular style of acting. When the theatre turned toward realistic literature, a new acting style became necessary. The rise of the director greatly influenced the evolution of acting style. The Saxe-Meiningen group (see Chapter 15) worked out very detailed movement and characterizations. One of the more important groups to be influenced by the Saxe-Meiningen troupe was the Moscow Art Theatre of Russia.

Realistic Acting

On June 21, 1897, Konstantin Stanislavsky (1863-1938) and Vladimir Nemirovich-Danchenko (1858-1943) drafted the general artistic principles and managerial procedures of the Moscow Art Theatre. Among the procedures set down was the stipulation that Nemirovich-Danchenko exercise authority over all literary matters and Stanislavsky over matters of production. Nemirovich-Danchenko had veto rights in the region of content, Stanislavsky in the region of form. As time went by, Stanislavsky became more and more interested in the actor. His theories on acting, particularly those theories concerned with reaching an intense psychological realism, became for some the ideal method of producing the needed acting style. Stanislavsky's influence on the theatre has been monumental, particularly after the Art Theatre's world tour in 1923. Many contemporary American directors acknowledge a debt to Stanislavsky's technique. The Group Theatre, the most distinguished troupe of the 1930's, was founded by several students of the Stanislavsky system, including Lee Strasberg and Harold Clurman. The system was taught in the United States by two Moscow Art Theatre members, Richard Boleslavsky (1889-1937) and Maria Ouspenskaya (1881-1949), who elected to stay in the United States and were co-directors of the American Laboratory Theatre between 1923-1930.

The Actor's Studio, founded by director Elia Kazan, Strasberg, and Cheryl Crawford in 1947, used a variation of the Stanislavsky system. The Actor's Studio utilized exercises derived from Stanislavsky in an effort to free actors from psychological inhibitions and to encourage imagination through emotion memory. Much of the Studio seemed to be

Top left: Konstantin Sergeivich Stanislavsky (nee Alexeyev), Russian actor, director, and teacher, shown on the occasion of the fiftieth anniversary of the Moscow Art Theatre. Courtesy Embassy of the Union of Soviet Socialist Republics.

Bottom left: Vladimir Nemirovich-Danchenko who, along with Stanislavsky, founded the Moscow Art Theatre. Courtesy Embassy of the Union of Soviet Socialist Republics.

Above: The Moscow Art Theatre in 1899. In the center (with hand on lapel) is Stanislavsky; to his left is Nemirovich-Danchenko. In the second row (third from left) is Olga Knipper, Chekov's wife; in the first row (far right) is Ivan Moskrin. Courtesy Embassy of the Union of Soviet Socialist Republics.

Left: Maria Ouspenskaya (1881-1949) toured America in 1923 with the Moscow Art Theatre. She and Richard Boleslavsky remained in America to head the American Laboratory Theatre, where they introduced the Stanislavsky system of acting. Ms. Ouspenskaya is pictured here in her role as Baroness von Obersdorf in Sidney Howard's *Dodsworth* (1934: Starring Walter Huston and Fay Bainter). She was rarely without her monacle hanging from her neck. Courtesy Joseph "Mac" Dixon.

Clara Morris (1846-1925) as Evadne. An American actress, her realistic acting and emotional outbursts gained her the label of "Queen of Spasms." Few actresses have possessed such personal magnetism; it is said she hypnotized her audience. Miss Morris never rehearsed, preferring instead to rely on her instincts and intuition. By 1880, she was billed as "America's greatest living actress." From *Dramatic Portrait Gallery*, 1880.

geared toward encounter sessions and self-understanding by the actor.

The Actor's Studio was often criticized for fostering the negligence of theatrical techniques and for encouraging self-indulgence of its actors. The success of Marlon Brando (1924-   ) as Stanley Kowalski, under the direction of Kazan, in Tennessee Williams' *A Streetcar Named Desire* (1947) placed the work of the Studio in the public light. Brando's lifestyle and the novelty of a serious actor mumbling lines created, fairly or unfairly, an image of the school. Nevertheless, some of the most famous actors were produced by Strasberg's techniques. James Dean, Marilyn Monroe, Lee J. Cobb, Paul Newman, Geraldine Page, Rip Torn, Jane Fonda, and Susan Strasberg were all graduates. Many actors who attempted to imitate the new style by mumbling lines and inventing endless amounts of inconsequential stage business, in spite of Strasberg's objections, were thought to be perpetrators of the Studio style. Strasberg's techniques, real or imagined, generated endless debates as to whether they were actually Stanislavsky's methods. An interesting paradox is that no one actually knows what Stanislavsky's method was, probably not even Stanislavsky. In truth his "system" was the result of years of evolution and testing and was compartmentalized by later writers.

The New Theatres

Because of the theatrical monopoly in England, the legitimate houses had grown tremendously in size. Both Covent Garden and Drury Lane could seat as many as 8,000 people. Playing without sound amplification and with some of the audience a considerable distance from the stage, an exaggerated acting style was necessary. Moreover, actors from the old school were not overly anxious to sanction legitimate drama in a small theatre. Charles Kemble (1775-1854), an actor-manager of some fame, commented in 1833 that "regular drama can only be presented in theatres of certain dimensions. I assure you a very small theatre is destructive of good acting; instead of being favorable to an actor, it brings him so near the audience that he cannot abstract his mind from the audience." Kemble maintained that anyone could hear in a major theatre. The fault, he commented, was with the audience, not the theatre.

Edmund Kean (1787-1833), also an actor of great popularity, agreed with Kemble that anyone could see from any part of the theatre. "I think the intellect becomes confined by the size of the theatre," he states. "The larger the stage the better the actor, and the less observable are his faults."

The Theatre Regulations Act of 1843 officially ended the theatrical monopoly and with it the large theatres. Smaller theatres, such as the Prince of Wales and the Princess, moved toward ensemble acting. These theatres were subject to theatrical censorships and would not or could not perform the new drama, even though the new theatrical techniques and scenery were utilized in the performance of the old. This phenomenon was also

Drury Lane Theatre, built in 1794 by Henry Holland. From *Londina Illustrata,* 1825.

true in other countries. Since the new drama was considered offensively immoral, theatres attempting productions were frequently denied licenses to perform. In an effort to provide a space for these new dramas, the independent theatre movement was formed.

In Paris on March 30, 1887, André Antoine founded the first of the independent theatres called the Théâtre Libre, or Free Theatre, after Victor Hugo's epigraph *A Theatre Set Free.* He began his first full season in the fall of 1887 and sold his tickets by subscription only. This in effect made the theatre a private organization open only to members, a device which was to be used throughout Europe to allow banned plays to be performed. Antoine left the Théâtre Libre in 1894 an artistic, if not financial, success.

Antoine's influence on the theatre of his time, and indirectly on the theatre of our time, is immense. First, in keeping with the tradition of the fair theatres, he demonstrated a method by which producers of new plays could bypass the censor through playing only for private audiences. Second, he showed how a theatre, playing for audiences too small to interest commercial producers, could be successful. When others of a similar mind saw the results of his experiment, additional independent theatres were formed.

Covent Garden prior to its opening in 1794. Below is the entrance from the piazza to the theatre. From *Londina Illustrata,* 1825.

Edmund Kean as Gloucester in *Richard III,* Act I, Scene 2. Kean was a major influence on the "star" system. From *The Kembles and Their Contemporaries,* 1890.

A collection of theatre tickets used at public theatres of the seventeenth and eighteenth centuries. From *Londina Illustrata,* 1825.

The Freie Bühne

In Germany Otto Brahm (1856-1912) became the first president of the Freie Bühne (Free Theatre) founded in Berlin in 1889. To avoid censorship, the Freie Bühne was organized along the lines of the Theâtre Libre as a private institution. Among its initial works were *Ghosts,* Tolstoy's *The Power of Darkness,* Zola's *Thérèse Raquin,* Becques's *The Vultures,* and several of Strindberg's plays including *The Father.*

Perhaps the most significant discovery by the Freie Bühne was the playwright Gerhart Hauptmann (1862-1946), one of Germany's most respected writers and recipient of the Nobel Prize in literature in 1912. The production of *Before Sunrise* by the Freie Bühne in 1889 is considered by many scholars to mark the birth of modern German drama. Hauptmann's most famous play, *The Weavers,* was first performed by a revived Freie Bühne in 1892, which had discontinued programming in 1891.

The Independent Theatre

On March 13, 1891, J.T. Grein (1862-1935), a Dutchman residing in London, created a group called The Independent Theatre. Their first production was *Ghosts,* which had been banned by the censor. A portion of Clement Scott's review of that performance was quoted earlier. The Independent Theatre became the second English group to produce plays by means of private subscriptions. The Shelley Society had produced *The Cenci* by that means in 1887. Grein primarily produced continental dramas because, for obvious reasons, English playwrights were not writing controversial plays in the new style. Grein appealed to a young Irish critic and novelist to fill the void. In 1892 at the urging of Grein, George Bernard Shaw (1856-1950) began his long career as a playwright, with the Independent Theatre's production of *Widower's House.*

Like the Freie Bühne, the Independent Theatre produced one of the greatest playwrights of all time and, for that reason alone, deserves a place in history. More than that, however, it provided an outlet for English playwrights for a number of years. The Independent Theatre was replaced by the Incorporated Stage Society in 1899. The Stage Society, by providing an outlet for young English writers whose works might otherwise have been emasculated by the stage censor, also provided a continuing service to the theatre.

Realism both in scenic technique and dramatic literature had established itself in the theatre by the turn of the century. It remains one of the most popular styles of the twentieth century on both stage and television. Scenic naturalism has become, more or less, a province of the cinema and has been, until recent times, the prevalent style. But realism was not the only style to come out of the latter part of the nineteenth century. Several new styles were to come forward that are equally important today.

Selected Readings

Jackson, Holbrook. *The Eighteen Nineties,* New York, 1913.

Meyer, Michael. *Ibsen.* New York, 1971.

Miller, Anne Irene. *The Independent Theatre in Europe.* New York. 1931.

Valency, Maurice. *The Flower and the Castle.* New York, 1963.

Vocabulary

1. Auguste Comte	oh GOO:ST KOHNT
2. Eugène Scribe	yoo ZHAYN SKREEB
3. Alexandre Dumas fils	ah leg ZAHND ruh doo: MAH fees
4. Émile Augier	ay MEEL oh ZHYAY
5. Victorien Sardou	sahr DOO
6. Henrik Ibsen	HEN rik IB suhn
7. Björnstjerne Björnson	BYAWRN styern BYAWRN suhn
8. J.T. Grein	GREEN
9. Émile Zola	ay MEEL ZOH luh
10. Henri Becque	ahn REE BEK
11. André Antoine	ahn DRAY ahn TWUHN
12. Konstantin Stanislavsky	kawn stahn TEEN sta ni SLAHF skee
13. Vladimir Nemirovich-Danchenko	VLA duh mir nuh MEER uh veech dahn CHEN koh
14. Maria Ouspenskaya	MAHR ee uh oo spen SKIGH uh
15. Elia Kazan	EE li uh kuh ZAHN
16. Théâtre Libre	tay AHT ruh LEEB ruh
17. Freie Bühne	FRIGH uh BYOO nuh
18. Richard Boleslavsky	boh luh SLAHF skee

CHAPTER TWELVE

Idealism and the Spirit: The Antirealists

The realistic analysis of man and his society had some interesting side effects toward the close of the nineteenth century. The validity of Judeo-Christian theological concepts had been seriously challenged by the implied atheism of the Darwinian theory. Realistic drama was in search of logical truths arrived at through the scrutiny of scientific observation. Therefore, objective proof obtained by the use of the five senses tended to overlook, ignore, or deny the existence of a spiritual realm. At first the new style received little negative criticism, and it quickly captured the imagination of the theatrical world. But slowly, almost analogous to the Biblical warning that "man cannot live by bread alone," a group of detractors rejecting the cold scientific view of human destiny was formed. While not yet ready to return to orthodox religion for answers, the detractors felt that scientific realism had left a vacuum in life by denying transcendental alternatives. In short, adjusting to a spiritualless world was difficult. The antirealists began to explore ways to fill the vacuum. Many studied the occult or looked to those areas seemingly beyond the comprehension of man. Still others probed deep into the psychological nature of the human mind in an effort to find new truths. For some the theatre became the sounding board of a new religion. The latter part of the nineteenth century seemed to beget a series of these new styles, the first of which were called symbolists.

Symbolists

The inspiration for the symbolist movement had come in part from the American poet Edgar Allen Poe (1809-49). Poe's poetry and literature explore the unknown and the mysterious. His works are filled with symbolic overtones which create emotional impressions. Poe's use of color at times is mind-boggling, an almost psychedelic beauty which bombards the senses and creates a feeling of horrified fascination.

Opposite: Bertolt Brecht (1898-1956). Courtesy German Information Center.

Richard Wagner

Poe's ideas were further reinforced by the antirealistic experiments of operatic composer Richard Wagner (1813-1883). Wagner, born in Leipzig in 1813, at first wanted to be a poet, but he became fascinated with music and studied composition. Wagner was unhappy with the growing trend toward realism in the theatre and he attempted to create alternatives in theatre and drama. Wagner's experiments in both were significant. His opera house at Bayreuth, which opened in 1876, inspired theatre design for many years. The theatre, designed to create a "mystic chasm" between the real world and ideal, featured, among other things, a hidden orchestra pit, a steam curtain to mask scene changes, and a double proscenium arch. Wagner felt that real truths could be found only in the ideal and that the dramatist should be a mythmaker. He argued that the dramatist's works are frequently violated by the actor's interpretation. Thus the accurateness of interpretation demanded of great tragedy is only possible with the help of music. To Wagner, music would allow the dramatist to control every nuance of sound that the actor makes, and thus would assure a work of art performed as it was intended by the dramatist-composer.

He states: "What was not practically possible for Shakespeare — to be himself the actor of each one of his roles — is practicable for the musical composer, and this with great definiteness — since he speaks to us directly through each one of the musicians who execute his works." Wagner felt that the author-composer should work to fashion all aspects of the drama into a unified work of art *(Gesamtkuntswerk).* His ideas are best conceptualized in his great tetralogy, *Der Ring des Nibelungen,* and in *Tristan and Isolde.*

Oscar Wilde (1856-1900), a leading member of the "Art-for-Art's-Sake" movement in England — a movement similar to the French Symbolist and German Neoromantic movements. As a dramatist, Wilde is best remembered for *The Importance of Being Earnest* (1895), *Salomé* (1893), and *Lady Windermere's Fan*. From Dircks' *Players of Today*, 1892.

Friedrich Nietzsche

The theoretical concepts of Wagner were further reinforced by the philosophical ideas of Friedrich Nietzsche (1844-1900). Born in Rocker, Germany, Nietzsche studied at the Universities of Bonn and Leipzig. He met Wagner in 1870 and became engrossed in the composer's operas. Nietzsche's first important work, *The Birth of Tragedy from the Spirit of Music* (1872), was an attempt to justify the theory behind Wagner's works. While Nietzsche later had reservations about his own treatise and certainly about Wagner, he wrote to his readers: "I beg to inform of my conviction that art is the highest human task, the true metaphysical activity such as it is under by the man [Wagner] to whom, as my great precursor on that path, I now dedicate these pages."

Nietzsche reinforces the idea that ritual and myth are at the very heart of the dramatic phenomenon, not only through his historical observation that tragedy began as ritual linked to the cult or myth of Dionysus, but also in his choice of terms. He writes:

> I have borrowed my adjectives from the Greeks who developed their mystical doctrines of art through plausible embodiments, not through purely conceptual means. It is by those two art-sponsoring deities, Apollo and Dionysus, that we are made to recognize the tremendous split, as regards both origins and objectives, between the plastic, Apollonian arts and the non-visual art of music inspired by Dionysus.

Nietzsche viewed the Apollonian as representing the dream world of clarity and order and the Dionysian as intoxication or irrational disorder. The Apollonian world of the dream where "nothing seems indifferent or redundant" tends to protect man against the terrors of reality. According to Nietzsche, it was the Apollonian spirit that demanded the creation of Olympian Gods as a way of giving meaning to human life. The Apollonian spirit thus provides the necessary illusions to fuel the human spirit. The myth of perfection which centers on man's superiority and individuality over nature is fostered by the Apollonian. The Dionysian spirit, on the other hand, fills the human mind with the intoxicating joy of primal nature.

> Man now expresses himself through song and dance as the member of a higher community; he has forgotten how to walk, how to speak, and is on the brink of taking wings as he dances. Each of his gestures betokens enchantment; through him sounds a supernatural power, the same power which makes the animals speak and the earth render up milk and honey. He feels himself to be godlike and strides with the same elation and ecstasy as the gods he has seen in his dreams.

The almost orgiastic Dionysian spirit, then, shatters all illusion of man's superiority, strips him of his individuality, and makes him one with nature.

Thus, according to Nietzsche, tragedy arose from the conflict between the desire for clarity and order and the wild primitive urge toward disorder. Tragedy exists as a "symbolizing of Dionysian wisdom by means of the expedients of Apollonian art." Tragedy, as Nietzsche saw it, reaffirms the value of life itself through the death of an individual because life will go on seeking perfection in any case. In a sense, the spirit of *all* men is reaffirmed through the death of *a* man. Nietzsche believed that in order to have great art, a balance between the Dionysian and Apollonian elements was necessary. He deplored the state of drama during his own time because he felt that realism (science and the Darwinian concept of progress) had blocked out the Dionysian vision.

The idea of a Dionysian vision manifested itself in the arts in many ways. For the symbolist school, it was art for art's sake. They postulated that art must be an expression of the inner voices if it is to be an expression of truth. In many ways, symbolism was similar to romanticism in its rejection of the concept that ultimate truth may be found only in rational thought processes. For that reason, the movement is sometimes called neoromanticism. But the symbolist believed that truth can be grasped only by intuition. Since ultimate truth cannot be understood logically, it cannot be expressed in logical language. Therefore, ultimate truth can only be suggested through symbols which evoke in the minds of the audience those feelings which are akin to the dramatist's intuition of reality. The dramatist, through a series of carefully selected symbols, attempts to intoxicate the audience by linking them with primal forces, or at least his intuition of those forces. Actually, the audience may reach a state of grace or ecstasy through the feelings evoked through the suggestiveness of the symbols. The symbolists argued that it was not necessary for drama to teach, because beauty was an end in itself.

Theophile Gautier

Theophile Gautier (1811-72) maintained that art and beauty need not exist for practical reasons, they exist for their own sake. He perhaps expresses it best when he writes:

> Nothing that is beautiful is indispensable to life. One could suppress the flowers, and the world would not suffer materially from it; and yet who would be willing for there to be no more flowers? I should sooner give up potatoes than roses, and I suspect that there is not more than one utiltarian in the world capable of digging up a tulip bed to plant cabbages.
>
> Of what use is the beauty of women? Provided that a woman is medically normal, in a condition to receive a man and to have children, she will always be good enough for the economists.
>
> What good is music? Or painting? Who would be so mad as to prefer Mozart to a republican politician like M. Carel, or Michaelangelo to the inventor of white mustard?
>
> There is nothing truly beautiful except what is no use; everything useful is ugly, for it is the expression of some need, and man's needs are ignoble and disgusting, like his poor, infirm nature. The most useful spot in the house is the bathroom.

The most important dramatists of the symbolist school were Maurice Maeterlinck (1862-1949) and Paul Claudel (1868-1955). The dramatist who popularized symbolist techniques was Edmond Rostand (1868-1918).

Maurice Maeterlinck

Maeterlinck was a Belgian-born lawyer who became influenced by the symbolist movement while living in Paris. Maeterlinck became a spokesman for the group during the nineties. He wrote three plays that became indicative of the symbolic ideals: *The Intruder* (1890), *The Blind* (1890), and *Pelléas and Mélisande* (1892). Maeterlinck maintained that the dramatist "must show us how, under what form and conditions, according to what laws, to what end, the superior powers act upon our destinies, the unintelligible influences, the infinite principles of which he as a poet is convinced the universe is full."

Pelléas and Mélisande is perhaps the most famous of Maeterlinck's symbolic plays. It is delicate in its rendering, weaving loosely-defined symbols throughout. Water, light, and darkness are recurring motifs throughout the play.

Other Symbolists

Paul Claudel (1868-1955) became perhaps the strongest of the symbolic dramatists after Maeterlinck. His three most famous plays are *The Tidings Brought to Mary, Break of Noon,* and *The Satin Slipper*. Claudel's plays are difficult to produce but have enjoyed a recent record of production in the post-World War II theatre.

Edmond Rostand remains famous for his *Cyrano de Bergerac* (1897). *Cyrano* was written as a vehicle for the actor Constant Coquelin (1841-1909). Since its original production, actors have coveted the role and the play is still frequently done. Rostand's *The Romancers,* a delightful satire on young love, is the story upon which the delightful musical, *The Fantasticks,* is based.

The symbolists found a champion in Aurelien-Marie Lugné-Poe (1869-1940). Lugné-Poe had worked with Antoine but quickly became intrigued with the symbolists. On May 17, 1893, Paul Fort (1872-1960) and Lugné-Poe opened the Théâtre de l'Oeuvre with the premier production of *Pélleas and Mélisande*.

No properties or furniture were used and the stage was semi-dark with a gauze curtain hung between the actors and the audience. The design created an air of mystery which astonished the spectators. The actors, costumed in vaguely medieval style, chanted their lines and, according to some critics, behaved like sleepwalkers. Lugné-Poe followed the motto of "the word creates the decor" and simplified his scenery a great deal. He used settings by such artists as Toulouse-Lautrec, Denis, Vuillard, Bonnard, and Odilon Redon among others. The Théâtre de l'Oeuvre was to become to the antirealist what Théâtre Libre had become to the realist.

Sigmund Freud

The concept of the unknown, of powerful forces existing outside the five senses, was given an odd twist by the father of psychoanalysis, Sigmund Freud (1856-1939). Freud was to have enormous influence on the drama during the twentieth century. He postulated that there were three aspects of personality: the id, the ego, and the superego. The id, which may be loosely defined as the primitive uncensored impulse, is roughly analogous to Nietzsche's Dionysiac spirit. The ego and the superego were similar to the Apollonian in that they represent the ordered element of character. Freud's ideas have affected both the realistic and the nonrealistic theatre. The nonrealistic drama was deeply influenced by his emphasis upon the subconscious. The idea that dreams might well be expressions from the id, and therefore inner truths, was fascinating to the dramatist. Actually, Freud considered the unconscious as the "real psyche." He argues: "Its inner nature is just as imperfectly reported to us through the data of consciousness as is the external reported to us through indications of our sensory organs." Freud found that through dreams the id finds expression. Since neurosis occurs when there is imbalance between the conscious and the unconscious, Freud found it necessary to identify repressions or drives locked into the id. The analysis of dreams became a diagnostic tool in bringing repressed desires and memories to the surface. He observed that fears and desires were rarely expressed logically. They were expressed in terms of symbols and were extremely difficult to interpret. A dream of flying, for example, is sometimes interpreted as indications of sexual frustration.

The whole concept of repression of the id by the superego is projected by Freud into society itself. He maintained that people fear the licentiousness of nature and its psychic components; culture tends to defend us against nature. A community is in itself a safeguard against individual license. Some societies, such as Victorian England, are constructed on the renunciation of instinctual gratification. All of this suggests difficulty in identifying the nature of moral truth since values seem to be dependent on public opinion. The question of universal morality has become a major theme in some of our more recent drama.

August Strindberg

The idea of the dream world as an expression of our inner selves was perhaps best expressed by August Strindberg (1849-1912), a Scandinavian who started his career as a naturalist. Strindberg had previously written a series of explosive realistic and naturalistic plays, such as *The Father* (1887) and *Miss Julie* (1888). He began to study the philosophies of Schopenhauer and Nietzsche and in 1902 he wrote *The Dream Play,* which was to become the most influential of early antirealistic plays. In the preface he states: "The author has tried to imitate the disconnected but seemingly logical form of a dream. Anything may happen; everything is possible and probable. Time and space do not exist. On an insignificant background of reality, imagination designs and embroiders novel patterns, free fancies, absurdities and improvisations. The characters split, double, multiply, vanish, solidify, blur, classify. But one consciousness reigns above them all — that of the dreamer; and before it there are no secrets, no incongruities, no scruples, no laws."

The play deals with our incapability of resolving the conflict between the spirit and the flesh. It has an ethereal beauty about it and has recently become extremely popular in the United States. The central character is probably Strindberg himself, or at least a revelation of his unconscious mind. Certainly Strindberg's sense of the contradictions of life are readily apparent. The Dreamer says:

> Why are we born like animals?
> We who stem from God and man,
> Whose souls are longing to be clothed
> In other than this blood and filth.
> Must God's image cut its truth?

August Strindberg, shown in his study about 1900. This Swedish writer's influence on modern drama is second only to that of Ibsen. Courtesy Swedish Information Service.

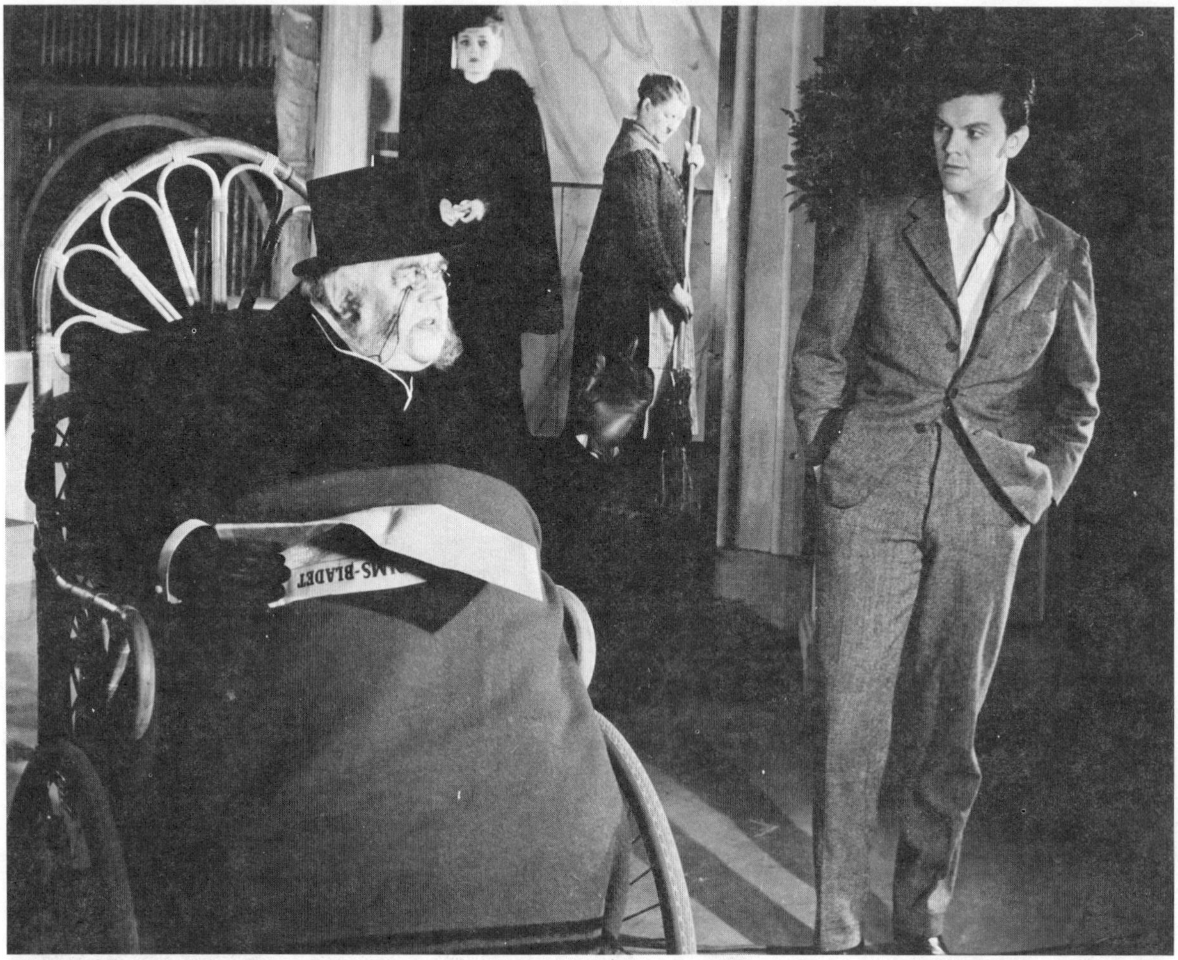

Above: A scene from *The Ghost Sonata* by Strindberg, directed by Ingmar Bergman, at the Malmo State Theatre in 1954. Courtesy Swedish Information Service.

Right: Strindberg's *The Road to Damascus,* Part I, Act III, Scene 2, produced in 1900 at the Royal Theatre of Stockholm. Courtesy Swedish Information Service.

Robert Lansing as the father in Strindberg's *The Father,* in the Roundabout Theatre Company's 1973 production. Courtesy Swedish Information Service.

Strindberg's vision of man as a tortured soul and his techniques of externalizing psychological concepts were to influence still another group of antirealists who called themselves expressionists. Strindberg's ideas later adapted by the expressionists were: (1) the destruction of the limitations of time, place and logical sequence by adopting the viewpoint of the dream; (2) flowing one event into another without any logical explanation; (3) characters who are dissolved and transformed into other characters; (4) blending time and place together.

Expressionism

Most scholars of the theatre credit the expressionistic movement with being the most important revolt against realism in the early twentieth century. The movement started in Germany around 1910, first with the visual arts and later with the theatre. Walter Hasenclever's *The Son,* produced in 1914, was the first Expressionist drama. Expressionism, as a term, denotes the intent of its followers to express a personal view of reality. The expressionist was not concerned with external reality. Everything portrayed on stage is placed within the context of the dramatist. Usually the central character becomes the spokesman for the playwright and the play is seen through his eyes. The audience views the play literally through the mind of the central character. The way in which the character sees an object may not be what one normally calls realistic at all. The expressionist frequently distorted the normal appearance of objects. At times actors were called upon to move in a rigid mechanical way, speaking lines with flat monotones. Any device was used to convey the playwright's viewpoint to the audience. In Georg Kaiser's (1878-1945) *From Morn to Midnight,* an expressionistic classic, the central character returns to his home, which is loveless, lifeless, and mundane. In a recent production of this play, the scene was played in the following manner. On a second level above the actors, several robed figures holding puppet strings manipulated the characters, who represented the cashier's family. Each actor moved and delivered lines as if he or she were merely a marionette. This, of course, portrayed for the audience how the cashier viewed his own family.

The Activists

The expressionistic school was divided into two basic groups — the activists and the mystics. The Mystic school was primarily concerned with expressing the varying human viewpoints and feelings. The activists, on the other hand, set out to save the world. The activists saw man as essentially noble and capable of greatness. But the industrialist society has reduced him to a machine, and deactivated his soul. The activists argued that realism tends to reinforce the idea that man is a machine because it focuses on his outward state alone, his external reality, without attempting to study his soul. The expressionist argued that if man and the world are to be saved, we must understand man's soul. We must view society from the perspective of the soul instead of interpreting the soul from the perspective of a corrupt society. In many ways, the expressionists were the most messianic theatre movement of the period. For that reason, much of their drama was concerned with the salvation of man and his world and is message-centered. Frequently, the central characters are Christ-like figures searching for truth, only to be martyred by a materialistic society. The Cashier, the central figure in *From Morn to Midnight,* dies with his arms outstretched in front of a cross, crying *Ecce Homo!* Usually the plot reduces character to basic stereotypes such as cashier, mother, daughter. All aspects of the production are geared to emphasizing the major thesis of the play. If, for example, the play strives to picture the dehumanization of man, every aspect of the play would be distorted to show dehumanization. The opening scene of *From Morn to Midnight,* for example, shows the cashier in his booth. In this case, the booth may be distorted to resemble an animal cage, or even a prison. Frequently realistic scenes may fade into dream visions or fantasy so that the whole production seems almost like a nightmare.

The expressionistic movement, with its hope for reformation of society, reacted strongly to the disaster of World War I. The very idea of a world at war was an anathema to the group, although some supported their country and even died in battle. During the latter half of 1914, many of the expressionists met in Weimar to oppose the war. Some moved to Switzerland to avoid being involved. The group became more disillusioned after the war during the peace settlement, when it became obvious that the terms of agreement would probably be a factor in sparking another war. For some, the belief in the nobility of man and his potential for greatness turned to a belief in the inevitability of his destruction.

The war with its own particular horrors, such as poison gas and the aerial bomb, shocked the world. In some ways, whatever innocence that man had left, was gone. The damage of the first modern war left indelible scars on the face of the ideal man, and into the vacuum rushed a plethora of new movements, each groping for new answers to horrifying questions.

Futurists

One of the earliest influential movements was the Futurist movement, actually founded before the war by Italian poet Filippo Tommaso Marinetti (1876-1944). Marinetti found redemption in the acceptance of the future and the rejection of the past. He extolled the creations of the machine age, citing the racing motor car as the modern equivalent of the winged horse of ancient mythology. He equated libraries and museums (a term he used also to describe the theatre) with the old and dying and not with the young whom he categorized as forty or under. "When we are forty," he said, "let others, younger and more valiant, throw us into the wastebasket like useless manuscripts." The Futurists were a highly aggressive group concerned with the creation of a masculine fighter driving forth the creation of a new society based on the future. "We wish to glorify War — the only health giver of the world — militarism, patriotism, the destructive arm of the anarchist, the beautiful ideas that kill, the contempt for women."

Based on the style of production found in the music halls of Europe, the Futurists called for a more vital theatre. They liked the idea of performers mingling with the audience and the use of modern technology to create multimedia productions. They were essentially antiliterary and even antiactor, creating actor lights and even actor gases.

Dada

The second movement to come out of the postwar psychosis was Dadaism. The name Dada was coined for its meaninglessness by a group of artists residing in Zurich in 1916. Its leader was the German poet Hugo Ball (1886-1927).

Reacting to the madness of war, the Dadaists set out to create a satisfying world based on discord and chaos, the Dionysian vision. Since the logical world of science had produced the logical war, truth would have to be found in the absence of order, in complete freedom. Since values of the past were considered destructive by the Dadaists, society must give the individual freedom to be spontaneous in the future. The movement produced antiartistic paintings and poems, illogical works, rubbish collages and noise music. The first theatrical presentations were done on March 20, 1920, at the Théâtre de l'Oeuvre. The performances included *The First Celestial Adventure of Mr. Fire-Extinguisher* by Tristan Tzara (1896-1963) and *The Silent Canary* by George Ribemont-Dessaignes. *The Silent Canary* deals with a megalomaniac who thinks himself to be Gounod and who teaches a canary to sing *Faust,* silently. Among the entr'actes was a "Cannibal Manifesto" read entirely in the dark. The performance concluded with the actors and the audience exchanging mutual insults.

Another performance by the group in May featured *You Would Have Forgotten Me* by André Breton and Philippe Soupault and a musical piece by Tzara called *Vaseline Symphonique,* which provoked the audience to lob eggs at the performers.

Surrealism

Probably the best-known of the minor movements was surrealism, which appeared shortly after the death of Dadaism in 1924. The leader of the new group was André Breton (1896-1966). Breton was highly interested in the works of Freud, particularly after meeting him in 1921. Breton was primarily interested in the truths that may be found in the subconscious. For that reason, he attempted to neutralize the censorship of the superego and the logic of the ego. In the visual arts, Salvador Dali's paintings are perhaps the best known examples of the style. Dali paints everyday objects, usually in a dream background, intertwining the familiar with the strange, thus visualizing the metaphor.

Guillaume Apollinaire (1880-1918) was the first to use the term *surrealism* to describe his own play *The Breasts of Tiresias* (1917). He also used the term to describe *Parade,* presented by the Ballet Russe in 1917. The ballet was written by Jean Cocteau (1892-1963), who was to write the most famous of the surrealistic plays, *Orpheus,* in 1926, composed by Erik Satie, designed by Pablo Picasso, and choreographed by Leonid Massine.

Antonin Artaud

Perhaps the definitive statement of the postwar antirealists was in the writing of Antonin Artaud (1896-1948). Certainly, his influence on the contemporary theatre is prominent. Artaud's approach to the theatre was original and yet influenced by the movements before him. His basic theory was that the theatre in the Western World was bankrupt in that it limited its concern to a narrow range of the human experience. It did not probe into the inner recesses of the mind where the real problem of existence lies. The present theatre, he argued, was a preserver of a culture that lulls the mind. He proposed a theatre which will not "numb us with ideas for the intellect but stirs us to feeling by stirring up pain." Artaud called his new theatre the theatre of cruelty. He believed that spectacle would act as a catharsis, almost a religious experience, removing violence from the spectator. He writes:

> The theatre will never find itself again — i.e., constitute a means of true illusion — except by furnishing the spectator with the truthful precipitates of his dreams, in which his taste for crime, his erotic obsessions, his savagery, his charisma, his utopian sense of life and matter, even his cannibalism, pour out, on a level not counterfeit and illusory, but interior.

Artaud proposed to place the spectator in the center of the theatrical space surrounded by the action, a complete break from traditional theatre. For Artaud, theatre was the pulse of civilization itself. He felt that one of the signs of the decay of Western civilization was that it had enshrined such lazy, unserviceable notions as art. "Art," he says, "is the expression of one man, while culture is the expression of all." Artaud wanted the theatre to investigate myth and ritual but not the old myths. New myths must be created, according to Artaud, out of severe disaster like the plague. For him, the beauty of the plague is its destruction of repressive social forms. He writes: "Order collapses, authority evaporates, anarchy prevails and man gives vent to all the disordered impulses which lie buried in his soul." Artaud wanted to hammer the conscious mind until it gave up its secrets. The truth, he felt, lay in the subconscious mind and must be explored. He was not concerned with physical cruelty, but moral cruelty which "goes to the extremity of instinct and forces the actor to plunge right to the roots of his being so that he leaves the stage exhausted."

Artaud felt that poetry and language had become opiates in the Western theatre and he proposed to borrow from the Oriental theatre. He wanted the drama taken out of theatres and placed into barns, factories, or even old airplane hangars. The theatre, he says, which is in *no thing,* but makes use of everything — gestures, sounds, words, screams, light, darkness — rediscovers itself at precisely the point where the mind requires a language to express its manifestations. He employed electronic devices along with what he called nonverbal sounds. In this way, he sought to break down the audience and force them to cleanse themselves through catharsis down to their inner reaches where the true person exists. Then and only then, he felt, can man exist in harmony with others.

Thus the antirealistic theatre had established itself well into the twentieth century. Contributions and ideas of the anitrealists were quite substantial. First, they all basically revolted against the concept that science will be the savior of mankind. Second, they agreed that ultimate truth cannot be found in external reality. Third, most felt that modern society tended to dehumanize man and was wasting away his basic goodness. Fourth, there was a general movement to myth and ritual as a means of studying true human feelings and desires. Fifth, the subconscious provided the key to truth and must be penetrated against the opposition of the logical mind. Sixth, the language in the theatre must be altered in order to reach the subconscious. Seventh, they all agreed that new theatrical techniques which would shatter the world of the familiar must be utilized. Eighth, their ultimate goal was the destruction of repressive social and mental controls.

To what extent these ideas have changed our theatre will be discussed later; to what extent these ideas have changed our lives, only the future can tell.

Along with the development of realism and the revolt of the antirealists, still another important movement, contributed to the theatre as we know it. This movement is what some theatre historians call the "theatre of social action."

Vsevelod Meyerhold

Vsevelod Meyerhold (1874-1942) began his career as an actor with Stanislavsky's company in 1905. He left the Art Theatre because he disagreed with the realistic style. By a quirk of fate, Meyerhold became the nominal head of Russian Theatre after the revolution. His work did not please the communist authorities, however, and in February, 1921, he resigned his position as head of the theatre section of the party. He was then appointed director of the State Higher Theatrical

Meyerhold State theatre, Moscow, during V. Mayakovsky's *The Hot Bath,* Act VI, produced by Meyerhold, 1930. Courtesy Novosti from Sovfoto.

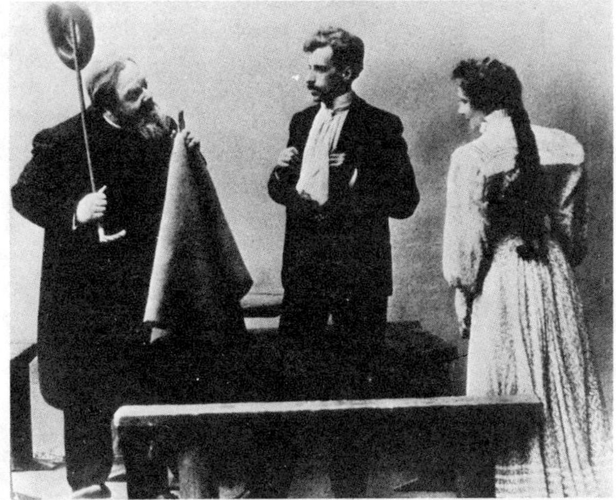

The Seagull by Chekhov, staged by the Moscow Art Theatre. Left to right: Luzhsky as Dorn, V. Meyerhold as Treplev, and Roksamova as Nina. Courtesy Novosti from Sovfoto.

Workshop, which trained young directors. He used this opportunity to engage in a series of experiments dealing with biomechanics, theatricalism, and constructivism. Meyerhold's basic premise was that in order to serve the socialist revolution best, he must also create a revolution in the theatre. Since realism was the basic philosophy of the revolution, he proposed to treat realistic social problems with completely nonrealistic means. Meyerhold believed that the stage, the actor, the scenery, the lighting, the costumes, and even the script, was a single complexity to be used by the director in interpreting society. To achieve his controlled machine, Meyerhold devised a system which he called biomechanics to train his actors.

Biomechanics was simply a method by which the actors trained their bodies so that they might respond as machines to anything demanded of them. They trained in gymnastics, dancing, fencing, and other physical disciplines which eliminated the superfluous from movement. This method of training allowed the actor to maintain the theatricalism necessary to Meyerhold's concept.

Theatricalism was a method by which the audience was made aware that it was in a theatre and that it was seeing a theatrical representation. Trapezes were hung from above, the curtain was removed, and lights were placed in full view. Since the audience was never allowed to confuse the action onstage with real life, Meyerhold hoped to focus their individual attention on isolating social problems. His hope was that the audience would leave the theatre with the goal of solving problems existing in the outside world.

While he did not originate the art form, Meyerhold's theatrical work has come to be associated with the term *constructivism*. He felt that the stage setting should be practical rather than decorative, and he stripped the stage of any identifiable decor and used platforms, intersecting planes, and other structural devices. In effect the stage was a machine for the director to run. Meyerhold's legacy may well be the way in which he inspired others. Sergei Eisenstein (1898-1948)

Second scene, "Near the gate of Velikograd," from *Les Soirs,* as staged by Meyerhold and Bebutov. The play, written by Emile Verhaeren, premiered November 7, 1920. Courtesy Novosti from Sovfoto.

utilized Meyerhold's ideas by bringing biomechanics, among other techniques, to the People's Theatre in Moscow when he became director in 1922. Eisenstein first used the concept of montage with this group when he juxtapositioned unrelated scenes to point up contrasts. He later used this technique during his career as a filmmaker.

Bertolt Brecht

Meyerhold's concept of theatre was further refined in Germany through the works of Bertolt Brecht (1898-1956). Brecht agreed with the expressionists that the then contemporary theatre was corrupt in that it had reduced the spectator to passivity. Brecht created a new theatre, which he called *epic* to distinguish it from the past. Brecht used three key terms to describe the dramatic change he wished to bring about: historification, defamiliarization or alienation, and epic.

Brecht wanted to achieve what he called *entfrendung,* which can be translated as alienation, a word which has become synonymous with Brechtian theory. Actually Brecht more often used the coined term *verfremdungseffekt,* which could mean defamiliarization or, as it is sometimes translated, to make strange. Historification is a part of the defamiliarization process. Brecht argued that the theatre should attempt to remove past events from the present. For example, in many of the Hollywood historical movies, history was viewed from the present. Characters were evaluated on the basis of today's values, morals, and in many cases, hair styles. If actors did not act in a manner acceptable to contemporary society, they did not succeed. Brecht felt that this kind of viewpoint perpetuated the myth that values have not changed and, therefore, it is useless to advocate change.

Defamiliarization was also a process of awakening the audience from its past stupor. Brecht wanted to make the audience aware that it was in the theatre. Lights and other technical devices were in plain view and, in some instances, were utilized to make a point to the audience. Songs, filmed sequences and narrative passages kept the audience from becoming too empathically involved in the story. Brecht wanted his audiences to watch productively. Each element of the production served as a focusing device, forcing the audience to be intellectually aware of what was said. Each independent aspect of the play contributed to the overall effect, which aimed to awake the spectator to his sense of social responsibility. Brecht wanted his audience to state: "If I had lived this, I would have done something."

To differentiate his theatre from the old, he used the term *epic*, because he felt that his theatre resembled the epic poem more than it did the traditional stage. Brecht's drama moved over a great span of time just as the epic poem, bridging gaps with narrative sequences. Brecht made the following comparison of his theatre with what he called the dramatic form:

Vsevolod Meyerhold in 1922-23. Courtesy Novosti from Sovfoto.

DRAMATIC FORM	EPIC FORM
1. The stage "incarnates" an event.	1. Relates the event.
2. Involves the audience in an action; uses up its activity.	2. Makes the audience an observer but arouses its activity.
3. Helps it to feel.	3. Compels it to make decisions.
4. Communicates experiences.	4. Communicates insights with an event.
5. The audience is projected into an event.	5. The audience is confronted.
6. Suggestion is used.	6. Arguments are used.
7. Sensations are preserved.	7. Impelled to the level of perceptions investigation.
8. The character is a known quality.	8. The character is subjected to changes.
9. Man unchangeable.	9. Man who can change and make changes.
10. His drives.	10. His motives.
11. Events move in a straight line.	11. In "irregular" curves.
12. The world as it is.	12. The world as it is becoming.

Brecht wrote several plays for his theatre. His first major success was *The Three-Penny Opera* (1928), which ran for over 400 performances. *The Three-Penny Opera,* with music composed by Kurt Weill, is based on Gay's *The Beggar's Opera*. Recently one of the tunes from the piece, recorded under the title "Mack the Knife" by Bobby Darin, became quite popular. Brecht fled Hitler's Germany in 1933, settling in the United States in 1941. During the period between 1935 and 1947 he wrote such magnificent dramas as *Mother Courage* (1937), a study of the endurance and brutalization of women during the Thirty Years War; *Galileo* (1938-39); *Good Woman of Setzuan* (1938-40), an intimate look at man's fading morality; and the *Caucasian Chalk Circle* (1944-45). After leaving the U.S. in 1947, Brecht chose to return to Germany. He later founded the Berliner Ensemble, which became one of East Germany's major cultural showpieces. He remained there until his death in 1956. Brecht's influence both in the drama and dramatic techniques is monumental.

Selected Readings

Hayman, Ronald., ed. *The German Theatre*. London, 1975.

Jasper, Gertrude. *Adventure in the Theatre*. New Brunswick, N.J., 1947.

Raymond, Marcel. *From Baudelaire to Surrealism*. London, 1933.

Marshall, Norman. *The Producer and the Play*. London, 1957.

Vocabulary

1. Richard Wagner	RI kahrt VAHG ner
2. Bayreuth	bigh ROYT
3. gesamtkuntswerk	ge ZAHMT koonst vairk
4. Friedrich Nietzsche	FREE drik NEE chuh
5. Apollonian	ap uh LOH nee uhn
6. Dionysian	digh uh NIZ ee uhn
7. Théophile Gautier	tay oh FEEL goh TYAY
8. Maurice Maeterlinck	moh REES MAY ter lingk
9. Paul Claudel	kloh DEL
10. Edmond Rostand	RAW stand
11. *Pelléas and Mélisande*	pe lay AHS me li ZAHND
12. Aurelien-Marie Lugné-Poe	awr re LYEN muh REE loo NYAY POH
13. Théâtre de l'Oeuvre	tay AHT ruh duh LER vruh
14. Georg Kaiser	ÇAY ohrg KIGH zer
15. Filippo Tommaso Marinetti	mahr uh NE tee
16. Tristan Tzara	TRI stan ZAH ruh
17. André Breton	ahn DRAY bruh TAWN
18. Philippe Soupault	fee LEEP soo POH
19. Guillaume Apollinaire	gee YOHM uh paw lee NAIR
20. Jean Cocteau	zhaw kawk TOH
21. Antonin Artaud	an tuh NEEN ahr TOH
22. Vsevelod Meyerhold	vuh SE vohlt MIGH er hohld
23. verfremdung	fer FREM doong

CHAPTER THIRTEEN

The Melting Pot: Modern Theatre

Each age covered in this book has had a distinctive theatrical style. The twentieth century, therefore, is unique in that there is no singular style. On the contrary, if one were to attempt to identify a twentieth century theatrical signature, it would best be described by the term eclectic. The modern theatre is, in many ways, a culmination of all that has gone before it. This can easily be seen in the growth of the American theatre.

Little has been said about the early American theatre during the course of this book. That is certainly not because it did not exist — it did. The American theatre was a young and dynamic institution beginning in the colonies, spreading west of the Alleghenies, crossing the Missouri by boat and the plains by covered wagon. The American theatre was in Colorado at the mining camps, sweated with the silver miners in Death Valley, and was shot up in California during the gold rush. The history of its growth is colorful and exciting, but in terms of its product it was almost a carbon copy of the English stage. Tracing the development and growth of the theatre phenomenon, therefore, negates an intensive look at America until the first half of the twentieth century.

The American Theatre

Theatre in America during the last half of the nineteenth century was a thriving business, and for that reason it demanded the box office return necessary to support it. America had no long tradition of theatre, as had England, for example, so its audiences had to be nurtured. Since Americans as a whole were working people, the theatre was geared primarily to the public's taste. This was not bad nor unique, as most of what was popular in England was popular in the United States. But what did make a difference was that in England there were enough theatre lovers to allow a variety of theatres to survive. Not so in America, where the audience preferred to see stars and their vehicles. The fact that America could import a quality product from England made it difficult for American-born playwrights and actors to survive in the beginning. Playwrights, actors, and designers did develop in America but, for most of the nineteenth century, their work was primarily in the commercial mainstream. Principles of economics had a great deal to do with shaping the American theatre. Because of the difficulties in traveling during the early part of the nineteenth century, most American cities had resident stock companies who produced a number of plays in repertory. It wasn't long, however, before producers began to realize that it was cheaper to mount a single production, and run it for as long as it made money, than to produce several plays for a short period of time. The length of runs at the Boston Museum increased from an average of fourteen days in the 1860's to seventy-five in the 1880's.

Opposite: Joseph Jefferson III (1829-1905) as Rip Van Winkle. Photo 1894 by Falk.

Producers also found that the public would pay more to see a "star" than they would to see local professionals; hence, stars were frequently booked in to play major roles. This practice was not unusual as foreign stars had been doing it for years. They came into a city, performed, and left. The resident company then went on as before. Soon, however, one star was followed by another and the resident company became merely a support team. Then the idea of traveling a single show to various cities was initiated with success.

New York: A Theatrical Center

Once traveling companies became popular with producers, it is not surprising that a tour base was needed. Even less surprising is the fact that New York was the most likely center for this activity. New York had held a leading position in the theatre business since 1830. It had the largest concentration of theatres in the United States and a

Above: The new Chestnut Street Theatre, Philadelphia, as it appeared in 1831. The original Chestnut Street Theatre opened February 17, 1794, but burned in 1820; the new theatre opened December 2, 1822.

Right: Edward Sheldon (1886-1946), American dramatist whose plays, *Salvation Nell* (1908), *The Nigger* (1909), *The Boss* (1911), and *The High Road* (1912), reflected the Progressive Reform movement in the United States. Photo 1914 by Pirie MacDonald.

population that was growing at a faster rate than the total population of the country. Because foreign stars usually landed in New York, managers were accustomed to booking out of Manhattan. Since the booking machinery for stars was already there, it was an easy matter to extend it to shows. By 1880 New York became the base for a large percentage of theatrical tours. In addition, if a producer expected to make money on the road, it became essential that the play be a New York success. Managers of various theatres throughout the country journeyed to New York to arrange for tours. Because of the centralization of the theatre and the difficulties involved with the enormous number of producers, controlling theatrical production in America became possible.

The Theatrical Syndicate

In 1896 Sam Nixon, Fred Zimmerman, Charles Frohman, Al Hayman, Marc Klaw, and Abraham Erlanger formed what was called the "theatrical Syndicate." Basically the Syndicate connected key routes between the large cities in the United States by building theatres or by forcing existing theatres into signing exclusive contracts. New York producers who refused to cooperate were denied bookings and noncomplying actors were punished by being blackballed from all tours. The American theatre fell under the complete control of the Syndicate by 1900. Because the Syndicate was primarily concerned with the commercial aspects of the theatre, scripts considered unlikely to appeal to a mass audience were not performed. The Syndicate, therefore, held what might be called de facto censorship over the American stage between the years 1900-1915.

Several stars, whose names are still mentioned with respect in the theatre profession, emerged during this period. Among them were John Drew II (1853-1927) and Otis Skinner (1858-1942), Ethel Barrymore (1879-1959), E.A. Sothern (1859-1933), and the lovely Maude Adams (1872-1958), who gained theatrical fame by her performance in *Peter Pan*.

Some actors and directors held out against the Syndicate: Mrs. Fiske (1865-1932), who was the first American to produce the new realistic drama; James O'Neill (1847-1920) (father of Eugene O'Neill), who became forever identified with the leading role in *The Count of Monte Cristo;* and David Belasco (1854-1931), who became the father of naturalistic staging in America. Belasco's productions were so much in demand that he was able to dictate his own terms to the Syndicate, which was the first crack in its power.

Charles Mathews, the Elder (1776-1835), English actor whose tours in America in 1822 and 1834 popularized the comic actor and the specialty performer. Actors specializing in such roles as the Yankee character, Jim Crow the Indian, and other native types were more readily accepted. Mathews achieved success through short satiric pieces containing a variety of characters, all of which he portrayed. From *The Kembles and Their Contemporaries,* 1890.

The Shuberts

Belasco joined forces with Lee, Sam, and J.J. Shubert, who had started in the theatre in Syracuse, New York. Their plan was to book shows into their own theatres. They initiated what was called the "open door" policy by allowing any production the right to play in a Shubert house. Because this practice appeared so liberal in comparison to the heavy-handed policy of the Syndicate, the Shuberts were called the saviors of the American theatre. The Syndicate fought back in several ways. First, they tried to persuade the Shuberts to limit the number of productions and the construction of new theatres. Second, they insisted on the exclusive rights to book all Shubert theatres. Third, they eventually closed all Syndicate theatres to Shubert productions.

In January, 1907, Belasco and the Shuberts took the Syndicate to court for criminal conspiracy in restraint of trade. The Syndicate won the case, but the decision of Judge Otto A. Rosalsky set a legal precedent that was to enable the Shuberts to hold control over the theatre for years to come. The decision included several interesting points. First, Judge Rosalsky ruled that the Syndicate had the right to exclude a business rival from the use of their premises. Second, the Shuberts and Belasco were not being prevented from practicing their trade. Third, and most important, the judge ruled that theatrical amusements could not be considered as "articles of trade and commerce" and, therefore, were not subject to the antitrust laws.

The Syndicate suffered a severe blow when their knowledgeable colleague, Charles Frohman, was killed with the sinking of the *Lusitania* in 1915. From that time forward, the Shuberts became the power controlling the legitimate stage. The crash of 1929 put them temporarily in bankruptcy, but in 1933 they were able to buy themselves out of bankruptcy. The last of the Syndicate members, A.L. Erlanger, died in 1930, leaving the Shuberts with a monopoly that, by virtue of Judge Rosalsky's decision, was nearly unchallenged.

The rule of the Shuberts was every bit as dictatorial as that of the Syndicate. The choice of productions was geared primarily toward fattening the box office and not the mind. Their control lasted until the Rosalsky decision was overturned in a federal antitrust suit in 1950. The Shuberts were forced to dispose of several of their theatres and the monopoly was broken by 1956. Although neither of the three Shubert brothers is living today, Shubert Theatre Enterprise is still the largest legitimate theatre chain in the world.

The commercialization of the American stage followed a relatively common pattern of industrial development. First, small local units were replaced by a large central unit. Second, the business aspects of the theatre were separated from the production element. Third, the products were standardized, as each play was produced by only one company or a number of duplicate companies. Fourth, theatre came under the control of big business. While the control over the theatre did little to improve the legitimate stage, the state of the theatre was not as vacuous as one might believe.

The power of the Shubert monopoly was, in many ways, similar to the governmental restrictions which had influenced the theatre in England and France. With the so-called legitimate stage effectively controlled, those who, for one reason or another, refused or were denied participation in the monopoly began to look elsewhere for the chance to make their livelihood in the theatre. Once again dissenters were to contribute an important new creative force to the American theatre, in particular, and the theatre in general.

The Universities

The first of these creative forces began in American colleges and universities. For the first time, courses were being offered in the drama. The most important course, known as English 47, was taught by George Pierce Baker (1866-1935), beginning at Radcliffe College in 1903 and then at Harvard in 1913. In 1925 Yale enticed Baker to move with a promise of a new theatre, a promise Harvard would not make. The first degree program was established in 1914 at Carnegie Institute of Technology by Thomas Wood Stevens (1880-1942). In 1918 Frederick Koch (1877-1944) established the Carolina Playmakers at Chapel Hill, listing playwright Paul Green, novelist-playwright Thomas Wolfe, and perhaps the greatest American theatre teacher to date, Hubert C. Heffner, as members.

Little Theatre Movement

The second creative force was the "Little" theatre movement. Following the pattern of the independent theatres in Europe, several little theatres were established as an American laboratory for the innovations that were being developed in Europe. Some of the most important were the Toy Theatre, founded by Mrs. Lyman Gale in Boston in 1912; Maurice Brown's Little Theatre, opening in Chicago in 1912; New York's Neighborhood Playhouse, formed by Irene and Alice Lewisohn in 1915; the Washington Square Players, established in New York in 1915; and the Provincetown Players, organized in Provincetown, Massachusetts, in 1915.

Provincetown

The Provincetown Players began as a group in the summer of 1915. They were not professionals of the theatre per se, but were journalists, painters, sculptors, teachers, and the like. These were restless individuals raised under Victorian morality who questioned why Strindberg was condemned and Ibsen was considered immoral. Values were being questioned and the commercialism in the American theatre further reinforced the concept that the older generation was essentially corrupt. Many of these young rebels from Greenwich Village spent their summers at Provincetown, a small Cape Cod settlement not far from Plymouth, Massachusetts. The group included, among others, John Reed, Mary Heaton Vorse, George Cram Cook, Susan Glaspell, Hutchins Hapgood, and Robert Edmond Jones. The first plays were given at Hutchins Hapgood's house and consisted of *Suppressed Desire* by Susan Glaspell (1882-1948) and George Cram Cook (1873-1924) and *Constancy* by Neith Boyce. The productions were designed by Robert Edmond Jones (1887-1954), who was to become one of the premier set designers of the American stage and a leading advocate of the "new stagecraft." Jones used the veranda with the ocean in the background for the first play, and then asked the audience to turn their seats around in order to view the set design for the second play which was a broad doorway at the opposite end of the room. As might be imagined, the Hapgood house was quite crowded for the first production. Consequently, a deserted fish house on the wharf, owned by Mary Heaton Vorse, was renovated with fish nets and circus benches for the next performances. The theatre was named "The Wharf Theatre," and interest in the colony reached a responsive note.

At a meeting called to discuss several new plays for production consideration, a member casually mentioned the name of a young man who was rooming with the vagabond philosopher, Terence Carlin. Carlin later introduced a shy, dark boy and read one of his plays called *Bound East for Cardiff.* The play was produced immediately, and the young Eugene O'Neill was made a member of the Provincetown Players.

For some, the founding of the Provincetown Players marks the birth of American drama. The players moved to 139 Macdougal Street in Greenwich Village in 1916. During the next two years at this location, six new plays by O'Neill were produced. The group moved to a larger place at 133 Macdougal and gained substantial notoriety considering that they were still an amateur group. A milestone was reached on November 1, 1920, with the opening of O'Neill's *The Emperor Jones.* When George Cram Cook read the play he already knew that it was going to take something special to capture the play scenically. He decided to build a dome of plaster and concrete. Starring as the Emperor in the play was Charles Gilpin (1878-1930), who as the first professional actor was paid the only salary among the cast, a stately sum of $50.00. Gilpin performed Brutus Jones 240 times throughout his career but was passed over during the 1924 revival of the play in favor of Paul Robeson. O'Neill did not want Gilpin to continue in the role because of a drinking problem. Later O'Neill was to say: "As I look back on all my work, I can honestly say there was only one actor who carried out every notion of a character I had in mind, that actor was Charles Gilpin."

The Emperor Jones was also significant in that it marked a change in the nature of the Provincetown Players. The success of the play provided an opportunity to move it to a Broadway theatre. At first there was a division of opinion among the players, but the possibility of making money for more new

The Emperor Jones. Western Kentucky University production, with Philip Cherry as the Emperor and Homer Tracy as Smithers.

plays overcame theoretical objections and the play opened at the Selwyn Theatre on December 28, 1920. After 1923 O'Neill, Kenneth Macgowan, and Robert Edmond Jones formed a branch of the players to perform period plays — foreign and non-commercial. The other branch continued in the old manner. Provincetown playhouse closed in 1929, finally succumbing to financial pressures. The discovery of O'Neill alone justified its existence, but others launched through its efforts read like a Who's Who of the American theatre. Susan Glaspell, Paul Green, E.E. Cummings, Norman Bel Geddes, Edna St. Vincent Millay, Robert Edmond Jones, Paul Robeson, Frank Wilson, Walter Abel, and Charles Gilpin, among others, went on to contribute significantly to the American theatre.

The Black Theatre

James Weldon Johnson (1871-1938) once said that "the Provincetown Playhouse was the initial and greatest force in opening up the way for the Negro on the dramatic stage." Johnson, a black poet-novelist, American counsel, and former secretary of the National Association for the Advancement of Colored People, was referring to the difficulty the black American had in making a living in the theatre. Part of the problem was that black characters were highly stereotyped. They were classified into five basic types: the lovable but ignorant clown; the tragic mulatto or half-breed who cannot find happiness in either the white or black society; the religious slave who is the soul of passivity and goodness; the amoral savage who breeds like an animal; and the beast who sets out to become equal so he can destroy white society.

The first type, the lovable clown, was by far the most popular. Thomas D. Rice (1806-1860), a white man, introduced a song and dance character of this type in 1828. He called his character "Jim Crow," creating a new expression in the language. Rice's success with the Jim Crow character helped develop the minstrel show, which was refined by E.P. Christy in 1846 with his Christy's Minstrels.

First Company

The first known company of black actors was developed in New York in 1821 by James Brown. Brown wrote the first play by a black American, a play entitled *King Shotaway.* The company performed a repertory which included *Othello* and *Richard III,* with James Hewlett, a West Indies native, in the leading roles. Brown's group was constantly harrassed by groups of white rowdies and was disbanded about 1823. Brown probably provided Ira Aldridge (1804-1867) with his first acting experience.

With the closing of Brown's theatre, Aldridge was unable to find work on the American stage, and in 1825 he traveled to England where he made his debut as Othello. He became immensely popular and was billed as the African Roscius. Aldridge toured throughout Europe and the British Isles, once playing Othello to Charles Kean's Iago. He received decorations from the rulers of Prussia, Russia and Saxe-Meiningen. All indications support the conclusion that Ira Aldridge was one of the finest actors of his age. He became enormously wealthy and successful in virtually every country but his own.

Outside the minstrel show and Jim Crow dancing, blacks in the theatre were relegated to stereotypes. In 1915 Anita Bush organized the All Colored Dramatic Stock Company, which gave black actors their first and longest period of stability. Ridgeley Torrence's *Three Plays for a Negro Theatre* (1917), which marked a movement away from the stereotyped black character, were the first plays which allowed black audiences in Broadway theatres. In addition, the *Emperor Jones, Porgy* by DuBose and Dorothy Heyward, and *The Green Pastures* by Marc Connelly provided acting opportunities for the black actor. *The Green Pastures,* based on *Ole Man Adam and His Children* by Roark Bradford, a white journalist, created the most impact. Canadian-born Richard B. Harrison, a speech and dramatics professor who played De Lawd, had to be trained by a white actor to speak in "Negro" dialect. The production had difficulty in finding rehearsal space, as few rehearsal halls in New York would allow blacks on the premises. But the play was a hit and blacks were given the opportunity to earn a decent living in the theatre. *Green Pastures* was also made into a film which marked the debut of several blacks, including Eddie Anderson, who was to become famous as Jack Benny's chauffeur, Rochester.

There were black musicals, notably *Shuffle Along* by Noble Sissle and Eubie Blake, produced in 1921. In addition, Sissle and Blake wrote *Chocolate Dandies* and *Runnin' Wild,* which were popular to both white and black audiences.

Black Playwrights

The first serious play to be produced on Broadway by a black American was *The Chipwoman's Fortune,* a one act play by Willis Richardson produced in 1923. The play was performed by the Ethiopian Art Players of Chicago for two weeks on Broadway. Garland Anderson's *Meek,* opening on February 6, 1928, was probably the first full-length play to be produced. Several other black playwrights wrote between the years of 1928 and 1935. For example, Langston Hughes's *Mulatto* had the longest Broadway run of a black playwright to date.

Several off-Broadway productions by blacks were produced before the war, including Langston Hughes' *Don't You Want To Be Free?* (1938) and Theodore Ward's (1902-) *Big White Fog* (1940). *Big White Fog* was perhaps the most vitriolic play about the black man's condition in America. The play contains the character of Marcus Garvey, the founder of the black Muslim movement in America, and is a stirring drama of despair. But even in the collapse of the Mason family, there was hope that blacks and whites would reconcile their differences. Theodore Ward was a theatre man throughout his life. Given a boost by the federal theatre project, Ward worked to achieve acceptance of the black artist by the theatre community. In spite of the many rebuffs that Ward suffered, he has never given up believing that eventually artists, black and white, would someday be judged by their art alone.

The most important play of the prewar black theatre was *Native Son,* written in 1941. *Native Son* was adapted for the stage by Paul Green, a Provincetown Player's product. Green, a white man, adapted his play from Richard Wright's novel of the same name.

One of the most refreshing achievements of recent years has been the development of an innovative black theatre movement, which has paralleled the world theatre in microcosm. It began in 1963 with the Free Southern Theatre, quickly radicalized in 1964 with the Black Arts Repertoire Theatre School, headed by Imamu Amiri Baraka (LeRoi Jones). Baraka's (1934-) group, influenced by Nietzche's condemnation of Western culture, set out to develop a new black culture. Larry Neal, writing about the movement, states: "We advocate a cultural revolution in art and ideas. The cultural values inherent in western history must either be radicalized or destroyed, and we will probably find that even radicalization is impossible." Baraka moved from comparatively mild plays, such as *The Toilet* (1964) and *Dutchman* (1964), to *Slave Ship* (1969), which advocates a total rejection of Western society and the evolution of a new black culture.

The Negro Ensemble Company, founded in 1968 in New York, produced a series of plays which were of concern to blacks. The company is probably the most prestigious black company in America today. Originally directed by Douglas Turner Ward, Robert Hooks, and Gerald S. Krone, the Negro Ensemble has consistently maintained a high quality in their works.

The New Lafayette Theatre of Harlem opened in 1967 with Robert Macbeth as its director. The company lasted until 1973, publishing the *Black Theatre Magazine* and providing an information service to black groups throughout the country.

Black playwrights, actors, and directors have distinguished themselves on the theatrical scene. Lorraine Hansberry (1930-1965) won considerable acclaim in 1959 with *A Raisin in the Sun,* the most successful play by a black writer to that date. Her second play, *The Sign in Sidney Brustein's Window* (1964), is still played frequently throughout the country. Another is Ed Bullins (1935-) who is perhaps the most respected of the current black writers. He has been associated with Joe Papp's Public Theatre since he left the New Lafayette in 1973. He is currently working on a series of plays about black life in the industrial North and West. In addition, Lonnie Elder III's (1933-) *Ceremonies in Dark Old Men* (1969) and Joseph A. Walker's (1933-) *The River Niger* have been successful. Other writers who seem to be developing are Richard Wesley, Alice Childress, Edgar White, Ted Shine, Vinette Carroll, Leslie Lee and Lorna C. Littleway.

The considerable talent of Ntozake Shange (1948-) has been recently displayed on Broadway with *For Colored Girls Who Have Considered Suicide When the Rainbow Is Enuf.* Shange, originally from the Bay Area (San Francisco), first produced her "choreopoem" at the Bacchanel, a woman's bar just outside Berkeley, California. The play was brought to New York where it attracted the eye of producer Woody King. It eventually played at the Public Theatre and then traveled to Broadway in September of 1976, where it was still running in 1978. The work, enhanced by dance and music, explores the reality of seven different kinds of women. The language is poetry and the effect is superb, all of which support the belief that the black theatre is a viable, growing phenomenon that has stimulated and is stimulating the stage today.

Anna Corey Mowatt Ritchie (1819-1870), actress and playwright, whose play *Fashion* (1845), established social comedy in America. From *The Interviewer's Album,* 1881-1882.

Eclecticism

The American "Little" theatre movement culminated in the formation of the Theatre Guild. This organization was the most respected theatre group in the United States between 1920 and 1930. Its artistic director was Philip Moeller (1880-1958) and its principal designers were Lee Simonson, Robert Edmund Jones, and Norman Bel Geddes (1893-1958), all advocates of "new stagecraft." Basically the "new stagecraft" was the result of a trend started by Swiss-born Adolph Appia (1862-1928) and the Englishman Gordon Craig (1872-1966). Appia is noted for his innovation in lighting

Gordon Craig as Arthur de St. Valery in Phillips' *The Dead Heart,* September 28, 1889, at Henry Irving's Theatre (Lyceum). From *The Theatre,* 1890.

Richard Boleslavsky (1889-1937), shown here with a student, Ruth Nelson, and Robert Edmond Jones, was a noted teacher of acting. A member of Stanislavsky's Moscow Art Theatre, Boleslavsky joined Maria Ouspenskaya in heading the American Laboratory Theatre. His text, *Acting, The First Six Lessons,* is still widely used today. Robert Edmond Jones (1887-1954) is generally credited with introducing the "new stagecraft" in America with his design for *The Man Who Married a Dumb Wife.* Courtesy Joseph "Mac" Dixon.

theory and Craig in theatre design. Another Englishman, William Poel (1852-1934), is credited with being one of the forerunners of theatrical eclecticism. Poel founded the Elizabethan Stage Society in 1894 and attempted to perform Shakespeare's plays on a stage similar to the Elizabethans. Up until this time, Shakespeare's plays were produced according to the style popular at the time of their production. If the prevalent theatrical style was wing and drop, pictorial realism, or realism, that was the way the play was produced.

Poel's ideas were reinforced by Max Reinhardt (1873-1943) in Germany. Reinhardt believed that each play should be approached differently and that theatre architecture and dramatic styles are related. Reinhardt's work was called "eclecticism" or "artistic realism." The new approach freed design from the rigidity of a particular style. All elements of theatre, the conventions of all periods, could be utilized in the design of the production.

The constructivism of Meyerhold, the distortions of the expressionists, the dream atmosphere of the symbolist, the epic staging techniques of Brecht, could be combined in a production with actors utilizing the acting techniques of Stanislavsky. The artist was given the freedom to use any device to enhance the artistic signature of the twentieth century theatre.

Original production of *The Emperor's New Clothes,* which opened in 1936 at the Adelphi Theatre (now the George Abbott Theatre) in New York and starred Joseph "Mac" Dixon. Courtesy Joseph "Mac" Dixon.

The new stagecraft designers opted to create a specific statement by utilizing all aspects of technical theatre to enhance the play. The design of Norman Bel Geddes for Dante's *The Divine Comedy* in 1921 remains one of the classic examples of the new school.

While it is true that Americans had been writing plays from Royall Tyler on, the plays were mostly based on European models. With the discovery of Eugene O'Neill at the Provincetown Playhouse, America began to establish itself to the theatrical world.

Eugene O'Neill

Eugene Gladstone O'Neill (1888-1953) was born in a Times Square hotel to a famous actor of the day, James O'Neill. His early education was as fragmentary as his home life. He attended Princeton before signing on as a seaman and making several voyages throughout the world. After a brief spell in a sanitarium in 1912, O'Neill developed an interest in playwrighting. In 1914 he enrolled in George Pierce Baker's playwrighting class (English 47) at Harvard, but left that spring (1915) for New York. While living in New York's Greenwich Village, he met Terry Carlin who in turn brought him to the attention of the Provincetown Players. The Provincetown Players were responsible for producing O'Neill's first play — a one act, *Bound East for Cardiff.*

The production of *Beyond the Horizon* (1920), O'Neill's first full-length play, established him as a major American talent. He also received the Pultizer Prize for his efforts. His subsequent production of *Emperor Jones* not only reinforced earlier acclaim for his talents, but projected him into the world spotlight. The production, designed by Cleon Throckmorton, utilized the new stagecraft concepts and represented the first major Expressionistic drama by an American.

O'Neill was awarded the Nobel Prize for literature in 1936, only the second American to receive such an honor to that date.

Niblo's Garden Theatre, New York, 1855. The theatre opened in 1827 as the Sans Souci, was reconstructed in 1828 as Niblo's, and continued through 1895. America's first "leg show," *The Black Crook*, was produced here in 1866. From *Ballou's Pictorial*, 1855.

Other Playwrights

Suddenly, all of the new ideas that had been taking shape in Europe seemed to melt into a potpourri of creative energy. From 1920 the American theatre changed from an imitator to a leader. O'Neill continued his almost incredible output of plays. During the years between 1920 and 1934 O'Neill wrote *Anna Christie, Gold, The Straw, The First Man, The Hairy Ape, Welded, All God's Chillun Got Wings, Desire Under the Elms, The Great God Brown, The Fountain, Marco Millions, Strange Interlude, Lazarus Laughed, Dynamo, Mourning Becomes Electra, Ah Wilderness,* and *Days Without End*. These plays themselves form a canon of literature of which any country might be proud. But O'Neill was not the only talent to emerge during this period. Others include George S. Kaufman, who opened a collaboration with Marc Connelly, called *Dulcy,* in 1921. Soon Maxwell Anderson, George Kelly, Elmer Rice, Sidney Howard, Robert Sherwood, Paul Green, S.N. Behrman, Edna Ferber, Clifford Odets, Archibald MacLeish, Irwin Shaw, Sidney Kingsley, John Steinbeck, Erskine Caldwell, Jack Kirkland, Lillian Hellman, Clare Boothe, Bella and Samuel Spewack, and Phillip Barry all made their theatrical debuts. Plays like Anderson's *High Tor,* Steinbeck's *Of Mice and Men,* Hellman's *The Children's Hour* and Shaw's *Bury the Dead* gave the

Scene from *The Black Crook* by Charles M. Barras. The first New York production opened September 12, 1866, at Niblo's Garden Theatre. *The Black Crook* was a major step toward the development of American musical comedy. Courtesy Harvard Theatre Collection.

theatre a vitality that it never had before. A total of 280 new plays were produced on the Broadway stage between 1927 and 1928, a record which has not been equalled to this day. The Theatre Guild, formed in 1919 by several members of the disbanded Washington Square Players, and the Group Theatre, discussed in Chapter 16, became the most important producing agents of the period.

The prewar period between 1920 and 1940 also saw the rise of the two other entertainment phenomena, the musical and the cinema.

Musical Comedy

Musical entertainment has been strong in the United States for many years. *The Beggar's Opera* was extremely popular when it was imported during the first part of the eighteenth century, as were other English ballad operas. Much of the popular English entertainment during the latter half of the eighteenth and the first part of the nineteenth century used music in the background. These entertainments were imported to the United States. Some were musical extravaganzas, some were burlesques. After the passage of the Theatre Regulations Act in 1843 in England, observers were quite surprised when it was discovered that, while very few new legitimate theatres were licensed between 1843 and 1853, sixty-seven music licenses were granted in 1845 and 255 in 1853. The reason was the rise in popularity of the music halls. The music halls specialized in light musical entertainments, short skits sometimes with music and sometimes without, Pose Plastiques, ballets, and burlesques. Pose Plastiques consisted of females in various skimpy attire posing in a manner describing a famous painting. The ballet was divided into two kinds: the *ballet divertissement* and *ballet d'action*. The former was primarily a drama-dance with spectacular costumes, scenery, and lightly-clad women.

Lydia Thompson (1836-1908), best known for her contribution to striptease. She and her "British Blondes," seizing on the popularity of *The Black Crook,* toured the United States in 1868-1869, introducing the modern concept of burlesque. Courtesy Lilly Library, Indiana University.

The music hall type of entertainment provided the basis for a new development in the United States. A group of ballet dancers in New York to perform the opera *La Biche au Bois* in 1866 were stranded when the Academy of Music burned. The manager of Niblo's Garden, William Wheatley

"A Vaudeville turn — I'm so glad you've found me. Oh, take me away." Drawn by William Glackens for *Scribner's Magazine* in 1901.

(1816-1876), conceived the idea of incorporating the ballet troupe into a play called *The Black Crook* by Charles M. Barras (1826-1873). The result was a musical extravaganza similar to those produced in the English music halls. There were spectacular scenery, scantily-clad ballet girls, and song. Significantly, it grossed over a million dollars at the box office. A reviewer in the New York *Tribune* wrote: "The scenery is magnificent; the ballet is beautiful; the drama is rubbish. There is always a bitter drop in the sweetest cup, a fly in the richest ointment. Mr. Barras' drama is the bitter drop and the superfluous fly in this instance."

The Black Crook ran for sixteen months and spawned numerous copies, including *Evangeline,* which introduced the term musical comedy. In

Canterbury Hall, opened in 1849, by Charles Morton (1819-1904), known as the "father of the halls." At first Morton did not charge admission to what is now considered the first organized music hall in England; he relied instead on the drinks sold. Note the wing scenery and the man being beaten in the box.

1869 Lydia Thompson (1836-1908), an English music hall actress-dancer, brought to New York a group of women which she called the British Blondes. The program, again at Niblo's, consisted of ballet and skits which were burlesques of famous works; i.e. *School for Scandal* and *The Forty Thieves*. Typical of music hall dance, the ballets were designed more to show off female pulchritude than artistry. Gradually, the term *burlesque* came to be associated with variety acts and musical numbers featuring beautiful women. Because of its sexual overtones and the addition of the striptease in 1929, burlesque has come to be associated with mostly male audiences. In 1880, however, Tony Pastor (1837-1908) initiated a burlesque form intended for the family. This form, called vaudeville, became one of the most popular types of entertainment to emerge in America, and many famous personalities got their start in show business on the vaudeville stage — Bob Hope, Jack Benny, Milton Berle, Groucho Marx, and Jimmy Durante, among others.

From 1870 to 1900, influences on the development of musical comedy included Edward Harrigan's *The Mulligan Guard Ball* (1883), the work of Otto Harback and Rudolph Friml (1879-1972), Edward Rice's *Evangeline* (1874) and the operettas of Gilbert and Sullivan. From the turn of the century until 1920, the names of George M. Cohan (1878-1942), Victor Herbert (1859-1924), and Jerome Kern (1885-1945) stand out as the dominant forces shaping the American musical. Whereas Victor Herbert is considered the first major American composer, he was European (Ireland) born and

William Schwenck Gilbert (1836-1911), English dramatist who collaborated with Arthur Sullivan (1842-1900) in writing *Trial by Jury* (1875), *H.M.S. Pinafore* (1878), *The Mikado* (1885), and *The Pirates of Penzance* (1885). Their first work led to a partnership with Richard D'Oyly Carte (1844-1901), who built the Savoy Theatre to present their plays. Gilbert and Sullivan discontinued their collaboration in 1896, perhaps because of Gilbert's temper and rigid disciplinarian attitude. Gilbert was knighted in 1907. From *The Theatre,* 1882.

his music reflected his Viennese training. George M. Cohan is considered the "father of American musical theatre." He made no improvement upon the form, but he did succeed in creating a truly American musical with his emphasis upon native themes, subject matter, and characters. Furthermore, he was born on July 3 (although he claimed he was "Yankee Doodle Dandy" being born on July 4) in Rhode Island, which made him native born. He was awarded an honorary Congressional Medal of Honor for his song, "Over There," which served to arouse patriotic fervor and support for America's participation in World War I. In the works of Jerome Kern during this period are to be found the beginnings of interlocking music, lyrics, and book. *Have a Heart* (1917) demonstrates this complete integration wherein the songs with their lyrics advance the action. In addition, Kern had the comedy based upon the situation rather than having it interjected by the comedians. By the end of 1917, the integration of the American musical in terms of book, music, lyrics, and settings was firmly established.

During the 1920's, American musical theatre added another dimension with Sissle and Blake's *Shuffle Along* (which included Josephine Baker and Paul Robeson). Noble Sissle and Eubie Blake (who is still active today) not only produced an excellent and successful musical in *Shuffle Along,* but were among the first to introduce jazz (ragtime) into the musical form. Such tunes as "I'm Just Wild About Harry" and "Love Will Find A Way" have more in common with today's musical comedies than "Indian Love Call" or the "Donkey Serenade." Certainly *Shuffle Along,* along with the later black reviews such as *Runnin' Wild, The Plantation Review* and *Blackbirds of 1928,* took full advantage of the ragtime beat. *Blackbirds,* incidentally, featured a young dancer by the name Bill Robinson, better known as Bojangles.

On December 27, 1927, at the Ziegfeld Theatre, Florenz Ziegfeld produced *Show Boat,* by Jerome Kern and Oscar Hammerstein II. The show was an outstanding hit and is still played with success today. *Show Boat* was innovative in many ways: it was a musical about America and its past; it was the first to deal with serious subject matter (miscegenation); it was based on a successful book by Edna Ferber; it utilized the "new stagecraft" technique of Joseph Urban; and it utilized American musical style, including jazz. A reviewer in the *New Republic* wrote: " 'Can't Help Lovin' That Man' is an interesting and successful experiment in negroid forms and inflections by a composer who til now had ignored them."

Several musicals of merit were to follow, notably *Of Thee I Sing.* Produced in 1931, *Of Thee I Sing* featured a libretto by George Kaufman (1889-1961). Kaufman's book was clever and well written, underscoring the importance of words in the

Opposite: "Love Will Find A Way," along with "I'm Just Wild About Harry," were two popular hits from *Shuffle Along* by Noble Sissle and Eubie Blake. *Shuffle Along* helped to establish the form of the American musical comedy. Courtesy Frank K. Carner.

LOVE WILL FIND A WAY

SHUFFLE ALONG, Inc. *Presents*

THE NEW YORK MUSICAL NOVELTY SUCCESS

Shuffle Along

Book by Flournoy Miller *and* Aubrey Lyle

Baltimore Buzz	60
Bandana Days	60
Daddy Won't You Please Come Home	60
Everything Reminds Me of You	60
Gypsy Blues	60
Good Night, Angeline	60
Honeysuckle Time	60
I'm Just Wild About Harry	60
If You've Never Been Vamped By a Brown Skin	60
I'm Craving for That Kind of Love	60
I'm Just Simply Full of Jazz	60
Kentucky Sue	60
Love Will Find a Way	60
Liza Quit Vamping Me	60
Low Down Blues	60
Old Black Joe and Uncle Tom	60
Oriental Blues	60
Pickaninny Shoes	60
Shuffle Along	60
Vision Girl	60

Lyrics & Music by Noble Sissle *and* Eubie Blake

M. Witmark & Sons
New York

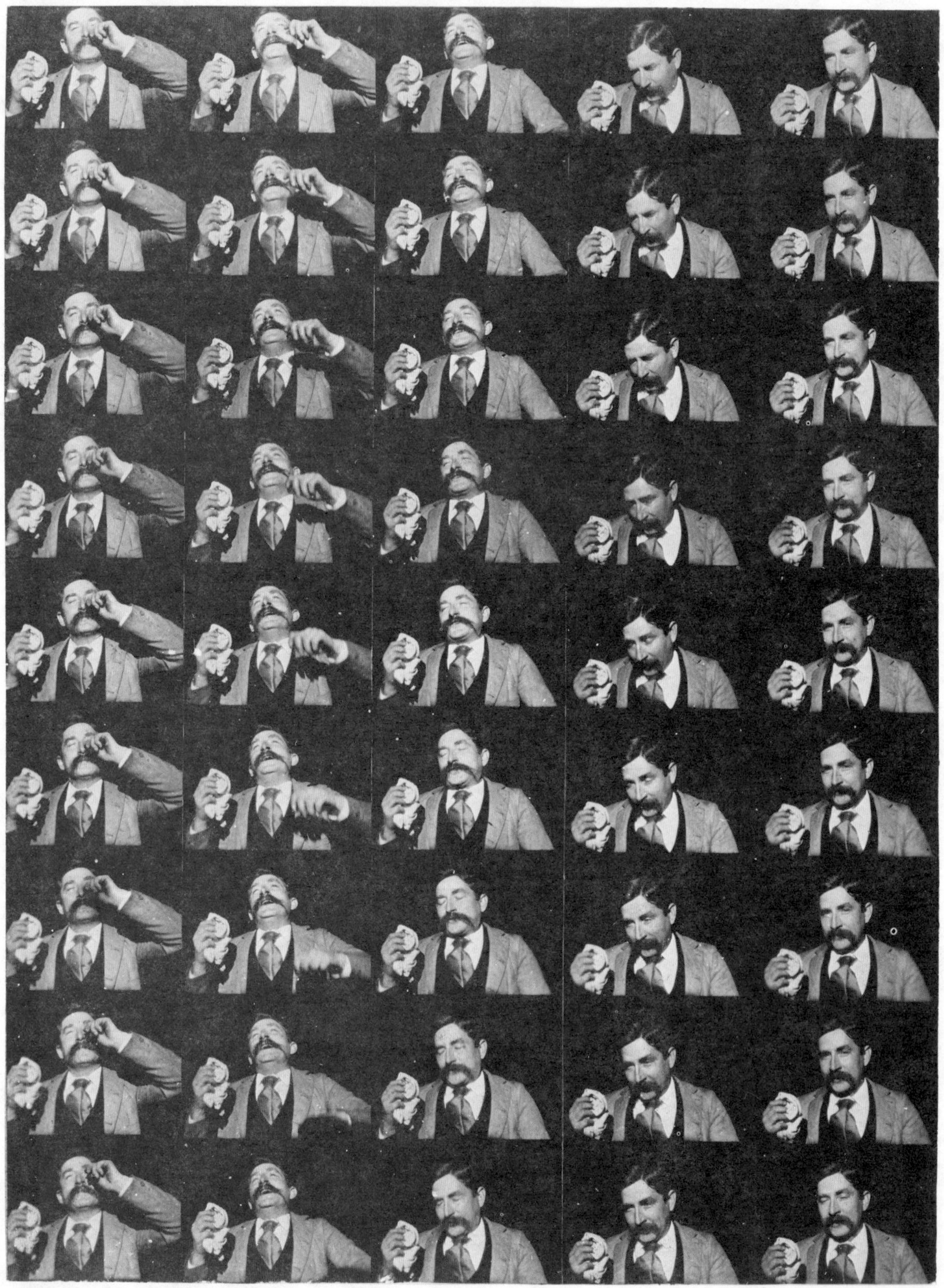

Above: The Vitascope was introduced by Edison April 23, 1896, at Koster and Bial's Music Hall, Herald Square, New York, after Edison purchased the manufacturing and market rights from Thomas Armat. Such projectors aided Edison in creating the film industry.

Opposite: The Sneeze, 1894. Edison's Kinetoscope, a forerunner to the Vitascope, was introduced April 14, 1894, at 1155 Broadway, New York. Unlike the Vitascope, the Kinetoscope was perfected at Edison's laboratory in West Orange, New Jersey.

musical. The show also featured the music of George (1898-1937) and Ira (1896-   ) Gershwin and became the first musical to win the Pulitzer Prize. Also during the 1930's musicals took a new turn when Russian-born George Balanchine created the first jazz ballet for *On Your Toes* (1936). This innovation marked the first use of ballet for story telling in a Broadway musical. In 1937 Balanchine again created a first when he unveiled a dream ballet for *Babes in Arms.* Balanchine added another first in 1938 when he had a dancer assume the lead in *I Married an Angel.* Balanchine's contributions created the basic framework for the integration of dance and story which is a trademark of the present-day musical. In addition, Balanchine's work proved to be a direct influence on Agnes DeMille's choreography for *Oklahoma.*

Perhaps the culmination of the new direction in musicals was reached in 1943 with the production of Richard Rogers (1902-   ) and Oscar Hammerstein II's lavish musical *Oklahoma.* The show, based on Lynn Riggs' (1899-1954) play *Green Grow the Lilacs,* played for 2,248 performances in New York alone. It featured an intelligent, well-written script, excellent music, innovative dance, and striking scenery, all beautifully blended to perfection. *Oklahoma* did not really do anything that had not been done by other American musicals but, in many ways, *Oklahoma* was the first American musical. All the elements from the past seemed to fuse together in the one indigenous theatrical form that America has produced, the musical comedy.

Cinema and Theatre

The development of the cinema out of the theatre was another important factor during the early part of the century. The invention of the motion picture can be divided into three phases: animated pictures, animated photographs, and finally, motion pictures. In 1877 Thomas Edison (1847-1931) joined with W.K.L. Dickson in trying to photograph and project motion. Utilizing the invention of photography on celluloid by William Friese-Greene, George Eastman quickly developed a flexible film. Edison and Dickson then developed the Kinetoscope, which used Eastman film with a shutter moving as fast as forty frames per second. The Kinetoscope utilized a light source under the film and a magnifying glass through which one looked at the moving picture. Thomas Armat then projected Edison's Kinetoscope on a screen with a projector called a Vitascope. Edison collaborated with Armat on an improved projector which they called, for reasons only they knew, a Kinetoscope. The year 1895, then, marks the birth of the motion picture industry. Since we are primarily concerned with the theatre and its influence, no attempt will be made to present a detailed history of the cinema. Yet there are factors in the relationship between the cinema and theatre that are important to consider. First, many developments in spectacle in the nineteenth century theatre were utilized in the early cinema. Second, the early cinema came at a time when realism was in vogue. And, third, cinema was effectively able to capture the mass audience market. The theatre had been rapidly moving toward spectacle by the end of the nineteenth century. Three producer-directors had developed styles of production which were to make them exceedingly popular to mass audiences. They were Henry Irving (1838-1905) in London and David Belasco and Steele MacKaye (1844-1894) in America.

Henry Irving took the popularity of melodrama and created spectacular theatrical effects. He spared little in devising various traps which could make an actor appear or disappear. One of the most famous was the vampire trap which enabled actors to "float" up from beneath the stage. Witches faded in and out of fog and castles dissolved into courtyards. Many of these devices were utilized in the production of Shakespeare as well. Irving used flashback techniques and even cross-cutting, all later absorbed into the cinema. In fact, when cinema arrived, Irving's theatre declined.

Belasco concentrated on making his sets and interiors as realistic as possible. Belasco, like Irving, used technical devices to cater to mass audiences. His was the naturalistic stage where drugstore bottles contained real pills. But Belasco, like Irving, found it difficult to survive when the cinema beat him at his own game. Photographic reality was simply more exciting than the illusion of reality.

Steele MacKaye was an important inventor in the America theatre. In addition to the hat holder that used to adorn the bottom of all theatrical seats, MacKaye invented several methods of eliminating pauses from scene shifting, thereby allowing

A Russian Honeymoon, presented in 1883 at the Madison Square Theatre, incorporated Steele Mackaye's ideas and naturalistic settings.

scenes to flow in and out of each other. The most important device was the elevator stage which he designed in 1879 for the Madison Square Theatre.

The elevator stage consisted of two levels, one built on top of the other, placed in a large elevator shaft. While one scene was playing, the stage crew either shifted to the next scene from below or from above the audience level. He also designed a sliding and floating stage. MacKaye was interested in controlled spectacle, not necessarily limited to the theatre stage. William Cody ("Buffalo Bill" 1846-1917) once hired him to stage a series of mammoth pictures that were to illustrate the growth and expansion of America. The panorama alone was half a mile long and fifty feet high. The production included a cyclone supplied by four six-feet exhaust fans which entirely destroys a Colorado mining camp. The production was filled with action and scene changes. Scene three, for example, reads in the following way: "A cattle ranch, where the cowboys' fun is interrupted by an Indian attack, which is beaten off at last by Buffalo Bill and a party of rescue . . . ."

MacKaye invented what he called the Spectatorium for the Chicago Exposition of 1893. The Spectatorium was a huge building which included twenty-five telescopic stages. The frame of the stages was 150 by 170 feet. They moved over six miles of railroad tracks and their aggregated weight would have been 1,000 tons. A new lighting system capable of reproducing any natural lighting effect and a cyclone system, which would have required over 400 horsepower to run, was to be constructed. MacKay's Spectatorium was similar, at least in concept, to the modern cinema sound stage. Unfortunately, it was never constructed.

Irving's romatic melodrama, Belasco's stage realism, and MacKaye's superspectacle, then, were made to order for the new art form. Many of the first pictures were merely melodrama photographed from a fixed camera, but in 1903 E.S. Porter discovered realism and sensationalism as methods of presenting melodramatic material. His film, *The Great Train Robbery,* was the first step by the cinema in its separation from the theatre. But it was not until the release of D.W. Griffith's *Birth of a Nation* in 1915 that the cinema reached a position to challenge the theatre. *Birth of a Nation* surpassed anything the theatre had ever done in terms of spectacle, realism, and melodramatic power. Hence audiences, which to this point had been fed the same formula in the legitimate theatre, logically turned to a media that could do it better. While Irving, Belasco, and MacKaye were cited as specific examples illustrating the kind of theatre being produced, they were by no means the only practitioners. Many affiliated with the commercial stage in America were, for the most part, equally guilty. Therefore, the effect on the American theatre was serious, particularly after the invention of the sound motion pictures in 1927. Certainly, cinema had to be a factor in the change which occurred in the American theatre between 1920 and 1940. There is, perhaps, a certain amount of irony when one listens to contemporary critics of the American movie business: "Too much spectacle, too much realism, and too much melodrama."

World War II and After

World War II was one of the most destructive events that we have ever known, and its resolution the least satisfying. The world was left divided into two potentially hostile camps with the threat of a nuclear holocaust hanging over its head, producing a kind of social paranoia during the 1950's. This paranoia was reflected in the theatre in a number of ways. First, dramatists questioned the moral validity of a generation which had committed such horrors. Second, there were questions about mankind as a whole being able to function in a responsible manner. Third, there were questions about man's ability to survive the anxiety about the future and guilt over the past. Fourth, there were questions about man's corruptibility.

Playwrights throughout the world began to explore these themes. Jean-Paul Sartre (1905-) found solace in a new philosophical movement called existentialism. Sartre reasoned that no just God would have allowed the holocaust; therefore, God does not exist. If there is no God, then there is no universal morality and, therefore, no fixed standards of conduct and no verifiable moral codes. Each person, he argued, is free to establish his own values and morals and to live by them if he chooses to do so. Conformity to the code of values of a society that produced the war was considered immoral by Sartre. He expressed his ideas in the French theatre through several plays. The most important of his existential plays were *The Flies* (1943) and *No Exit* (1944). Sartre and Algerian-born Albert Camus (1913-1960) were instrumental in laying the foundations of the theatre of the absurd, which will be discussed later.

The Swiss playwright Friedrich Duerrenmatt (1921-) studied the question of the corruptibility of man in many of his works. He is best known for *The Visit* (1956), which was performed on Broadway by one of the finest theatrical teams of the American stage, Alfred Lunt and Lynn Fontaine. *The Physicists* (1962), *Play Strindberg* (1969), and *The Collaborator* (1973) have also received critical acclaim. Existentialism and theatre of the absurd will be explored in the next chapter.

Postwar English Theatre

The English theatre was in shambles after the war, both literally and figuratively, as only one theatre in London remained open after the German blitz. Terence Rattigan (1911-1978), Christopher Fry (1907-), and American expatriot T.S. Eliot were the most important writers on the commercial stage.

The most significant company immediately after the war was the Old Vic. Initially under the direction of Tyrone Guthrie, the management passed on to Lawrence Olivier, Ralph Richardson, and John Burrell. The group declined as Richardson and Olivier turned more and more to other commitments such as the cinema. To fill the void, the Stratford Festival company with its group of exciting actors, both new and old, became critically acclaimed. The company boasted Peter Brook (1925-), Paul Scoffield (1922-), John Gielgud (1904-), Anthony Quayle (1913-), Michael Redgrave (1908-), Peggy Ashcroft (1907-), and Olivier, among others. In spite of these companies, however, the English stage was declining, if not doomed, in the eyes of many critics. The year 1956 marked both the low point and the beginning of a revival which once again would thrust it into favor. During that

Dorothy Tulin as Natalya Petrovna, Genma Craver as Katya, and Derek Jacobi as Mikhaylo Rakitin in Ivan Turgenev's *A Month in the Country,* at the Chichester Festival Theatre, 1974. Courtesy British Tourist Authority.

The National Theatre, London, which opened in October 1963. England was the last country in Europe except Italy to form a national theatre. Courtesy British Tourist Authority.

year, two producing units were formed in London — the English Stage Company and the Theatre Workshop. The Theatre Workshop, operating as a private club, organized in 1945 under the direction of Joan Littlewood. The group was instrumental in the development of Brendan Behan (1923-1965) and Shelagh Delaney (1939-).

The English Stage Company (known as the Royal Court because it is housed in the Royal Court Theatre) was started by George Devine (1910-1966), who had taught at Michel Saint-Denis' London Theatre Studio from 1936-1939. Devine's theatre was to have a major effect on the English stage in two ways: first, it introduced several major playwrights; second, it was instrumental in ending the almost ancient struggle for a free stage in London.

By the mid-fifties there were a number of young playwrights who were unable to get their plays produced in the commercial theatre. One of the major reasons for the problem was the Lord Chamberlain's insistence that the scripts be altered. In short, many of the new dramatists refused to be intimidated by the office of the play examiner. As in the past, when the government imposes restriction, theatre people find a way around it. They resorted to the private club ruse as others had done before them. The English Stage Company was a private club and charged a small entrance fee. Card holders were then permitted to purchase tickets and see unlicensed plays. As a result, a kind of symbiotic relationship existed between the commercial stage, the Lord Chamberlain, and the private theatre clubs. The commercial stage had no desire to produce plays by new writers and was not bothered by the loss of audiences, since those who attended the private showings did not necessarily frequent the commercial stage anyway. The Lord Chamberlain tolerated the arrangement because it allowed the playwrights a place to perform, and kept them from criticizing the play examiner. The private clubs tolerated it because it was the only way for them to keep open. The only fly in the ointment was that it was illegal to perform an unlicensed play if the actors were paid; it was simply against the law. Yet, no one pursued the point, and the Royal Court produced John Osborne's (1929-) play *Look Back in Anger* (1956). The play attacks the established society with such vehemence that the central character soon became a symbol of England's "angry young men." *Look Back in Anger,* by the way, had been banned on the commercial stage by the Lord Chamberlain. Osborne has since written a number of plays, notably *Luther* (1961) and *Inadmissible Evidence* (1965).

The Royal Court also introduced John Arden (1930-), who wrote *Sergeant Musgrave's Dance* (1959), N.F. Simpson (1919-), who concentrated on theatre of the absurd with such plays as *A Resounding Tinkle* (1956) and *One Way Pendulum* (1959), and Ann Jellico's (1928-) *The Knack,* produced in 1961.

The Repeal of Censorship

The Royal Court continued to produce through the sixties, introducing playwrights Joe Orton (1933-1967), David Storey (1933-) and, probably the most important, Edward Bond. Devine retired from the English Stage Company in 1965. He was replaced by William Gaskill (1930-), who maintained two theatre spaces at the Royal Court. The upstairs was devoted entirely to new works and the downstairs to mixture of old and new. In 1965 Gaskill produced a play by the young playwright Edward Bond (1935-). The play, called *Saved,* had been banned by the censor as immoral. The scene in question involves a group of young thugs who abuse a baby by rubbing the baby in its own excrement and then stoning it to death in its carriage. The play deals with the decadence and violence of London's East Side and this scene underscores the point. Gaskill's direction was subtle and intentionally geared to get the idea across without being vulgar. Nevertheless, some members of the press condemned the scene without having seen it performed and supported the censor. Buoyed by unexpected praise from the press, the Lord Chamberlain's office sought to close the play. When a member of the Lord Chamberlain's office was admitted to the play without a membership card by a harried box office ticket seller, the Chamberlain closed the theatre and a court trial followed. The Chamberlain's office maintained that the Stage Company had violated its status as a private club by selling a ticket to a nonmember. Selling tickets to the general public constituted a public theatre which was subject to the Lord Chamberlain's jurisdiction. The Stage Company, on the other hand, maintained that the ticket error had been an individual mistake by busy office personnel

Stratford Festival Theatre, summer home of the Royal Shakespeare Company, Trevor Nunn, artistic director. Courtesy British Tourist Authority.

and not at all the general policy of the organization. The trial aroused a great deal of interest as the great and the near-great of the English theatre came to testify on behalf of the Stage Company. Sir Lawrence Olivier's impassioned plea for the defendants was considered the high point among the theatrical community. At the end of three months' testimony, the judge rendered his verdict. Gaskill and the Company were found guilty but not for the reasons cited by either the prosecution or the defense. The judge knew what many scholars of the theatre had known for years. According to the Theatre Regulations Act of 1843, if a theatre paid its actors, it was a public theatre whether or not a membership card was needed.

Both the Chamberlain and the Stage Company were shocked with the decision. For the Chamberlain, the safety valve allowing for the private showing of new plays was effectively destroyed. For the Stage Company, its very raison d'être, the production of new playwrights, was now under the control of the Lord Chamberlain who, by the very nature of his charge, must ban them from production. Parliament addressed itself to the situation. A hearing was held featuring testimony from numerous theatre and theatre-related personages. During the latter part of 1968, Parliament abolished censorship, freeing the English stage from the control of the Lord Chamberlain for the first time in almost 300 years.

English theatre has been a product of its environment, socially, psychologically, and physically. Censorship over what could not be seen on the English stage first became a tool of the monarchy to influence the minds of the common man. During the Walpole regime it evolved into a means of controlling political dissent, and with the act of 1843, censorship became a reflection of the Victorian conscience.

Falsely or not, the Victorian middle class aspired to the morals (or what they thought to be the manners and morals) of the aristocracy and, in many ways, did not desire equality or the breakdown of the English caste system. One cannot help but remember Crichton's words in Barrie's *The Admirable Crichton:*

> The divisions into classes, my Lord, are not artificial. They are the natural outcome of a civilized society. There must always be a master and servants in all civilized communities, my Lady, for it is natural, and whatever is natural is right.

Lillie Langtry (1852-1929), English actress-manager, whose beauty and position created a sensation when she went on stage. Prominent in English society and a friend of Edward VII, she was one of the first women from society to become an actress. From *The Theatre,* 1882.

So it was with the Victorian middle class. To the middle class, the rise of the lower class was synonymous with the movement toward equality and, with it, permissiveness. A similar development took place after the war when the commercial theatre continued to cater to middle-class values of the past. The new theatre was viewed with a certain amount of fear by the middle class. The battle between the Lord Chamberlain who became the upholder of past values, and the new theatres was symptomatic of this fear. Because of its revolutionary slant, the new theatre was suspected of being a kind of theatrical Frankenstein capable of destroying or undermining the traditional values of

Johnson Forbes-Robertson (1853-1937), actor-manager who in 1882 performed what some critics called the finest Hamlet of all time. Forbes-Robertson was knighted in 1913. From *The Theatre,* 1882.

English life. But it began to be more and more obvious after World War II that the values of the past were not always applicable to today's society. As long as the voice of the new drama was allowed expression, the archaic office of the censor lived on. But when the old threatened to strangle the new, the inevitable battle producing the inevitable conclusion began. As a result, theatrical censorship, one of the last vestiges of Victorian England, was dead.

The modern English theatre is once again one of the world's best. Playwrights such as Peter Shaffer *(The Royal Hunt of the Sun,* and *Equus),* Edward Bond *(Lear* and *The Fool),* and Harold Pinter *(The Caretaker* and *The Homecoming),* have gained world-wide fame. The English stage has produced the finest actors and directors in the world, such as Lawrence Olivier, John Gielgud, Ralph Richardson, Geraldine McEwan, Paul Schofield, Peter Brook, William Gaskill, Nichol Williamson, and Joan Littlewood, to name but a few. It is alive and well today, with a superb system for the training of young actors. Significantly, its policy of reduced-rate tickets for students will build future audiences. Because of the quality of the theatre, many English productions are finding their way to Broadway.

The American Theatre

The American theatre after the war was clearly a product of trends established before the war. Playwrights such as Tennessee Williams and Arthur Miller were to achieve fame with primarily realistic plays, although both were to experiment with other styles later in their careers. Williams produced a number of excellent dramas, usually based on the survival of love and beauty in a brutal world. His *The Glass Managerie* (1945), *A Streetcar Named Desire* (1947), and *The Rose Tattoo* (1951) all had a delicate, almost poetic, quality to them. In 1955 he turned briefly away from realism to expressionism with his *Camino Real,* which failed on Broadway but may yet survive the test of time as one of his best plays. Recently Williams completed *This Is an Entertainment* (1976) and reworked *Summer and Smoke* into an entirely new script called *Eccentricities of a Nightingale* (1977). His latest play *Vieux Carré* (1977) was not well received. He remains a force in the American theatre, even though his output has declined considerably.

Arthur Miller (1916-) was, like Williams, a product of university training. His *Death of a Salesman* (1949) remains one of the classics of American theatre. Miller has been concerned with values in a highly materialistic society. His *The Crucible* (1953) was written during the time of the McCarthy hearings of the House Un-American Activities Committee. The parallel between the Salem witch hunts and this committee are not lost. Miller's more recent plays include *After the Fall* (1964), *Incident at Vichy* (1964), *The Creation of the World and Other Business* (1972), and *Archbishop's Ceiling* (1977).

Musicals continued to be popular on the American stage. Rodgers and Hammerstein maintained their successful collaboration with *Carousel* (1945), *South Pacific* (1949), and *The King and I*

The original Broadway production of Arthur Miller's *Death of a Salesman,* directed by Elia Kazan and designed by Jo Mielziner, opened on February 10, 1949, at the Morosco Theatre. Mielziner's design extended the new stagecraft of the 1920's to what was called theatricalized realism. Courtesy New York Public Library at Lincoln Center.

(1951), which was just recently revived on Broadway. Probably the most successful musical of the period was *My Fair Lady* (1956) by Alan Jay Lerner and Frederick Loewe. *My Fair Lady,* based on *Pygmalion* by George Bernard Shaw, received unanimous critical acclaim and is still played throughout the world. In the late 1960's, the dominant rock beat was noted in such musicals as *Your Own Thing* (an interpretation of Shakespeare's *Twelfth Night*) and *Hair. Hair* was significant because it established the rock musical by introducing new concepts in stage lighting, dancing, music, and blocking.

Because the New York stage is a business enterprise, the singular most important factor in its survival is that it must make money. This is not new; Shakespeare's theatre had to make money and so did Garrick's. But the difference is in the amount of money needed before expenses are paid. For Shakespeare, overhead expenses were minute compared to Broadway. Production costs in the theatre today are astronomical and producers are forced to concentrate on plays that will appeal to the tastes of mass audiences. For that reason, New York has once again become the center for commercial theatre. Broadway must leave the work of discovery to either the regional theatres, off-off-Broadway, or the English stage. Neil Simon has been the most successful of the Broadway writers, producing a string of hits; *Barefoot in the Park* (1963), *The Odd Couple* (1965), *The Last of the Red Hot Lovers* (1970), *California Suite* (1976), and *Chapter Two* (1978) have dominated the New York stage. Edward Albee (1928-) exploded on Broadway with *Who's Afraid of Virginia Woolf* in 1962. Albee's later works have not been financially successful, but he remains an important American writer whose output is awaited eagerly by the theatre public as well as critics.

Arthur Kopit (1938-) gained success with his *Oh Dad, Poor Dad, Mama's Hung You in the Closet and I'm Feeling So Sad* (1960). Kopit's *Indians* (1968) was even more successful and was made into a screen play.

The Regional Theatres

The real excitement in the American theatre, then, is not on Broadway. Although Broadway can be exciting, the most exciting theatre has been and is being done by the off-off-Broadway groups described in the next chapters, with two notable exceptions — the regional theatre and the New York Shakespeare Festival.

The most important of the regional theatres is the Tyrone Guthrie Theatre of Minneapolis. The Guthrie theatre opened in 1963 and has inspired other cities to follow suit. The Actor's Workshop in San Francisco, The Alley Theatre in Houston, Actors Theatre in Louisville, and the Arena Stage in Washington are fully professional and excellent companies.

The New York Shakespeare Public Theatre was initiated by Joseph Papp (1921-). Papp is probably the most energetic producer in America. He has sent quality productions to Broadway after their public theatre openings. These include *Hair* (1967), *Chorus Line* (1975), and Pulitzer Prize plays, *No Place to be Somebody* by Charles Gordone and *That Championship Season* by Jason Miller.

The sixties and seventies have seen the rise of several experimental groups which are in the process of revolutionizing the theatre in America and elsewhere. Most are continuations of developments which started in the early part of the century, but all have created their own innovations and some have achieved an entirely new direction. These new developments, plus the eclecticism of Broadway, *are* the contemporary theatre.

Selected Readings

The American Theatre: A Sum of Its Parts. New York, 1971.
Mitchell, Loften. *Black Drama*. New York, 1967.
Schaffer, Louis. *O'Neill*. 2 vols. Boston, 1968-1973.
Ziegler, Joseph. *Regional Theatre*. Minneapolis, 1973.

Vocabulary

1. eclecticism	ek LEK tuh si zuhm
2. Imamu Amiri Baraka	im AH moo: uh MEER ee buh RA kuh
3. Ntozake Shange	en toh ZAH kee SHAN guh
4. S.N. Behrman	BAIR muhn
5. William Poel	pohl
6. *La Biche au Bois*	lah BEESH oh bwuh
7. Steele Mackaye	muh KIGH
8. Jean-Paul Sartre	zhaw pohl SAHR truh
9. Albert Camus	ahl BAIR kah MOO:
10. Friedrich Duerrenmatt	FREED rik DOO: ruhn maht
11. Lawrence Olivier	oh LIV ee ay
12. *Camino Real*	KA mi noh REEL
13. *Vieux Carré*	vyer kah RAY

Above: Anna Cora Ritchie's *Fashion* (1845) as produced at the University of Georgia. Directed by Fay Head; costume design by Jackson Kesler. Courtesy Jackson Kesler.

Below: Christopher Fry's *The Lady's Not for Burning.* Directed by D. Whitney Combs; set design by James Brown; produced at Western Kentucky University.

CHAPTER FOURTEEN

Theatre in the 1960's Revolt against Tradition

During the 1960's, attempts by theatre practitioners to break with traditional theatre were decidedly widespread. This was motivated in part by the turmoil of the times and in part by Actors Equity (the union for actors and stage managers) unionizing the off-Broadway theatres, which financially could no longer afford to be experimental. Off-Broadway was, in all practicality, Broadway one step removed. It had to worry about making money and, consequently, could not afford to take a chance on new talent or new experimental productions. It catered largely to the traditional theatre goer who expected to sit in a soft seat while being entertained by actors who, dressed in costume and wearing makeup, appeared on a stage pretending to be somebody else. The actor and the audience relationship was thus one in which the actor was set apart from the audience by appearing on a stage which was physically removed from the audience. Seeking to fill the gap left by off-Broadway as well as rebelling against traditional theatre, experimental theatres and ensemble groups emerged. What resulted was a redefinition of the relationship between the actor and the audience.

Traditional theatre places the audience in the position of an outside observer and seeks to communicate illusion to the audience. With illusion comes passiveness, which in traditional theatre strongly suggests a desire on the part of the audience to be entertained. In the 1950's Bertolt Brecht and his Berliner Ensemble were the most noted example of a theatre group seeking to break with the theatre's traditional actor-audience relationship. Brecht wanted audiences to become directly involved, to become active, and his productions aimed at dispelling illusion through a number of devices aimed at incongruity. Despite his innovations, the actor-audience remained basically traditional; the audience was still basically apart from the production as opposed to being an integral part of it. Brecht had not physically combined the actor and the audience into one area where the audience could directly (actively) participate in the production.

In an effort to make the audience an integral part of the performance, the experimental theatres redefined the traditional boundaries separating the actor and the audience. Among the innovations were the elimination of fixed seating and a permanent stage. The action took place amidst the audience, which greatly minimized (if not altogether eliminated) illusion. To make the audiences part of the action, actors engaged the audiences in dialogues. Actors listening to the audience could also be classified as audience, and the audience responding to the actors could be considered actors. Audiences were no longer passive; Brecht's concept of an active audience was created.

Generally speaking, experimental theatre was an effort to demonstrate that behind all the masks and facades, people are universally the same, and that society has been largely responsible for the differences created. The task of the theatre is to create an atmosphere where audiences can discover their true natures. They are challenged by the actors to respond as well as share their dreams, fears, and attitudes. By having members of the audience share with the actor, as well as with each other, the audience and actors will become united as a community. Theatre is thus conceived much like a place of worship, where one can reveal one's self. It is a place where mankind will recognize the absurdity of life and having recognized its absurdity, will not be overly concerned about it. It is taking life too seriously that causes man to hate and cry. Freeing himself from this concern will enable him to laugh instead of cry, and love instead of hate. It is another way to purge one's emotions.

Opposite: The Moscow Theatre of Drama and Comedy on Taganka Square, better known as Taganka Theatre, is traditionally the most experimental and liberal in Moscow. Founded in 1964, the theatre is under the direction of Yuri Lyubimov, who is shown here congratulating the cast after the production of *Under the Skin of Liberty Statue.* Courtesy Tass from Sovfoto.

Eugene Ionesco, a Rumanian by birth, is among the most successful of the so-called absurdists. *The Bald Soprano* (1949), *The Lesson* (1950), *The Chairs* (1952), and *Rhinoceros* (1960) remain classics from the Theatre of the Absurd. Photo Agnes Varda, courtesy New York Public Library at Lincoln Center.

Theatre of the Absurd

Samuel Beckett (1906-), Eugene Ionesco (1912-), Arthur Adamov (1908-1971), and Jean Genet (1910-) are considered the mainstays of absurdist drama. Although theatre of the absurd is a French phenomenon, Genet is the only native Frenchman. Beckett is Irish; Adamov, Russian; and Ionesco, Rumanian. All came to France, and all wrote their plays in French. All four writers share a similar philosophy which suggests that the human condition is one of isolation and futility, and that man is at the mercy of unknown forces. These writers have influenced a host of dramatists throughout the world, including Edward Albee, Harold Pinter, Gunter Grass, Max Frisch, Slawomir Mrozek, Vacláv Havel, Fernando Arrabal, and Friedrich Duerrenmatt.

The absurdist playwrights believe that life is absurd because it has no "purpose or goal or objective." We are born without asking to be born, and we die without really seeking death. Our entire lives are spent like puppets hanging in limbo. We don't know where we came from, and we don't know where we are going. Taking a cue from Camus' *The Myth of Sisyphus* (1942), who spent eternity rolling a boulder up a hill only to have it roll down again, the absurdists see our lives spent in futile, hopeless labor. We do the same things day in and day out with slight variation. Life seems meaningless because we do not know the answers; we possess only functional knowledge. We therefore invent religion and fill our lives with meaningless devices to rationalize our existence and to keep our minds off the fact that we will one day die. We are not only ignorant of life, but incapable of doing anything about our ignorance. This makes us insecure. Furthermore, in that all things are doomed to death and decay, we cannot create anything of significance. Life is thus a senseless, meaningless concept devoid of purpose of significance — it is absurd.

The classic example of absurdist drama is Samuel Beckett's *Waiting for Godot* (1953); more properly, the title, *En Attendant Godot,* should be translated *While Waiting for Godot.* Essentially a novelist and poet in the thirties and forties, Beckett turned to the dramatic form in the 1950's and *Godot* represents his first effort. It has been translated in over a dozen languages, has sold over 50,000 copies in French, and over 350,000 copies in Beckett's English translation. For this play as well as his other efforts, Samuel Beckett was awarded the Nobel Prize for literature in 1969.

Existentialistic in philosophy, the play focuses on two tramps, Estragon and Vladimir, who wait on the side of a road for someone named Godot. While waiting, they occupy their time playing games, complaining about life, sleeping, calling each other the nicknames of Didi and Gogo, and generally engaging in various diversions.

Joining Vladimir and Estragon is Pozzo, a tyrant, and his terrified slave, Lucky, who is forced by Pozzo to show his tricks, do a dance, and demonstrate that he can think (which he really cannot). These two disappear into the darkness. Later they return — Pozzo is blind and Lucky, dumb. They are unable to recall who they are, let alone, who they were. The entire play focuses not on who the characters are, but what the characters do while waiting. As Estragon reflects, "Nothing happens, nobody comes, nobody goes, it's awful."

The play has two acts, each of which ends with a boy delivering the message that Godot cannot come today but maybe tomorrow. Estragon then asks "What shall we do?", to which Vladimir replies, in true existentialistic fashion, "Wait for Godot." Like Vladimir and Estragon, mankind occupies itself in a variety of diversions while waiting.

Historically, the term *absurdism* was coined by Martin Esslin in the book *Theatre of the Absurd* (1961). The roots of absurdism are generally traced back to Alfred Jarry's (1873-1907) *Ubu Roi* (1896), which was first produced in Paris. Ubu is the false King of Poland, who personifies human greed, brutality, selfishness, and cruelty. The manner in which Ubu was characterized became a trademark of the theatre of the absurd — the external characterization of a character's internal qualities. Rather than infer the character's psychological nature, dramatists of the absurd theatre blatantly express the character's nature. For example, Ubu's human grossness is shown to us by his enormous belly, mask, and exaggerated costume. The character is made larger than life.

Influences upon absurdism are many; however, many of its characteristics come from several sources. In addition to Jarry, Guillaume Apollinaire (1880-1918), Antonin Artaud (1896-1948), August Strindberg (1849-1912), Franz Kafka (1883-1924), and the existentialist, Camus (1913-1960), lent their influences. The influences can be noted in some of the outstanding characteristics of the absurdist theatre.

Gunter Grass (b. 1927), Germany's best known contemporary author. The majority of his plays belong to the absurdist tradition. As a novelist, he is best known for *The Tin Drum*. Grass was awarded the Georg Buchner Prize in 1965. Courtesy German Information Center.

1. Conventional language is degraded. This device is utilized to emphasize that there is a lack of communication between people. The absurdists believe language is empty of substance and thus has fallen into a mere convention of slogans and cliches.
2. The focus of absurd drama lies in the action. No connection exists between what the characters say and what they do.
3. Characters are patterned after Ubu; they are not literary characters, but are cardboard figures who entertain.
4. Conventional logic is rejected.
5. The audience is forced into a position of asking not what will happen next, but basically what is happening.

The Living Theatre

The Living Theatre of Julian Beck and his wife, Judith Malina, was "the mother of them all." The Becks are the forerunners to a host of experimental theatres, a great many of which are located in New York City and are grouped under the label of the off-off Broadway theatres. The Living Theatre was basically a political theatre whose members sought a revolution in the theatre as well as society; hence, its name became synonymous with anarchy and radicalism. The Becks chose their name in 1947 to emphasize their philosophy: a commitment to contemporary works which in turn concerned issues germane to society's social, economic, and political institutions.

Historically, the Living Theatre started in a theatre on Wooster Street (New York) where the Becks presented miracle plays, Japanese Noh dramas, Strindberg, and Ibsen. From there they moved their theatre to their West End Avenue apartment, where in August 1951 they presented four short plays. This performance is generally considered to mark the beginning of the Living Theatre. In December 1951, they were able to open their own theatre, the Cherry Lane in Greenwich Village, with *Many Loves* (1959) by William Carlos Williams. The Cherry Lane Theatre closed after three performances and over the next years, the Becks continued to perform wherever they could. The company was unheralded until their realistic production of *The Connection* in May 1959, which received good reviews and brought them national attention. Consequently, in 1961 they were asked to perform at the Théâtre des Nations in Paris, where they won the Grand Prix for the best acting company.

The Becks were anticapitalistic, both politically and artistically, and cared very little about making money. Consequently, the company was in a constant state of poverty, which was overcome, to a degree, by living as a commune. Their lack of concern about money also manifested itself in the Becks' refusal to pay the government its taxes. Because of this, in 1963 their theatre was closed and the Becks were sent to jail. Upon their release they went to Europe where they remained until 1966, when they returned to the United States. Two years later they went to Brazil, where they were expelled for drugs and again returned to America. The group disbanded in 1970 perhaps because of financial reasons as well as dissatisfaction in the group.

Before breaking up in 1970 into what Beck asserted were "cells" ("as part of a plan to attack the entire structure from many sides"), the Living Theatre underwent change. Their intent was the same however; they were still a theatre group who worked together, lived together in a communal society, and together subscribed to the same ideological position. The change was philosophical. Their performances of *Antigone* (1962) and *Mysteries – And Smaller Pieces* (1964) demonstrated this change. The productions were philosophically eclectic in that they contained Hindu mysticism, Greek mythology, Christianity, and the theories of Artaud, and were designed to rouse the audience against immorality, environmental pollution, and capitalism.

The Living Theatre's approach to their performances is based upon a hostility against the value system represented by the capitalistic society. At times, Julian Beck would verbally assault the audience by calling them "mother f — bourgeois intellectuals" because the money they spent for a ticket could have been used for feeding the poor. At other times, the actors engaged the audience in conversation, sometimes trying to provoke the audience. On other occasions the audience members were caressed by the actors, who encouraged them to join in the performance. For example, in the rite of the "love pile" in *Paradise Now* (1968), some audience members joined the actors in taking off their clothes. The nude actors and audience then lay side by side or atop each other in a pile where they could explore each other's bodies. The actors were symbols of the antiestablishment cult of the 1960's: their dress consisted of beads, long hair, beards, and tattered clothes, and they would often perform "stoned." Their performances stressed hostility against society and traditional theatre. The Living Theatre was indeed the foremost experimental theatre to emerge thus far in the twentieth century.

Grotowski

Jerzy Grotowski (1933-) is the director of the Polish Laboratory Theatre in Wroclaw, Poland, where in 1959 he began his work which revolutionized the theory of acting. Presently, his work has evolved in what he terms "paratheatre."

Grotowski's ideas about acting and the theatre were popularized in the 1960's through his book *Towards a Poor Theatre* (1968). In this book he stresses a complete redefinition of the relationship between the actor and the audience. The traditional relationship is discarded, and the actors and audiences are mixed. In addition, Grotowski argues that the scenic arrangement for every production should be different, implying no fixed seating or fixed stages. Furthermore, Grotowski suggests the elimination of makeup, costumes, stage lighting, set design and sound effects. These are elements of the "Rich Theatre." The only elements necessary for theatre are the actor and the audience. In that he has no need for all the elements which go into staging a traditional production, except the actor and the audience, Grotowski applies the label *poor* to this theatre.

Grotowski's concept of poor theatre is really a way of applying self-renunciation (as practiced by many religious orders) to art. Self-renunciation is another way of removing all externals, and in terms of theatre, this is what Grotowski suggests. This concept of Grotowski is predicated on the Biblical notion that man's "naked spirit" has been clothed in violence, social hypocrisy, greed, and oppression, and that these force people to assume a variety of personalities (masks) in order to survive. This is not our true nature, and thus, a stripping away of all the masks is required so that we can have a spiritual reawakening and reveal our true selves.

This underlying philosophy is inherent to Grotowski's acting techniques. Everything in the theatre stems from the actor. He is the basic element. Instead of makeup, properties and costumes, the actor's facial muscles can create masks, and a piece of cloth can suggest a costume (if one is really needed). The rhythm of the body muscles can convey emotion. Music can come from the actor's voice, hands, and feet. Traditional scenery can be eliminated in favor of mixing actors and audience to create stronger bonds of communication. In terms of plays, Grotowski advocates using old myths and updating them to make them more meaningful to contemporary audiences. It is a way of reconciling the past with the present.

Grotowski's acting techniques are engineered to uncover feelings which he believes are hidden in our "collective unconscious." The Swiss psychologist, Carl Jung (1879-1961), was responsible for the term which defines a part of the mind in which is stored a person's true feelings, intuitions, attitudes, knowledge (racial memory), and experience. Everyone inherits their "collective unconscious," which, says Jung, is responsible for our general or universal behavior. To arouse these emotions, states Grotowski, requires physical stimuli; thus, there is a relationship between the mental and the physical. Further, the relationship between our emotions and our physical actions involves another step. Grotowski sees the physical action being linked to basic impulses (physically, impulses are nerve fibers and require stimuli), and these in turn being connected to the "collective unconscious." For Grotowski, then, the idea is for the actor to find stimuli for those basic impulses. This process involves exploring the "collective unconscious" for specific stimuli for the desired impulse. Grotowski believes that the actor, upon discovering the stimuli, can re-create it spontaneously before that impulse becomes a premeditated thought. By having complete knowledge and physical control of the body and voice, an actor can re-create the living impulse. The use of impulses to create an artistic performance is, for Grotowski, part of the actor's goal.

The other task of the actor is to create for the audience an opportunity for self-renunciation. Grotowski is extremely concerned about the audience, and thus has gone on record as allowing only a select audience (usually not over forty members) for each performance, which lasts only fifty-five minutes. These audience members are individuals who are willing to give of themselves and wish to analyze themselves and remove their masks. With the spectator as a primary concern, Grotowski's staging is designed to establish a close relationship between the actor and audience. As the actor suffers, the audience is to suffer with him. This suffering will lead to a state of grace. Grotowski's ideas thus are intended to create a "holy theatre," a religious experience for the audience through the aid of the actor.

This close relationship concept as well as the reconciliation of the past with the present proved to be fundamental to the experimental theatres of the 1960's. Of all the influences, Grotowski and the Living Theatre proved to be the most influential.

Open Theatre

The immediate successor to the Living Theatre and, in many ways, an American parallel to Grotowski's Polish Laboratory Theatre was Joseph Chaikin and Peter Feldman's Open Theatre. Although both Feldman and Chaikin were originally responsible for the company's formation, it was under the leadership of Chaikin that the company made its significant contribution.

Chaikin and Feldman were both members of the Living Theatre but opted to remain in America when the Becks made their trip to Europe in 1961. In February 1963 the company was formed, with such members as Jean Claude Van Itallie, Megan Terry, Gordon Rogoff, Mary Irene Fornes, and Gerry Ragni (one of the composers of the musical *Hair),* and later, Sam Shepard. They called themselves the Open Theatre to distinguish them from the closed theatre of Broadway. Their intent was to develop an acting style "that would depict the individual's response to a depersonalized society." Like the theatre of the absurd, the Open Theatre believed that language was empty of any substantive content. They were antitraditional theatre, and, consequently, were against characterization as found in naturalistic drama. Seeming to parallel Grotowski's ideas, the group sought an acting style in which the actor relied upon his root impulses (intuition and instinct) in order to achieve a true uncensored response to modern events. Unlike leaders of the Living Theatre, however, they did not see their group as communal nor their performances as a political forum. They were primarily interested in the art of acting.

At first the company experimented with a variety of techniques, such as the theatre games of Viola Spolin which eventually became the mainstay of the Open Theatre's work. Despite their progress, the group refused to commit themselves to a specific acting approach, to focus on specific long-range goals, or to resolve artistic and commercial questions relating to their organization. This lack of self-definition was, in the long run, the factor causing the Open Theatre's demise.

Among the significant productions to emerge from the group were *America Hurrah* (1968, later called *Motel), Viet Rock* (1966), and *The Serpent* (1969). It was through *The Serpent,* their first full-length production, that the philosophy of the company was best expressed. That philosophy was based on the concept of collaboration. It was out of the actors' own personal responses, dreams, meditations, and perceptions that *The Serpent* was created. *The Serpent* reflects the collective world of the Open Theatre but things like responses, meditations, dreams, and perceptions are hardly explicit. Much of what is expressed is at the "gut level," and acts as a stimulus to similar feelings within the audience. The Open Theatre, like many experimental theatres, expresses an acting style which goes back to ritual and myth; it is part of a strong desire to find a relationship between past and present.

In 1969 the Open Theatre went on a European tour, and by the time it returned, the company had become embroiled in a crisis. Some members wanted to use their work as an instrument for political expression (like the Living Theatre), and others wanted to continue as they had in the past. Chaikin favored reorientation toward a leftist political position, but he did not favor playing the same production daily, like a commercial theatre, even though it brought financial benefits. He sought a middle ground between the company's radical beliefs, their artistic concepts, and "living in America." The middle-of-the-road policy reflected a lack of commitment on the company's part. This created a host of divergent views and thus in 1973 the company dissolved. Nonetheless, Chaikin is still active with another group with whom he is exploring the ideas of the anthropologist Joseph Campbell, who contends all ritual and myth are concerned with either pleasure, power, or duty.

Bread and Puppet Theatre

The Bread and Puppet Theatre was founded in 1961 by Peter Schumann who had been a puppeteer, choreographer, and an instructor at the Putney School in Vermont. His first New York production was in 1962, when he directed *Dance of Death* at the Sheridan Square Playhouse. By 1963 Schumann's group was performing regularly in a loft in Greenwich Village. Although presently unknown to many commercial theatre goers, Schumann's group continues to flourish, playing wherever it can — in the streets, parks, or in a traditional theatre.

Influenced by Grotowski, Peter Schumann organized his group around two concepts: bread and puppets. Like Grotowski, Schumann holds that theatre is a religious experience. Thus, before, during, or after a production, bread is passed around free for the audience to share. Bread is basic and emphasizes not only Schumann's desire to feed the hungry, but also stresses the religious ritual of communion. The use of puppets is directly related to the religious connotation of bread. Following the precepts of Jesus that "man does not live by bread alone," Schumann has added a puppet show.

These puppets vary in size from hand puppets to his most notable ten-foot rod puppets. The Bread and Puppet Theatre will perform any place their puppets can fit, but prefer street performances for which there is no admission charge. The theatre will perform indoors, however, for which Schumann generally charges a small admission. The most noted puppets are his "gray ladies," who are completely gray and symbolize the mother figure, specifically the suffering woman of Vietnam or the Virgin Mary.

The main purpose of the Bread and Puppet Theatre is to persuade the audience to abolish violence and hunger in the world and to place their priorities on water, air, and soil (ecology) and not on materialism. In light of his purpose, Schumann's goals are threefold:

1. *Poverty:* Eliminate dependence on material objects.
2. *Moderation:* Emphasize love and de-emphasize lust.
3. *Resistance:* Oppose the warmongers and the tenets of capitalism.

The usual format for the Bread and Puppet Theatre is similar in some ways to a Greek production. There is a pre-production parade (in which the audience may join), which leads to the performance area. Schumann announces the program. A loaf of bread is passed around; each audience member breaks off a piece and passes on the loaf. The plays consist of dances, gestures, chants, masks, music, songs, varying sounds, and minimal dialogue (if any). Illusion, in the traditional sense, is not attempted; the medium is the message. For Schumann that message is a desire to reawaken man's spiritual nature.

El Teatro Campesino

The founder of the *El Teatro Campesino* (The Farm Workers Theatre) is Luis Miguel Valdez (1941-   ), who worked for Ronnie Davis' San Francisco Mime Troup before organizing his own company. It is from his experiences with the Mime Troup that Valdez was able to form El Teatro Campesino in 1965 in Delano, California. This company is not to be confused with the Teatro Compesino of Mexico, organized in the 1930's, whose goals was improving sanitary conditions. Valdez's group was organized out of the strike by Cesar Chevez's Mexico-American National Farm Workers Association against the grape ranchers. Valdez formed the group to support the strike by dramatizing the better life as well as to teach the farmer how to survive politically.

At first the plays were improvised, but now the company relies on the written word. This change has fostered a Chicano literature for which the playwrights, such as Valdez, have been an important force. The scripts are a mixture of Mexican and English slang. To help those in the audience who do not speak English, the actors wear signs to tell the character's name or role. For example, *patroncito* (grower), *huelgista* (striker), and *contratista* (contractor).

The company was originally dedicated to the organization of the Farm Workers, but its focus has shifted toward the racial heritage *(la rasa)* of the Mexican-American. Probably the first play to indicate this shift was Valdez's *La Carpa Rasquachi*

(1976). The stress on the "roots" of the Mexican-American has encouraged the formation of other such groups. The most notable is the El Teatro Bilingüe whose focus is upon producing literary works from Latin America. This company is more traditional in its approach and philosophy. Nonetheless, its formation alongside that of El Teatro Campesino indicates a strong push on the part of ethnic minorities to resurrect their cultural past. The dramatization of the cultural heritage of varying ethnic groups may well be a continuation of the ritual performances begun in the 1960's. The theatre groups of the sixties and seventies have placed a strong emphasis on their "roots."

Guerrilla Theatre

Guerrilla theatre is not a specific theatre group but rather a political activity to be used by varying theatre companies. As a conscious theatre activity, guerrilla theatre developed as a result of the Vietnam War. Although the term was coined by Peter Berg, a member of the San Francisco Mime Troupe it was popularized by Ronnie Davis, the leader of the San Francisco Mime Troup in the early 1960's. Its name was derived from guerrilla warfare; guerrilla theatre seeks to imitate its namesake. In adhering to the tactics of guerrilla warfare, the guerrilla theatre employs these devices: mobility, small groups, simple tactics, surprise, and pressuring its opponents' weak points. The main purposes of guerrilla theatre are to teach, seek change (revolution), and be an example of change. This change can be created, if necessary, by disrupting the proceedings of rallies, conventions, trials, college commencements, or other formal meetings. Some ideas recommended by Ronnie Davis are:

1. Use a portable stage.
2. Keep the length of production under one hour.
3. Emphasize commedia dell'arte techniques (masks, gags, music).
4. Perform Saturday and Sunday afternoons.
5. Use any cheap place for rehearsals (parks, for example).

These ideas of Davis suggest a formalized presentation for guerrilla theatre. Guerrilla theatre was used, however, by many political activists in a nonformal arrangement; for example, boycotting grapes and lettuce. Actors went to grocery stores and placed pictures of hungry migrant workers in the grape and lettuce sections of the store. When customers went to purchase these products, the pictures were intended to dissuade them. The political ideas of guerrilla theatre found a strong outlet in such ensemble groups as the El Teatro Campesino.

Happenings

Happenings are another theatrical activity. They were originally known as "painter's theatre," because the first happenings were given by painters in their galleries and studios. Although John Cage gave what is considered the first American happening in 1952, the first painter's happening as well as the coining of the term is generally credited to Allan Kaprow, who in 1959 invited a select group to view *18 Happenings in 6 Parts.* Kaprow's theatrical event was not intended for the theatre, but rather was an experience aimed at the painter. As Kaprow indicated, he wanted to expand his environment to express his artistic ideas rather than be limited to a canvas. Happenings are thus a form of environmental theatre (a term originated by Richard Schechner), which means that the first scenic principle is to use actively all the space in the performance area.

Compared to traditional theatre, happenings seek an opposite approach. Plot is replaced by what is termed *compartmented structure,* with each scene or unit of a happening completely independent of the other scenes or units. There is no cause-to-effect relationship. It is much like a three-ring circus, with all the acts occurring simultaneously. Unlike traditional drama, scenes in a happening may or may not contain people. A scene might be only a scene of sound. If people are involved, there is frequently little interplay between them. The actors do not attempt characterization; that is, they do not embellish the part with detail trying to convince the audience that they are another person. They play themselves. Furthermore, there are no designated entrances or exits, and the actor has greater freedom in performing the tasks designated in the script. The actor is much like a property or a stage effect which is used to demonstrate the actor's creation. Unlike the traditional theatre, a happening does not function in terms of expected logic — that is, everything has

Joseph Dixon, Edith Groome, and Clarence R. Chase in a scene from ". . . *one-third of a nation* . . .," A Federal Theatre Project, 1938. Courtesy Joseph "Mac" Dixon.

a cause-to-effect relationship. Traditional drama is structured to create illusion and impart information to the audience. A happening does not seek to impart information; it serves as a direct experience rather than an illusionary one. All meaning must be intuited; that is, interpreted through our subconscious. Next, in keeping with the experimental theatres, happenings are performed anywhere. To avoid the traditional use of theatre space, Kaprow suggests that a happening should take place over several widely separated locales and time should not be a factor in a happening. Lastly, a happening may or may not have dialogue, may be performed only once, seeks no audience as audience, and above all, makes no separation between art and life. The happening is life actually occurring at a particular moment; it is a "slice of life."

Off-Broadway

Off-Broadway refers to New York theatres located in an area bounded by Fifth and Ninth Avenues from 34th Street to 56th Street to 72nd Street not having a seating capacity above 499 (originally this was 299), and in its inception, dedicated to providing opportunities for writers, actors, directors, set designers, and other specialists in the

The Straight Wharf Theatre's (Nantucket) production of *The Fantasticks,* currently the longest running musical on or off Broadway. Directed by Joseph "Mac" Dixon. Courtesy Joseph "Mac" Dixon.

theatre. Productions were nonunion, and ticket prices were lower than Broadway. Profit was not the motive, art was. Unfortunately, off-Broadway became unionized in the early 1960's, limiting the opportunities for new talent and for experimentation in productions. Thus, the concept behind the birth of the off-Broadway movement was dead, and for all intent and purposes, off-Broadway had severed its ties with its past.

The origin of the off-Broadway movement is generally linked to what is known in America as the "Little theatre" movement. The "Little theatre" movement was nationwide and was developed in direct reaction to the commercialism of Broadway, as noted earlier. From two little theatre groups, notably the Washington Square Players and the Provincetown Players, the format as to what constitutes an off-Broadway theatre was derived.

Prior to its unionization, off-Broadway gave every indication of becoming America's "art" theatre. Although its expansion was halted by World War II, its growth continued immediately thereafter. In 1949 the off-Broadway League of Theatres was formed in an effort to keep the actor's union, Equity, from interfering. Three years later in 1952, Jose Quintero and Theodore Mann produced *Summer and Smoke,* starring Geraldine Page, at the Circle in The Square Theatre. This production marks the turning point in the off-Broadway movement. Brooks Atkinson's favorable review for the New York *Times* heralded recognition for the Circle in The Square and subsequently for off-Broadway.

During the 1950's and 1960's, off-Broadway expanded to its present state, which is merely an extension of Broadway. In direct reaction to off-Broadway's commercial state, off-off-Broadway emerged.

Cast of *Tales of Maine,* created and directed by Thomas A. Power. The Children's Theatre of Maine is one of many organizations using chamber theatre style productions which require little or no scenery.

Off-Off-Broadway

There are roughly 150 theatres which can be classified as off-off-Broadway. These theatres are dedicated first and foremost to giving new dramatists a hearing, as well as providing an atmosphere where artists can perfect their art. Geographically, these theatres are scattered throughout Greenwich Village and are located in churches, lofts, coffee-houses, and cellars. Historically, the first off-off-Broadway theatre developed in 1958 at Joe Cino's Café Cino. This coffeehouse had impromptu poetry readings, art exhibits, and dramatic readings. The dramatic readings led to mini-productions which provided an outlet for new scripts. Whereas Joe Cino's coffeehouse is considered the first off-off-Broadway theatre, the first off-off-Broadway production is usually cited as that of *Ubu Roi,* presented in 1960 at the Take 3 Theatre.

Significant off-off-Broadway groups include the Manhattan Project, Theatre of the Ridiculous, the Performance Group, the Open Theatre, Cafe LaMama, Theatre Genesis, Judson Poet's Theatre, and the Living Theatre, which is the forerunner to all experimental groups including those of off-off-Broadway. The experimental nature of off-off-Broadway was tested in 1975, when Equity tried to require that the actors in off-off-Broadway belong to Equity. The effort was resoundingly defeated, signifying, at least for the present, that the artistic endeavors of off-off-Broadway are more important to the actors than two on the aisle. It is on that note that off-off-Broadway continues today, but for how long is the question.

Selected Readings

Brockett, Oscar G., and Findlay, Robert R. *Century of Innovation.* Englewood Cliffs, New Jersey, 1973.

Croyden, Margaret. *Lunatics, Lovers, and Poets.* New York, 1974.

Kostelanetz, Richard. *The Theatre of Mixed Means.* New York, 1968.

Sainer, Arthur. *The Radical Theatre Notebook,* New York, 1975.

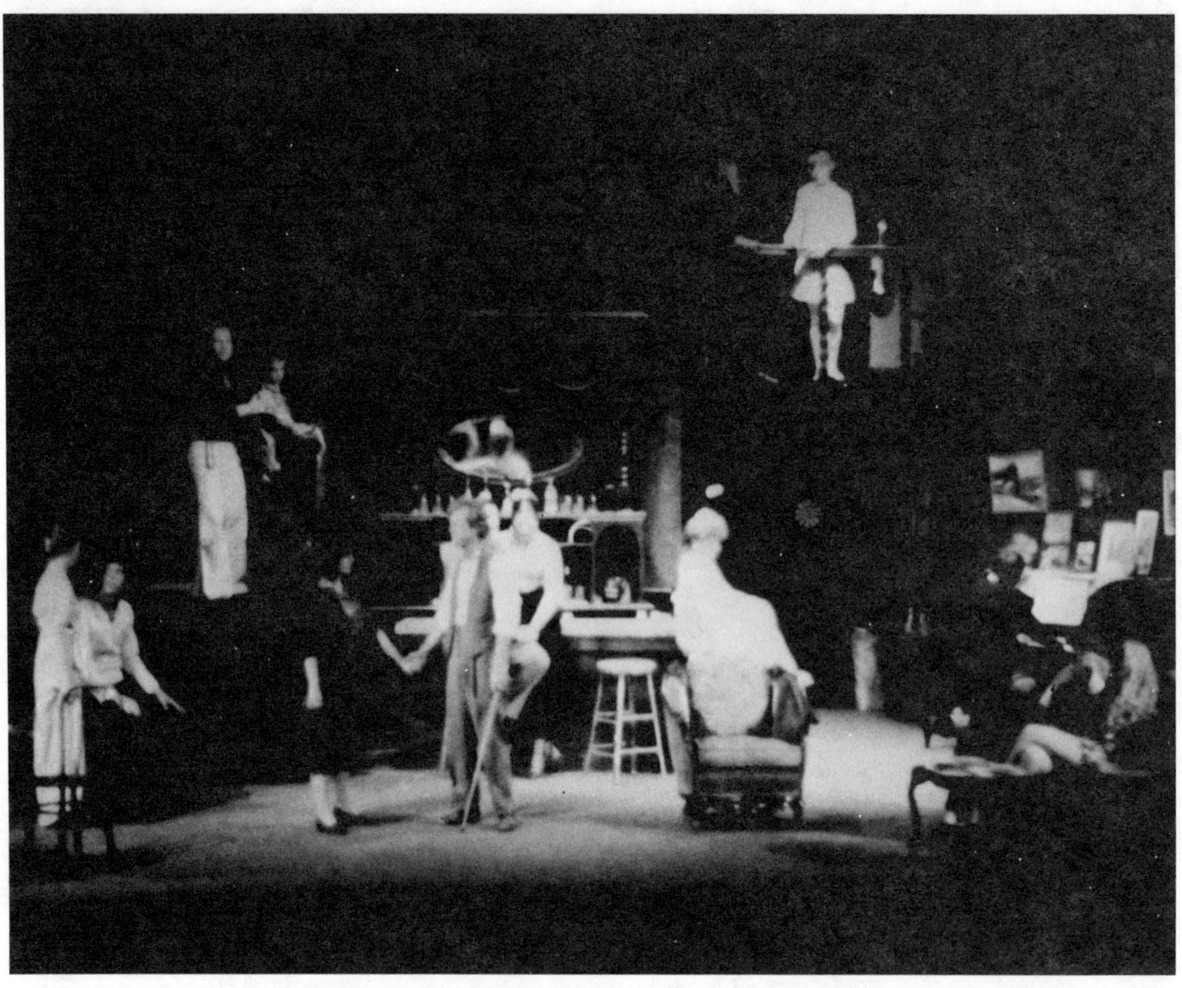

Brendan Behan's *The Hostage* as presented at Western Kentucky University. Directed by William Leonard; setting by James Brown.

Vocabulary

1. Berliner ensemble	bair LIN uhr
2. Jean Genet	zhaw zhe NAY
3. Arthur Adamov	AH duh mawf
4. Slawomir Mrozek	swahv OH meer MROH zyek
5. Vacláv Havel	vahs LAHF hah VEL
6. *Ubu Roi*	OO boo rwuh
7. Alfred Jarry	jah ree
8. Noh drama	noh
9. Jerzy Grotowski	YE zhee gruh TOW skee
10. Wroclaw, Poland	VRAWT slahf
11. Joseph Chaikin	CHAY kin
12. Jean Claude Van Itallie	zhaw klohd van i TAHL ee
13. Mary Irene Fornes	fohrns
14. Jerry Ragni	RAG nee
15. Gordon Rogoff	ROH gawf
16. El Teatro Campesino	el tay AHT roh cahm pe SEE noh
17. Luis Miguel Valdez	loo EE mee GEL vahl DEZ
18. La Carpa Rasguachi	lah KAHR puh rahs GWAH chee
19. patroncito	pah truhn SEE tuh
20. contratista	kawn trah TEES tuh
21. huelgista	whel GEE stah
22. La Rasa	lah RAH sah
23. Chicano	chi KAH noh
24. Allan Kaprow	KA proh
25. Richard Schechner	SHEK nuhr
26. Joe Cino	CHEE noh
27. Judith Molina	maw LEE nuh

CHAPTER FIFTEEN

The Creative Process

Drama is the one literary genre that requires components other than the script itself in order to be fully formulated. A play is written to be produced as a theatrical event. As a theatrical event, it must have a space, possibly scenery, costumes, and some kind of actor or interpreter.

All drama begins with a basic idea to be demonstrated. If the idea of the action to be imitated is manifested in written language, the maker of that idea is a playwright. Makers of plays have been with us at least since the fifth century B.C. and perhaps longer. From the great classical Greek period to the present day, writers of drama have recorded and are recording the lifestyles, conflicts, and philosophies of their individual worlds. Writers such as Aeschylus, Sophocles, Euripides, Aristophanes and Menander left us with insights into the very nerve center of Athenian thinking. History is filled with dramatists who have supplied the various theatres of their day with some of the most stimulating literature ever written. Each play was, in a sense, a record of its maker's life experience and a view of the civilization of which he was a part. Many of these playwrights have left to posterity a masterpiece, written in a genre which has been hailed as the highest form of literature. The chapter on form and style describes some of the structural characteristics of the drama, but what of the entire creative process involving the playwright, actor and director? How does the idea start, and how is it carried through?

The Germinal Idea

Playwrights vary in the way in which the initial concept of the play is formulated. Some writers begin the playwrighting process out of an idea arising from some sort of personal anxiety or experience. Arthur Laurents (1918-   ), for example, wrote *Home of the Brave* (1945) out of his combat experiences during World War II. He brooded on the discrimination he had suffered as a Jew and finally created his study of religious bigotry. The Drama Critics Circle Award play, *Raisin in the Sun,* was based upon Lorraine Hansberry's memories of her own childhood, when at the age of eight, she moved into an all-white neighborhood. Archibald MacLeish (1892-   ) was tormented by the meaning of suffering after witnessing the results of a Nazi bombing raid on the English town of West Hamm. Some victims had had their homes bombed as many as four times. The idea of meaningless suffering and persecution seemed to MacLeish to be the universal theme of war. It was this idea that led to the completion of perhaps his most famous play, *J.B.* (1958).

Ideas for a play, then, can be philosophical ones. Jean-Paul Sartre, with almost messianic fervor, composed his modern version of the Greek myth of Orestes, *The Flies,* to detail the philosophical idea of existentialism. Eugene Ionesco touted a similar idea in *The Bald Soprano.* Ionesco tells us: "The non-metaphysical world of today has destroyed all mystery; and the so-called "scientific" theatre of the period, the theatre of politics and propaganda, anti-poetic and academic, has flattened mankind out, alienating the unfathomable third dimension which makes a whole man. The theatre of ideologies and thesis, proposing political solutions and presuming to save humanity — to wish to save it is to kill it — and there are no solutions. To realize that is the only healthy solution."

Still other playwrights find their germinal seed in history, newspaper articles, mythology, or stories. One of the great teachers of playwrighting, George Pierce Baker, once said: "Undoubtedly, he who begins with a story is nearer his goal than he who begins with an idea or character." William Shakespeare himself was a frequent adapter of material. *Plutarch's Lives, The Holinshed Chronicles, Euphues,* and *Ur Hamlet* all furnished the

Opposite: George Bernard Shaw (1856-1950), considered second only to Shakespeare as a dramatist.

Maxim Gorky and Anton Chekhov in 1900. Courtesy Tass from Sovfoto.

basis for such plays as *Julius Caesar, Richard II, As You Like It,* and *Hamlet.* Lillian Hellman's (1907-) reading of "The Great Drumsheugh Case" from one of William Roughead's (1870-1952) anthologies of criminal law trials was the spark that resulted in *The Children's Hour* (1934).

Aeschylus, Sophocles, Euripides, Seneca, Racine, Anouilh, Anderson, Giraudoux, and O'Neill are among the many authors who wrote plays based on Greek mythology. Some of Henrik Ibsen's early plays were based on Norse mythology, and *The Black Mass* (1966) by LeRoi Jones was based on the Muslim myth of Yacub. The Tevye story of Sholom Aleichem provided Joseph Stein (1912-) with the background to create the book for the musical *Fiddler on the Roof* (1964).

Plays based on an idea of a character have been universally popular with playwrights. Joseph Kesselring (1902-1967), the author of *Arsenic and Old Lace,* admits "I got the idea for *Arsenic* by deliberately selecting my grandmother as a focal point and trying to imagine the most improbable thing she could possibly do." Both *All My Sons* (1947) and *After the Fall* (1964) by Arthur Miller were based on real life characters. The main character in *All My Sons* evolved out of Miller's aquaintance with a businessman who was turned in by his own daughter for manufacturing defective machinery during World War II. The character of Maggie in *After the Fall* was patterned after Miller's former wife, Marilyn Monroe.

Sometimes the character is fictitious from the onset and takes the form of a type. George Axelrod (1922-), author of *The Seven Year Itch* (1952), describes that play's genesis in this manner: "As everybody who writes down words on paper for a living knows, once in a while you get an idea that's a natural. One that can't miss. As I say, the idea came in one piece. The summer bachelor. The girl upstairs. The wife we only see in the hero's imagination. The whole business."

Sometimes the original germinating idea, be it philosophy, story, personal experience, or character, will become disguised as the playwright begins to formulate his work. In some cases, a playwright may not remember what started the creative process at the onset. Perhaps he may begin with a philosophical idea and evolve to a study of character. Whatever, at a certain point the playwright must begin to select and order his material in a way that will cause his audience to react in the desired manner.

The Play Plan

Some playwrights will plan their play in much the same way as an architect develops a set of plans. A plan for a play is sometimes called a scenario. The kind of scenario developed by the playwright varies from a relatively complete narrative of the entire play broken down into units initiated by the entrance or exit of a character, to a sketchy one page outline. Units set up by the entrance or exit of a character are called french scenes.

Henrik Ibsen wrote extremely detailed scenarios, which gave character motivational sketches as well as intended impact of the scene. Eugene O'Neill not only wrote a rather complete scenario, but also kept a work diary in which he recorded ideas and impressions of the play. August Strindberg, Anton Chekhov, Tennessee Williams, Moss Hart, John Millington Synge, Lillian Hellman, Somerset Maugham and Arthur Wing Pinero are among the writers who worked out an almost excessively complete scenario.

Other playwrights seem to be able to compose the entire play in their heads. Noel Coward was one of the most famous writers who seemed to thrive using this method. In his autobiography, *Present Indicative* (1937), Coward relates how he wrote *Private Lives* (1930). He had promised to write a play for Gertrude Lawrence while on a trip to Yokohama. For quite some time he was unable to produce anything of consequence until one evening in Shanghai after going to bed. "The moment I switched out the light, Gertie appeared in a molyneux dress on the terrace in the south of France and refused to go again until four a.m. by which time *Private Lives*, title and all, had constructed itself."

There are, of course, other methods of developing a play. Some writers create character to such a degree that the character begins to dictate story. Still others will take the climactic moment of the play, develop it, and gear the rest of the play to that moment. Sometimes a writer will "think on paper;" that is, he will start off with a vague idea and allow the play to develop as it will. This technique can be rather painful and is not recommended by most playwrights. Oddly enough, it is the method most frequently used by the beginning playwright.

Regardless of what technique is used to develop the play, one thing should be noted: a play is rarely, if ever, produced from a first draft. It has been said that a play is not written, but is rewritten. Lillian Hellman not only spent a great deal of time writing a scenario, but also went through no less than fourteen complete drafts of *The Children's Hour*. Every professional playwright knows the agony of creating a work of art; indeed, some playwrights have developed bizzare creative habits. Lord Alfred Douglas (1870-1945), writing in *Oscar Wilde and Myself* (1914), tells us that Wilde started drinking around four in the afternoon when he began to write and did not stop either activity until three the next morning; yet he was rarely drunk. Most playwrights, however, are more like Neil Simon, who tends to work on a diet of coffee, cookies, and dry roasted peanuts. Ibsen, Chekhov, Shaw, and Williams almost completely abstained from food while working. Whatever the condition of the body and mind, whatever the technique, many playwrights really do not know how they create their plays. Alexandre Dumas fils once remarked: "Well my dear friend, if you want me to be quite frank, I'll own up that I don't know how to write a play. One day a long time ago when I was scarcely out of school, I asked my father the same question. He answered 'It's very simple; the first act clear, the last act short, and all acts interesting.' "

After the playwright is satisfied that his play is "interesting," he will probably attempt to have it performed. He may, for example, attempt to find a producer to finance it and go through the agonies of a major professional production as described in Chapter 16. For a revealing account of this process, young playwrights are advised to consult William Gibson's (1914-) *See Saw Log* (1959). The *See Saw Log* is a day-by-day description of the evolution to Broadway of Gibson's play *Two for the See Saw* (1958). Although most plays do not reach Broadway, most are produced somewhere, somehow. One of the first requirements for production is a director.

Tooth of Crime by Sam Shepard with Joan Mackintosh as Becky and Spaulding Gray as Hoss, performed by Richard Schechner's performance group. Photo by Clem Fiori.

The Evolution of the Director

The modern director is a relative newcomer to the theatrical scene. Historically, actor managers were fairly common, but the director as we know him did not emerge until the later part of the eighteenth century. Scholars disagree as to who was the first modern director, per se. Several early actors were close to being in total control of the production. The great English actor David Garrick (1717-1770), for example, revolutionized many of the theatrical conventions of his time and was one of the first actor-managers to insist upon a rather lengthy rehearsal schedule from his company. Garrick is perhaps best known for his success in eliminating the ancient custom of seating spectators on the stage proper. The practice had done much to hamper Garrick's sense of aesthetic unity and his lead was quickly followed by other managers.

Lucia Elizabeth Bartolozzi Vestris (1797-1856), sometimes called Madame Vestris, was not only one of the first female managers to enjoy a long career, but was also a very discriminating artist. Madame Vestris maintained considerable artistic and practical control over her company. Among other things, she introduced real, instead of fake, properties to the stage and moved production techniques to a more realistic style.

William Charles Macready, who did much to elevate the status of the actor, also extended the duties of the actor-manager to an unparalleled degree. Macready exercised control over many facets of the total production. He was one of the first managers to restore many of the bowdlerized cuts in Shakespeare, cuts which had occurred during the latter part of the seventeenth and early eighteenth centuries. He restored, among other parts, the tragic ending to *King Lear*. Macready was considered by his company to be somewhat of a dis-

Madame Vestris, nee Lucia Elizabetta Bartolozzi, shown in the role of Apollo in *Midas.* Madame Vestris managed the Olympic Theatre from 1831-1839 and is credited with introducing the box set (but not originating it) in England in 1832. From Coleman's *Players and Playwrights,* 1890.

ciplinarian. He required his actors to attend lengthy rehearsal sessions which were quite unusual during this period. Furthermore, Macready required his actors to act during rehearsals, a custom which prompted one of his older actors to retort, "Sir, I never act a rehearsal, but I will do it tonight." Macready, it is said, replied briskly, "Sir, if you cannot do it in the morning you will not do it at night."

Most historians seem to agree that the first director was probably Georg II, Duke of Saxe-Meiningen (1826-1914), the ruler of one of the many small German states. The Saxe-Meiningen company was a highly disciplined troupe under the absolute control of the Duke. His approval was a necessity for virtually every aspect of the production, and he demanded lengthy preparation from his actors, who were relatively unknown. The Saxe-Meiningen company shunned the use of stars; consequently, much time and effort went into the preparation of supernumeraries as principals. The Duke insisted on and got absolute obedience and subordination from his actors. For this and other reasons, the Saxe-Meiningen troupe electrified audiences with its controlled and realistic crowd scenes and ensemble acting. The success of this company and its methods was duly acknowledged in theatrical circles. There is general agreement that Georg II, Duke of Saxe-Meiningen, influenced either directly or indirectly many of the young emerging directors, including Andre Antoine and Konstantin Stanislavsky.

An empirical observation of the techniques of contemporary directors and directors of the past suggest certain similarities in approach: a director establishes a concept of the play, a director applies his concept to the technical aspects of the play through his designers and technicians, and a director actualizes his concept through rehearsal and control over all aspects of the finished production.

The Director's Concept

Directing is sometimes analogous to conducting an orchestra. What, for example, makes a piece of music seem more exciting when the orchestra is under the baton of a distinguished conductor? The answer must lie in the way in which a maestro approaches the music — his concept. Similarly, a director approaches each production through an intense study of the script itself. Some of what the director does will be discussed in Chapter 16. After the play has been thoroughly analyzed so that the director understands its meaning and powers, he will ponder a way by which those meanings and powers may reach an audience. Sometimes a director may discuss the play with the author. In some cases, a director may even have a hand in helping the playwright shape the final draft. Elia Kazan frequently contributed to the final script of such playwrights as Arthur Miller and Tennessee Williams. Foremost in the director's mind must be his concept of what the meaning and powers of the play are. If the play was written in another era, the director may feel that in order for a modern audience to fully comprehend the meaning of the play and be affected by it, some alteration must be made. Peter Brook (1925-   ), one of England's finest directors, chose to use a set with three white walls festooned with circus apparatus to stage Shakespeare's *Midsummer Night's Dream*. The production was a complete success with the audience ostensibly coming away with a fresh understanding of the play.

Robert L. Benedetti (1939-), Dean of California Institute of the Arts, directed *King Lear* using a set based on an ancient Chinese puzzle with the actors wearing unisex costumes on a stage covered with hay. The audience was reportedly electrified and filled with new insights into the play. The English director Peter Bucknell played the fairy scene in *Midsummer Night's Dream* with the cast dressed in Kabuki costumes. Bucknell reasoned that an Oriental fairyland would have been startling to an Elizabethan audience, and since the style of the production and trappings (i.e., recorder groups and dancing on the lawn) was Elizabethan, the Kabuki fairyland, it was hoped, would produce a similar reaction in a contemporary audience. Shakespeare's great masterpiece *Hamlet* has been done in as many ways as there are imaginative directors.

Certainly care must be exercised in order to prevent diluting a concept by virtue of directorial gimmicks which have little or no relevance. The true test as to the relevant value of the directorial approach is whether or not the approach clarifies the meaning and enhances the power of the play. If the approach itself becomes the center of audience focus, then the director has failed and a new approach becomes necessary.

The Director: Visualization

When the director has formalized his concept of the production, the next step is to explain the guiding idea to the technical designers. Each technical discipline (i.e., scene design, lighting design, costume design) should be approached individually. The set designer should be the first approached because what is done with the scenery may well influence what is done in the other areas. The degree to which the director becomes involved with the actual design varies but, in most cases, a director will have the final say on the design.

One of the most successful producer-directors in America during the first part of the century was a man who liked to be referred to as the Bishop of Broadway, David Belasco. Belasco sometimes took his designers in hand into his theatre. Once they were seated, Belasco would indicate to them on an empty stage every entrance, exit, and movement in the play, the entire process sometimes taking up to five days. Other directors, such as Robert Lewis, allow their designers a great deal of latitude.

Most directors list only important specific necessities such as entrance ways, necessary furnishings, and the like for their designers, preferring to see how the artist reacts artistically to the general concept. A series of meetings may then take place where thumbnail sketches are used to visualize the developing set. When a director approves the visual idea, a color rendering or model may then be made. The approval of a scenic design sets off a flurry of activity. Colors and style of costumes may now be conceived, and the lighting technician has the space upon which to focus his lights.

Through it all, the director must always question whether or not each technical element is enhancing his general overall concept of the play. Nothing scenically must call attention to itself to detract from the play. One of the most important decisions that a director must make is to cut from the production anything that does not follow this criterion. Many designers and technicians have wept real tears as an effect or a much admired costume has been dropped because it was actually too good.

In a production of *Thurber's Carnival* (1960) at a major university, the scenic director assigned a graduate student to perfect an anesthetizer for the Walter Mitty sequence. The student worked for two months perfecting a machine that was capable of lighting up like a computer, with individual lights operating in orderly rows. At command, the lights could deviate in a crazy fashion with a fireworks display complete with sirens and bells at the finale. The device was first used at a technical rehearsal and received a standing ovation from cast, crews, and observers in the audience. The director, after a five minute eulogy on the ingenuity of the inventor, promptly cut the machine for breaking the aesthetic flow of the play. "It performed not poorly," he paraphrased, "but too well."

David Belasco (1853-1931), sometimes called the "Bishop of Broadway," is noted for his naturalistic staging, his battle against the Syndicate, and his lighting innovations. Courtesy, Harvard Theatre Collection.

Some directors, on the other hand, thrive on scenic effects. Considerable money has been spent on spectacular devices which can be unnecessary accouterments. David Belasco spent considerable sums to perfect lighting effects which were to influence, if not revolutionize, lighting in America. In the play *The Darling of the Gods* (1902), Belasco spent a small fortune attempting to capture a Japanese sunrise. Part of the publicity package ballyhooed the authenticity of the effect, only to have an indignant Japanese student write in *The Critic* magazine: "Real Japanese scenery is not bathed in such strenuous light, such as the colored electric contrivances which Mr. Belasco's machinery fairly pours upon his scene. The Belasco sun is too familiar. It is as attainable as any red apple at a fruit stand."

When the designs have been approved and construction is underway, the director is temporarily free to concentrate on the most visible personnel in his production: the actors. His first duty must be to select them.

The Director: Casting

Selecting a cast can be difficult and rewarding. The director's concept of the play must be translated into the kinds of people who will be best

Ludwig Devrient (1784-1832) is pictured in the roles of King Lear, Duke of Gloucester, and Shylock. Devrient, said to have possessed a demonic artistic nature, was an outstanding tragedian who made his first stage appearance at age twenty and later appeared at court in Berlin. Courtesy, German Information Center.

suited for the available roles. Physical characteristics and demeanor may or may not be important, depending on how the director visualizes his characters. For example, a director who sees Hamlet as weak and indecisive may want a slim, slightly built actor to play the role. A strong-willed, decisive Hamlet would require, perhaps, a more powerfully built actor. The director must have a fairly strong idea of his characters in order to cast the right person in the role. He may then set up tryout dates and advertise them. There are several types of tryouts from which the director would select.

The most popular audition for educational and community theatre is the open tryout, where all interested persons are invited to attend and compete for roles. The advantage of the open tryout is that everyone ostensibly has a chance to show their talent. This type of audition is rarely used in New York where an abundance of aspiring actors live. In New York in the early 1960's, a trio of young directors used the open tryout system, advertising in at least two trade journals that they would hold two days of auditions for a summer theatre company. All interested actors were invited to try out for five acting positions. Near riot conditions erupted as over 300 people, many with no previous acting experience, clogged the small rehearsal room, filled the corridors and stairwell, and blocked the front sidewalks. After listening to some of the most incredible performances by the most bizarre, if not downright dangerous, people in New York for two gruelling days, only two actors were hired.

As noted in Chapter 16, most knowledgeable directors in New York use the closed or invitational tryout method. Actors may be located through *The Players Directory,* which is internationally recognized as "the casting director's Bible." Actors' agents are notified and only the most experienced actors are heard. In some instances, a director may invite actors with whom he has worked or actors in whom he is interested. The closed rehearsal is also used by some community theatre groups when casting is limited to members only.

Tryout methods vary from director to director. Some prefer that the actors perform a memorized section from a play. Others will ask an actor to sight read material from a new play. Sometimes a director will furnish the actor with a detailed description of the character so that he may see if the actor can adjust to the interpretation. Some directors prefer to read groups of actors. Still others will read only one actor at a time.

Casting is always a difficult experience for the director. Ideal casts are rarely, if ever, found. There is no way to tell whether an actor can handle a role save through the experience of doing it. For that reason, directors are always a bit unsure until the actor has proven to be a good one.

The Director and the Actors

When the cast has been assembled, the director must now begin his work with the actors. There is an interesting paradox about actors and acting. An actor's art is an interpretive one and comes into being only when the actor is in the process of interpreting. A playwright, a designer, and a director may sit out in the audience and watch their work. However, unless a sequence is filmed, an actor may never see his work. Even filmed sequences never really capture the live audience experience. Yet it is the actor who first comes to mind when one normally discusses the theatre, and it is the actor who reaches the heights of popularity and adulation. On the other hand, after the act of creation by the actor is passed, it is the playwright who is remembered in history. Actors must constantly reaffirm their artistic place in the sun, while a playwright's place is guaranteed as long as his work is admired.

After selecting the cast, most of the director's time and effort must be concentrated on actualizing his concept in space and time through the means of the actor. Generally, the actor, as an interpreter, has at his disposal two means, his body and his voice. The director must utilize those means as he actualizes his concept through interpretation and stage picture.

The Voice

The voice is, of course, one of the chief tools of the actor; how the actor uses his voice is of prime concern to the director. If at all possible, actors should be able to sing and should have vocal training. Even if the actor is not blessed with a musical

George Frederick Cooke (1756-1812), English actor shown in the role of Richard III. Cooke's career and reputation were ruined by alcoholism; however, when sober, he was considered one of the finest actors of his generation. He was given to playing his roles intuitively rather than studying them. On tour in the United States, he remarked that President James Madison was "the contemptible King of the Yankee Doodles." From *The Kembles and Their Contemporaries,* 1890.

ear, it is important to have an ear for sounds. Human sounds, both verbal and nonverbal, form the basis for the actor's interpretive skills. Verbal sound or diction is the most frequently used sound by the actor because, in most cases, plays are written in a language composed of words. Words have both denotative and connotative powers. Actors must be aware that in certain artistic combinations it is important that the denotative power of the words come through above all else to clarify the idea. It may be important in a script to render the simple line, "I like you," in a denotative way. The line denotatively means I have a fondness or affection for you, and if read in a normal way, will mean just that. However, the way in which the line may be read can vary considerably from this denotative meaning. These are its connotative powers. Both the director and the actor must be able to understand the connotative powers of words and their effect on an audience. It is possible, for example, to say "I like you" with passionate intensity which means more than the denotative meaning of having a fondness for a person. Conversely, it is possible to read the line in a manner so as to suggest that you really do not like the person at all. Note that in both cases the denotative power of the words do not change on the written page, but because of the way in which the line has been rendered by the actor, the connotative power of the words has changed. Since only the director can judge the connotative value of the words an actor utters, he must constantly control the use of volume, pitch, articulation, pronunciation and other factors involved in producing the desired effect.

Conceptually the director must always guard against the possibility of an actor overdoing it, or for that matter, underdoing it. Every director, one would imagine, has chuckled to himself when he has heard the classic directorial pontification from Shakespeare's *Hamlet,* which still carries an important lesson for the actor:

> Speak the speech, I pray you, as I pronounced it to you, trippingly on the tongue; but if you mouth it, as many of you players do, I had as lief the town-crier spoke my lines . . ."

Nonverbal sounds can also be an effective tool for the director. Screams, moans, sighs, and other controlled nondenotative sounds can be utilized by the actor and director for effect. The famed Bread and Puppet Theatre Group frequently utilizes nonverbal sounds with startling effectiveness. One play has no words at all, but the way in which the actors use sound connotatively clearly projects the meaning of the play to an audience. The sounds carry connotative powers of sadness, joy, hate, or whatever emotional quality the director desires to create.

Silence may also be used effectively by the actor and the director. In a production of Bertolt Brecht's *Mother Courage* by the Berliner Ensemble theatre, the scene in which Mother Courage is forced to

The Beggar's Opera by John Gay. University of Maine, Portland; scene design, Minor Rootes. Directed by Walter R. Stump.

Eugene O'Neill's *The Emperor Jones* as produced at Western Kentucky University. Directed by Loren K. Ruff; set design by James Brown.

Top: From Morn to Midnight (1916) by Georg Kaiser. A contemporary production by the University of Southern Maine with lighting and scene design by Michael Roderick; directed by Walter Stump.

Bottom: Clifford Odet's *Paradise Lost* as produced at Western Kentucky University. Directed by Loren K. Ruff; set design by Greg Ross Hambleton.

Top: Set for *H.S.M. Pinafore* by W.S. Gilbert and Arthur Sullivan. Minor Rootes, Designer.

Bottom: Set for *Oedipus Rex.* Fullerton College, designer Charlie Kading, director James Henderson.

Mother Courage by Bertolt Brecht as performed by Richard Schechner's performance group. The performers are singing the song of Mother Courage's Boots in Scene 1. Courtesy Clem Fiori.

view the body of her son was done with superb use of silence. In the scene, in order to protect her daughter, Mother Courage must not utter a cry of recognition or she faces instant death. To intensify the horror of the experience and still maintain Mother Courage's silence, the director instructed the actress playing Mother Courage to scream silently. She lifted her head toward an overhead down light, which had the effect of distorting her features, and arranged her facial demeanor to suggest a scream without any kind of vocalization. The audience, we are told, was electrified as they heard in their minds a soul-piercing scream which had never been vocalized at all.

Dramatic pause and other nonverbal devices are normally augmented by gesture or movement as was the case in the *Mother Courage* scene. The way in which a director arranges his movements is extremely important to the total effect of the production. Probably no other single technique better separates an experienced director from the one who lacks experience than the way in which he moves his actors. On the other hand, nothing will identify an inexperienced actor as quickly either.

Movement

Movement in the theatre can include anything from dance or highly stylized body language to a simple cross by an actor from one side of the stage to another or even a simple gesture. Motivated movement will pull focus faster than any other device on stage. For that reason, movement will naturally pull the audience attention to the actor who is making the move. Conversely, if an actor moves

Midsummer Night's Dream performed at University of Southern Maine, directed and designed by Minor R. Rootes. Note the shift in focus as Albert Duclos as Oberon moves downstage. The shift is accomplished both by the head and the body. Courtesy Don Johnson.

who should not be moving, it is possible that he will pull focus away from where it should be. The way in which the movement is made may also demonstrate character. It is possible to show age, sex, general physical condition, attitude, and even the emotional state that the character is in, through movement.

Certain theatrical styles require different kinds of movement. An actor performing in a play in which a hoop skirt is used as a costume must move in an entirely different manner than she would if she were wearing contemporary garb. Expressionistic plays may require actors to move in more non-realistic ways. In a recent production of Georg Kaiser's *Morn to Midnight,* the actors in the cashier's home scene were required to move as if they were puppets on a string. Sometimes the nature of the play itself demands a particular kind of movement from the actor. Aeschylus' *Orestia,* with its long choral passages, requires much different movement than *Waiting for Godot.*

Movement may be used by the director to establish probability, build to climax, or even develop emotional effects. A group of machine-like figures

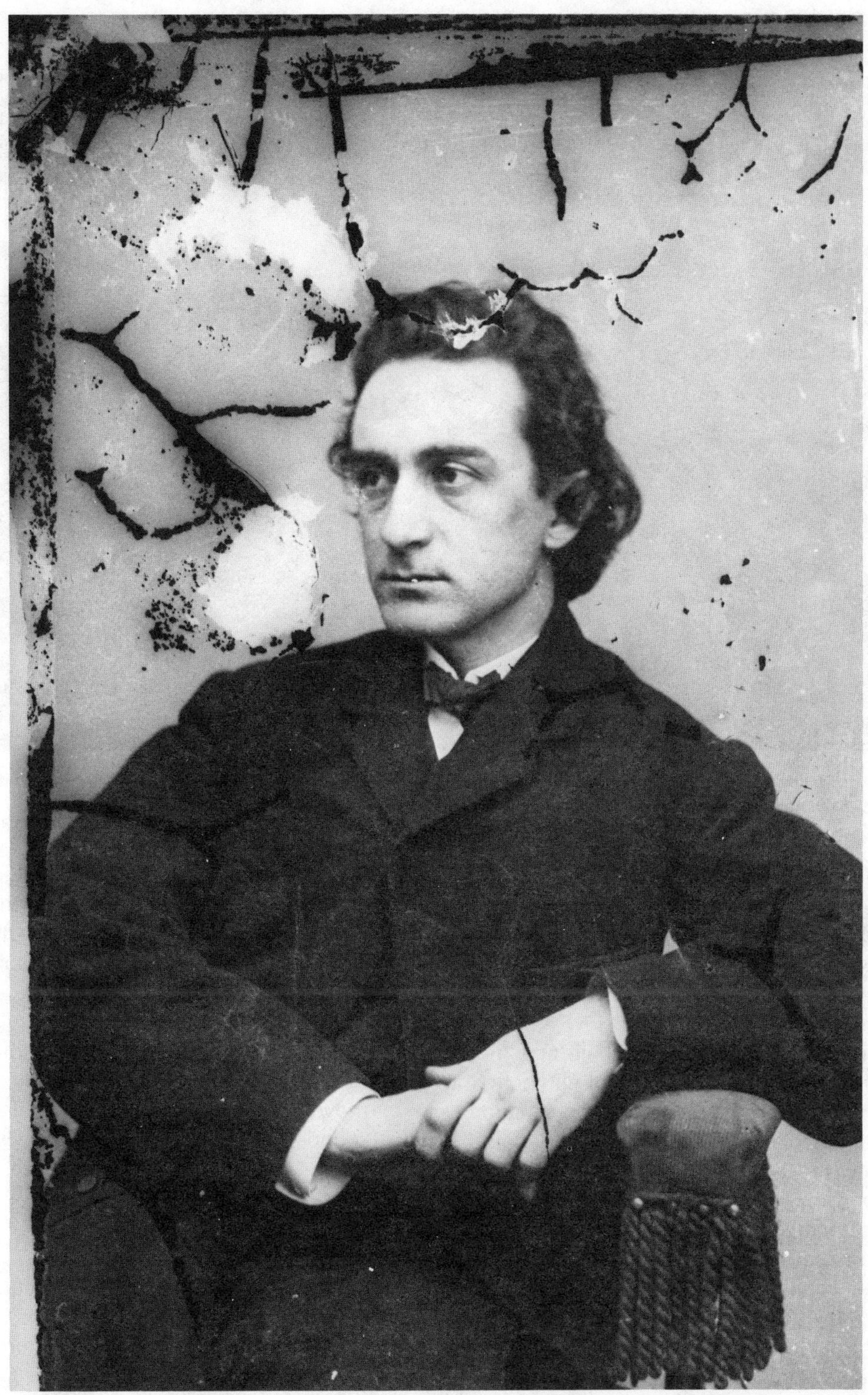

Edwin Booth (1833-1893), considered by many historians to be the finest actor America has produced.

Midsummer Night's Dream, performed at University of Southern Maine, directed and designed by Minor R. Rootes. Courtesy Don Johnson. Note how focus is on Oberon by the positioning of the sprites.

at the beginning of a play would establish for an audience the nonrealistic intent of the production and, therefore, the probability of the play itself.

Movement should be used to build climactic moments. The classic movement of two lovers coming toward one another, slowly at first, and then running to a reuniting embrace, is rather simplistic but a good example of climactic movement. The confrontation of two opposing forces or the stalking of one character by another also demonstrates the use of movement as preparation for or climax itself.

Emotional effects through movement are frequently used by the director. Scenes filled with intense conflict are often translated into strong, rapid moves, while relatively tranquil scenes are usually marked by somewhat slow movement.

Gestures and stage business, such as smoking a pipe or wiping one's glasses, can be utilized to gain emphasis, build to climactic moments, and strengthen emotional response. Movement, gesture, and stage business are all utilized by the director to form the general stage picture. The use of the actor in creating story through movement is the sum total of all the visual elements. It is at this point that the director strives to create a harmonious balance between his actors and their environment.

A teacher of directing once told a children's theatre class that the true test of effective stage movement and composition is, if all words and sounds were deleted from the performance, the stage composition would still tell the story.

Stage Picture

Every element of the stage picture must be arranged in a meaningful way that will emphasize some necessary element of the story. For that reason, every movement of an actor must be a motivated, meaningful contribution to the play itself. Movement into stage pictures must never be constructed separately but as a development which has grown out of the story. While every stage picture should maintain its own kind of aesthetic balance, it must never be allowed to exist for picture's sake. Stage pictures must be set up by the director so that they maintain what might be called theatrical equilibrium. Equilibrium can be easily seen in paintings because, unlike the theatre, groupings in the visual arts remain static. A quality painting of, let us say a landscape, will probably impart to us a sense of repose. This is because of the painting's artistic equilibrium which appeals to our own sense of equilibrium through the process of association. Now imagine somebody putting an ink splotch on the picture. The anger we feel is not necessarily because of the destruction of the picture, as the spot may well have been added by the artist himself. What does destroy our sense of repose is a breakdown of artistic equilibrium. The same effect can be achieved if someone dumps a load of trash at a favorite viewpoint. The sense of equilibrium has been outraged.

Stage pictures differ compositionally from paintings or real landscapes not from their sense of equilibrium, but in the fact that stage pictures constantly change. One picture may become temporarily off balance in order to achieve a new focal point.

There are many ways of using line, mass, and proportion in stage pictures. Such means as height, use of stage space, and technical methods of pulling focus — i.e., costumes and light — can be useful in achieving emphasis. It is possible, for example, to shadow large areas so that a source of light automatically pulls focus. In a production of John Steinbeck's *Of Mice and Men* (1937), the scene in which Curley's wife is killed by Lennie takes place on a hay pile in a barn. Picture the hay pile at down left center in the barn. Most of the barn is in shadow with shafts of light from cracks in the barn door filtering across and lighting the hay pile. Here you have the main acting area, the hay pile, emphasized through use of lighting, while the rest of the stage remains in shadow.

The stage picture must always support the movement of the story, and like the anesthetizer in *Thurber's Carnival,* must never call attention to itself. When used with discrimination and artistic taste, it can be a mighty tool in the repertoire of a director. No directorial tool, technique, or idea can function artistically if the actors do not carry it off. When the curtain goes up, it is an actor's world.

The Actor

Much has, can, and will be said about the art of acting. Systems and methods come and go. No technique is universally beneficial for all actors. Basically, there are two acting ideas on which all acting methods are founded. One idea is based on the concept that acting is an imitative art. Actors must be trained observers and technicians. The study of human emotional behavior is paramount in this technique. Once the actor is aware of how emotion is manifested he may attempt through technique to imitate the trappings of that emotion on stage. The so-called Stanislavsky method would fall into this category. It is possible to summarize some of Stanislavsky's techniques.

An interesting paradox here is that no one actually knows what Stanislavsky's method was, probably not even Stanislavsky. In truth his "system" was the result of years of evolution and testing and was compartmentalized by later writers. First, he believed that the actor must develop the two obvious tools of his trade, his body and his voice. Second, contrary to later misreadings of his advice, the actor should school himself in theatrical techniques so that he may appear more natural as he *projects* his characterization. Third, in keeping with the concept of the realist which he remained at heart, Stanislavsky demanded that his actors be skilled observers of reality. Fourth, the actor must be able to relate some similar emotional situation in his own life to the dramatic situation. A young actor once asked a Stanislavsky-schooled director how he should portray a man committing a murder without having murdered. The director handed the actor a fly swatter and ordered him to kill a pesky insect that had been tormenting the class. The student pursued the task with glee, dispatching the bug with one well-aimed blow. While the student stalked his prey, the teacher directed the others to watch the hunter's reactions. At the moment of the kill, the terrifying expression on the face of the swatter brought home the point of sense memory to the gathered group. Stanislavsky believed in the magic "if" where the actor must say: "If I were in this situation, I would . . ." Fifth, the actor must analyze the play, by dividing it into component parts or units. With each unit there is a task which the actor, as character, executes. This task or objective, when analyzed, is expressed by an acting verb. (I must *kill* this man.) The units of the play,

Richard III as portrayed by Edwin Booth.

together with the creative objectives of which they are composed, merge into and form the through line of action. Every action, whether inner or outer, has its logical and coherent place within the through line of action. The through line of action is directed toward and intricately linked with the superobjective of the play. The superobjective is the playwright's main idea expressed in terms of an action verb. The superobjective is the essential principle of analysis used to obtain a unified production of the written script, yet it is the most difficult principle for the actor to grasp and define as he studies and rehearses the play for production. But the understanding of the role in relation to the play is the only way that he can effectively contribute to the overall ensemble effort. Stanislavsky demanded of his actors discipline and hard work in an effort to better their skills.

On the other hand, some actors believe that an actor must be able to project himself into the character and re-create the emotional responses. Whichever of the two techniques or variations thereof the actor chooses to utilize in his preparation, certain similarities can be derived empirically. They are (1) analysis of character in terms of the play; (2) analysis of the character in terms of his psyche; and (3) analysis of the character in terms of technique.

Analysis of the character in terms of the play is not unlike that outlined in Chapter 2. Simply, an actor must determine how the character he must create functions in terms of the play itself. What are his goals, motivations, relationships, and characteristics in terms of the total work? How does the character function as a part of the aesthetic whole? All too often, inexperienced actors tend to isolate their roles from the play itself, some commit the unforgivable sin of having never read the play. Just as the director must understand the playwright's concept before he fashions his own, so must the actor.

Analysis of character in terms of his psyche is simply internalizing the character. What kind of emotional responses will be forthcoming from this type of individual? The methods by which these responses are manifested on stage are moot unless an actor is sure of what they will be. Character motivation is important here as a guideline to determine the degree and kinds of emotional response.

Analysis of character in terms of technique includes the kinds of physical movement best suited for the character, the appropriate vocal characterization, and the way in which the character must be constructed in terms of build.

All of these functions are important for the actor to consider, regardless of the method used in their actualization. Careful preparation and intelligent discrimination are part of what makes an actor succeed, and an actor's success on the stage is the one absolute necessity in the art of the theatre. The playwright's idea translated to the stage by the director and actualized by the actor is what the theatre is all about.

Selected Readings

Bellman, Willard F. *Lighting the Stage*. San Francisco, 1967.

Dean, Alexander. *Fundamentals of Play Directing*. Rev. by Lawrence Carra. New York, 1965.

Kesler, Jackson. *Theatrical Costume Bibliography*, Detroit, 1979.

Sellman, Hunton D. *Essentials of Stage Lighting*, New York, 1972.

Stanislavsky, Konstantin. *An Actor Prepares*. Trans. by Elizabeth Reynolds Hapgood. New York, 1936.

CHAPTER SIXTEEN

Management and Production
The Business of Theatre

The business of the theatre is business. In fact, the theatre has been called the worst-run business in America. Nonetheless it does pay attention to its management. Good management means a well-run organization, and even more importantly, it means money. Management includes a broad spectrum of activities from the box office to backstage. It includes operating, financing, and staging a production from the initial purchase of a script to the final curtain. This chapter is about management. It is not intended to be a handbook for management but simply a statement of what goes into producing a theatrical production. Bear in mind that, due to inflation, the various amounts of money indicated could change, even as this line is being written.

Producing A Play

Let's suppose you are a producer who wants to put a play on Broadway. The first step is to get a property, a play intended for production. You can purchase an original play or perhaps you have found a translation or an adaptation that suits you. You could even produce a play that is in public domain — which means no copyright and therefore no expenditure for the rights. On the other hand, you don't own the rights. Whatever type of property you choose, when you find a script that you want to produce, you take an option on that property; you purchase the right to produce the play. By paying the owner of the script money to produce his script, you are in essence saying, "I will pay you money for the exclusive right to produce your play within a designated time — usually six months or one year." This is an option.

Opposite: Actor-manager Henry Irving in the role of Shylock. Irving was the dominant force in English theatre between 1880 and 1900 and was the first performer to be knighted (in 1895) for his achievements. From *The Theatre,* 1880.

The Dramatists Guild

The Dramatists Guild is the union designed primarily to protect the author's rights. The right to produce a play in America or Canada is known as the Dram. Guild Contract which is short for the Dramatists Guild, Inc. Minimum Basic Protection Contract. The Guild contract is thus a type of license requiring you to pay the author royalties on his script. A royalty is a fixed amount of money paid to the author or owner of the work being produced. The contract also requires that the author's name appear on all programs and advertisements. The contract is lengthy, detailed, and confusing to the layman. For example, the contract provides that the author is entitled to purchase (not comps. — complimentary) a certain number of seats for each performance of his play. Also, prior to the closing or one month after the New York opening (whichever is earlier), the producer must furnish a neat copy of the script to the author. This script includes the information about lighting, costumes, properties, set, sound, and actors' cues. This is the stage manager's script and is called also the prompt script. The Dramatists Guild Basic Production Contract is only one contract which this union uses. There are also a Revue Product Contract, a Collaboration Contract, a Stock Tryout Production Contract, a Dramatic Contract, and a Dramatico-Musical Production Contract.

Financing the Production

Assuming you have an option, you must next decide who will produce the play. Will you do it by yourself or will you seek help? Most producers get help — that is, they get financial assistance rather than pay the cost themselves. A common method used by producers is to form a "limited partnership" with outside investors (sometimes

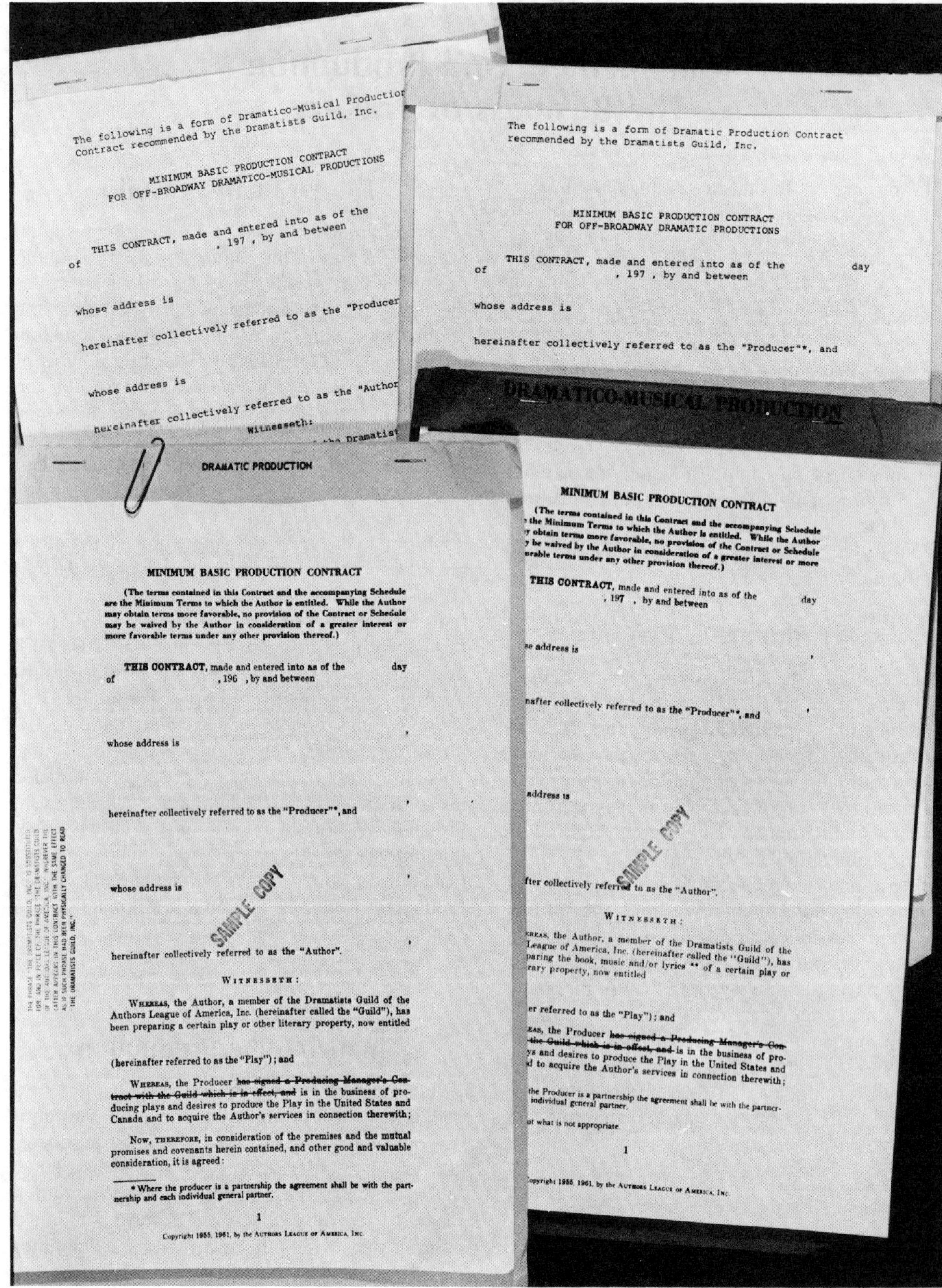
The following is a form of Dramatico-Musical Productio
Contract recommended by the Dramatists Guild, Inc.
MINIMUM BASIC PRODUCTION CONTRACT
FOR OFF-BROADWAY DRAMATICO-MUSICAL PRODUCTIONS
THIS CONTRACT, made and entered into as of the
of , 197 , by and between
whose address is
hereinafter collectively referred to as the "Producer
whose address is
hereinafter collectively referred to as the "Author
Witnesseth:
The following is a form of Dramatic Production Contract
recommended by the Dramatists Guild, Inc.
MINIMUM BASIC PRODUCTION CONTRACT
FOR OFF-BROADWAY DRAMATIC PRODUCTIONS
THIS CONTRACT, made and entered into as of the day
of , 197 , by and between
whose address is
hereinafter collectively referred to as the "Producer"*, and
DRAMATICO-MUSICAL PRODUCTION
DRAMATIC PRODUCTION
MINIMUM BASIC PRODUCTION CONTRACT
(The terms contained in this Contract and the accompanying Schedule are the Minimum Terms to which the Author is entitled. While the Author may obtain terms more favorable, no provision of the Contract or Schedule may be waived by the Author in consideration of a greater interest or more favorable terms under any other provision thereof.)
THIS CONTRACT, made and entered into as of the day
of , 196 , by and between
whose address is ,
hereinafter collectively referred to as the "Producer"*, and ,
whose address is ,
SAMPLE COPY
hereinafter collectively referred to as the "Author".
WITNESSETH:
WHEREAS, the Author, a member of the Dramatists Guild of the Authors League of America, Inc. (hereinafter called the "Guild"), has been preparing a certain play or other literary property, now entitled
(hereinafter referred to as the "Play"); and
WHEREAS, the Producer ~~has signed a Producing Manager's Contract with the Guild which is in effect, and~~ is in the business of producing plays and desires to produce the Play in the United States and Canada and to acquire the Author's services in connection therewith;
NOW, THEREFORE, in consideration of the premises and the mutual promises and covenants herein contained, and other good and valuable consideration, it is agreed:
* Where the producer is a partnership the agreement shall be with the partnership and each individual general partner.
1
Copyright 1955, 1961, by the AUTHORS LEAGUE OF AMERICA, INC.
THE PHRASE "THE DRAMATISTS GUILD, INC." IS SUBSTITUTED FOR, AND IN PLACE OF, THE PHRASE "THE DRAMATISTS GUILD OF THE AUTHORS LEAGUE OF AMERICA, INC." WHEREVER THE LATTER APPEARS IN THIS CONTRACT WITH THE SAME EFFECT AS IF SUCH PHRASE HAD BEEN PHYSICALLY CHANGED TO READ "THE DRAMATISTS GUILD, INC."
MINIMUM BASIC PRODUCTION CONTRACT
THIS CONTRACT, made and entered into as of the day
, 197 , by and between
hereinafter collectively referred to as the "Producer"*, and
SAMPLE COPY
WITNESSETH:
the Author, a member of the Dramatists Guild of the League of America, Inc. (hereinafter called the "Guild"), has
1
Copyright 1955, 1961, by the AUTHORS LEAGUE OF AMERICA, INC.

called "Angels," possibly from the guardian angel or from the phrase "Isn't he an angel," meaning that he is a doll, which a backer certainly is). The investors are considered the limited partners and the producer is the general partner. Limited means that the investors are limited in terms of how much input they have in the actual production and, more importantly, it means that they are limited in terms of how much money they have to put into the production. Usually a limited investor is liable for a fixed amount plus an overcall, which is additional money ranging from ten to twenty percent of the limited partner's original investment. When the investor gives the money to the producer, the producer must put it into a bank until he has enough money to produce the show. He cannot spend it before time, unless the contract so states. When the producer reaches the amount he has estimated is needed to produce the show, he may withdraw the money.

Assuming that a producer chooses to form a limited partnership, his next step is to convince investors to put their money into his production. One method used, though doubt has been raised as to its effectiveness, is the backer's audition. At a backer's audition, prospective investors view a sampling or a condensed version of the play. The presentation can be held in an apartment, dining hall, rehearsal hall, etc.; food and drinks are usually served; questions are answered by the producer; and the entire program lasts about an hour.

Regardless of how a producer chooses to raise funds, he must treat the play as he would a stock listed on the stock exchange. For example, if the producer wishes to raise money outside the state of New York (whether by phone or mail or in person), he must file appropriate forms with the Securities and Exchange Commission (SEC). The forms are designed to insure that the investors are protected against "shady" schemes and to aid the SEC in determining whether the producer and his associates are entering into a legal business endeavor. The SEC forms ask for such information as:

1. Where you will be doing business.
2. People with whom you are associated.
3. Pertinent information about you and your associates.
4. The name of your attorney.
5. The state in which you intend to raise money.

Opposite: Samples of contracts issued by the Dramatists Guild, Inc. Courtesy Dramatists Guild.

Charles Fechter (1824-1879), English actor-manager, pictured here in the role of Hamlet. Fechter is credited with popularizing realistic acting, reviving interest in the box-set, and aiding the vogue of "gentlemanly" melodrama. He also wrote several dramatizations of novels. From *Dramatic Portrait Gallery,* 1880.

Along with the questionnaire, a detailed prospectus must be mailed to all potential investors. The prospectus describes all those involved with the production, the financial arrangements, and a brief summary of the play; it also contains a "risk to the investor clause." This clause requires that the producer, in essence, try to discourage would-be investors. The clause must therefore contain the following information:

1. The investor should be prepared for a total loss.
2. The number of Broadway plays which lost money the prior season.
3. The odds against the play being successful and thus the remote chance of having your investment pay off.

If you, as producer, decide to confine your money-making activities to New York, you also need to file with the New York attorney general. If you raise money outside New York state, you must always file with the attorney general in the particular state. All states have what are known as "blue sky laws." The term stems from the idea that when the individual invests his money, he will have nothing but blue skies — meaning the investment will automatically be successful. All investments are not assured, however, and many producers may be dishonest. To protect the consumer from being literally robbed by a fraudulent scheme, many states require the producer to file with the attorney general or the appropriate officials.

In addition to limited partners who will help you finance the actual production, you will more than likely need help with the pre-production expenses. Even if your show is a hit, it usually takes three to four weeks for the money to begin accumulating so that you can pay expenses as well as the investors. Thus you will need front money — perhaps $20,000. Funds will be needed to post the bonds demanded by various unions. The actors' union, Actors Equity Association, requires a bond of two weeks' salary for each actor plus a bookkeeping charge of $50.00 per week. The Association of Theatrical Press Agents and Stage Managers requires two weeks' salary. A week's salary is demanded by the American Federation of Musicians (that is, if you do a musical or hire musicians), and the theatre owner requires a deposit of three to six weeks for rent plus $1,000 for possible damages. As a producer, you will need money for other pre-production expenses such as buying the option, printing the scripts, advertisements, auditions, rehearsals, payments to a "star" and/or director, and other such items. To assist with these expenses, a producer may choose to have an associate or coproducer in addition to limited partners. This associate may or may not be part of the actual production. His primary function is to assist with pre-production expenses in return for a percentage of the producer's share of the profits.

The Theatre Owner and the Unions

Assuming that you have an option, have satisfied all the unions, have filed with the SEC and attorney general, and have sufficient funds, your next step is to obtain a theatre. A good location is fundamental, and according to some sources, Greenwich Village is the best location for walk-in trade. In obtaining a theatre, a producer must deal with the League of New York Theatres. The League was founded in 1930 and acts as the bargaining agent for theatre owners with producers, theatre owners and producers with the unions, theatre owners with unions, and producers with unions.

Those contracts negotiated between the theatre owners and unions include the Theatrical Protective Union. This union includes electricians to service the electrical equipment and maintain public address systems, carpenters to build sets, a curtain man, a property master, fly men to raise and lower the scenery, soundmen, and "taking in" and "taking out" personnel — those concerned with taking in and taking out of the theatre all equipment in front of the house as well as backstage. In addition to this crew, theatre owners must provide ticket sellers and ticket takers, and thus must negotiate a contract with the Legitimate Theatre Employees Union. This Union not only controls the hiring of ticket takers, but has jurisdiction over employing ushers and backstage doormen as well.

The hiring of ticket sellers comes under another union — The Treasurers and Ticket Sellers Union. The personnel involved in this area comprise the box-office staff. The box-office staff usually consists of a box-office treasurer and two assistants who are responsible for handling ticket sales and monies. Inasmuch as a ticket is a legal contract, the implication is that the theatre is liable for the information printed on the ticket.

Tickets usually are of two types — general admission and reserved seats. However, theatres sometimes issue special types of tickets known as hardwood. In New York, for example, many commercial establishments handle a hardwood ticket known as a "twofer." The "twofer" is a pass given out free which, on redemption at the box-office, enables the customer to purchase two tickets for (two-fer) the price of one. Hardwoods are thus a form of complimentary tickets, or as a free pass is termed in the theatre, "Annie Oakley." The term is so known because Annie Oakley, whose real name was Phoebe Anne Oakley Mozee Butler (1860-1926), gave out free passes with her picture on the tickets. Another explanation is that the holes punched in tickets look as if Annie Oakley used them for target practice.

The issuance of complimentary tickets is part of the contract agreement that theatre owners sign with producers. In fact, the theatre owner has sole

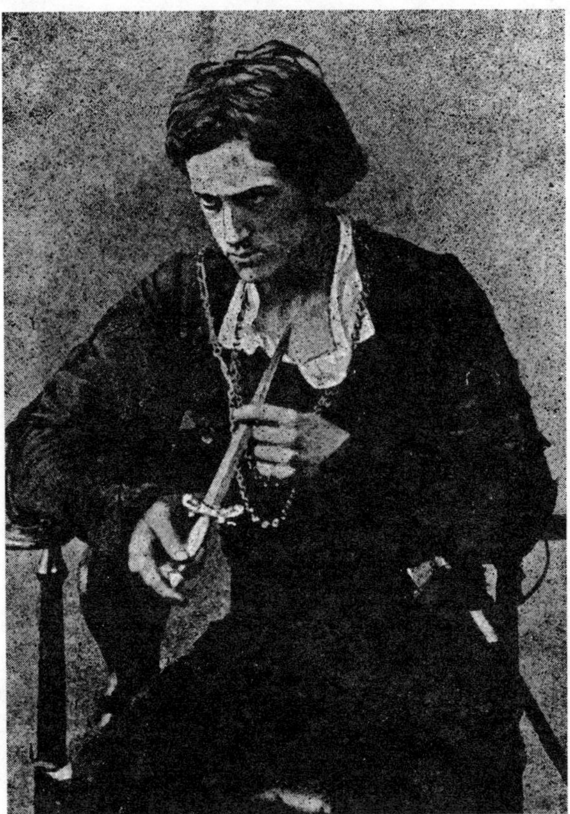

Above left: Charles Kean (1811-1868), famous for his management of the Princess Theatre from 1850-1859. Among his many contributions were the development of historical accuracy in his 1852 production of *King John* and his 1853 *Macbeth* (the audience was given a list of authorities he had consulted); efforts to establish the director as the main artist of the theatre; elimination of the afterpiece, which he placed before the main production; and the elimination of variety acts which led to specialization acts. From Coleman's *Players and Playwrights,* 1890.

Above right: Frank Benson (1858-1939), English actor-manager whose Shakespearian productions contributed to a non-realistic approach in staging. Benson, an athlete at Oxford, subjected his company, The Bensonians, to rigorous physical training. From Dirck's *Players of Today,* 1892.

control over the box-office and all that goes with it. The producer cannot, for example, "paper the house" (give away tickets without the theatre owner's consent). The idea is to sell all the tickets (go clean) and not have any unsold tickets (deadwood).

Computerized ticket sales have facilitated greatly the job of the box office personnel. Computerizing also helped overcome, to a great extent, the mishandling of ticket sales. Although illegal, box office treasurers have sold tickets above the ticket price, keeping the difference for themselves. Because such activities are illegal as well as difficult to determine, the term ICE (Incidental Company Expenses), which refers to all shady box-office activities, is applied. Historically, the term seems to have been used by bookkeepers to account for the shortages which occurred when managers took box-office money or issued free tickets. Computerizing box-office sales, however, has done a great deal to minimize any illegal activities with regard to tickets.

Two additional unions with which theatre owners must negotiate are the Theatre Amusement and Cultural Building Service Employees, and the International Union of Operating Engineers. The latter is the bargaining agent for those employees involved in the operation and maintenance of the theatre's heating and cooling systems. The former bargains for the cleaning women, the porters, the elevator operators, and the night watchmen.

The Producer and the Unions

Like the theatre owners, the producers must enter into a series of contractual negotiations with the various employees of a production. The union that most affects the producer and, for that matter, the entire production is Actors Equity Association, known as Equity. Equity represents the entire cast, as well as the stage manager and assistant stage managers. Equity derives its charter from the Associated Actors and Artists of America (the four *A's*) which is a voluntary association governed by the AFL-CIO. Equity is therefore subject to the influence of the labor unions; the actor and the laborer have a common bond.

Initial casting of actors is usually done by the stage manager and the casting director (if there is one). This spares the director, author, and producer, who ultimately make the final casting decisions, from having to deal with the many Equity actors who by Equity laws are entitled to an audition. Separate auditions are held for chorus and principal actors. Equity also requires an open call for auditions in order that any Equity member may try out. If auditions require more than two days for a chorus role and four days for a principal part, the actor must be paid. After the initial cuts, the remaining actors are called back for final auditions.

The final choices are determined and contracts issued. Equity provides many types of contracts, including a production contract, a resident stock contract, a nonresident stock contract, resident theatre contracts (called L.O.R.T.), children's theatre contracts, dinner theatre contracts, off-Broadway (this refers solely to the New York area), and the "Hat-Bat" contract (this refers to the Hollywood Area Theatre — Bay Area Theatre). The three "floor" (basic) contracts from which all contracts are drawn are the (1) production, (2) stock, and (3) children's. The actor who is doing a Broadway show would be involved with a Standard Minimum Production Contract for principal actors, a Standard Minimum Production for chorus, and a Standard Run of the Play Production Contract. The Standard Minimum Contract for principal actors provides a good example of some of the provisions which Equity requires in its contracts. The actor, for example, is guaranteed salary for two weeks but he is also placed on probation, during which time he may be replaced or leave (Equity permitting). If the contract is signed seven days or less before the first rehearsal, the probationary period is five days for the producer to replace the actor or for the actor to request to be replaced. If the contract is signed seven days or more, then written notice and salary for two weeks are to be given by the person requesting a change. Two weeks' notice is the required period once the production has opened.

In terms of actual parts to be cast, directors, writers, and producers are primarily concerned about the "star" and other principal roles. A star is defined as a performer whose name appears above the title or whose name carries the phrase *starring* or *also starring*. Stars, however, are generally excluded from auditions and are approached through friends or agents, whose function is to get jobs for actors and entertainers in their respective media. The agent in return receives a commission. The agent was proverbially known as the ten percenter, since this was his commission, but inflation has increased the percentage. Stars will usually be cast as hired. This means they perform a specific role and do no other parts. Other principal actors, however, may be cast as hired or understudy as cast, which means they play one part and understudy other parts.

In addition to the rules for stars and principal actors, Equity has rules for other cast members. If a part requires a juvenile actor, then the juvenile must be fourteen years old or younger. Equity also requires that if extras are used, they cannot be a definite character, cannot sing, dance, understudy, speak lines except in omnes (in a group), and cannot rehearse until two weeks before the show's opening. They are to be used for atmosphere and background only. Supernumeraries, known as "supers" or "supes," must be mute on stage, cannot travel with the company, and can rehearse only on the day they are to appear. In a musical, chorus members are hired not only as dancers and singers, but may be contracted to understudy a role, play a part or be hired as a swing (a nonperforming member of the chorus who "swings chorus members performing chorus numbers"). Once the cast is assembled, one of the members is chosen by a cast vote to be a deputy. The deputy is the designated representative for Equity members in dealing with the producer should a problem arise.

Because Equity has jurisdiction over the actor, it controls the rehearsal and performance schedule as well. Only eight performances are allowed per week and, according to Equity, a week is six days. This means that two matinees are given on two days of the week and on one day the theatre is dark — no performance is scheduled. Furthermore, when rehearsals are ongoing, they can only be for eight and one-half hours, of which one and one-half hours must be given for breaks. In other words, Equity allows only seven hours for rehearsal. The exception is the final week before production. During that time, a company may rehearse ten out of twelve hours.

Although rehearsal pay for a dramatic presentation is limited to four weeks (five weeks for a musical), regulations govern additional monies for extended rehearsals. Ten days, however, is the maximum additional rehearsal allowed before the producer must begin to pay the actor his regular performance salary as opposed to the rehearsal salary. To hold down costs, rehearsals are held in a hall or rented studio until the final week before opening, and thus, the producer is conscious about adhering to a strict rehearsal schedule.

Equity is not the only union with which the producer must deal. He is also responsible for negotiating a contract with the director, who belongs to the Society of Stage Directors and Choreographers if the production is a first class theatrical production. Night clubs, concerts, theatre restaurants (except Las Vegas), or readings are not considered first class. Should the production require dancers, then the producer must hire a choreographer, a person who composes the dance movements. Choreographers have the privilege of naming a dance captain whose duties are to call dance rehearsals in order to "maintain the quality of the dancers' performance."

The most famous actor-manager from 1900-1914, Sir Herbert Beerbohm Tree (1853-1917). Tree developed an acting school which later became known as the Royal Academy of Dramatic Arts. From Dirck's *Players of Today*, 1892.

Unions for Wardrobe, Costumer, Lighting, and Scenic Designers

The Theatrical Wardrobe Attendants Union is another union with whom the producer must negotiate a contract. The personnel protected by this union are the wardrobe supervisors, assistants, and dressers. The rules are very strict with regard to the duties of these employees. The wardrobe supervisors and assistants may not help the actors change costumes nor may another performer help. This function belongs to the dresser. Conversely, the dresser may not perform the duties of the wardrobe supervisors except in an emergency. The duties of the wardrobe supervisors include making, cleaning, repairing, and remodeling costumes.

The lighting, scenic, and costume designers are all members of the United Scenic Artists (USA). The minimum salary for a scene designer is presently $1,500; $750 for a lighting designer; and costumers are paid $75 per costume for stars or featured players, $35 per costume for the first fifty costumes for supporting players, and $25 for each costume over fifty.

The scenic or set designer must construct, color, and provide working sketches (to scale) of the set for the construction carpenter to build and paint the set; get estimates for materials; design, select, and approve properties, including furniture and draperies; attend the first out-of-town and New York openings and dress rehearsals; and perform all of these functions for road companies. Unlike the professional theatre, in colleges and universities, high schools, and community theatres, the set designer will also double as the technical director (TD). This position focuses on building, setting up, and striking (removing) the scenery.

The lighting designer must provide a list of all equipment and a light plot, which is a ground plan of all the lights drawn to scale showing position, color, media, and type of all instruments. In addition, the lighting designer needs to provide all information requested by the contract electrician; supervise special effects as well as get estimates on their cost; supervise hanging and focusing of all instruments, and set up the light cues; attend first out-of-town and New York openings and dress rehearsals and conduct the lighting rehearsals for these performances; and perform all of these functions for road companies.

The costumer must submit complete costume sketches with color samples for all characters; provide a costume plot, which itemizes all costume changes for each character scene by scene; get estimates of materials from three costume shops; select all costumes, including those used by an actor from his personal wardrobe; be responsible for all accessories, footwear, and headwear (wigs, beards, and moustaches included); approve hair styling and supervise all necessary fittings and alterations (wardrobe makes the costumes); and attend the same rehearsals and performances required of the set and lighting designers.

The Theatre Owner-Producer and the Unions

The remaining series of contracts to be negotiated are between the theatre owner and producer as an entity and the unions. The Association of Theatrical Press Agents and Managers, known as ATPAM, is one such union. ATPAM covers the employment of press agents, house managers, and company managers. Each area covered is considered a specialized position; doubling is not allowed. A house manager, for example, may not also be a company manager.

The duties of a press agent begin four weeks before the first paid New York performance. His function is to publicize the production; the object is SRO — standing room only. He also functions as an advance man. In this capacity, he goes out on the road in advance of the production and will publicize the show, set up interviews for cast members, check on housing, transportation, and the theatre facilities for the technical crews. The press agent also works with an advertising agency which the producer has hired to do all the paid ads, such as those that appear in the trades (theatre papers) or the dailies (New York newspapers which are published daily).

The individual responsible for managing the front of the house (auditorium and lobby) is the house manager. The house manager functions as the representative of the theatre owner; he works for the house. He oversees the ushers, ticket-takers, box-office personnel and doormen, and checks the box-office statement. The house manager functions primarily in front of the house and keeps things running orderly. Before the curtain goes up, the house manager and stage manager are in contact with each other should something be askew either backstage or in the front of the house.

Whereas the house manager attends to the front of the house, the stage manager supervises the backstage area. He must be a member of Equity, but he is not permitted to act. During the rehearsals he assists the director, but once the production begins, he is in charge of the entire backstage as well as the stage area.

Inasmuch as the house manager attends to a particular theatre building, he will not tour with the company as does the company manager. The company manager handles the company's administrative problems and is the producer's representative. This explains why in reality one person could not be a house manager and a company manager for the same production.

The last union with whom the theatre owners and producers must negotiate is the American Federation of Musicians. The ATPAM and the musicians' contract are the only two which the producer and theatre owners enter into jointly. Some theatres decide at the start of each season not to enter into a contract with AFM for the forthcoming year. In one way this is advantageous as the owner is not required to hire any musicians unless needed. A signed contract between the AFM and the theatre owner at the beginning of the year obligates the theatre owner to hire a set number of musicians for each production whether he needs them or not. If a production requires musicians, however, and the theatre owner has not entered into an agreement, he then must pay more for the musicians than if he had entered into a contract. In other words, he is penalized. Noncontracted theatres are known as penalty houses. When musicians are needed, they are selected by a contractor, much as a casting director is used to select actors. It should be pointed out that musicians who invest in a production cannot be hired for that production or vice-versa. Also, if a cast album is made, the musicians in the production must be used for recording the album. This is also true for actors and the stage manager.

Pre-Broadway Tryout

Having cast the show, rehearsed, and negotiated with the various unions, the producer is now ready to try out the show before opening on Broadway. Cost is an important factor in determining whether to attempt a pre-Broadway run. The purpose behind the tryout is to test the production on an audience as well as out-of-town critics, and based on their reactions, adjust the production or rewrite if necessary. If rewriting is required, a play doctor is sometimes hired. He might be a writer or a director and his job is to reshape the script in order to save the show. There is the story about Kermit Bloomingdale, owner of the famous department store, who had a production requiring a play doctor. He called in the well-known playwright and director, George Kaufmann, to doctor the show. After Kaufmann viewed the show, Bloomingdale asked him for advice on how to save the show. Kaufmann suggested that Bloomingdale keep the store open late and close the show.

Creator of "The Greatest Show on Earth," Phineas Taylor Barnum (1810-1891). Barnum was noted for his showmanship and his circus, which he created in 1871. From Seilhamer's *The Interviewer's Album,* 1881-1882.

Pre-Broadway tryouts are designed to have the show in the best condition possible so that it can be ready for the Broadway critics. Often a producer will discover through a pre-Broadway tryout that the production will not survive and will, therefore, close the show before it ever opens in New York. The expense of trying a show out of town first, say in New Haven, Boston, or Philadelphia, or if a musical, the O'Keefe in Toronto or the Fisher Theatre in Detroit, has become extremely expensive. Consequently, a producer may have a Broadway preview. This means the play will stay on Broadway for one to three weeks before officially opening. On the other hand, if the production is toured first before opening on Broadway, then the show will probably remain on tour anywhere from four to six weeks if a drama, and six to ten weeks if a musical. The production would then spend a few days in New York before opening.

The Bancrofts (Marie Wilton: 1839-1921) and Squire Bancroft (1841-1926). During their career as managers the Bancrofts managed their own theatre, The Prince of Wales from 1860-1880, and the Haymarket from 1880 through 1885. They established the "long run" for plays, the "run of the play contract," abandoned the benefit system, raised actors' salaries, and introduced domestic realism to England. From *The Theatre,* 1885.

Broadway

Once a producer determines that the production is ready for Broadway, he must negotiate a license agreement with the theatre owner. The license or theatre agreement is issued by the New York City Department of Licenses. The license varies with each theatre but contains such items as:

1. The date the show is to open.
2. The date the producer may occupy the theatre.
3. What the theatre owner is to provide (see contract negotiations required for the theatre owners and for the producers).
4. What the producer is to provide (perhaps that a particular staff is to be provided by the producer).
5. The percentage of the box-office receipts against a guaranteed payment which the theatre owner is to receive.
6. A stop clause. If gross box-office receipts fall below a specified mark for two weeks, the producer or the theatre owner may break the agreement. The producer or theater owner may not purchase tickets to increase the gross weekly receipts.
7. That a producer must "strike" (remove) the set and be out of the theatre within anywhere from twelve to forty-eight hours.
8. Provisions for free seats for the press as well as specifying the number of seats the theatre may purchase as well as get free.

There are numerous other provisions relating to expenses and who is responsible for these expenses. This agreement is similar with slight variations to the out-of-town agreement which is also used for pre-Broadway tryouts. If the license agreement is not used, then a form is furnished by the Independent Booking Office. This agency is designed to supply out-of-town bookings for pre-Broadway shows.

The cost for a dramatic show or a musical is a minimum of $75,000. According to available statistics, a dramatic show grosses between $45,000-$70,000 and a musical $70,000-$100,000. Of course, these figures fluctuate according to the size of the theatre and inflation. With so much money invested, a producer has to weigh carefully the reviews his show receives. The reviews come out in the early morning after the opening. After reading the reviews, the producer meets with members of his staff (company manager, press agent) to determine, in essence, what to do — close or stay open. This decision will be based upon reviews, advance ticket sales, and other potential income. If the show is a success, then the producer plans the advertising campaign. A big hit in New York will probably result in the formation of another company for touring. The stage manager will put the touring show together while he proceeds with rehearsals. This is a relatively easy task because the stage manager will duplicate (using his stage manager's script) the Broadway production. During the last week of rehearsal for the touring company, the original director takes over and continues with the show through opening night. Often before a production goes on tour or closes, it will be staged about midnight for members of the profession who couldn't see it because they were working at the same time the production was playing. This particular performance is called a "Gypsy Run-Thru," and is usually done without benefit of sets, costumes, or the other elements of spectacle used to stage the production.

From option to closing, producing a show requires good business practices. To enter into the producer's role for the so-called glamour of the entertainment world should be a minor consideration. The business of show business is to make money, and this means sound management.

Selected Readings

Faber, Donald C. *Producing on Broadway*. New York: Drama Book Specialists/Publisher, 1968.

Langley, Stephen. *Theatre Management in America. New York:* Drama Book Specialists/Publishers, 1974.

Nelson, Charles A. and Turk, Frederick J. *Financial Management for the Arts*. New York: ACA Publications, 1975.

Reiss, Alvin H. *The Arts Management Handbook*. New York: Law-Arts Publishers, 1970.

STUDY GUIDE

Chapter 1

Name________________________________

KEY WORDS

Art	Claude Levi-Strauss	Ritual Theory
Judicial Metaphor	Artistic Theory	Carl Jung
Tomb Theory	Sir James Frazer	Imitation
Coleridge	The Year	*The Poetics*
Aristotle	Aesthetic Distance	

PROGRAMMED QUESTIONS

1. "A useful skill systematically applied" is antiquity's definition for _____________.	art
2. That art was a useful skill prompted _____________ in part to prove that drama was an art. His argument was put forth in his treatise _____________.	Aristotle *The Poetics*
3. In addition to writing *The Poetics,* Aristotle also wrote that _____________ is natural and pleasurable and man learns best from it.	imitation
4. Imitation is a fundamental concept to theatre. By imitating the actions of people, the noted Swiss psychologist _____________ believed theatre and drama are a useful tool in helping man analyze himself.	Carl Jung
5. Carl Jung's idea about the nature of theatre and drama relating directly to man's immediate environment has also been suggested in the theories surrounding the origins of theatre. The oldest theory was developed by the Cambridge School of Anthropologists under the leadership of _____________, whose theory was labeled the _____________.	Sir James Frazer ritual theory
6. Sir James Frazer's ritual theory contended that a mock battle was given once a year in which the combatants represented summer and winter. This battle was called _____________.	The Year
7. The ritual theory, with its mock contest called "The Year," was questioned by William Ridgeway, whose _____________ suggested funeral rites contained the origins of theatre and drama.	tomb theory
8. Ridgeway's tomb theory, as well as Frazer's ritual theory, have been questioned by Arrowsmith's _____________, and Gerald Else's _____________.	judicial metaphor artistic theory

9. Arrowsmith's judicial metaphor theory and Else's artistic theory are simply trade-offs, one theory for another. The French anthropologist, ____________, attacks Frazer's underlying assumption that all societies go through similar patterns of development. Levi-Strauss argues that societies develop randomly rather than uniformly.

Claude Levi-Strauss

10. Underlying all theories is the belief of audience identification with the performance; that the actions being performed closely resemble life. This close identification suggests a fundamental relationship between the theatre and its audiences. This ability of a performance to transport the audience mentally into the world of the stage was viewed by ____________ as a "willing suspension of disbelief" on the part of the audiences. Coleridge suggests that theatre is easily palpable for audiences; their only requirement is a detachment from their immediate environment. This state of detachment is termed ____________.

Coleridge
aesthetic distance

ESSAY QUESTIONS

1. What is the nature of the theatre? Consider the concept of imitation in your answer.

2. Discuss the various theories surrounding the origins of theatre and drama.

Chapter 2

Name ______________________________

KEY WORDS

Action	Crisis	Tragic Flaw
Plot	Climax	Tragic Fault
Thought	Obligatory Scene	Pity
Character	Characters	Fear
Beginning	Characterization	Catharsis
Middle	Psychological	Ridicule
End	Spectacle	Laughter
Exposition	Tragedy	Fear
Point of Attack	Comedy	Hate
Inciting Incident	Melodrama	Double
Complications	Genuinely Serious	Normal
Discovery	Serious	Styles
Probable	Expedient	Undeserved Misfortune
Necessary	Moral	Deliberate
Probability	Stylizing	Relative

PROGRAMMED QUESTIONS

1. ______________ is defined as a change.	action
2. Action in drama is structured. This means that the thoughts, sayings, and doings of the characters are organized. Of the six elements of drama given by Aristotle, ______________ is concerned with organizing the characters into action.	plot
3. Plot may be created in drama in three ways: ______________, ______________, and ______________.	thought, character, action
4. Action, character, and thought are three types of plot. Aristotle recommended that plots should organize the action within a play by means of a ______________, ______________ and ______________.	beginning, middle, end
5. The beginning, middle, and end have distinctive functions within a play. The beginning includes background information about events which happened before the curtain went up. This background information is termed ______________.	exposition
6. The amount of exposition is determined by where the author chooses to start the story. Where he starts is known as the ______________.	point of attack
7. Although the point of attack indicates where the story begins within a play, it does not necessarily start the main action. The beginning of the main action requires an ______________.	inciting incident

8. The inciting incident causes all subsequent action. The subsequent action is in the middle of the play. It is made up of____________. — complications

9. A complication is any factor which alters the course of action. The basis for all complications is a ____________. — discovery

10. A discovery is a change from ignorance to knowledge and serves to answer questions which are raised throughout the play. The time for a question depends upon when the author has exhausted all possible answers except one. This answer will be the____________answer as well as the ____________one. — probable necessary

11. The probable and the necessary ending given to a play demonstrates the concept of____________. — probability

12. Probability means that what happens within the play's structure is logical, believable, and consistent. When an author creates complications, characters, and events properly, they will eventually lead to a major turning point which is known as the____________. — crisis

13. A crisis is any turn in the action and is always followed by a ____________. — climax

14. A climax is the high point of interest; it is the culmination of the action. The climatic scene is usually a "showdown" scene between the hero and the villain. This scene occurs in the end of the play and is termed an ____________. — obligatory scene

15. The obligatory scene is a device in drama. Not all dramas have an obligatory scene, however. Obligatory scenes are found most often in plots unified by action. Inasmuch as plot is concerned with structuring the play's action, plot can be said to structure or form____________. — characters

16. Characters are created differently and the way the author chooses to differentiate his characters is known as ____________. — characterization

17. Characterization can occur on four levels. Conflict results from the____________level. — psychological

18. The psychological level of characterization is concerned with a character's thoughts. Thoughts when uttered are achieved through sound. Whereas plot organizes what a character thinks, says, and does,____________represents those actions on stage. — spectacle

Chapter 2, *Continued* Name______________________________

19. Spectacle represents the written word brought to life. It is all the elements which make up theatre; plot, character, thought, and diction are those elements which make up a drama. When a playwright organizes plot, character, thought, diction, sound and spectacle, he is creating a form. There are three basic forms:____________, ____________, and____________.	tragedy comedy, melodrama
20. Tragedy, comedy, and melodrama have specific characteristics. A tragedy is concerned with____________action.	genuinely serious
21. Whereas tragedy requires a genuinely serious action, comedy and melodrama require only a____________action.	serious
22. That melodrama and comedy use only serious actions means that the decisions made are____________.	expedient
23. Expedient decisions are designed to solve the immediate situation and are not long-lasting. Tragedy requires ____________decisions.	moral
24. A moral decision is made by a protagonist in a tragedy, and requires that the character____________about the decision before making it. That decision results in____________and is brought about by an error in judgment on the part of the protagonist. This error is termed a____________.	deliberate undeserved misfortune tragic flaw
25. Instead of a tragic flaw, another interpretation suggests that the character is a victim of circumstances and terms the decision a____________.	tragic fault
26. Whether tragic fault or tragic flaw, the decision which the character makes will aid in arousing certain emotions. In a tragedy these emotions are____________, ____________, and their____________.	pity fear catharsis
27. Pity, fear, and their catharsis means that these emotions have been created and must be removed or reduced (catharsis). The emotions for a comedy are____________, ____________, and their catharsis.	ridicule laughter
28. Ridicule, laughter, and their catharsis define the emotions for comedy. Melodrama arouses the emotions of ____________, ____________and their catharsis.	fear hate

29. The arousal of fear and hate in a melodrama achieves catharsis by the____________ending. Tragedy's emotion achieves catharsis by removing the fear and changing pity into another emotion such as admiration. Because comedy requires a deviation from the____________without any serious injury befalling the normal, its emotions are purged by restoring the norm. double normal

30. Stylistically, to deviate from the norm (or what is considered real) is termed____________. stylizing

31. Stylizing a production, however, is an imprecise term, when referred to as a style or restricted in its definition. By definition, a distinctive method of construction in art is termed ____________. style

32. Style is a____________term and thus the terms realism and naturalism should be thought of as realisms and naturalisms. relative

ESSAY QUESTIONS

1. Determine the point of attack of a Greek, Elizabethan, and modern play. Ascertain also whether the point of attack in these plays is early or late. Why?

2. Structurally analyze *Hamlet* as a tragedy, *The Front Page* as a comedy, and *Night Must Fall* as a melodrama.

Chapter 3

Name ________________________________

KEY WORDS

Dithyramb	Archon	Parabasis
Dionysus	Satyr	*The Grouch*
Arion	Pratinas	Menander
Thespis	Aeschylus	Three Actor Rule
534 B.C.	Sophocles	Choregos
486 B.C.	Euripides	Chiton
City Dionysia	Aristophanes	Himation
Rural Dionysia	*The Oresteia*	Buskin
Lenaia	*The Persians*	Epidaurus
Anthesteria	*The Cyclops*	Periaktoi
Episkenion	*Oedipus Rex*	Theatre of Dionysus
Skene	Pinakes	Phallus
Ekkyklema	32	Padded tights
Parados (paradoi)	Agon	449 B.C.
Deus ex machina	Theologeion	11

PROGRAMMED QUESTIONS

1. Aristotle contended that tragedy originated out of the improvisations of the leaders of the ____________.	Dithyramb
2. The Dithyramb was a hymn sung about the god ______________.	Dionysus
3. The Dionysia hymn was said to have been formalized by____________.	Arion
4. Arion's contribution is said to have been improved upon with the addition of the first actor, for which ____________ was responsible.	Thespis
5. Thespis's addition probably was responsible for his winning the first contest for the best writer of tragedy. The date was____________.	534 B.C.
6. 534 B.C. not only marks the beginning of tragedy contests but also marks the first governmental recognition of theatre and drama. In addition to tragedy, comedy was officially recognized in____________, the best actor in____________, and dithyramb in 509 B.C.	486 B.C. 449 B.C.
7. 486 B.C., 449 B.C., as well as 534 B.C. were the dates for which contests were instituted for the best writers of tragedy, comedy, as well as contests for the best dithyrambic chorus and best actor at the____________festival.	City Dionysia

8. The City Dionysia was one of four festivals held yearly honoring Dionysus. The other three were the____________, the____________, and the____________.	Anthesteria Rural Dionysia Lenaia
9. Whereas the Lenaia and the Rural Dionysia presented drama in the fifth century, the exception was the____________.	Anthesteria
10. The Anthesteria seems to have had a connection with drama in the fourth century. At all festivals sponsoring dramatic events, the official responsible for its operation was the ____________.	archon
11. The archon was responsible for selecting three writers for the tragedy contest. Each writer was required to write three tragedies and one____________drama.	satyr
12. The satyr drama is said to have been invented by ____________.	Pratinas
13. Whereas Pratinas was noted as a writer of satyr drama, the real founder of Greek tragedy was____________.	Aeschylus
14. Aeschylus was responsible for adding the second actor, having written the oldest extant drama, and having written the only extant trilogy in Greek drama. His trilogy____________is the oldest extant trilogy, and his play____________is the oldest extant play.	*The Oresteia* *The Persians*
15. *The Oresteia* (458 B.C.) and *The Persians* (472 B.C.) account for four of the seven extant plays of Aeschylus. The work of Aeschylus was technically improved upon by____________, who added the second actor.	Sophocles
16. Sophocles' play____________served as a model for Aristotle's *Poetics*.	*Oedipus Rex*
17. *Oedipus Rex* accounts for one of the seven extant dramas of Sophocles. After Sophocles the next great writer of Greek tragedy was____________, of whom we possess eighteen extant dramas. Of these eighteen, Euripides' play ____________is the only complete extant satyr drama.	Euripides *The Cyclops*
18. *The Cyclops* is one of____________extant dramas which constitute the total number of surviving plays written by Aeschylus, Sophocles, and Euripides.	32
19. Whereas 32 plays survive for Greek tragedy, ____________ survive for Greek old and middle comedy.	11

Chapter 3, *Continued* Name______________________________

20. The eleven Greek comedies were written by______________. — Aristophanes

21. Aristophanes' old comedy demonstrates two unique literary devices: the debate over the happy idea, known as the______________, and the cessation of action wherein the audience is addressed, known as the______________. — agon, parabasis

22. The agon and the parabasis are seemingly standard devices for old comedy. Again this information is based upon eleven plays. Our information about New Comedy is even scantier. We possess only one complete extant New Comedy, entitled ______________written by______________. — *The Grouch*, Menander

23. *The Grouch,* by Menander, along with other partial plays and fragments of Greek New Comedy, indicate that the subject matter is prevalent in present-day television comedies. Another present-day concept developed by the Greeks is the use of individual financial backing. This person is termed an "angel" in modern theatre, whereas the Greeks called the backer a ______________. — choregos

24. The choregos's willingness to spend money determined, in a large measure, success or failure for the writer. In addition to obtaining a choregos, the writer of a tragedy had to obtain three speaking actors which was all he was allowed. This is known as the ______________. — Three Actor Rule

25. The Three Actor Rule allowed extras and a chorus. The Three Actor Rule was not applicable to comedy which allowed three to five actors. Another basic difference between tragedy and comedy was the costume. The basic dress for old comedy was the ______________, ______________, a ______________, and a soft-sole slipper called a______________. — phallus, padded tights, short chiton, buskin

26. Whereas the phallus, padded tights, a short chiton, and a buskin were basic for comedy, the basic actor's costume for tragedy and satyr drama featured a basic dress garment called a ______________. — chiton

27. In addition to the chiton, a rectangular cloth garment known as a______________was also worn. — himation

28. The himation and chiton represent the basic garments for tragedy, comedy, and satyr drama. These garments represented a basic dress of the Greek people and indicate a dress suited for warmer climates. The Greeks were outdoor people as the structure of their theatres testify. The best preserved Greek theatre is at______________. — Epidaurus

29. Although Epidauraus has the best preserved Greek theatre, the Theatre of____________is where all the extant Greek tragedies and comedies were presented and, hence, commands the greatest attention. — Dionysus

30. The Theatre of Dionysus consisted of an orchestra behind which was built the____________where the actors changed costumes. — skene

31. The skene had a second level from which the god-actors spoke. This was called the____________. — theologeion

32. The theologeion was part of the second level of the skene. This second level was termed the____________. — episkenion

33. The episkenion had a back wall with door openings into which were inserted painted panels called ____________. — pinakes

34. The pinakes were one scenic device. Another was a revolving triangular prism called the____________. — periaktoi

35. The periaktoi was used to enhance the scenic illusion. Also used as a device for illusion was a couch on wheels used to reveal dead bodies. This was called the____________. A physical crane which enabled an actor playing a god to be lifted to the second level of the skene was also used. This device was termed the____________. — ekkyklema; deus ex machina

36. The ekkyklema was rolled out through the central doorway of the skene, whereas the deus ex machina was probably located behind the skene. Bordering each side of the skene were passageways into the orchestra. These were the____________. — paradoi

ESSAY QUESTIONS

1. Discuss the concept of the polis as it relates to theatre and drama.

2. Trace the development of Greek tragedy from its formalization in 534 B.C. through the end of the fifth century.

Chapter 4

Name ______________________________

KEY WORDS

Livius Andronicus	Ludi Scaenici	Ludi Romani
240 B.C.	240-86 B.C.	Atellan Farce
Mime	Pantomime	Plautus
Terence	Theatre of Pompey	Scaena Frons
Auleum	Siparium	Fabula Palliata
Fabula Crepidata	Fabula Togata	Fabula Praetexta
Seneca	Closet Drama	533 A.D.
Octavia	Naevius	Afranius

PROGRAMMED QUESTIONS

1. Roman drama is said to have begun with the translation of____________in the year____________B.C., and the last record of a performance was in____________.

   Livius Andronicus
   240 B.C.
   533 A.D.

2. The dates 240 B.C. and 533 A.D. can be said to encompass the period for Roman theatre and drama. Livius Andronicus' translations in 240 B.C., however, started the golden age of Roman drama which stems from 240 B.C. to____________.

   86 B.C.

3. During the years 240 B.C. to 86 B.C., Roman drama was presented at festivals called ludi. The oldest festival which presented drama was the Ludi____________.

   Romani

4. At the ludi Romani, as well as at other ludis presenting drama, the scenic plays were called the ludi____________.

   Scaenici

5. The ludi Scaenici essentially consisted of tragedy and comedy until these forms became unpopular. A minor form to replace tragedy was____________.

   Pantomime

6. Whereas pantomime replaced tragedy,____________replaced comedy.

   Atellan Farce

7. The Atellan farce was replaced by another minor form which was in part violent and obscene. This form was the ____________.

   Mime

8. The mime was directly connected to the introduction of a curtain called the____________.

   Siparium

9. The siparium was one type of curtain used by the Romans at the first permanent Roman theatre called the____________.

   Theatre of Pompey

10. The Theatre of Pompey also used another type of curtain called the____________.

    Auleum

11. The auleum was a type of drop curtain which fronted the stage house known as the____________. — scaena frons

12. The scaena frons had a number of uses. Its basic use was a scenic background particularly for comedy and tragedy. Comedy and tragedy were classified in the Roman theatre according to whether the subject matter found its source in Greek or Roman life. Those forms of tragedy and comedy based upon Greek life were called respectively____________ and____________. — fabula crepidata, fabula palliata

13. Fabula crepidata and fabula palliata found their counterparts in plays based upon Roman life. These forms of tragedy and comedy were called respectively____________ and ____________. — fabula praetexta, fabula togata

14. Fabula praetexta was a form used by the Roman dramatist____________, and fabula togata had as its chief writer____________. — Afranius, Naevius

15. Afranius and Naevius were not the most noted dramatists to emerge from Roman drama. The immediate successor to Naevius was____________. — Plautus

16. Unlike Plautus, who wrote to please his audience, ____________wrote a more literary form of comedy for his immediate constituents. — Terence

17. Both Plautus and Terence served as influences on succeeding generations of writers of comedy. The strongest influence in terms of human tragedy was the dramatist____________. — Seneca

18. Seneca wrote plays which were seemingly designed not to be performed. Such plays are termed____________. — closet dramas

19. The nine closet dramas of Seneca do not constitute all the surviving Roman tragedies. There is one additional work by an unknown writer called____________. — *The Octavia*

20. *The Octavia* is an example of fabula praetexta, whereas Seneca's works are examples of fabula____________. — crepidata

ESSAY QUESTIONS

1. Read the play *Hamlet* and indicate Senecan influences.

2. Describe the relationship between Roman theatre and drama, and Roman society.

Chapter 5

Name ______________________________

KEY WORDS

Secular	Liturgical	*Regularis Concordia*
Hroswitha	Mystery or Cycle Play	Miracle
Morality	Interlude	*Fulgens and Lucrece*

PROGRAMMED QUOTATIONS

1. The earliest extant medieval drama is____________.	*Regularis Concordia*
2. The *Regularis Concordia* is an example of church drama which is better known as ____________drama.	liturgical
3. The opposite of liturgical drama is____________drama.	secular
4. Early examples of secular drama are the plays written by a Saxon nun called ____________.	Hroswitha
5. Hroswitha's secular plays were in rhymed Latin, not in the vernacular. The use of vernacular can be noted when the church allowed drama to be presented outdoors by the guilds. The major form of medieval drama associated with the guilds was____________or____________.	mystery cycle play
6. Mystery or cycle plays were concerned with Bible stories. The other major form of liturgical drama was the____________.	miracle play
7. The miracle plays were based upon the lives of the saints. In terms of secular drama, the form which emphasized allegory was the____________play.	morality
8. In addition to the morality play, another form which in actuality covered all plays presented during the Middle Ages was the____________.	interlude
9. The oldest English interlude is____________.	*Fulgens and Lucrece*

ESSAY QUESTIONS

1. Trace the development of Medieval theatre and drama from the beginning of the Middle Ages through the fifteenth century.

2. Briefly discuss the relationship between Medieval theatre and drama and the Medieval society from 300 A.D. to the fifteenth century.

Chapter 6

Name______________________________

KEY WORDS

Ubaldus
Vitruvius
Serlio
Teatro Novissimo
Sabbattini
Glory
The Art of Poetry
Commedia Dell'Arte
Comic
Academies
De Architectura
Brunelleschi
Teatro Farnese
Torelli
Furttenbach
The Poetics
Lazzi
Pastoral
Courts
Intermezzi
Teatro Olimpico
Aleotti
Chariot and Pole System
Horace
Aristotle
Tragic

PROGRAMMED QUESTIONS

1. Two institutions responsible for the development of Italian Renaissance theatre were the____________ and the ______________.

   academies
   courts

2. The academies and the courts developed theatre in Italy by devoting themselves to a study of classical dramatists, theorists, and architects. One of the most influential studies centered on the Roman architect,____________, whose work, ____________, remained an unquestioned authority for years.

   Vitruvius
   De Architectura

3. Vitruvius and his work, *De Architectura,* was one of the chief interests of the academies. Another interest of the academies, as well as the courts, was in the lavish spectacle entertainments called____________.

   intermezzi

4. Intermezzi, along with opera, did much to develop the concepts of scenes and machines associated with the Italian Renaissance. One of the fundamental concepts of Italian scenery was perspective which was rediscovered and developed by____________.

   Brunelleschi

5. Brunelleschi's ideas as well as Renaissance theatre practices are depicted in the *Architectura* by____________.

   Serlio

6. Serlio's treatise recommends three settings:____________, ____________, and____________.

   tragic, comic, pastoral

7. The tragic, comic, and pastoral sets were composed of angle wings, and hence, were designed *not* to be changed. The oldest surviving Renaissance theatre displaying Serlio's ideas of permanent scenery, as well as the first surviving theatre displaying a proscenium arch, is the____________.

   Teatro Olimpico

8. In the Teatro Olimpico, as well as in any theatre desiring the scenery to be shifted, in order for the sets to be changed the principles of perspective had to be applied to flat wings. This problem was solved by_____________. — Ubaldus

9. Ubaldus's principles were first applied to a set of flat wings in 1606 by_____________, who employed them at the _____________, which is the first surviving theatre to have a proscenium arch. — Aleotti; Teatro Farnese

10. Aleotti's transferrence of perspective to flat wings led to the next step which was the rapid shifting of scenery. This was developed by _____________, whose use of carriages and poles to accomplish the quick change of scenery led to the name of the_____________ system. — Torelli; chariot and pole

11. Torelli's chariot and pole system was perfected at the public opera house,_____________in 1641. — Teatro Novissimo

12. The Teatro Novissimo's display of flat wings in perspective being shifted rapidly via a machine represents a scenic innovation which occurred in the public opera house. Another scenic innovation developed at the public opera houses was a device for lowering heavenly figures from the clouds. This was termed the "_____________." — glory

13. The "glory" and other scenic investitures are discussed in detail by the German set designer_____________. — Furttenbach

14. Furttenbach's treatise, *The Noble Mirror Art,* is considered the only detailed account of Renaissance stage lighting. The standard work on stage practiced at the courts is summed up in_____________*Manual For Constructing Theatrical Scenes and Machines.* — Sabbatini's

15. Whereas Sabbattini and other scenic artists were influenced by the Roman architect, Vitruvius, the chief influences on literary criticism were the Greek,_____________, and the Roman,_____________. — Aristotle; Horace

16. Aristotle's work,_____________, and Horace's _____________were responsible for instituting literary criticism in the Renaissance. — *The Poetics*; *The Art of Poetry*

Chaper 6, *Continued* Name

17. Theorizing about *The Poetics* and *The Art of Poetry* led to the rules which constitute French and English classicism. In addition to the scenic artists and the literary critics developing a format for their art, the actors in the Renaissance also had a format. One of the most influential forms of comedy to emerge from the Renaissance was done by professional actors. This form of comedy is called____________. Commedia dell'arte

18. The Commedia dell'arte techniques were extremely influential to succeeding generations. A good example of that influence is the use of stage business called____________. lazzi

ESSAY QUESTIONS

1. How did the Italian Renaissance theatre reflect its social, political, and cultural institutions?

2. Describe the development of literary criticism.

Chapter 7

Name ____________________________

KEY WORDS

Popular Drama	Classical Drama	*Ralph Roister Doister*
Gammer Gurton's Needle	*Gorboduc*	University Wits
Christopher Marlowe	John Lyly	Robert Greene
William Shakespeare	Thomas Kyd	*The Spanish Tragedy*
First Folio	1572	1574
1576	Interlude	The Theatre
First Blackfriars	James Burbage	Earl of Leicester
Ben Jonson	Master of Revels	Inigo Jones
Stuart Masques	1642-1660	Second Blackfriars
Plautus	Terence	Seneca

PROGRAMMED QUESTIONS

Question	Answer
1. Elizabethan drama resulted from the merger of two forces: ____________ and ____________ drama.	popular classical
2. Popular drama included such entertainments as the medieval morality play and the ____________.	interlude
3. Whereas the interlude demonstrated the medieval influences on popular drama, the classical drama demonstrated the influence of Roman drama through the plays of ____________ and ____________ for comedy, and ____________ for tragedy.	Plautus Terence Seneca
4. The influence of Plautus and Terence for comedy, and Seneca for tragedy, can be noted in the English plays ____________ by Nicholas Udall, ____________ by Mr. "S," and ____________ by Sackville and Norton.	*Ralph Roister Doister* *Gammer Gurton's Needle* *Gorboduc*
5. *Ralph Roister Doister, Gammer Gurton's Needle,* and *Gorboduc* were the forerunners to the golden age of Elizabethan drama, which resulted from the work of a group of writers known as the ____________.	University Wits
6. The University wits were comprised of such writers as ____________, ____________, ____________, ______, and ____________.	Robert Greene, John Lyly Thomas Kyd Christopher Marlowe
7. Whereas John Lyly, Thomas Kyd, Christopher Marlowe and Robert Greene had attended the university, the greatest dramatist of all times, ____________, had not and, hence, was not a University Wit.	William Shakespeare

8. William Shakespeare's work owes much to the writings of the University Wits. Thomas Kyd popularized the vogue for tragedy with his play,____________, which influenced *Hamlet.*	*The Spanish Tragedy*
9. In addition to *The Spanish Tragedy's* influence, the perfection of blank verse is credited to____________; the forerunner to English tragi-comedy is seen in the work of____________; and the concept of euphuism belongs to ____________; all were influences on William Shakespeare.	Christopher Marlowe Robert Greene John Lyly
10. Christopher Marlowe, Robert Greene, and John Lyly's works are, for the most part, obscure. The survival of William Shakespeare's writings is to be credited to Condell and Hemings, whose collection and publication of Shakespeare's work is referred to as the____________.	First Folio
11. The First Folio (1623) contains a dedication from England's first poet laureate who was____________.	Ben Jonson
12. Ben Jonson wrote primarily for the court entertainments known as____________.	Stuart Masques
13. Stuart Masques were the means by which Italinate scenery was introduced to England. The set designer responsible for this introduction was____________.	Inigo Jones
14. Inigo Jones' set designs and introduction of machines demonstrates that the major advances in English scenery were done at court. The other advances in English theatre and drama were made at the public and private theatres. The first public theatre was built by____________, in the year____________, and was called____________.	James Burbage 1576 The Theatre
15. James Burbage built The Theatre in 1576. Also in that year, the first private theatre was built by William Farrant. It was called the____________.	First Blackfriars
16. The First Blackfriars was not the most important private theatre. The most important was the____________.	Second Blackfriars
17. The Second Blackfriars, built by James Burbage in 1596, was probably intended to have an adult company. Burbage was originally a member of The Earl of Leicester company, which had received the first royal patent in____________.	1574
18. The 1574 licensing act also granted the power to approve plays and to license acting companies to the____________.	Master of Revels

Chapter 7, *Continued*

Name______________________________

19. The Master of Revels' power was an attempt by Elizabeth to improve upon the____________act, which in *de facto* legalized the acting profession. 1572

20. The 1572 act enabled actors to perform without fear of arrest. The ability of actors to perform with a license continued until____________when the theatres were closed. 1642

21. The 1642 closing of theatres remained until____________, when the Restoration period began. 1660

ESSAY QUESTIONS

1. Discuss the relationship between the Elizabethan theatre and the Elizabethan government. Consider both the local as well as the royal government.

2. Trace the emergence of Elizabethan drama.

Chapter 8

Name ____________________________________

KEY WORDS

Lope de Vega	Time	Calderón
Place	Hôtel de Bourgogne	Action
French Academy	*Phèdre*	Neoclassical
Jean-Baptiste Poquelin	Verisimilitude	Molière
Reality	Character and Manners	Morality
Comédie Française	Abstraction	William Davenant and Thomas Killigrew
Essence	Letters Patent	Purity of Dramatic Types
William Wycherley	Decorum	*Country Wife*

PROGRAMMED QUESTIONS

Question	Answer
1. The Golden Age of Spain produced two outstanding writers: ____________ and ____________.	Lope de Vega Calderón
2. The ____________, built in 1548, was the birthplace of the new French Theatre.	Hôtel de Bourgogne
3. The ____________ was charged with maintaining the purity of the French language, being the final arbiter in all things literary, and from which the standards of drama were postulated.	French Academy
4. The ____________ doctrine demanded that the playwright follow certain rules so that reality might be shown.	neoclassical
5. The neoclassical doctrine has at its core the concept of ____________.	verisimilitude
6. Verisimilitude can be reduced to three basic ideas: ____________, ____________, and ____________.	reality, morality, abstraction
7. The neoclassicist believed that no two classes of things were exactly alike; however, all things may be identified by certain characteristics which all members of a class share. Those common elements are called ____________.	essence
8. ____________ was essential; tragedy must not contain comic elements nor should comedy be serious.	Purity of dramatic types
9. The rule of ____________ called for each character portrayed to be appropriate in terms of the universal standard of the norm being depicted.	decorum
10. The neoclassicist decreed that a play should be unified in terms of ____________, ____________ and action.	time place

11. Racine's ____________ is perhaps the crowning achievement of the neoclassical style. *Phèdre*

12. The idiosyncrasies of the seventeenth century French society fell under the satirical eye of ____________ , better known as ____________ . Jean-Baptiste Poquelin Molière

13. Although Molière wrote different types of comedy, his most admired works were comedies of ____________ . character and manners

14. When Louis XIV issued orders joining the theatrical companies in Rue Guénégaud and the company at the Hôtel de Bourgogne, the ____________ was formed. Comédie Française

15. ____________ and ____________ were granted a monopoly over theatrical productions in London by Charles II. William Davenant Thomas Killigrew

16. Theatrical monopolies were granted by virtue of ____________ . Letters Patent

17. No writer epitomized the style of Restoration Comedy more than ____________ , whose ____________ is usually considered a classical example of Restoration comedy. William Wycherley *Country Wife*

ESSAY QUESTIONS

1. Using the outline of *Le Cid,* show why the Academy might have objected to its abuse of the neoclassical rules.

2. Compare the theatrical monopolies of Louis XIV with those of Charles II.

Chapter 9

Name______________________________

KEY WORDS

Sentimental Drama	*The Beggar's Opera*	Middle Class Protagonist
Robert Walpole	Johann Christoph Gotthsched	Henry Fielding
Carolina Neuber	Licensing Act of 1737	Ackerman Troupe
La Serva Padrona	David Garrick	Querrelle des Bouffons
James Quin	Nicholas Medard Audinot	Charles Macklin
Jean Baptist Nicolet	Lewis Hallam	Melodrama
Fair Theatres	Burletta	Pantomime
Theatre Regulation Act	Comédies en vaudeville	Opéra Comique

PROGRAMMED QUESTIONS

1. ____________reflected the philosophical beliefs of David Hume and others who believed that man is by nature good, and that one must follow the dictates of the heart, of the instinct, to remain good.

   Sentimental drama

2. The second important development during the eighteenth century was the use of a ____________in tragedy.

   middle class protagonist

3. ____________and____________were instrumental in the growth of the German theatre.

   Johann Christoph Gotthsched
   Carolina Neuber

4. The____________was one of the most popular acting companies in Germany.

   Ackerman Troupe

5. England produced three noteworthy actors,____________, ____________and____________.

   David Garrick, James Quinn, Charles Macklin

6. The eighteenth century saw the beginning of the American theatre with the arrival of____________ at Williamsburg.

   Lewis Hallam and Company

7. The Foire Saint-Germain and the Foire Saint-Laurent produced plays which defied the neoclassical rules. These ____________caused the Comédie Française to feel the pressure of competition.

   Fair Theatres

8. After Louis XIV extended theatrical restrictions to include any spoken entertainment, fair managers turned to____________.

   pantomime

9. After Louis banned pantomime, the fair managers devised a method whereby the audience could understand and actually participate in the play. This ingenuous device was called a piéce â ècriteaux, later to be called ____________.

   Comédies-en-Vaudeville

10. ____________had no single composer and was made up of vaudeville or rewritten popular tunes.

    Opera Comique

11. John Gay wrote____________, a political satire, in which he made fun both of the London he knew as well as ____________, England's first prime minister. — *The Beggar's Opera*; Robert Walpole

12. *The Beggar's Opera* did much to infuriate the Prime Minister, but it took the satirical pen of ____________ to move Walpole to action. — Henry Fielding

13. ____________ stated that players could not perform unless their managers had been licensed by the Lord Chamberlain. — The Licensing Act of 1737

14. Louis XV authorized a return to opera comique in 1751. ____________ was produced in Paris by the bouffons Italian. It initiated a craze for Italian music and opera. The fair theatres set out to supply the demand. — *La Serva Padrona*

15. The ____________ featured the supporters of the Queen, who favored the Italian style opera, versus the King, who favored Opéra Comique. — Querrelle des Bouffons

16. The most important theatres of the Boulevard du Temple were those of ____________ and ____________. — Nicholas Medard Audinot; Jean Baptiste Nicolet

17. The new pantomime gradually assumed all the characteristics of ____________. — melodrama

18. Restrictions on the theatre were lifted shortly after the ____________. — French Revolution

19. The ____________ was an outgrowth of the Licensing Act of 1737. — Burletta

20. In 1843 ____________ restored legitimate drama to the theatres of London. — The Theatre Regulations Act

ESSAY QUESTIONS

1. Compare the development of the fair theatre with the illegitimate theatre in England.

2. Show the immediate developments leading to the passage of the Licensing Act of 1737.

Chapter 10

Name ______________________________

KEY WORDS

Romantic Ideals	Macready	August Wilhelm Schlegel
The Lady of Lyons	Johann Wolfgang von Goethe	Royall Tyler
Friedrich von Schiller	Charlotte Cushman	Heinrich von Kleist
Edwin Forrest	Germaine Necker (Mme. de Staël)	Victorians
Equality	Theatre Regulations Act of 1843	Idealism
Play Examiner	George Alexander Redford	

PROGRAMMED QUESTIONS

1. According to the ____________, all things are of a single creation. To know truth, one may study any individual aspect of creation and by doing so gain knowledge of the whole. — romantic ideals

2. Romanticism began in Germany. ____________ (1767-1845) is generally credited with formulating and disseminating romantic theory through a series of lectures and essays. — August Wilhelm Schlegel

3. Perhaps the two greatest German playwrights were ____________, who wrote *Faust,* which stands as a classic, and ____________, who wrote *The Robbers* and *Don Carlos.* — Johann Wolfgang Goethe; Friedrich von Schiller

4. The most popular German playwright of the era was considered to be ____________. Among his best known works are *The Broken Jug, Penthesilea* and *Prince of Homburg.* — Heinrich von Kleist

5. With the publication of *Of Germany,* ____________ is credited with introducing romanticism to France. — Germaine Necker (Mme. de Staël)

6. Romanticism was concerned with these aspects, ____________ and ____________, among other things. — equality; idealism

7. The Bulwer-Lytton and ____________ partnership produced the most popular plays in England during the first half of the nineteenth century, one of the most famous being ____________. — Macready; *The Lady of Lyons*

8. The first American comedy to be professionally produced was *The Contrast,* written by ____________. — Royall Tyler

9. ____________ was the first native-born actress, and was considered the finest tragic actress of the English-speaking world. — Charlotte Cushman

10. The first true star of the American stage was ____________. — Edwin Forrest

11. Perhaps in no other age have people been so hypocritical and concerned with the appearance of respectability as were the ____________. — Victorians

12. The____________legitimized censorship while freeing minor theatres from the domination of the Patent houses. — Theatre Regulations Act of 1843

13. A____________was appointed by the Lord Chamberlain to read and alter manuscripts. — play examiner

14. Perhaps the most famous, or infamous, of the play examiners was____________, who refused to license Sophocles' *Oedipus Rex,* Ibsen's *Ghosts* and Gilbert & Sullivan's *The Mikado.* — George Alexander Redford

ESSAY QUESTIONS

1. Trace the development of romanticism and its influence on the theatre.

2. Write a brief sequence on William Charles Macready showing his influence on the theatre.

Chapter 11

Name________________________________

KEY WORDS

Industrial Revolution	Emile Zola	Positivism
Realistic Scenery	*The Origin of the Species*	Realistic Acting
Charles Darwin	The Theatre Regulations Act of 1843	Eugene Scribe
André Antoine	Father of Modern Drama	Gerhart Hauptmann
Naturalists	Independent Theatre	

PROGRAMMED QUESTIONS

1. With the coming of industry, theatre took a major twist. The injustices that occurred during the____________to women and children gave rise to a serious study by dramatists. — industrial revolution

2. August Comte was the first philosopher to speak out against Romanticism. His theory of ____________ equated the study of nature with the study of society. — positivism

3. One of the most controversial books of all time, ____________ by____________, was published on November 24, 1859. The theory put forth in the book basically says (1) all forms of life evolved from a common ancestry; (2) there is a natural selection process moving toward perfection. — *The Origin of the Species* Charles Darwin

4. The French playwright____________formed the ideal dramatic structure, sometimes called the "well-made play formula" employing cause-effect development geared to carefully prepared climax. — Eugene Scribe

5. Henrik Ibsen became known as the____________ because of his accurate reflection of the life around him and his sensitive dealing with social problems. — Father of Modern Drama

6. Developing along with realism was a movement that believed that all behavior is directly related to heredity and environment. The adherents of this movement were called ____________. — naturalists

7. ____________became the principal spokesman for this naturalist school of thought. — Emile Zola

8. To go along with realistic drama was____________. Three-dimensional stage pieces and real properties were introduced. — realistic scenery

9. The outgrowth of realistic literature in the theatre gave way to a new style of ____________. Stanislavsky left a monumental mark on the acting styles in the theatre because of his methods of teaching acting. — realistic acting

10. The____________officially ended the theatrical monopoly and with it, the large theatres. — Theatre Regulations Act of 1843

11. ____________founded the first of several new theatres in Paris. The Théâtre Libre was open only to subscription members, making it, in effect, a private organization. — Andre Antoine

12. In Germany the Freie Bühne was the beginning point for Nobel Prize winner ____________. His production of *Before Sunrise* is considered by most scholars to mark the birth of modern German drama. — Gerhart Hauptmann

13. J.T. Grein on March 13, 1891, in London created a group called the____________. — Independent Theatre

ESSAY QUESTIONS

1. Show how societal conditions in the nineteenth century directly influenced the development of realism and naturalism.
2. Show how realistic plays differed from the romantic.

Chapter 12

Name ______________________________

KEY WORDS:

Edgar Allen Poe	August Strindberg	Richard Wagner
Expressionists	Unified Work of Art	Activists and Mystics
Friedrich Nietzsche	Messianic	*The Birth of Tragedy from the Spirit of Music*
Antonin Artaud	Theatre of Cruelty	Art for Art's Sake
Dionysian and Apollonian	Theatre of Social Action	Biomechanics
Vsevolod Meyerhold	Theophile Gautier	Théâtre de l'Oeuvre
Maurice Maeterlinck	Bertolt Brecht	Historification and Defamiliarization
Epic Theatre	Sigmund Freud	To Make Strange
Analysis of Dreams	Superego	

PROGRAMMED QUESTIONS

1. The inspiration for the symbolist movement came in part from the American poet ____________.	Edgar Allen Poe
2. Poe's ideas were further reinforced by the anti-realistic experiments of operatic-composer ____________.	Richard Wagner
3. Wagner felt that the author-composer should work to fashion all aspects of drama into a ____________.	unified work of art
4. Wagner's theories were championed by the German philosopher ____________.	Friedrich Nietzsche
5. Nietzsche's first important work ____________ was an attempt to justify the theory behind Wagner's work.	*The Birth of Tragedy from the Spirit of Music*
6. Nietzsche believed that in order to have great art, a balance between the ____________ elements was necessary.	Dionysian and Apollonian
7. The idea of a Dionysian vision manifested itself in the symbolist school as the ____________ concept.	art for art's sake
8. The leading exponent of the art for art's sake school was ____________.	Theophile Gautier
9. The most important dramatists of the symbolist school were ____________ and Paul Claudel.	Maurice Maeterlinck
10. The two writers' plays were produced at the ____________, opened by Paul Fort and Aurelien-Marie Lugne-Poe.	Théâtre de l'Oeuvre
11. The concept of unknown, powerful forces existing outside of the five senses was reinforced by the father of psychoanalysis, ____________.	Sigmund Freud

12. Freud postulated that there were three aspects of personality: the id, the ego, and the ____________. — superego

13. The ____________ became for Freud a diagnostic tool in bringing repressed desires and memories from the id to the surface. — analysis of dreams

14. The idea of the dream world as an expression of our inner selves was perhaps best expressed by ____________. — August Strindberg

15. Strindberg's ideas about the dream world were later adapted by the ____________. — expressionists

16. The expressionists were divided into the ____________ and ____________. — activists, mystics

17. In many ways the activist school of expressionism was the most ____________ theatre movement of the period. — messianic

18. Perhaps the most active of all the postwar antirealists was ____________. — Antonin Artaud

19. Artaud proposed a theatre which does not numb us with ideas for the intellect but stirs us to feeling by stirring up pain. He called his new theatre ____________. — Theatre of Cruelty

20. Along with Artaud's revolt against realism still another movement called ____________ evolved. — Theatre of Social Action

21. ____________ was one of the most important forerunners of the above group. — Vsevolod Meyerhold

22. Meyerhold's method of training actors for the new theatre was called ____________. — biomechanics

23. ____________ was directly influenced by Meyerhold. — Bertolt Brecht

24. Brecht's theatre was called the ____________. — Epic theatre

25. Epic was one of the three terms that Brecht used to describe his theatre. The others were ____________ and ____________. — historification, defamiliarization

26. *Verfremdung,* which means defamiliarization, is sometimes translated as ____________. — to make strange

ESSAY QUESTIONS

1. Compare Nietzsche's influence on the theatre with that of Freud's.

2. Show how Antonin Artaud's techniques utilized in his Theatre of Cruelty were derived from earlier movements.

Chapter 13

Name______________________________

KEY WORDS

New York
Thomas D. Rice
Minnie Fisk
Richard B. Harrison
Lee, Sam, and J.J. Shubert
Ceremonies in Dark Old Men
Lyman Gale
William Poel
Susan Glaspell
Eubie Blake
Emperor Jones
E.S. Porter
Saved
Paul Green
Charles Frohman
Ira Aldridge
David Belasco
Lorraine Hansberry
Little Theatre Movement
Eclecticism
Provincetown Players
Noble Sissle
Eugene O'Neill
Steel Mackaye
Edna St. Vincent Millay
Sam Nixon
King Shotaway
James O'Neill
Imamu Amiri Baraka (LeRoi Jones)
George Pierce Baker
Ntozake Shange
Maurice Brown
Charles M. Barras
Robert Edmund Jones
Kinetoscope
E.E. Cummings
The Visit

PROGRAMMED QUESTIONS

1. Once traveling companies became popular with producers, a tour base was selected in____________.

   New York

2. Because of the centralization of the theatre in New York,____________and____________along with others gained control of the theatre through their organization called the Syndicate.

   Sam Nixon
   Charles Frohman

3. Some theatre people such as____________,____________, and____________ fought against the syndicate.

   Mrs. Fisk, James O'Neill,
   David Belasco

4. Belasco joined forces with____________to break the back of The Syndicate.

   Lee, Sam, and J.J. Schubert

5. Among the forces against the monopoly of the Shuberts was the new interest in the theatre by United States colleges. For the first time, courses such as____________'s Harvard 47 workshop were being taught.

   George Pierce Baker

6. The____________was also a creative force against commercialism.

   Little Theatre movement

7. ____________'s Toy Theatre in Boston and____________'s Little Theatre in Chicago were important members of the little theatre movement.

   Lyman Gale
   Maurice Brown

8. The____________, however, became the most famous of the little theatre groups.

   Provincetown Players

9. The Provincetown Players were founded by a group of intellectuals including playwright______________and designer____________.

   Susan Glaspell
   Robert Edmund Jones

10. The most important young playwright to come out of Provincetown was ________.	Eugene O'Neill
11. O'Neill's ________ solidified the reputation of the Provincetown Players.	*Emperor Jones*
12. Throughout its lifetime, the Provincetown Players produced many important playwrights including ________, ________, and ________.	E.E. Cummings Edna St. Vincent Millay Paul Green
13. Black Americans had difficulty making a living in the theatre. Most were relegated to Jim Crow type song and dance introduced by ________.	Thomas D. Rice
14. The first play by a black American was ________ by James Brown.	*King Shotaway*
15. The most important early black actor was ________.	Ira Aldridge
16. *The Green Pasture* by Marc Connelly provided many acting opportunities for blacks. ________, a professor of speech, played the leading role.	Richard B. Harrison
17. Probably the most radical of the black playwrights is ________.	Imamu Amiri Baraka
18. *A Raisin in the Sun* by ________ was the most successful play by a black writer to that date.	Lorraine Hansberry
19. Lonne Elder III's ________ was also widely acclaimed.	*Ceremonies in Dark Old Men*
20. The "choreopoem," *For Colored Girls Who Have Considered Suicide When the Rainbow is Enuf,* by ________, enjoyed a recent long run on Broadway.	Ntozake Shange
21. The American theatre is probably best described by the term ________.	eclecticism
22. One of the first eclectic directors was the Englishman ________.	William Poel
23. The beginning of the American musical is generally traced to *The Black Crook* by ________.	Charles M. Barras
34. *Shuffle Along* by ________ introduced ragtime to the American musical.	Noble Sissle and Eubie Blake
25. In 1877 Thomas Edison joined with W.E.L. Dickson in trying to photograph motion. The result was the ________.	Kinetoscope
26. Early cinema utilized the theatrical work of Henry Irving, David Belasco, and ________.	Steele Mackaye

Chapter 13, *Continued*

Name ______________________________

27. The first step by the cinema in its separation from the theatre was ______________'s *Great Train Robbery*. — E.S. Porter

28. One of the better plays written since the war is Fredrick Duerrenmatt's ______________. — *The Visit*

29. Edward Bond's play ______________ was indirectly responsible for the repeal of the licensing act in England. — *Saved*

ESSAY QUESTIONS

1. Show why eclecticism is a good term to describe the present-day theatre.

2. Discuss the influence of theatrical conventions upon cinema.

Chapter 14

Name______________________________

KEY WORDS

Alfred Jarry
Peter Schumann
Julian Beck
Guerrilla Theatre
Towards a Poor Theatre
Off-Broadway
Open Theatre
Bread and Puppet Theatre
The Living Theatre
Luis Valdez
Jerzy Grotowski
Allan Kaprow
Root Impulse
Collective Unconscious
Ubu Roi
El Teatro Campesino
Judith Malina
Happenings
Joseph Chaikin
Off-Off-Broadway

PROGRAMMED QUESTIONS

1. Chicano Theatre was given a strong push in its development when____________started____________.

   Luis Valdez
   El Teatro Campesino

2. Luis Valdez's El Teatro Campesino was conceived as a political organization. Consequently, it made use of a theatrical activity designed to aid political activists. This activity emerged as a result of the Vietnam War and is termed____________.

   Guerrilla Theatre

3. In addition to Guerrilla Theatre, another widely used theatrical activity, which was originally called "painters theatre," is____________, whose development is credited to____________.

   Happenings
   Allan Kaprow

4. In addition to happenings developed by Allan Kaprow, Guerrilla Theatre also became a standard activity during the 1960's for politically oriented theatre companies. The Living Theatre was the forerunner not only for political theatre companies, but for experimental theatres as well. It was the strongest influence on the____________movement, which eventually gave way to the____________theatres.

   off-Broadway
   off-off-Broadway

5. The off-Broadway and the off-off-Broadway theatres were influenced by____________.

   The Living Theatre

6. The Living Theatre was founded by ____________ and his wife____________.

   Julian Beck
   Judith Malina

7. Julian Beck and Judith Malina were also influential on another experimental theatre company which is considered an immediate successor to The Living Theatre. This group was formed by a former member of the Beck's company, and took the name____________as opposed to the closed theatre of Broadway.

   Open Theatre

8. The Open Theatre was developed by Peter Feldman and____________.

   Joseph Chaikin

9. Joseph Chaikin's Open Theatre paralleled the Polish Laboratory Theatre whose leader was_____________.	Jerzy Grotowski
10. Jerzy Grotowski expressed his ideas about the theatre in his book_____________.	*Towards a Poor Theatre*
11. *Towards A Poor Theatre* contains Grotowski's ideas about acting which stresses Jung's concept of the "_____________."	collective unconscious
12. The "collective unconscious" was to provide stimuli to the_____________.	root impulses
13. Root impulses were, according to Grotowski, to be the bases of a performance. Grotowski's ideas about theatre, particularly that theatre is a religious experience, provided an influence on a German puppeteer named_____________.	Peter Schumann
14. Peter Schumann formed the_____________.	Bread and Puppet Theatre
15. The Bread and Puppet Theatre performances often contain no conventional dialogue. Another movement which rejected conventional dialogue because it was thought to be empty of substance was the_____________.	Theatre of the Absurd
16. The theatre of the absurd traces its beginnings back to the play,_____________, which was written by_____________.	*Ubu Roi* Alfred Jarry

ESSAY QUESTIONS

1. Discuss how the theatre of the 1960's summarized the prevalent attitudes of that decade's society.

2. Compare and contrast traditional theatre with nontraditional theatre.

Chapter 15

Name________________________________

KEY WORDS

Scenario
Voice
Georg II, Duke of Saxe-Meiningen
Gesture
Costumes
Build to Climax
Detract
Imitative Art
Body
William Charles Macready
Connotative Power
David Belasco
Establish Probability
Call Attention
Motivated
Madame Vestris
Denotative Power
Set Designer
Movement
Lighting Designer
Develop Emotional Effects
Open Tryout

PROGRAMMED QUESTIONS

1. A plan for a play is sometimes called a_____________. — scenario

2. _____________was not only one of the first female managers, but is often credited with introducing the box set into England. — Madame Vestris

3. _____________, who did much to elevate the status of the actor, also extended the duties of the actor-manager to an unparalleled degree. — William Charles Macready

4. Most historians seem to agree that the first director was probably_____________. — Georg II, Duke of Saxe-Meiningen

5. When the director has formalized his concept, the first designer approached should be the_____________. — set designer

6. One of the most successful producer-directors in America during the first part of the nineteenth century was_____________. — David Belasco

7. Once the set has been approved_____________colors and style may be conceived and the_____________ may now proceed with his design. — costume; lighting designer

8. Nothing scenically must_____________to itself or _____________from the play. — call attention; detract

9. The most popular audition for educational and community theatre is the_____________. — open tryout

10. The actor has at his disposal two means, his_____________ and his _____________. — body; voice

11. Actors must be aware of certain times when the _____________or simple meaning of the words must come through to clarify the idea. — denotative power

12. If the way in which the actor renders the line is changed, the_____________power of the words is changed. — connotative

13. Dramatic pauses and nonverbal devices are normally augmented by_____________or_____________. — gesture, movement

14. It is possible to show age, sex, general physical condition, attitude, and even emotional state that the character is in through_____________. — movement

15. The director may use movement to_______________, _____________, or even _____________. — establish probability, build to climax, develop emotional effects

16. Every movement of an actor must be a_____________, meaningful contribution to the play. — motivated

17. Basically, there are two acting ideas upon which all acting methods are based. One idea is based on the concept that acting is an_____________. — imitative art

ESSAY QUESTIONS

1. Choose a one act play and prepare a complete director's interpretation of the play.

2. Choose a character from either a Shakespearean drama or a contemporary drama (post 1960) and prepare a character analysis.

Chapter 16

Name______________________________

KEY WORDS

Property
Option
Dramatists Guild
Dram. Guild
Limited Partnership
Backer's Audition
SEC
Blue Sky
Associate
Coproducer
League of New York Theatres
Actors Equity Association
Star
Extra
Supernumerary
Society of Stage Directors and Choreographers
United Scenic Artists
Wardrobe Supervisor
American Federation of Musicians
Association of Theatrical Press Agents and Managers
House Manager
Company Manager
Stage Manager
Hardwood
Papering the House
Deadwood
Go Clean

PROGRAMMED QUESTIONS

Question	Answer
1. A ____________ is the term used to designate a play which is intended for production.	property
2. Once a producer determines the property he wants to produce, he then must purchase the right to produce the play. This purchase is called an ____________.	option
3. When a producer takes an option, he must negotiate with the union protecting the author's rights. This union is called the ____________, Inc.	Dramatists Guild
4. The Dramatists Guild, Inc., gives the producer the right to produce a particular play when a producer signs the basic production contract, which is known as the ____________ Contract.	Dram. Guild
5. After the Dram. Guild Contract has been signed, the producer usually forms a partnership with many investors. This partnership is termed a ____________.	limited partnership
6. If a producer chooses to finance his production by forming a limited partnership, his task is to convince investors to put their money into his production. One method to interest would-be investors is the ____________.	backer's audition
7. The backer's audition is often insufficient and the producer must look elsewhere for funds. Regardless of his methods, he must file the appropriate form with the ____________.	SEC
8. In addition to the SEC, the producer must also file with the New York attorney general's office as well as the attorney general of any state in which the producer chooses to solicit funds. To protect would-be investors every state has what are known as ____________ laws.	Blue Sky

9. Blue Sky laws are a form of insurance for the investor. Some investors may choose to become an _____________ or _____________ and therefore will assist or completely finance pre-production expenses in return for a percentage of the producer's profits.

associate
coproducer

10. Once an associate or producer is determined, the producer must next obtain a theatre. He must negotiate with _____________, which is the bargaining agent for theatre owners.

The League of New York Theatres

11. The League of New York Theatres is only one of the many unions with whom a producer must negotiate contracts. The union representing actors or stage managers is _____________.

Actors Equity Association

12. Actors Equity defines performers as follows: a _____________ is defined as a performer whose name appears above the title, or whose name carries the phrase *starring* or *also starring*.

star

13. A star is a principal actor. If a performer is cast as an _____________, then that person cannot sing, dance, understudy, assume a definite character, and may only speak in a group.

extra

14. Unlike the extra, the _____________ cannot even speak in a group, and is allowed to rehearse only on the day of performance.

supernumerary

15. A supernumerary is usually chosen by the casting director. Directors belong to the _____________ union.

Society of Stage Directors & Choreographers

16. The Society of Stage Directors and Choreographers negotiates with the producer. The scenic, lighting, and costume designers are represented by the _____________, with whom the producer must also deal.

United Scenic Artists

17. The United Scenic Artists strictly define the functions of those professionals which it represents. Unlike nonprofessionals, the costumer, for example, does not construct costumes. This is the function of the _____________.

wardrobe supervisor

18. The wardrobe supervisor also is the responsibility of the producer. The only other unions which concern the producer are those which the producer and theatre owner jointly deal with as an entity. These two unions are _____________ and _____________.

The American Federation of Music
The Association of Theatrical Press Agents & Managers

Chapter 16, *Continued* Name________________________________

19. The American Federation of Musicians and the Association of Theatrical Press Agents and Managers negotiate for the musicians and the press agents, house managers, and company managers. The____________is responsible to the theatre owner, whereas the____________is responsible to the producer.

house manager
company manager

20. Inasmuch as the house manager and the company manager have different bosses, in reality they cannot be the same person. The house manager attends to the front of the "house" and the____________oversees the entire backstage and stage area.

stage manager

21. The stage manager assumes the role of director during a production. His authority, however, is confined to the stage and backstage area. The front of the house belongs to those unions with whom the theatre owner has dealt. A primary area is that of the box-office. The Treasurers and Ticket Sellers Union bargains for box-office employees as well as ticket-takers. A special type of ticket which is actually a complimentary ticket is termed a ____________.

hardwood

22. Hardwoods are issued only with the theatre owner's authorization. The theatre owner may decide to give away free tickets in an effort to fill the theatre. This is termed____________.

papering the house

23. When papering the house occurs, it means that there are a lot of unsold tickets which are called ____________.

deadwood

24. Somewhat opposite of deadwood is to sell every ticket or to____________.

go clean

ESSAY QUESTIONS

1. Discuss the relationship existing between the author and the producer. What must the producer do to protect the author's rights?

2. Outline the sequential steps involved in producing a play on Broadway.

INDEX